The Musical Representation

The Musical Representation

Meaning, Ontology, and Emotion

Charles O. Nussbaum

A Bradford Book
The MIT Press
Cambridge, Massachusetts
London, England

© 2007 Massachusetts Institute of Technology

All rights reserved. No part of this book may be reproduced in any form by any electronic or mechanical means (including photocopying, recording, or information storage and retrieval) without permission in writing from the publisher.

MIT Press books may be purchased at special quantity discounts for business or sales promotional use. For information, please email special_sales@mitpress.mit.edu or write to Special Sales Department, The MIT Press, 55 Hayward Street, Cambridge, MA 02142.

This book was set in Stone Serif and Stone Sans on 3B2 by Asco Typesetters, Hong Kong and was printed and bound in the United States of America.

Library of Congress Cataloging-in-Publication Data

Nussbaum, Charles O.
The musical representation : meaning, ontology, and emotion / Charles O. Nussbaum.
   p.   cm.
Includes bibliographical references (p.   ) and index.
ISBN 978-0-262-14096-6 (hardcover : alk. paper)
1. Music—Philosophy and aesthetics. 2. Representation (Philosophy). 3. Emotions in music.
I. Title.
ML3800.N92   2007
781′.1—dc22   2007000510

10 9 8 7 6 5 4 3 2 1

For Sherry and Renée

To the memory of my parents and godson

In the mountains the shortest way is from peak to peak: but for that one must have long legs.
—Nietzsche, *Zarathustra* 1

Contents

Preface: Unwrapping the Riddle

What is spatial and yet non-spatial, in motion and yet not in motion, meaningful and yet meaningless, sophisticated and yet primitive, universal and yet particular, voluptuous and yet austere, material and yet immaterial, religious and yet not religious?

I spent the prime of my youth as a professional symphony musician, pursuing philosophy as a second interest. When I began thinking seriously about philosophy as a profession, and even after I actually had entered the profession, there seemed to be little connection between the inamoratas of my youth and middle age that was of philosophical interest. But as time passed and my philosophical preoccupations shifted, I began to think of music less as a topic for traditional philosophical aesthetics and more as one for cognitive psychology, philosophy of mind, and philosophical semiotic. At that point, my opinion about interesting connections between music and philosophy altered, and I embarked upon the path of investigation that has led to this book.

It takes only a small amount of perspicacity to realize that music is a remarkable, indeed an astounding, phenomenon. The emergence of human musical experience from the audition of organized tones remains deeply puzzling, truly "a riddle wrapped in a mystery inside an enigma," a riddle, moreover, of very long standing. For the naturalist, the solution to this riddle is to be found nowhere but in the collusion between the physics of sound and the organization of the human body and mind–brain. For the cognitivist, the human mind–brain is an organically embodied representational system, a system that enters into states that are systematically interrelated and that stand in intentional relations to the environment in which the human organism is embedded, or, with some cognitive luck (a nod here to epistemological and semantic externalism), into states that are supposed to stand in such intentional relations. The embodied mind–brain also represents its internal milieu, the body in which it is ensconced: it functions to regulate homeostasis and to monitor behavior. But as it regulates and monitors the body, the mind–brain also represents its environment perceptually by means of the body. Because all human sensory perception is mediated by bodily states, all human thought, even abstract thought, is permeated with the body image. These facts, as we shall see, are crucial for unraveling the riddle of musical experience.

The direction of explanation undertaken here will not, however, be exclusively unidirectional. It will proceed not only from biology, psychology, and philosophy to music but will occasionally jog back from music to biology, psychology, and philosophy. As a product of evolution, the human mind–brain displays a layered structural organization that stands as a living record of its evolutionary history. Human representational function is similarly layered. Relatively recent cognitive acquisitions, most obviously the ability, characteristic of our species, to employ linguistic representations, did not arise *de novo* but were "exapted" or co-opted from older representational functions of which we may retain but little awareness. Consideration of the arts, and of musical art in particular, can help bring to light the more ancient cognitive functions that underlie modern human cognition, precisely because the arts, and most especially musical art, continue to exploit these older functions. The biology, psychology, and philosophy of musical representation have something to tell us about what we are, based on what we have been.

My debts are not numerous, but they are substantial. I owe special thanks to Robert McCauley, who talked through the entire manuscript with me in detail and who has been a source of unfailing professional support throughout my career. Copious thanks are also due Denny Bradshaw, Mark DeBellis, Stephen Hiltz, and Martha C. Nussbaum, who commented on the whole manuscript. I also wish to thank Thomas Dorn, Mark Johnson, and Rudolf Makkreel, who commented on parts of the manuscript; Robert L. Nussbaum, M.D., and Sherry R. Nussbaum, M.D., who advised me on matters genetic and biological; Amy N. Mack, who helped with French translation; Alan J. Nussbaum, who helped with Greek terminology; J. Scott Darnell and the *Phoenix Graphics Group* of Fort Worth, Texas, for their work on the diagrams and musical examples; Tom Stone, the wonderfully supportive MIT Press Bradford Series editor; and Judy Feldmann of MIT Press, who saw the manuscript through the editing process and offered many useful suggestions. Ronald de Sousa, Lydia Goehr, Jerrold Levinson, and Jenefer Robinson provided invaluable assistance along the way, and three anonymous readers for the MIT Press gave me some important matters to ponder. Finally, I wish to thank my home institution, the University of Texas at Arlington, for a Faculty Development Leave awarded during the fall of 2003, without which the completion of this book would have required significantly more time, and for the unstinting generosity I have received since joining the faculty here.

One final note: For stylistic reasons only, I have used masculine personal pronouns throughout.

1 General Introduction: What Is a Naturalistic Philosophical Theory of Musical Representation?

1.1 Introduction and Chapter Conspectus

If we are to unravel the riddle of musical experience, we need a thread on which to tug. Construing music as representational, as a symbolic system that carries extramusical content, I hope to persuade you, exposes such a thread. This will require showing (1) that music *can* be representational, that is, that musical events are physically *capable* of performing representational functions; and (2) that musical events *are* representational, that is, that they are used to represent by their producers and consumers. In the preface, I asserted that for the philosophical naturalist, the solution to the riddle of musical experience is to be found in the collusion between the physics of sound and the organization of the human body and mind–brain. But what exactly is philosophical naturalism? What are representations, and what, specifically, are musical representations? What, indeed, is a philosophical theory? In this general introduction, I attempt to outline what I take a naturalistic philosophical theory of musical representation to be and what such a theory might be expected to accomplish. Readers unconcerned with these philosophical framework issues may skip over the next three sections and go directly to section 1.5, perhaps opting to return to the omitted sections at some later juncture.

Section 1.2 presents a dialectically organized sketch of the version of naturalism I endorse. A naturalist must develop a view concerning the integration of scientific description and philosophical analysis, and a developed view on this matter is indispensable to the task of clarifying the explanatory strategy of any philosophical work that avows naturalist commitments. The treatment of representation in a naturalistic setting is a case in point. How does a naturalist reconcile naturalism with the normative requirements, expressed as correctness conditions, of meaning and content? Section 1.2 endorses a physicalist functionalist approach: a representation (or representational token) is construed as a physical (or physically implemented) item that is used by an interpreter to carry out one or more representational functions. Although interpretation need not be anything as sophisticated or explicit as the metalevel paraphrase discussed in section 1.3 below, it will minimally involve the extraction of informational content from informational vehicles and the subsequent internal representation of that content, which is an implicit mode of paraphrase. Without pretending to an exhaustive treatment of representational function, a task that extends beyond the scope of a book directed specifically at musical representation, I provide in section 1.2 an account of what these representational functions are and what sense of "function" will be in play.

Section 1.3 opens with a discussion of representation and metarepresentation, or the representation of representation. There are two reasons for this. First, the argument of the book relies, though not in an entirely uncritical way, on the generative theory of musical understanding proposed by Lerdahl and Jackendoff (1983). I argue in section 1.3 that generative theories both of language and music are fundamentally metarepresentational because their subject matter consists of representations and rules. Second, metarepresentation is central to the conception of philosophical activity I endorse. In section 1.4, I ally myself with those who see philosophy as an ongoing attempt to elucidate, or make explicit, normative principles implicitly in force in a range of venues and to bring principle and judgment of cases into reflective equilibrium. Making explicit is a mode of interpretation, and interpretation is a mode of metarepresentation.

One such venue of making explicit is Western tonal art music since 1650. This musical tradition, I shall argue, is a norm-governed, representational practice. A naturalistic philosophical theory of musical representation, then, will be a theory that attempts to make normative principles of musical representation explicit and bring them into reflective equilibrium with the intuitions of competent listeners concerning a specified range of musical experience, while respecting a specific set of naturalistic commitments. By "competent listeners" I mean, first, those who are familiar with the stylistic conventions of Western tonal art music, but who are not necessarily technically trained in performance or music theory. Second, these are listeners who actually have a body of experience to call upon, listeners who have an interest in and have spent some significant amount of time interacting with music of this style. The aim is to specify what such music is supposed to be doing for such listeners. Section 1.5 completes the general introduction with a conspectus of the entire book.

1.2   Naturalism

"Naturalism" is a multiply ambiguous term. In epistemology alone, where, owing to Quine's pioneering efforts, contemporary naturalism first stimulated significant interest, a variety of distinct naturalistic positions can be discerned. We shall be taking up these and other niceties presently. According to my usage, a philosophical naturalist will (minimally) be committed to three theses:

1. The *ontological* thesis: pending future developments in basic science, nothing exists, including representational tokens themselves, that is not some form of physical mass-energy falling under the principle of the conservation of energy (which is not to deny that complex physical systems may possess emergent properties, including intentionality and other mental properties, not present in simpler arrangements of mass-energy).

2. The *metaphysical* thesis: all existing entities are enmeshed in the causal order of the physical universe and as such fall under the counterfactual-supporting causal laws of the basic sciences of physics and chemistry, or the successors of such laws (which is not to make the reductivist claim that these laws are sufficient to explain satisfactorily the origins and behavior of all complex emergent phenomena, including biological, mental, and social phenomena).

3. The *epistemological* thesis: all material descriptive knowledge claims must in principle be empirically testable, that is, evaluable before the tribunal of sensory experience, and that any such claim must cohere with (minimally, be consistent with) evolving scientific theory (which is not to subscribe to a verificationist criterion of meaningfulness or to a falsificationist principle for demarcating science from nonscience; nor is it to deny that observation is theory laden and that some version of confirmation holism may be tenable; nor is it to insist that all scientific-theoretical entities at various levels of functional and structural abstraction be in principle observable).

The expression "material descriptive knowledge claims" is meant to exclude

1. formal (mathematical and logical) knowledge;
2. knowing how;
3. the knowledge of behavioral norms and rules; and
4. the knowledge (i.e., the understanding) of meanings.

None of these modes of knowledge is empirically evaluable in the way putative material descriptive knowledge claims are. For the naturalist, therefore, they will all be subject to different modes of evaluation.

The first two exclusions are, I think, not very contentious. So consider just the third and the fourth. Knowledge of behavioral norms and rules is best seen as competency, or a mode of knowing how. Such knowledge tends not to be manifested verbally, although, of course, it may be; rather, it tends to be manifested in action. If knowledge of behavioral norms is manifested verbally at all, it is expressed by stating or paraphrasing rules. Knowledge of rules is rarely expressed by describing them, and even when it is, the description will contain a quotation of the rule or a paraphrase of the content of the rule: "The rule that . . .". Knowledge of behavioral norms is characteristically evaluated not by judging the correctness of any verbal expression of rules, but by judging the correctness of behavior.

Knowledge of meanings is a mode of knowledge of norms that apply to behavior and thus also a mode of knowing how. A speaker may know that a word has a certain meaning, but this knowledge is metalinguistic, and the speaker must be able to use the words in the metalanguage in which this knowledge is stated. Denying that knowledge of meanings is a mode of knowing how thus threatens a regress. Meanings, however, are not disembodied; they are carried by representations. But what exactly is a representation? Representations, I shall argue, are families of representational tokens, and a representational token, on the view I shall recommend in this book, is a physical (or physically implemented) item that acquires meaning or content by being used by an interpreter in one of two fundamental ways: (1) to derive information from an object (or objects), or (2) to guide action directed toward an object (or objects) by exploiting a link between the representational item and those objects. These two functions are not mutually exclusive, but rather complementary; and "guiding action" must be understood broadly enough to include the directing of attention. A representational token is linked with an object either by its being connected causally with it, or by correlating reliably with it, or by being linked with its object by habit or association, or by convention or stipulation. The object of a representation, moreover, may be another representation or even itself. In these cases the linkage between representation and metarepresentation will be conventional when the representations in question are external. Internal metarepresentational tokens may be linked with their objects causally or by reliable correlation or association. In addition, representations that have attained a certain level of logical sophistication may be inferentially linked with other representations.

Nothing, then, means anything unless and until it is pressed into representational service by an interpreter (or a community of interpreters).[1] This makes it possible both to misuse a representation and to use it in a "conniving" or fictional way with the awareness that its object is only virtual. With the possibility of misuse come correctness conditions, and with these, normative standards. So meanings themselves are normatively constrained. Because the use of certain types of representational tokens will exploit causal relationships between representational tokens and the world, the meanings of such token-types will have an externalist component that cannot be eliminated. But contrary to purely externalist causal-informational accounts of meaning and content, on this view causal relations on their own are incapable of fixing meanings. Any representation has many causal antecedents, both proximal and distal; and referentially vacuous representations lacking distal causal antecedents are not necessarily meaningless. To be in a representational state with a specific causal provenance, therefore, is not to have knowledge of meanings. To know the meaning of a representational item is to know how to use it correctly, to be competent to use it according to implicit or explicit norms, including inferential norms. Representation use, therefore, is also subject to sanctions, and knowledge of meaning is also evaluated by judging behavior, which in the central case is verbal behavior.

The three minimalist naturalist theses enunciated above are obviously philosophical theses. But are they descriptive knowledge claims? If so, are they material claims, or are they something else? To address these questions we cannot avoid considering what a naturalist should say about the relationship between generally empirical knowledge, science, and philosophy. Confining our attention for the moment to epistemology, we may distinguish five distinct versions of naturalism, ordered here from the least to the most radical (see Haack 1993, 118–119, for this formulation):

1. an extension of the term "epistemology" to refer not only to the philosophical theory of knowledge, but also to natural-scientific studies of cognition;

2. the proposal that epistemology be reconstrued as the philosophical component of a joint enterprise with the sciences of cognition, in which the questions about human knowledge tackled by philosophy will be extended to include new problem areas suggested by natural-scientific work;

3. the thesis that traditional problems of epistemology can be resolved a posteriori, within the web of empirical belief;

3'. the thesis that results from the sciences of cognition may be relevant to, and may legitimately be used in the resolution of, traditional philosophical problems, either

(a) all the traditional problems; or

(b) some of the traditional problems;

4. the thesis that traditional problems of epistemology can be resolved by the natural sciences of cognition, either

(a) all the traditional problems; or

(b) some of the traditional problems;

5. the thesis that traditional problems of epistemology are illegitimate or misconceived, and should be abandoned, to be replaced by natural-scientific questions about human cognition, either

(a) all the traditional problems; or

(b) some of the traditional problems.

The (a) and (b) variants of (3), (4), and (5) are termed, respectively, "broad" and "narrow." Where (1) and (2) are "expansionist" but still "a priorist" versions of naturalized epistemology, (3), (4), and (5) are all "a posteriorist." In addition, where (3) and (4) are "reformist," (4) and (5) are "scientistic." Finally, (5) is "revolutionary" because it adopts an eliminativist position regarding the traditional problems of epistemology.

Quine's adversions to the continuity of science and philosophy might suggest that he is committed to a variant of (3). But he then makes two covert moves, first a shift from (3) to (4), and, from there, a shift to (5). The first shift is abetted by an ambiguity in the meaning of the word "science," which supports both narrower and broader construals. Interpreted narrowly, "science" refers to a specific set of disciplines; but interpreted broadly, it refers to the entire web of empirical belief (Haack 1993, 122). Quine's first shift is the direct result of an unacknowledged slide from the broader to the narrower usage of the word "science," a transition from the claim that epistemology is continuous with the web of empirical belief to the claim that goals of epistemology may be entirely realized using the methods of the empirical sciences of cognition. But (4) is an inherently unstable position. Among the "traditional problems" of epistemology are the normative issues of establishing standards for justification of belief and the appraisal of evidence: like logic and ethics, traditional epistemology is a normative, prescriptive discipline. Since the empirical sciences (narrowly construed) are in the business of description and explanation, and not of prescription, they are ill equipped to address these normative questions, and therefore unable to realize the goals of traditional epistemology. Version (4) thus tends to collapse into (5), which solves the difficulty by simply eliminating the concerns of traditional epistemology. (5) replaces norms of epistemic evaluation with descriptive notions like reliability (a reliable cognitive procedure is one that, as a matter of fact, produces true beliefs with a relative frequency of 50 percent or better) or biological proper function (the proper function of cognitive mechanisms present in modern humans is to produce true beliefs because, as a matter of fact, homologues of these mechanisms produced true beliefs in ancestral forms enough of the time to contribute to the differential reproductive success of those organisms, which is why the mechanisms are present in us, the modern forms). Essentially, (5) puts normative epistemology out of business, a less than desirable result.

One Quinean response to this is to assert that the normative concerns of traditional epistemology are not tossed aside, but reconfigured in revolutionary naturalized epistemology as a set of "engineering problems": the questions, "What is knowledge?" and "How do we justify knowledge claims and evaluate evidence?" give way to the question "How do we build an effective epistemic engine?" (see also Churchland 1979, ch. 5). But an effective epistemic engine is, for Quine, a successful predictor or, somewhat less cautiously (Quine 1986, 664–665), a discoverer of truth. I shall pass over the normative issues of how predictive success (empirical adequacy) and truth (the proportion of true beliefs to false ones) are to be weighted against other theoretical virtues such as systematicity, consilience, and entrenchment of predicates. Suppose we did engineer an effective epistemic engine. It might be a classically computational design like Thagard's PI (an acronym, pronounced like the Greek letter, for the LISP program "processes of induction" [1988]) or like Pollack's computational robot Oscar III (Pollack and Cruz 1999); or it might be a trained-up connectionist network able to categorize novel objects not belonging to its training set (Churchland 1989, 1995). To predict successfully is, in part, to categorize properly, to project appropriate, and not grue-like,[2] predicates (or their connectionist functional equivalents). To the extent such a system was successful, it would be doing these things right and not wrong, and we would also have an explanation of how it was doing so: after all, we built it. Right and wrong, however, are determined according to our norms of logic and epistemology. We, the engineers, evaluate the system, albeit from the outside. We may, however, also explain our own successful cognitive activity. And when we do, Quine would suggest, we will have naturalized epistemology simply by explaining how we human cognizers get from stimulus to science.

But explaining *how* we get things right says nothing about why what we do *is* right. What exactly is unscientific or illegitimate about grue-like predicates? After all, they are empirically adequate, and the sentences in which they occur are, as far as we can tell, true, assuming the definitions of the grue predicates. Perhaps, then, there is something amiss in the definitions of these predicates. Perhaps, the answer might go, legitimate predicates are legitimate because they correspond to natural-kind categories (or at least track them: "is green" is not a natural-kind predicate). Natural-kind categories are stuffs or classes of entities whose causal powers (due to microstructure or causal-functional organization) maintain rich clusters of inductively projectible properties like the property of being green. But what is the status of this metalevel claim about predicates, the claim that the genuine predicates track natural kinds? The metalevel claim is a philosophical one: it has a normative flavor, since it seems to lay down criteria for legitimate predicates. For a revolutionary naturalist, however, the claim must be a scientific one. But of what sort? Perhaps a functional evolutionary-biological claim. One of Quine's responses (1969a, 126) hints at the type of evolutionary story later developed in sophisticated detail by Millikan (1984): genuine predicates track natural kinds because it is their direct and derived[3] proper functions to do so.

The problem with this approach is that evolution, because it is not an intelligent engineer but a satisficer, doesn't "care about" engineering effective epistemic engines per se. It cares about empirical adequacy, truth, and "genuine" natural-kind predicates only to the extent that they enhance fitness. As it happens, tracking some natural kinds is important to natural selection, while tracking others is not. It is important for living things to track hydrogen hydroxide and to distinguish it from hydrogen peroxide, but unimportant to distinguish jadeite from nephrite. Evolutionary considerations, while placing important constraints on any adequate version of naturalized epistemology, or, for that matter, on any adequate naturalized theory of representation, cannot by themselves vindicate any epistemological norm that places unqualified value on the tracking of natural kinds. Quine also has recourse to a rather different empirical claim about natural-kind predicates, the Goodman proposal that the genuine predicates are just the ones that are entrenched in established usage (1969a, 129). But this seems hardly more promising than the pure evolutionary approach: what endows past practice with normative force? We shall return to the issue of entrenchment later in this introduction, and to the evolutionary issues in chapter 4.

Since the integration of a genuinely normative epistemology with robust naturalistic commitments is her aim, it will come as no surprise that Haack endorses (3) and/or

(3'), "a narrow, reformist, aposteriorist naturalism" in epistemology. I shall be taking a similar line with regard to the philosophical theory of representation, an area where similar tensions between the descriptive and the normative appear. But the adoption of such a position levies certain demands. If one adopts a narrow version, it follows that only *some* of the traditional philosophical issues in the area in question can be resolved, using results from the sciences of cognition, within the web of empirical belief. But which ones, and how are the remaining issues resolved *without* using these results? Will the philosophical theory in question, be it epistemology or a theory of representation, rely on any material a priori principles either analytic or synthetic, that is, on any a priori principles other than formal truths of logic and set theory? If so, what is *their* epistemic warrant and how can we integrate our epistemic access to them with the naturalistic framework within which we, as natural cognizers, are included? If not—if the philosophical principles are one and all a posteriori—what makes them specifically philosophical? How are they distinguished from the results of the sciences of cognition? Are they to be held immune from empirical pressure, and if so, how? If, on the other hand, one adopts, as I am inclined to, the broad version of (3'), which holds that results from empirical science are relevant to all *legitimate*, that is, *nonchimerical*, traditional philosophical issues and which (in effect) denies the legitimacy of material a priori principles across the board, then the logical and the epistemological status of the specifically *philosophical* sentences of the theory and the role they play in "the web of empirical belief" both remain unclear. It is to these and related questions in the philosophical theory of representation that we now turn.

1.3   Representation, Metarepresentation, and Generative Theories of Language and Music

Whatever a theory of representation is, this much is clear: the sentences that constitute the theory will be metarepresentational, precisely because they are about representations or take representations as their objects. But there are, for the naturalist, two available modes of metarepresentation, the first descriptive and causally explanatory, the second interpretive and normative. The first mode explains the behaviors of representational tokens, both internal ("in the head") and external (public), in part by describing the causal roles they play in the behaviors of representational systems. The second mode elucidates the *meanings* of representational tokens by paraphrasing them. Tabling for the moment the second, interpretive mode, consider the first, causal-explanatory one. This mode sits well with functionalist approaches in the philosophy of mind that individuate representational mental states in terms of their causal roles in the economy of a cognitive system. Internal representations function as causal intermediaries between the input (stimulation) and output (behavior). The causal-explanatory mode also sits well with purely externalist informational-semantic theories (e.g., Fodor 1987, 1998), which attempt to individuate mental contents by invoking nomic causal relations between distal objects and tokens of types of mental representations. Finally, it is consonant with externalist natural teleological accounts of mental content (e.g., Millikan 1984), as well as with Darwinian selectionist (e.g., Dawkins 1976; Hull 1982; Durham 1991; Plotkin 1993; Blackmore 1999; Aunger 2002) and epidemiological (e.g., Sperber 1996) accounts of the replication and proliferation of cultural representations, both internal and external.

Subject to a caveat to be introduced presently, internal representational tokens considered descriptively may be said to instantiate a high-level natural functional kind, namely *natural representation*. External representations, also considered descriptively, instantiate (assuming they are conventional) a high-level artifactual-functional kind, namely *artifactual representation*. This suggests a parallel with evolutionary biology. Whereas biological species these days are generally regarded as historical individuals and not as natural kinds because terms designating species do not appear in any unrestricted evolutionary laws, high-level functional kinds like *predator* and *prey* or *host* and *parasite* are natural-kind candidates. *Predator* and *prey* or *host* and *parasite* are kinds of populations interacting in a state of equilibrium. Unrestricted, if only statistical, evolutionary laws concerning these high-level biological kinds can be formulated, laws that are empirically testable using species populations that instantiate these kinds, say, wolves and caribou (see, e.g., Rosenberg 1985, 145–146, 212–225). Artifacts like chairs, on the other hand, constitute artifactual functional kinds. If *natural* and *artifactual representation* are functional kinds, then they, like *predator* and *prey*, are kinds on a high level of functional abstraction; and if the universally quantified (but still obviously statistical) causal "law of the epidemiology of representations" propounded by anthropologist Dan Sperber (1996, 74)[4] is true, it is to instances of these kinds that this law applies.

But here is the caveat: the instances of the representational kinds are not the tokens themselves, but rather "strains or families of concrete representations related both by causal relationships and by similarity of content" (Sperber 1996, 83). These causally related families of concrete representations, as I shall be arguing in chapter 4, are types considered as tokens-of-a-type. Putting aside for the moment Sperber's claim of similarity of content, the parallel with biology remains close: biological species are also strains or families of "concrete" particulars (organisms) related by causal-historical relationships; and species, not individual organisms, instantiate the high-level biological functional kinds that are the referents of any unrestricted laws of evolutionary biology. The natural and artifactual representational functional kinds themselves, moreover, realize a three-place logical relation: a representational token (I have assumed, with only minimal argument so far) is a physical item used by an interpreter to stand for or to stand *in* for something else.[5] In this descriptive, causal-explanatory usage, "representation" is a theoretical term at home in the natural sciences of representation: cognitive psychology, evolutionary biology, and causal-explanatory as opposed to interpretive anthropology like the epidemiological theory proposed by Sperber. Thus although an epidemiological theory of the production, replication, and proliferation of representations in cultural environments is fundamentally Darwinian in inspiration, it differs, or is held by Sperber to differ, from a strictly Darwinian selectionist explanatory model in certain important ways. This is also a topic we shall take up in detail in chapter 4.

Let us now recur to the second, interpretive mode of metarepresentation. Back in 1996, it seems, Sperber did not regard the sort of descriptive-explanatory theorizing about representations characterized above as metarepresentational at all. At that time all metarepresentation was, for him, interpretive:

> humans have a meta-representational, or *interpretive*, ability. That is, they can construct not only *descriptions*—that is representations of states of affairs—but also *interpretations*—that is, representations of representations. Now, humans use this interpretive ability to represent meanings, intentions, beliefs, opinions, theories and so on, whether or not they share them. (1996, 87, emphases in original)

Sperber now seems to be willing to allow for representation of representation that is not interpretive (2000, 117). But this representation of representation is still not (for him) metarepresentation "in the relevant sense"; metarepresentation "in any useful sense" (118) concerns the representation of the *contents* of representations: "In order to represent the content of a representation"—in order to metarepresent the representation (in the relevant or useful sense)—"we use another representation with a similar content. We don't describe the content of a representation; we paraphrase it, translate it, summarize it, expand on it—in a nutshell, we intepret it" (1996, 34). The paradigmatic metarepresentation, for Sperber, is a metalevel sentence, such as "The claim that *John is a creationist* is slanderous" (2000, 120), that embeds a first-order sentence and translates or otherwise comments on the semantic content of the embedded sentence. It is true that some metarepresentations do embed and comment on the semantic content of first-order representations, as Tarskian T-sentences or the second-order sentences of indirect discourse do; but surely this is not the only appropriate or "useful" sense of the expression "metarepresentation." In what follows, I shall regard any representation of representations, descriptive-explanatory or interpretive, as metarepresentational. Descriptive-explanatory metarepresentation (the "causal metavocabulary") is no less metarepresentational than is interpretive metarepresentation (the "vocabulary metavocabulary") (Brandom 2000).

It is evident that for Sperber, interpretation and translation live in the same neighborhood. But this means that interpretation requires something that descriptive metarepresentation either largely ignores (as in the case of purely externalist semantic theories) or presupposes (recall Sperber's adversion to "families of representations related by *similar content*" [emphasis mine]): interpretation requires the interpreter to take into account the norms governing the *correct* use of the representations being metarepresented.[6] A field linguist who attempts radical translation of an alien language, for example, must regard certain noises and marks not merely as items in the physical causal order, but also as tokens of types to which syntactic (formation) and semantic (truth) rules apply, including rules of truth-preserving inference and material exclusion. Not all these rules need be made explicit by the field linguist; but it seems clear that when we translate we are doing something distinguishable from giving the sort of causal explanation of the behaviors of representational tokens and their users offered by a pure functionalist, a pure informational, or a selectionist/epidemiological theory of representation replication and proliferation.

Throughout the process of translation, the metarepresented representations may remain unendorsed and embedded in the referentially opaque expressions of indirect discourse, such as "...means that...," "...believes that..."; or they may be endorsed and held as true, thereby becoming first-order descriptive representations to which the translator is or becomes committed. This is the distinction between interpretation *de dicto* and interpretation *de re* (Brandom 2002). Suppose, now, that a linguistic interpreter undertakes the further task of making explicit, as far as he is able, the rules of the object language. Such an interpreter would be engaged in a mode of metarepresentation rather different from that of the original field linguist, a mode of metarepresentation that might be termed "meta*interpretation.*" As a metainterpreter, such a theorist would be attempting to metarepresent the *implicit rules of the object language*, not just translate the linguistic expressions that *fall under* the rules. Translation (a variety of Sperber's metarepresentation) requires use of the rules implicit in the object language; metainterpretation requires *mention* of these rules: it makes these implicit rules explicit by (meta)representing them. Still another interpreter, say an ethnographer (an interpretive anthropologist), might not limit metainterpretation to *linguistic* rules but extend consideration to other norm-governed practices of the object culture, say adult initiation rites or religious ritual. For this ethnographer, however, issues of endorsement and commitment still apply. The alien rules are likely to remain unendorsed by the ethnographer and embedded in metarepresentational sentences. If they were to be endorsed, these previously embedded rules would become *acknowledged norms*, rather than metainterpretive claims.

The case of linguistic metainterpretation, however, differs from ethnographic metainterpretation in two important ways. First, if we assume a version of the principle of charity, some of the rules that are presumed to govern the interpreted language, namely the rules of formal logic (noncontradiction, truth-preserving inference rules), will be endorsed by the interpreter and will perforce apply to the interpreting metalanguage as well. Second, if the metainterpreting linguist has cognitivist ambitions and subscribes to generative principles, as most cognitive linguists these days seem to do,[7] certain universal grammatical rules that constrain the grammar of the interpreted language will also constrain the interpreting language.[8] In the case of the linguistic metainterpreter, that is, many of the metarepresented rules will also apply at home. Because of the metainterpreter's endorsement of and commitment to grammatical rules applying to the alien language, then, at issue here will also be the achievement by the metainterpreter of something like "reflective equilibrium" between judgments of grammatical correctness, semantic meaningfulness, and inferential validity ("speaker-hearer intuitions"), on the one hand, and *his own* logical and grammatical governing rules, on the other.

"Reflective equilibrium" is, of course, a Rawlsian expression (1971) that concerns the process of reciprocal adjustment between moral principle and judgment of specific morally relevant cases. As such, the role of reflective equilibrium in moral philosophy bears some analogy to the integration of observation and descriptive-explanatory theory, sometimes referred to as the "interpretation" of data. Strictly speaking, however, reflective equilibrium apples only to the adjustment of *normative*, not descriptive, principle and specific judgments of correctness. But the notion of reflective equilibrium has broader application even with regard to normative principle, having been derived, as Rawls acknowledges, from Goodman's (1983) discussion of the reciprocal adjustment between specific judgments of inferential correctness and inferential principle in both deductive and inductive logic: *"A rule is amended if it yields an inference we are unwilling to accept; an inference is rejected if it violates a rule we are unwilling to amend"* (Goodman 1983, 64, emphasis original).

It is not uncommon to see metainterpretation by the ethnographer or the linguist referred to as "description": the ethnographer *describes*, but does not evaluate, the rules of the practices he studies; the linguist *describes*, but does not evaluate, the grammar of the object language he studies. The nonevaluative ethnographical metainterpretation that goes under the rubric of "description" is, however, fundamentally a mode of interpretation—a mode of interpretation subject only to conditions of very "narrow" reflective equilibrium, narrow because the interpreted normative principles are held isolated and deliberately not evaluated by being brought by the anthropologist into reflective equilibrium with his own principles; nor are his own evaluated with respect to the alien principles. The interpretation remains strictly *de dicto*. The rules of the alien practices are individuated by their contents; but, as Sperber says, we don't describe contents, we *interpret* them. Still, although the rules do express norms but do not, strictly speaking, carry truth values, they may also, insofar as they remain strictly *de dicto*, be taken to be descriptive *of the alien practices*: they both describe (for the interpreter) what is done and prescribe (for the interpretees) what is to be done.

Cognitive-linguistic metainterpretation, however, differs from ethnological metainterpretation not only because its rules must be evaluated (since they apply at home), but also because the rules of generative linguistics are supposed to be not merely "observationally" or "descriptively" adequate, but "explanatorily" adequate. A grammar of a language is observationally adequate if it "correctly predicts which sentences are (and are not) syntactically, semantically, and phonologically well-formed in the language" (Radford 1981). That is, it correctly predicts which sentences *will be judged* to be well formed by native speakers. A grammar is descriptively adequate if it "*also* correctly describes the . . . structure of sentences in the language in such a way as to provide a principled account of the native speaker's intuitions about this structure" (ibid.). Like the metainterpreted normative principles of ethnography, a descriptively adequate grammar is both prescriptive and descriptive: it both *prescribes* (provides "a principled account of the native speaker's intuitions about [sentence] structure") and *describes* the structure of the correct sentences. Observationally and descriptively adequate grammars, I submit, are products of metainterpretive activity, the metarepresentation of the contents of implicit grammatical rules. Recall, we interpret contents; we don't describe them. Finally, a grammar attains explanatory adequacy if it accurately predicts, correctly describes, and "also does so in terms of a highly restricted set of optimally simple, universal, maximally general principles which represent psychologically plausible natural principles of mental computation, and are 'learnable' by the child in a limited period of time, and given access to limited data" (ibid., 25–26). Generative linguists take themselves to be explaining language acquisition by hypothesizing universal principles internal to the mind–brain, much as physicists explain light emissions of the sun by hypothesizing thermonuclear reactions in the sun's interior (Chomsky 1980, 191). They attempt to make a shift, not always explicitly acknowledged, from the vocabulary metavocabulary to the causal metavocabulary and then to apply the latter to the vocabulary of grammatical principles.

Notice, though, what is required to support this analogy between physics and linguistics. The grammatical principles as stated can be nothing other than metainterpretations of implicit, indeed unconsciously followed, task-level internal rules: they "*represent* [metarepresent] psychologically plausible natural principles of mental computation." In order for these task-level internal principles to be scientifically explanatory, however, they (or their tokens) must be shown to be "psychologically real," that is, causally efficacious in the mental economy. The standard strategy is to prescind from the semantics of the grammatical principles and to focus on their computational syntax in functionally defined areas of the brain, considered as a classically computational language-acquisition device. As a result of this move, the generative theorist in search of psychological reality faces an explanatory burden the physicist does not face. Whereas on any realist interpretation of physics, the processes *described* by physical law are certainly physically real, the physicist need not show the laws themselves to be "physically real" (whatever that might mean), short of accepting recent and controversial cosmological views that construe the physical universe itself as a computational entity.

In *Knowledge of Language*, Chomsky (1986, 27, 48n15, 239) reiterates his commitment to methodological parity among the empirical sciences, placing the explanations provided by physics on all fours with computational explanations of psychology and linguistics. But there is, again, this difference: where the human visual and language acquisition systems arguably are computational devices, the physical universe most likely is not. Chomsky asks (ibid., 256), "Would it have been reasonable to ask nineteenth-century chemists to state explicitly the conditions that would justify their saying that the entities they postulate [valences, benzene rings] are 'represented' in physical mechanisms?" No, but that's just the point: such postulated "entities" are *not* representations, whereas classically computational principles are. If the language-acquisition device is not classically computational, however, then the principles that adequately *describe* human linguistic competence might not *cause* competent performance (see Schwartz 1978; Feagin 1997).

But they *may* cause it; and there are, it seems, only two ways to show this. Either one devises specific experimental tests designed to yield determinate answers, and then, depending on what these answers are, mounts an argument to the best explanation for the psychological reality of appropriate internal representational structures; or one argues on the basis of an indirect "how else" argument that grammatical competence cannot be explained without hypothesizing internal principles that compute over the syntactically structured representations in a language of thought.[9] Explanatory adequacy can also be bolstered by adducing an "existence proof": a biologically plausible computational design that implements these rules and is able to distinguish grammatical and ungrammatical sentences of an E-language, as Marr's computational theory of vision (1982) relies on a biologically plausible computational model that is able to construct representations of three-dimensional physical objects by extracting information from two-dimensional arrays.

Although experimental evidence for generative linguistics has been hard to come by, it is not entirely unavailable. A "trace" is a gap in the surface structure of a sentence that becomes filled when a category is moved by transformation (Chomsky 1986, 66). Consider the sentence "The policeman saw the boy that the crowd at the party accused (trace) of the crime." After transformation, "the boy" is placed in the position of the trace as the direct object of the verb "accused" in the deep structure of the sentence.[10] When parsing the sentence, a hearer must hold "the boy" in memory until the appropriate insertion point arrives. Experimental tests have shown that carrying out this task imposes a cognitive load: speakers detect extraneous signals more slowly and EEGs show effects of this cognitive strain (Pinker 1994, 219–220). There are, in addition, empirical data concerning so-called garden path sentences, sentences that motivate a structural hypothesis that turns out to be wrong. Generative theory hypothesizes that readers begin to process a sentence using a single structural hypothesis. If the hypothesis fails, a new one is tried. In the sentence "The student forgot the solution was in the back of the book," one is first inclined to read "the solution" incorrectly as the direct object of "forgot," not as the subject of an embedded clause. Recorded eye movements show that readers go back to the beginning of the sentence when they hit the word "was," just at the point at which the generative phrase-structure tree predicts they will (Pinker 1994, 235). The generative principles and tree structures can, then, be inferred by way of inference to the best explanation of these psychological and neurological phenomena.

Indirect "how else" arguments are not as compelling as empirical arguments to the best explanation; but they are not worthless either. In this case, however, success depends on establishing (or rendering plausible) a strong negative universal modal claim, namely, that no biologically plausible mental representations other than the rules of a language of thought *could* account for human grammatical competence. The problem with such modal arguments is that they are only as good as the conceptual repertoire they employ, and in this case the concepts are empirical: what seems impossible may turn out to be possible after all. In addition, connectionists have mounted arguments that grammatical competence is possible without the rules of a language of thought, indeed without a language of thought at all (see, e.g., Clark 1989, 1997; Cussins 1990; Bechtel 1994). Elman's (1992) connectionist sentence parser might be thought to provide an existence proof that actualizes this possibility. As a result, "how else" arguments in favor of the language of thought hypothesis are not decisive. This may be why some critics, much to Chomsky's continued annoyance (1980, 189ff; 1986, 245ff), persist in denying the psychological reality of the principles of generative grammar.

Generative theory does, however, advance compelling explanatory hypotheses of a more general nature as well. By postulating innate mechanisms similar to mechanisms that support other functions like vision, hearing, and motor control, it explains, as behaviorism utterly fails to explain, how children are able to learn the complex grammar of a spoken language as effectively as they do from very limited and degraded inputs. This proposal coheres with and motivates neuroscientific research, yielding testable hypotheses concerning specific areas of the brain, including Wernicke's and Broca's areas, that are thought to support linguistic functions. The proposal also coheres with developmental neuroscience and with what is known about the evolutionary history of the brain. Although Chomsky himself has expressed considerable skepticism concerning the usefulness of such interdisciplinary parallels, the postulated hierarchical structure of linguistic trees coheres with explanatory structures postulated in other branches of cognitive neuroscience, especially those concerned with the functional organization of the motor system (see Lashley 1951; Miller et al. 1960; Jackendoff 1987). We shall take up the functional organization of the motor system in more detail in chapter 2.

The evidence for the psychological reality of the principles of generative grammar may not, then, be conclusive, but it is far from negligible. I have belabored this issue a bit here in the introduction not only in the interest of clarifying description, explanation, interpretation, and metainterpretation, but also because I shall be relying in later chapters on the generative theory of tonal music advanced by Chomsky's former student and current intellectual ally, Ray Jackendoff, a theory that seems to be less well supported empirically than is generative linguistics and seems, therefore, to rely more heavily on reflective equilibrium between its principles and the intuitions of listeners. As a result, its credentials as a metarepresentational descriptive-explanatory theory, as opposed to a theory that is only metainterpretive, are a little weaker. But as we shall see, empirical evidence in its favor is also not entirely lacking.

According to Sperber's conventions, which I have adopted here and which, incidentally, are remarkably similar to Quine's, description is limited to the propositional representation of causally implicated physical entities, including representational tokens and their users. Description that is not embedded, explicitly or implicitly, in metarepresentational interpretive sentences carries with it existential commitment: a singular description can always be expressed as an existentially quantified variable with a predicate, and "to be is to be the value of a variable." According to the naturalist ontological and metaphysical principles stated at the outset, nothing exists other than causally implicated forms of mass-energy. Interpretation, on the other hand, carries no existential import. Contents are objects of interpretation, not description; and rules, as treated by the ethnographer and by the cognitive linguist at the task level, are individuated by their contents. Meanings and contents, however, are not causally implicated physical entities. They are, therefore, not existents, but rule-constituted "abstracta":[11] they are constituted from implicitly rule-governed behaviors, in this case linguistic behaviors including utterances, inscriptions, and sanctions belonging to the social language game.[12]

1.4 Reflective Equilibrium, Socratic Reflection, and Naturalism

Typical of one sort of criticism inveterately brought against reflective equilibrium as a justificatory process is Siegel's essay, "Justification by Balance" (1992).[13] Goodman's account of justification, he argues (36–37),

makes clear that principle can correct practice as readily as practice can correct principle. It is on his account the *mutual accommodation* of practice and principle that serves to justify both. But if practice can be criticized and corrected, then why is fit with practice justificatory? If practice can be criticized and improved, then justification cannot be a matter of fit with practice. For the relevant practice will have to be justified in terms of some independent criterion of justification—since fit with itself will hardly afford justification to some pattern of practice—in order for fit with that practice to afford justification to the principles which fit it.

Unfortunately, Siegel takes insufficient notice of two crucial words (italicized below) in the relevant passage from Goodman he himself quotes (28): "Principles of deductive inference are justified by their conformity with accepted deductive practice. Their validity depends upon accordance with the particular deductive inferences we actually make *and sanction*" (Goodman 1983, 63, emphasis mine). Since actual deductive practice already includes sanctions, it is already (implicitly) normatively vetted, hence (provisionally) justified. "Deductive principle" merely makes the implicit norms explicit, thereby facilitating their evaluation in wider contexts, both logical and extralogical, and their inclusion in systems with wider reflective equilibrium. There can, on pain of infinite regress, be no explicit rules for achieving reflective equilibrium, precisely because it is within this process that explicit rules are codified. Any explicit rules *for* achieving reflective equilibrium would themselves have to be products of a process of achieving reflective equilibrium. For a naturalist, the problem is to explain how even implicit norms can emerge from the prenormative, merely behavioral ooze (cf. Rosen 1997, 170). I cannot claim to be in possession of such an account, which would anyway extend well beyond the scope of this book.[14] But I believe a convincing story could be told by way of a judicious use of evolutionary biology, psychology, and anthropology. A certain primitive version of normativity first appears in the natural world with the emergence of living forms that possess organ systems, even relatively simple and undifferentiated ones, with proper functions[15] accorded by natural design; a social species like *Homo sapiens* is an evolutionary product; and sanctions are socially significant behaviors.[16] Some hints as to how this story might go are provided in chapters 4 and 6.

As a mode of reflection on implicitly normative practices already up and running, and to the extent it charts a course between regulism (behavioral governance by explicit rules) and regularism (mere regularity of behavior), the process of effecting reflective equilibrium is a close relative of Brandom's "reflectively rational Socratic practice," despite the fact that the modification of established normative principle in the face of recalcitrant cases that is an important aspect of effecting reflective equilibrium is only implicit in his common-law analogy.[17] Principles of inference, says Brandom (1994, 130),

may be likened to the principles formulated by judges at common law, intended both to codify prior practice, as represented by precedent, expressing explicitly as a rule what was implicit therein, and to have regulative authority for subsequent practice. The expressive task of making material inferential commitments explicit plays an essential role in the reflectively rational Socratic practice of harmonizing our commitments.

With this, we have arrived at a second mode of metainterpretation, something that might be called *reflexive* metainterpretation. Suppose an interpreter undertakes the ambitious task of making explicit *all* the rules governing the central practices, both representational and otherwise, of his own cultural community, including scientific, legal, artistic, and religious practices, with the aim of bringing judgment of specific cases and general principle into global reflective equilibrium, of "harmonizing" the implicit commitments of the members of his own community. Suppose, further, that this theorist attempts, as far as he is able, to include in the mix metainterpretations of normative principles governing all culturally alien practices he judges significant, both contemporary and historical. Some of these might be endorsed; others might remain unendorsed and embedded in metarepresentational discourse. Such a reflexive metainterpreter would be a philosopher—a philosopher, moreover, of Hegelian ambition. He would be engaged in a project of achieving wide, indeed the widest possible, reflective equilibrium between judgments of cases and principle. This mode of wide reflective equilibrium extends beyond the global commitments of the individual or the isolated group to the principles endorsed within a community in which a division of cognitive labor prevails, thus allowing deference (but also challenges) to experts. How these expert groups are identified is a difficult problem, raising complex issues of sociopolitical organization and of training, apprenticeship, testing, and qualification that I cannot explore here. Wide reflective equilibrium must also, like Brandom's common-law analogy, have a genuine diachronic dimension: what is justified now because it is in reflective equilibrium with current practice or principle may not remain so in the future.

A less ambitious reflexive metainterpreter might attempt to render explicit the implicit norms of some specific domestic cultural practice or other, as Rawls did with regard to liberal democracy, thereby facilitating a more narrow reflective equilibrium regarding some set of relevant normative commitments and judgments of cases. To attempt such a thing, provided the reflexive metainterpretation remains wide enough to extend beyond narrow disciplinary boundaries, is nothing other than to mount a philosophical treatment of that practice. A philosopher, whether more ambitious or less, is, I suggest, someone (a "polypragmatic Socratic conversationalist"?) in the business of reflexive metainterpretation, someone who attempts to bring to awareness some set of norms, to make them explicit by codifying them as rules or principles, in the interest of facilitating reflective equilibrium with regard to a domestic norm-governed cultural practice;[18] and the specifically philosophical sentences of a theory are nothing other than *reflexive metainterpretative sentences*.

Western tonal art music since 1650 is an example of such a domestic norm-governed representational practice; and making our normative commitments explicit so as to achieve reflective equilibrium regarding principle and practice is the aim of this book. Accordingly, I shall provide throughout the book a number of well-known musical examples to serve as intuitive test cases. That Western tonal art music since 1650 is a norm-governed practice is beyond question: musical compositions of this genre and their performances are subject to critical evaluation.[19] That it is in any sense a *representational* practice is yet to be argued. But this much we can already say: musical passages and compositions are intentionally produced structures that are susceptible to *misunderstanding* by performers and listeners. In such cases, we say they have missed the musical "sense." Intentionally produced, sense- or meaning-carrying items are, however, nothing other than representations. Saying what normative principles are violated by those who miss musical sense will be one task of the succeeding chapters.

Whatever the ambitions of the reflexive metainterpreter, however, the descriptive explanatory option remains: the representational tokens may be regarded as items in the natural causal order. And, if the metainterpreter is a naturalist, that is, if he subscribes to the three principles (ontological, metaphysical, and epistemological) enunciated above, the tokens must be so regarded. For whatever he may propose metainterpretively, this is what representations fundamentally *are*, both in themselves (ontologically and metaphysically) and as possible objects of descriptive knowledge (epistemologically), given commitment to these three principles. This serves to cool down breathless Goodmanesque irrealist longings, the temptation literally to impute "worldmaking" powers to representational (or "symbolic") activity. Interpretations of certain representational types[20] may be many; but we, the interpreting organisms, along with the representational tokens themselves, are physical particulars in this very physical world. *Norms and meanings* are not part of the causal fabric of the world, but *behaviors, including sanctioning behaviors*, are; and the interpretations of declarative sentences asserted by speakers, a special class of public representations, express commitment to unitary truth and may either be endorsed or negatively sanctioned by hearers within the social context. To assert a declarative sentence is to endorse it as true. Verbal commitment, endorsement, and sanctioning are behaviors that constrain interpretations of this special variety of representations.

The naturalist philosopher may say anything descriptively about his chosen set of representations or behaviors that he is prepared to endorse as true and may proffer any causal explanations he deems adequate. But any material descriptive claims or causal hypotheses advanced must be in principle empirically evaluable, even if not individually testable; inferences, both material and formal, and claims presented as logically true must fall under explicit rules of inferential practice or be brought into reflective equilibrium with those rules. Logically true statements may not be empirically testable; but even they (and the valid inference patterns they instantiate) are empirically *sensitive* to the extent they are subject to modification under conditions of (narrower or wider) reflective disequilibrium that is, to the extent they sanction (negatively) inferences we wish, in the interest of more virtuous theory, to make, or sanction (positively) any inferences that turn out, again in the interest of virtuous theory, to be unacceptable. Any empirical descriptions or explanatory hypotheses the naturalist philosopher employs must, moreover, cohere with theories of the descriptive sciences of representation and behavior, namely neuroscience, evolutionary biology, cognitive psychology, and descriptive anthropology (and with the basic sciences of physics and chemistry).

Alternatively, while the naturalist philosopher will not pretend to be doing empirical science from the armchair, he will not hesitate to make use, including inferential use, of descriptions and explanations deriving from reputable scientific sources to the extent they further the overall reflexive metainterpretative project. The present project, once again, is to engage in the reflexive metainterpretation of Western tonal art music since 1650 as a representational practice so as to bring judgment concerning the meaning and significance of musical experience into reflective equilibrium with normative principle, while situating musical experience firmly within a descriptive, broadly Darwinian evolutionary theoretical framework. As a result, dialectical movement back and forth between description and interpretation will be considered a virtue and not a vice. Indeed, it will be considered a necessity. For one thing, such a project requires that the naturalist philosopher remain ever cognizant of scientific description and explanation if he is to keep to his ontological, metaphysical, and epistemological commitments. For another, since the acceptance of a broad, reformist, aposteriorist naturalism precludes the practice of traditional philosophical a priori analysis, representational types must be identified and described empirically if they are to be reflexively metainterpreted.

What, then, is the status of the three naturalistic principles enunciated at the outset of this introduction? The third, the epistemological principle, is clearly reflexively metainterpretational: it is the codification of an empiricist norm implicit in centrally important domestic cognitive practices like science and law for the evaluation of truth claims and explanatory hypotheses. The first two principles, the ontological and metaphysical principles, on the other hand, could be taken to be descriptive and explanatory themselves. If so, they would be, for the naturalist, very abstract, high-level empirical hypotheses, validated by inference to the best explanation, and not philosophical sentences at all. But they need not be taken this way, and perhaps they should not be. Both these principles have significant modal force: they limn the limits of the possible, and Quine taught us that the logical status of descriptive modal claims is problematic. It is not clear what such principles explain, nor what claim they have to be the best explanation of anything. Rather than wielding explanatory power, they may be taken as normative principles that *set* explanatory *parameters*: any explanation that violates these norms is counted (provisionally) as unacceptable. To take them this way is to construe them as prescriptive rather than descriptive, as regulative principles that codify a certain "stance" or set of pragmatic attitudes with regard to explanation (cf. van Fraassen 2002, 60–63). As such, they, too, are reflexive metainterpretational principles, the result of reflection on the norms implicit in current scientific practice. If taken as normative principles, not as descriptive doctrine, they could be seen as part of an ongoing attempt to "harmonize" (by Socratic reflection) principles of musical representation with scientific principle and the web of empirical belief.

1.5 Conspectus

The remainder of the book falls into five chapters, which present the following account of musical representation, meaning, ontology, and emotion.

Chapter 2: The Musical Affordance: Three Varieties of Musical Representation. Three modes of musical representation are identified, one external (the heard musical surface) and two internal (the hierarchical plan representations of the goal-directed structure of the music and the musical mental models constructed on the basis of these hierarchically organized representations). These constructed mental models, which are nonconceptual analog representations, represent virtual layouts and scenarios in an imaginary musical space in which the listener acts (off-line). Musical space is a joint product of the physical acoustics of sound, the physiology of the human ear and neural auditory system, and the motor systems of the human brain and body.

Chapter 3: The Musical Utterance: How Music Means. The musical performance is a public representational token that functions as a nonconceptual or gestural utterance. Extrinsic musical meaning arises by way of an exemplification relation (modeling by way of shared properties) between musical mental models constructed by the listener and the actual world of human experience, including human cognitive experience concerning abstract realms of thought. Such modeling occurs in two distinct modes. First, the musical surface contains an elaborate field structure that models the structure of lexical semantic fields. This mode of musical meaning I term *extramusical form*. The second mode of musical meaning I term *extramusical content*. The listener constructs models of layouts and scenarios in virtual musical space in which he moves in imagination. Because motor experience is strongly implicated in musical understanding, extramusical content arises on the basis of a "body-in-the-mind" metaphorical transference, following the theory proposed by George Lakoff and Mark Johnson.

Chapter 4: The Musical Work. Like biological species, musical works are best regarded as reproductively established families of tokens. In the case of species, the tokens or replicas are individual organisms; in the case of musical works, the tokens are performances. Musical works are neither discovered Platonic abstract objects nor merely invented artifactual types, but created historical entities. Unlike biological species and their traits, which may be said to be *inventions* of undirected natural design because they are relatively accessible in the space of possible designs at certain historical junctures, musical works are creations (albeit not creations *ex nihilo*) because they occupy relatively remote positions in a finite but still vast possibility space.

Chapter 5: From Musical Representation to Musical Emotion. Because human emotions are intentional mental states normally directed at definite objects and states of affairs, actual or fictional, and because, given problems of individuation and reidentification of objects and locations in musical space, there can be, strictly speaking, no virtual musical objects; musical emotions are problematic and may generally be more properly

characterized as affective feelings. Still, talk of musical emotion is not entirely inappropriate, in part because certain global emotional states, namely moods, lack definite intentional objects, in part because some emotions can take rather indefinite features of
egocentric scenarios for their objects. Because internal musical representations have
the structure of plans and activate the motor system off-line, musical experience also
activates the motivational-emotional system, thereby giving rise to emotions and affective feelings. Because musical representation is nonconceptual, musical experience
tends to weaken the metaphysical distinction between subject and object and the
epistemological barrier between subject and subject. Objectification, the distinction between subject and object, requires the individuation and reidentification of independent objects, and that, in turn, requires conceptual abilities. Because of this, because
of the touch-like aspects of musical sound, and because emotions are valent (i.e., evaluative) perceptions of scenarios or indefinite situations, the musical environment
presents itself with a distinctively direct affective presence and intimacy.

Chapter 6: Nausea and Contingency: Musical Emotion and Religious Emotion. The intimacy of the musical environment and the thoroughgoing intentional determination
of musical performance down to very densely ordered nuance properties appeal to
human emotional needs and aspirations that are religious in character. Religion is, at
least in part, an attempt to assuage the human horror of the contingent, the existential
dread of the possibility that human existence is a mere accident of cosmic history and
biological evolution, that human existence constitutes no drama of consequence concerning dispensation regarding any immortal soul, but is rather a pointless sequence of
events significant to no conscious being other than human beings themselves. Owing,
in part, to its origins in the ritual practices of the Upper Paleolithic Magdalenian era,
musical experience derives some of its affective impact by evoking moods that are religious in character. The musical listener is temporarily immersed in a benignant virtual
environment where contingency and brute, "superfluous" (*de trop*) material existence
have been vanquished and where everything that happens, happens exactly as it
ought.

2 The Musical Affordance: Three Varieties of Musical Representation

2.1 Introduction and Chapter Conspectus

In the general introduction, I proposed that Western tonal art music since 1650 is a representational practice. But what reason is there to think that this (or any) style of music is representational at all? And if it is, *how* is it representational?

The aim of the present chapter is to begin to answer these questions. In section 2.2, I argue that the musical surface functions as an informationally structured entity, that is, as a carrier or vehicle from which information can be extracted by performing appropriate transformational operations that are supported by representations in the human mind–brain. In section 2.3, I propose that a musical performance presents itself as a two-dimensional surface defined by axes of pitch and time. On the basis of information contained in this musical surface, the listener constructs internal mental models of layouts and scenarios in virtual musical space.[1] Section 2.4 then takes up the phenomenon of motion heard in musical space by considering the contributions to musical experience made by the human motor system and the structure and function of the inner ear. After introducing at the end of section 2.4 the notion of simulated animate action in musical space, I consider in section 2.5 some relevant issues of motor neurophysiology and cognitive deficit. Section 2.6 takes up the question of the modularity of musical processing systems, and 2.7 provides a chapter summary and conclusion. A brief discussion of representation in cognitive psychology is appended in section 2.8.

The approach of this chapter will be largely descriptive. We shall be concerned here principally with musical performances as highly structured physical events that function as informational vehicles. Accordingly, the questions we shall be asking about the existence and nature of the internal representations that process the information latent in the musical surface will look to neuroscience and cognitive psychology for answers. Once the representations in question have been identified and described, we shall then be in a position to adopt in chapter 3 a normative, metainterpretational stance that shifts from description to interpretation. At that point, we shall attempt to make explicit the syntactic, semantic, and pragmatic principles governing the use of these varieties of musical representation.

2.2   Gibson, Representation, and Information

I find no fault with the Gibsonian program, as far as it goes. I find, however, that it does not go far enough. To say that there is sufficient information in the proximal stimulus and even to point to some of the higher-order variables in which the information resides is not to describe the mechanism that extracts the information and uses it to control appropriate behavior or additional cognitive processing.
—Roger Shepard (1981, 285)

Although James J. Gibson was no friend of internal representations, he did pay some close attention to external representations or "surrogates,"[2] especially external visual representations that are pictorial and cinematic. In "direct" visual perception of the world, the information in the optical array specifies stable objects or "invariants" in the environment.[3] The information in a photograph or a motion picture also specifies invariants. But in this case the stable objects are "virtual" objects of "indirect" awareness (Gibson 1986, 283). For Gibson, any external representation presents two aspects. It is a structured object in its own right; and it is a carrier of information about something else. It contains "information considered as structure"; and it contains "information about" (Gibson 1966, 245). Interestingly, Gibson does not confine his observations concerning external representations to photographs and so-called representational art. The "bleeding heart in the inkblot" (Gibson 1986, 283) is also a virtual object;[4] and pure music (music without words or attached program) also contains information considered as structure, although Gibson declines to speculate as to whether pure music has any "meaning," that is, whether it also contains any "information about." This is one of the central questions I mean to address in this chapter: what sort of information about, and what sorts of virtual objects[5] (if any) might there be said to be "in the music"?[6] If the musical surface can function as a Gibsonian surrogate, then music can be a representational art. In subsequent chapters I shall adduce additional reasons why music should be considered representational.

2.2.1   Ambiguities in the Notion of Information

Dretske reports (1981, 255n10) that at a 1976 conference, Gibson denied that his notion of information could be identified with Claude Shannon's information-theoretic notion, the version Dretske adopts in his *Knowledge and the Flow of Information* (1981). Dretske then produces the following quotation from Gibson (1966, 187), which, in his view, calls that denial into question:

Let us begin by noting that information about something means only specificity to something. Hence, when we say that information is conveyed by light, or by sound, odor, or mechanical energy, we do not mean that the source is literally conveyed as a copy or replica. The sound of a bell is not the bell and the odor of cheese is not the cheese. Similarly the perspective projection of the faces of an object (by the reverberating flux of reflected light in a medium) is not the object itself. Nevertheless, in all these cases a property of the stimulus is univocally related to a property of the object by virtue of physical laws. This is what I mean by the conveying of environmental information.

Dretske surely has a point. According to his version of information theory, the transfer of information from source to receiver must bring about the reduction, by virtue of nomic dependency or reliable correlation, of uncertainty at the receiver concerning which of a number of possible states of affairs obtains at the source.[7] And such information transfer does seem to be part of what Gibson is talking about here. Yet we can also see why he may have wanted to resist any direct identification of his notion of information with the information-theoretic one: there is no such information transfer from the bleeding heart "in" the inkblot or from the nonexistent subject of a representational painting. In neither case do we have nomic dependency or reliable correlation. Gibson's surrogates, that is to say, are not mere uncertainty-reducing signals. Because they contain "information considered as structure," they are what I shall be calling *informationally structured objects and events.*[8]

These objects, as we shall see in the next section, certainly may function as uncertainty-reducing signals, but they are more. They are informational vehicles that possess enough internal complexity to require sophisticated computations for the extraction of the information they contain *or can be taken to contain.* It is this mode of information extraction that allows for the tracking of so-called invariants in perceptual arrays and makes it possible for objects to be "seen in" representational surrogates. The ringing of a bell or the odor of a piece of cheese is certainly informational in the information-theoretic sense: both are capable of reducing uncertainty with regard to events and states of affairs at their sources. But they contain no invariants and no information considered as structure: no object is "heard in" the ring or "smelled in" the smell. These are not informationally structured objects or events, for they lack requisite internal complexity.[9] A fortiori, bell rings and odors are not *syntactically* structured objects or events: they may be signals, but they are not symbols. As we shall see in the next chapter, some surrogates are not only informationally structured, but are also syntactically organized symbols.

This difference of opinion between Gibson and Dretske not only highlights the distinction between signals and surrogates; it also highlights certain pervasive ambiguities in the use of the expression "information," ambiguities that infect both the Dretskean and the Gibsonian versions. Since I have characterized the musical surface as informational, we must attempt to sort these out. A signal with *de re* informational content, a locution Dretske (1981, 66) actually employs, carries information *of* an existing object, that it has a certain property or stands in a certain relation. In order to carry such information, a signal must depend nomically on or correlate reliably with events at its source; and it must reduce uncertainty at the receiver regarding these events. The informational content of a signal that does not reduce uncertainty at all is zero; for example, that particular signal would have been produced regardless of which of a number of possible states of affairs obtained at the source. Moreover, a signal carrying *de re* informational content is not true or false, veridical or nonveridical, for these are terms of semantic and epistemic evaluation that are out of place in mathematical information theory, which is primarily concerned with *average* amounts of information measured in binary units (or bits) transmitted across an information channel: the transmitted information can only be more or less equivocal or more or less noisy. Equivocation is relevant information at the source that is not transmitted, while noise is information arriving at (or perhaps deriving from) the receiver *independently* of information generated at the source in question. "Misinformation" is, therefore, a misnomer; and "reliable information" is a redundancy. Compare Dretske (1981, 45): "In this [information-theoretic] sense of the term, *false* information and *mis*-information are not kinds of information—any more than decoy ducks and rubber ducks are kinds of ducks. And to speak of certain information as being reliable is to speak redundantly." A signal either communicates some quantity of information measurable in bits or it does not; and any information actually transmitted is reliable because it is nomically dependent on (or reliably correlated with) objects and properties at the source of the signal and reduces uncertainty regarding them.

Unfortunately, Dretske does not always heed his own wisdom:

The pointer [on a voltmeter] carries information about voltage *in virtue of* carrying accurate and reliable information about these more proximal events [occurring in its own mechanism] (in the same way our sensory experience carries information about Elmer's death by carrying accurate and reliable information about the configuration of ink on a newspaper page). (Dretske 1981, 187)

Dretske does stipulate, it must be said, that to get *de re* informational content out of mathematical information theory, which is concerned only with average amounts of information transmitted over an information channel and not with the informational content of particular signals, uncertainty must be reducible to zero. That is, for a signal to carry the specific semantic content that some state of affairs obtains, the conditional probability that that state of affairs obtains at the source must be one, given information received and conditional on the information the receiver already has (1981, 52–53, 65). If conditional probability were to be less than one, then, by (violation of) the "xerox principle" (ibid., 57), repeated transmissions of a particular signal could ultimately alter its content; and this would make information theory unusable for semantic theory.

But I cannot see that this affects the point at issue. If informational content with a conditional probability of less than one cannot be misinformation, then neither can informational content with a conditional probability of one. As a result, Dretske should not be saying "accurate and reliable information," since "accurate" is a term of epistemic evaluation, and all information, if it is information at all, is reliable to some degree. He should be saying "information that is unequivocal or noise-free (to some specified degree)." And Dretske should *not* be saying that "our subject [trained to categorize as red white objects viewed under red light] did not acquire his concept in response to information about the color of objects. He did it in response to *mis*information" (1981, 223). Again, what Dretske should be saying is not that the subject acquired his color concept in response to misinformation, but in response to *information* (deriving from white objects) *under abnormal lighting conditions*. Compare Millikan (2000, 232): "The miscalibrated gauge carries informationL ["hard" information based on lawful or nomic dependencies] telling the actual level of gas in the tank. If we interpret it wrongly, that does not make it carry the informationL we wrongly take it to carry."

If we assume (as seems reasonable) that, like Dretske, Robert Stalnaker is referring to *de re* informational content, he commits a similar error: "the 'information' [that a zebra is striped] might," he says, "be misinformation: . . . it might be that the state of the visual system merely indicates that the zebra is striped, meaning that it is in a state that, under normal conditions, would constitute receiving the information that the zebra is striped" (Stalnaker 2003, 102). Again, what should be said (or implied) is not that the visual system contains misinformation, but that it contains *information* deriving from some object, say, a donkey, in unusual, say, highly dappled, lighting. Notice also the shift from "information" to "informational state." The latter expression is ambiguous: to say that the visual system is in an informational state can mean that it is in possession of *de re* informational content, which, as we saw, is neither veridical nor nonveridical; or it can mean that the visual system is in a state such that it *would* contain that information *if* it stood in certain causal relations or was reliably correlated with an object of a certain kind. "Would contain" easily slips into "would be *taken* to contain."

This shift from "information" to "informational state" allows Stalnaker, inappropriately, I believe, to regard informational content as *eo ipso* intentional, as *indicating* that a state of affairs obtains: "One can say that *x* *indicates* that *P* if it is in a state that *would* carry the information that *P* if the appropriate background conditions obtained" (Stalnaker 2003, 101). But no object in an informational state indicates anything until it is *used* to represent by an interpreter. An informational state, that is to say, *is not per se a representational state*. If it were, the rings in tree trunks would be representational and therefore intentional states, which, I submit, is absurd.[10] Stalnaker, therefore, should not say that "information is by definition veridical" (ibid.). To repeat, "veridical" is a term of epistemic evaluation that does not properly apply to *de re* informational content. The cross-section of the tree trunk is indeed an informational vehicle with *de re* informational content. But again, it does not indicate anything until it is used to represent.[11] Once it is so used, it achieves representational status and indicates, *for an interpreter*, that certain states of affairs obtain or obtained, say, that the tree is one thousand years old and has survived several forest fires. Compare, once again, Millikan (1984, 118): "There are no signs without potential interpreters."

If we take signs to be external representations, Cummins (1996, 90) rejects this basic semiotic principle. He defends a "picture theory" of representation according to which a "structure" represents another structure simply by virtue of being "isomorphic" with it (1996, 90ff). "Represents" is, thus, a two-place relation between structures, not a three-place relation between structures and a user. The mind, he says, "must be able to simulate nature" (1996, 92), a view with which I shall be agreeing. The problem I see with Cummins's version of the view concerns the heavy lifting he assigns the notion of "isomorphism." Isomorphism is structural similarity; and similarity, as Goodman (1972) taught us, is a slippery notion (see also chapter 3, section 3.2 below). Any attempt to identify representation with isomorphism motivates at least three questions:

1. "Is isomorphic with" is a symmetrical relation; "represents" is nonsymmetrical, if not asymmetrical. Of two isomorphic structures, which, then, is the representation and which is the represented, if not the one used to represent the other? Without a potential user, moreover, isomorphism is insufficient for representation. If it were sufficient, then any any snowflake would be a representation of any other structurally similar snowflake. This seems an embarrassment of representational riches.
2. Is the structural similarity first- or higher-order (isomorphism versus paramorphism)? Is it metrical (magnitude covariant), topological (order preserving), or neither? If neither, then even linguistic symbols (or their propositional contents) may be said to be "isomorphic with" the states of affairs they represent, as in the early Wittgenstein's "logical picture" theory of meaning. But Cummins rejects this version of the theory and denies that natural language represents at all (1996, 90, 111). It only communicates. He defines a structure as "a set of things and a set of relations on them" (ibid., 90n6). Examples of structures include abstract objects or "formalisms" like the series of natural numbers along with the relation of being greater than, maps, and other map-like analog representations. In the ensuing discussion, I shall be terming analog representations internal to the mind–brain "mental models" (see section 2.3.1 below).
3. Entities and events have various and sundry structural properties. Which are the representational ones?

Cummins does not explicitly address the first two questions, but he has an answer to the third: the representational properties are those, whatever they may be, that establish relations of isomorphism. This answer, however, conflates *representations* with mere *informational vehicles*: "If your map is not properly oriented, you won't get to your destination, *but that is not the map's fault. The correct information is there; you just do not or cannot exploit it*" (ibid., 99, some emphasis mine). Since Cummins uses representation-as-isomorphism as a theoretically primitive notion on which to build an account of cognition, representation is intrinsic to isomorphic structures, nonconventional, nonintentional, and entirely independent of use. As a result, the information that "is there" in the map is natural information, in this case, something very much like Gibson's "information considered as structure." Isomorphisms abound in nature, but, once again, natural information is neither correct nor incorrect. Either the map contains some quantity of natural information or it does not. Notice that Cummins, though not invoking the name of Gibson, characterizes maps and maplike entities as "surrogates" (ibid., 111).

For Millikan (2004, 37), "A natural sign of a thing is something else from which you can learn by tracking in thought a connection that exists in nature," which essentially is the view I advocate. But, like Cummins, she apparently has decided that a representation need not be intentional. "For your true representation to be an *intentional* representation," she says, "it must be a function or purpose of the system that produced it to make representations" (ibid., 67, emphasis in the original). Only representations produced by a system in accord with its proper function (Millikan 1984), it would seem, now qualify as intentional representations. A representation that is not intentional, we learn, is simply a natural sign with a certain degree of complexity: "When natural sign systems have more significant variables than time and/or place, it becomes natural to call them [i.e., the signs] not just 'natural signs' but 'natural representations,' and to speak of the (local) information they carry" (Millikan 2004, 50).

Distinguishing between representations that are produced by a representational system in accordance with its proper function and those that are not is unexceptionable. But I question the legitimacy of the distinction between natural representations and intentional representations, as well as the propriety of evaluating representations that allegedly are not intentional as true or false. The "true beliefs" of Davidson's Swampman, says Millikan (2004, 67n30), "are representations, but not intentional representations." A natural or "plain" representation, we discover, is simply a "bearer of natural information" (ibid., 71), albeit natural information that may be "local" (ibid., 31ff) and does not, in contrast with Dretske's "context-free natural information" (ibid., 35), require nomic or logical dependencies. In my terms, Millikan's bearers of natural information are nothing other than informational vehicles. An (uninterpreted) bearer of natural information is not intentional, but it is also not representational. She had it right in 1984: there are no signs (and, I would add, no representations) without potential interpreters. As a consequence, an uninterpreted bearer of information is neither true nor false. It merely carries some quantity of natural information.

Once used by an interpreter *as* a representation, an informational vehicle, including one that is internal ("in the head"), can also be *mis*used (misinterpreted). For an interpreter to be in a representational state is for that interpreter to use an internal informational vehicle (say, the retina in a certain informational state) as a representation. To use an internal informational vehicle as a representation is not, of course, to represent *it*, to make of *it* an intentional object: the intentional object is the distal object from which its *de re* informational content derives and regarding which the informational vehicle causally guides the interpreter's actions. These actions enable the interpreter to "triangulate," by way of sequences of causal interactions, on the distal object. How the *de re* informational content in an informational vehicle is exploited is up to the interpreter. Therefore, what that vehicle *represents* (zebra under normal conditions or donkey under abnormal conditions), how it is taken, is also up to the interpreter, even if what information the vehicle *contains* (donkey under abnormal lighting conditions) is not up to the interpreter but remains a matter of physical fact. With the representational use of an informational vehicle, however, comes the possibility of misrepresentation: things are not as the informational vehicle *is taken to indicate* they are: it is a donkey in dappled lighting, not a zebra, standing in the copse.

Many animals enter into representational states but are not able to metarepresent: they have no implicit theory of mind and cannot represent representations, neither their own nor those of others. As Bermudez (2003, chapter 9) convincingly argues, intentional ascent (i.e., metarepresentation) requires semantic ascent; and semantic ascent requires language. This distinctively human metarepresentational ability opens up another possibility, the possibility of a distinctive mode of representation without *de re* informational content: the deliberate interpretation of objects as Gibsonian informationally structured "surrogates" in full awareness that they have no *de re* informational content at all. Upon this "conniving" representational use of informational structures depends much visual art (cf. Evans 1982, 124).[12] And insofar as music is representational, I shall be arguing, it also depends on a similar conniving use of states of what Evans (1982, chapter 5, sect. 2) calls "the human informational system."

The distinctions I have pressed between informational vehicles, informational content, informational states, and representations, are, I believe, implicit in Evans. Here he refers to an informational vehicle with *de re* informational content:

We can speak of a certain bit of information being of, or perhaps from, an object, in a sense resembling the way in which we speak of a photograph being of an object. . . . A certain mechanism produces things which have a certain informational content. . . . And we can say that the product of such a mechanism is *of* the objects that were the input to the mechanism when the product was produced. (Ibid., 124–125)

But then he adds:

A photograph should not be said to represent . . . at least, not in the way in which a painting may be said to represent, e.g., that Christ is on the cross. We see, here, the need for a distinction between, on the one hand, an *a*-representation (i.e., a species of particular-representation, in a specification of whose content mention of *a* would figure: something which represents, or misrepresents, *a*) and, on the other, something which, without being an *a*-representation, is a representation *of a*. (Ibid., 125n10)[13]

Evans's distinction between a (photographic) representation of *a* and an *a*-representation is close to the one I have proposed between an informational vehicle with *de re* informational content and an object used as a representation, perhaps in a conniving way. But there is this difference: I maintain that a photograph of *a*, like a cross-section of the trunk of a tree, is *merely* an informational vehicle and not a representation at all.[14] But when the photograph is used to represent *a*, as it normally is,[15] it becomes not only a representation of *a*, but also an *a*-representation. We shall revisit Evans's views in chapter 5.

2.3   Musical Virtual Layouts and Scenarios

With the distinctions between information, informational vehicles, informational states, and representations now in hand, let us now take up once again the main thread of argument and explore Gibson's account of external visual representations a little further. A photograph or a work of pictorial art presents a two-dimensional surface that displays information "frozen in time" (Gibson 1986, 71). This means that a voluntary change in position on the part of the perceiver brings about no systematic change in perspective, and therefore does not enable disclosure of underlying invariants in the scene. The disclosure of information is in this case largely under the control of the artist or photographer. Exactly the same is true of cinema, indeed more so because of the added control of the order and tempo of presentation in time. Applying a similar Gibsonian analysis to music would require that it too be construed as presenting a two-dimensional surface. But one such construal is quite familiar and has been given extensive consideration (Kubovy 1981, 80ff; Julesz and Hirsch 1972, 299): the musical surface can be interpreted as a two-dimensional surface defined by an ordinate of pitch (heard frequency) and an abscissa of time.[16]

It is important to distinguish between music considered merely acoustically as a set of physical sound events and music as an informationally structured set of tones. As a set of physical sound events, a musical episode is a physical, spatial phenomenon and is perceived as such. A listener is generally able by means of head turning and asynchronous onset to individuate and locate sounds in the surrounding three-dimensional physical space. "Pitch streaming" phenomena (the tendency to group successive sounds of similar pitch together) will aid the individuation and location of sounds, but pitch is not an "indispensable attribute" (Kubovy 1981) for such individuation and location: the members of a set of simultaneous or serially arranged nonpitched sounds can be individuated and located in three-dimensional space. In the case of musical perception (the perception of a set of sound events as musical tones), however, the priority of spatial location over pitch for individuation is reversed, whether the tones are considered to be types or tokens.[17] Two simultaneous, equally loud, timbrally similar, and identically pitched tones emanating from two loudspeakers, each placed in front of a listener at angles of 45 degrees from the sagittal plane, will be difficult or impossible to individuate: they will be heard as a single tone emanating from a source directly in front of the listener. Two simultaneous, equally loud, timbrally similar, but differently pitched tones emanating from a single loudspeaker placed directly in front of the listener, on the other hand, are easily individuated (Kubovy 1981, 85ff). Since all sounds, pitched or nonpitched, musical or nonmusical, are events, time is an indispensable dimension for their individuation. There is, then, good reason to single out pitch and time as the indispensable attributes for the individuation of musical tones; and this, in turn, provides good reason to interpret the musical surface as a two-dimensional one.

This is not to deny that location in physical space *can* play some role in the individuation of musical tones. The standard audience-left to audience-right arrangement of high- to low-pitched stringed instruments in a symphony orchestra or a string quartet[18] identifies high tones as "left tones" and deep tones as "right tones," and makes use of these identifications to help the hearer individuate tones. The piano keyboard reverses this arrangement: left is low and right is high. Such identifications are nonessential to tone individuation and are merely conventional. At one time it was standard to place the second violins of an orchestra on the right where the cellos are now normally found, as was Toscanini's practice with the NBC Symphony Orchestra. Stokowski placed the woodwind and brass on the right, the cellos in the center, and the contrabasses in a line stretching across the back of the orchestra. One could imagine the performers in a string quartet seated in single file at right angles to the first row of audience seats. Ensemble would be extremely difficult in this bizarre arrangement, and the balances would suffer distortion. But as long as all four of the voices remained audible, the musical effect would not be destroyed. With adroit placement of microphones, such an arrangement might go undetected in a recording.

Like music, cinema creates an illusion of motion by way of a carefully ordered sequence of perceptions.[19] A certain contrast between cinema and music is, however, revealing. While a motion picture does not allow the unlimited exploratory eye movements permitted by a still picture, it does allow some such movements: one may visually explore a scene or a face in a motion picture. The cinematographic surface, that is to say, presents itself phenomenologically as a field with simultaneously present regions. With the exception of temporally extended, simultaneously sounding chords, however, music allows no such voluntary explorations of its surface.[20] While this is of course due to the physiological differences between the organs of hearing and seeing, it is also due to the nature of music itself. Sounding tones are events, and events are evanescent. Once consummated, they are gone forever. This suggests, if we are to pursue the present Gibsonian project of discovering virtual objects in music as a two-dimensional informational structure, that we might do well to compare musical audition not with vision, but with the only sensory modality other than vision and hearing that is capable of apprehending a surface as an informationally structured object, namely the haptic modality.[21] Tastes may be organized in taste space and smells in smell space; and they may convey information about the objects that cause them. But neither tastes nor smells are easily organized so as to contain Gibsonian informational invariants, though to say that this is impossible is perhaps to claim too much. As a point of phenomenology, haptic exploration of a surface does not, as in the case of vision, yield the presentation of a field, despite the possibility of simultaneous exploration of a small surface with independent but coordinated limbs and digits. During haptic exploration of a physical surface we may retrace our path at will. But haptic exploration has a far more pronounced serial form than does vision. And although we cannot literally retrace our musical path, musical structure allows the creation of the *illusion* of retracing a path, as when, to take the simplest case, we move step-wise along the diatonic scale from tonic to dominant and then back again.[22]

Jackendoff (1987, 257) points out that "[c]entral to most music is the notion of a maximally stable pitch that can serve as a point of departure and arrival and whose return can be recognized as a point of relaxation. Also central seems to be the notion of relative stability (consonance) or instability (dissonance) of the intervals between pitches." He goes on to claim that "[t]hese aspects of music have no formal parallel in other cognitive capacities (imagine organizing colors or smells that way!), and they are essential to getting any musical system off the ground." But there are formal parallels to these aspects of music in at least one other domain of sensory experience, namely kinesthetic experience, the experience of bodily motion in a gravitationally affected environment; and the kinesthetic sense is an aspect of the haptic. These are parallels Jackendoff himself acknowledges elsewhere (1987, 238–239). Structural symmetries and parallelisms abound in music, and these, I shall be arguing, can suggest invariances in a virtual landscape. In addition, musical polyphony allows the simulation (by independent but coordinated voices) of simultaneous haptic exploration using independent digits and limbs. But just as in cinema the order of informational disclosure is controlled by the director and not the viewer, in music, it is controlled by the composer, not the listener.

Consider now Gibson's signature doctrine of affordances. His idea was that environmental invariants present themselves to perceiving organisms as affording possibilities of action: animal and human perception is related to a range of possible relevant motor responses. Indeed, the relevant motor responses affect the quality of the perceptual presentation for a given creature. The fact that a flat, uncluttered terrain affords the possibilities of unimpeded motion makes it look runnable to a creature with appropriate capacities. Since external visual *representations* like pictures, photos, and motion pictures also present invariants, they present affordances as well. But in such cases the affordances, like the objects represented, are virtual: one can see that the fruit in the still life is not there for the eating. The human informational system has been exploited in a conniving way.

The idea of virtual objects present in a musical surface may seem at first an implausible one. With very few exceptions,[23] the musical surface (like Gibson's inkblot) contains no obvious representations of objects or events, nor does it, like a discursive symbol system, possess the conceptual and referential structure requisite for the individuation and reidentification of objects. This second difficulty is of signal importance, and I shall postpone discussion of it until chapter 5, where it can be addressed more adequately. The notion of the musical affordance, however, is suggestive because of the intimate connection between affordances and motor responses. But in order to put Gibson's idea to work, we shall have to take Shepard's opening epigraph to heart and depart from the Gibsonian anti-internal-representationalist line.[24] Gibson is suspicious of internal representations because he is understandably hostile to the traditional philosophical view of them as epistemically privileged objects of awareness that stand between perceiver and world. Contemporary philosophy of mind and cognitive psychology have largely rejected this view of internal representations, interpreting them instead as representational vehicles, that is, physical structures that carry out representational functions, rather than as Cartesian immanent intentional objects.

We may, then, countenance internal representations that mediate the extraction of information from the ambient informational array and mediate the appropriate motor responses. As Shepard observes (1981, 1984), the orthodox Gibsonian position—that the sensory systems engage in no constructive activities but simply resonate to already structured information in the ambient array—may be plausible, if inaccurate, when these systems are functioning smoothly in the relatively unambiguous and informationally rich environments for which they are designed. In these circumstances, their constructive activities go on unnoticed. But degraded and ambiguous inputs immediately reveal the extent to which information extraction depends on pattern completion, which in turn requires internal representations and constructive procedures that operate on these representations. Such processes are the means by which any sentient creature solves the general problem of recovering a three-dimensional world of stable objects from the two-dimensional patterns of stimulations on its sensory surfaces.[25] Shepard characterizes the relationship between the spatiotemporal world outside the skin of the organism and the representations inside its head as one of "psychophysical complementarity" rather than first-order isomorphism or similarity. The complementary relationship between key and lock is his preferred metaphor. The information from the three-dimensional ambient surround encoded in the sensory surfaces is extracted and transformed into internal representations by way of (mathematical) functions that stand in an inverse relationship to the functions that map the three-dimensional world onto the two-dimensional sensory surface. I shall not attempt here to specify these mathematical functions, a task that extends beyond my competence. The fact that the visual sensory surfaces are *informational structures*, that is, informational vehicles with significant internal complexity, allows the mapping and the performance of inverse transformations that establish the psychophysical complementarity relationship. The internal representations, in turn, effect appropriate motor commands that proceed outward to muscle effectors. Since affordances implicate possible *actions*, motor commands inhibited and run off-line play an important role in any experience of affordances. To run commands off-line is to simulate actions imaginatively without engaging the relevant motor systems.

In fact, as Shepard and others have recognized, any very sharp separation of perceptual and motor functions is artificial (Churchland 1995, 92ff; Clarke 2005, 19; Edelman and Tononi 2000, 96; Gibson 1974, 391; Heft 2001, 174ff; Lakoff and Johnson 1999, 581; Prinz 2004, 228–229; Shaw and Hazelett 1986; Shepard 1981, 330–331). Just as perception requires constant muscular readjustment, muscular control requires constant perceptual feedback.[26] The brain, Shepard points out, evolved as the control center of a motor guidance system in an environment that is locally three-dimensional and Euclidean, with a gravitationally stable frame conferring upright orientation and stability; an environment that contains rigid or semirigid objects subject to spatial transformations consisting of three modes of rigid spatial translation and three of rigid rotation; and an environment in which the *individual organism itself* is a semirigid, partially symmetrical object possessing the same six degrees of freedom of rigid translation and rotation. Much of the empirical evidence that he and his colleagues rely on to support the complementarity thesis concerns the systematic relationship between the times required for the performance of various mental rotations of imagined objects and the times required for the rotations of corresponding real objects in physical space.[27] In order to perform such mental rotations, the subject must implement (off-line) relevant motor programs, for example, the oculo-vestibular motor programs that would enable the eyes to track the rotation in physical space.

When we shift attention from visual to haptic perception, any sharp separation between cognitive and motor representation is especially artificial. Gibson (1966, 99) observes that

the haptic system, unlike the other perceptual systems, includes the whole body, most of its parts, and all of its surface. The extremities are exploratory sense organs, but they are also performatory motor organs; that is to say, the equipment for feeling is anatomically the same as the equipment for doing.

With regard to the haptic system, the *representation* of a rigid object includes an *action plan* for its exploration. The analogy between musical processing and haptic perception, when combined with an appropriate theory of internal musical representation, is, as I now shall argue, capable of yielding an account of musical virtual layouts and scenarios.

The most sophisticated and currently the most widely accepted cognitivist story concerning musical understanding is the generative account provided by Lerdahl and Jackendoff (1983). Like the generative linguistic theory that inspired it, the generative theory of tonal music has an important metainterpretive component: it renders explicit the implicit rules of musical "grammar," and these rules must achieve reflective equilibrium with the intuitions of the comprehending listener who is able to parse the musical surface correctly. These listener intuitions include the sort of "departure and arrival" experiences to which Jackendoff refers. But the theory also aspires to explanatory adequacy. As we saw in the general introduction, that requires showing these rules to be psychologically real, that is, causally efficacious in the mental economy of the listener. Although the claims of the generative theory of music for psychological reality are weaker than the claims of generative linguistics, they are not unsupported. Because there is, to my knowledge, only limited experimental evidence supporting these claims (but see chapter 3) and because of the weakness of indirect "what else" arguments,[28] there remains, as best I can tell, only one other cognitivist strategy available for establishing psychological reality: an argument from analogy that enlists structurally similar, but better established, theoretical objects of cognitive psychological theory, including cognitive linguistic theory, in support of the generative theory of musical understanding. The aim would be to locate the generative musical structures under more general principles of cognitive psychology.[29] If the earlier suggestions in this section are close to the mark, however, the part of cognitive psychology most germane to such a strategy is the cognitive psychology of *action*. Because my overall aims are primarily philosophical (reflexively metainterpretive) and not psychological (causal-explanatory), I shall not attempt to mount a full-fledged argument for the psychological reality of the Lerdahl and Jackendoff representations, an undertaking that would in any event be beyond my competence. But sketching the contours of such an argument, while taking a look at some of the results of the cognitive psychology of action, will yield some philosophical dividends before we are done.

The listener, Lerdahl and Jackendoff propose, extracts the structural information latent in the musical surface by accessing internal representations along with certain implicit well-formedness and preference rules. To say that these rules are implicit is to deny that they are consciously represented by the listener. I would go further still, denying that they are necessarily programmable, representation-level rules at all. As we shall see in the next chapter, they may be realized by a dynamic, connectionist system. The representations fall into four classes: metrical structure representations, phrase-grouping representations, time-span reduction representations, and prolongation reduction representations. All four classes of representations are hierarchically organized, and three of them (all but the phrase-grouping structures) are strictly nested and "headed." To say they are strictly nested is to say that subgroups do not overlap.

To say they are headed is to say that there is one tone or sound event in each group and subgroup that is the most important one.

The metrical structure representations divide bars into strong and weak beats. Smaller durational values are included within larger ones, and these within even larger ones. A piece in common (4/4) time, for example, will contain four quarter-note beats in each bar, the first and third strong and the second and fourth weak. Normally, the first beat is the strongest one and functions as its metrical head. Each quarter value will include two eighth-note values, two quarters will make up a half-note value, and the two half-note values will make up a whole-note value. Musical lines are also hierarchically grouped into phrases. The first large phrase of Beethoven's highly symmetrical *Ode to Joy* theme, for example, consists of eight bars in common time which, in turn, comprise two groups of four bars, each of which further comprises two groups of two bars (see figure 2.1). Unlike metrical structure representations, phrase groupings are not headed (there is no designated single most important event), nor are they strictly nested. For example, on occasion, the last note of one phrase group can also be the first note of the next.

The metrical and phrase grouping structures exhibit an atomistic, "bottom-up" mode of hierarchical organization, whereas the time-span and prolongation reduction structures are represented as generative treelike structures and are organized, like the trees of generative linguistics, in a more holistic, "top-down" fashion. (For a very

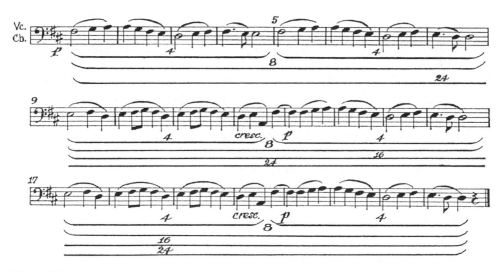

Figure 2.1
Grouping structure (time-span segmentation) of Beethoven's *Ode to Joy* theme. (From Lerdahl and Jackendoff 1983, 124, reprinted by permission of MIT Press.)

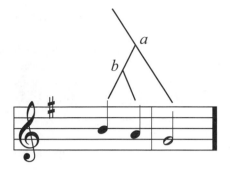

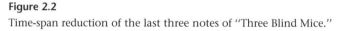

Figure 2.2
Time-span reduction of the last three notes of "Three Blind Mice."

simple typical time-span reduction tree, see figure 2.2. For a more typical one, see figure 2.3.) "Bottom-up" organization combines lower-level into higher-level groups in a cumulative way, whereas "top-down" organization expands hierarchies "from the inside." In generative linguistics, for example, sentences are regarded as indefinitely expandable from the inside by the addition of various modifiers (including words, phrases, and relative clauses) to the basic noun-phrase/verb sentential structure.

According to Lerdahl and Jackendoff, the same is true of the time-span and prolongation reductions. Whereas the former organize the musical tones with regard to their relative structural importance, the latter organize tones with regard to their roles in the increase and decrease of harmonic tension in a musical passage. Since harmonic role contributes strongly to structural importance, there is an intimate relationship between the two. Both varieties of representation are termed "reductions" because they construe musical phrases (and indeed compositions) as expansions or "elaborations" of much simpler series of tones and harmonic progressions. Both are headed (there is a most important event in each group and subgroup) and strictly nested (there is no overlap of membership between groups and subgroups).

The Lerdahl and Jackendoff theory does, however, pose a problem: many of their structures and rules (though not all) apply exclusively to tonal music, indeed to the cadential-harmonic variant of tonal music that has flourished in Europe, the Americas, and (more recently) elsewhere from the seventeenth century to the present. To avail ourselves of their theory would be to narrow the scope of discussion to this particular style of music. Let us so stipulate, but let us also not forget that these rules could be modified so as to apply to any style of music so long as it is tonal.[30] Still, I wish to emphasize following point: *I make no claim that any of the general conclusions regarding music reached in this book apply to any musical style other than that of the tradition of Western tonal art music since 1650.* This style of music, of course, constitutes one, and only one, of a wide variety of cultural expressions supported by the musical capacities

Figure 2.3
A complete time-span reduction of a Bach chorale. (From Lerdahl and Jackendoff 1983, 144, reprinted by permission of MIT Press.)

of the human phenotype. Nevertheless, Western tonal art music since 1650 seems to put these capacities on display in a particularly spectacular way. Some of my conclusions could perhaps be generalized to other musical styles, but I shall not attempt to do anything of the sort here. I shall, however, allow myself, when appropriate, the occasional allusion to other styles, including non-Western and premodern styles.

Another factor will serve to narrow the focus of my discussion still further. Western tonal art music since 1650, and especially Western instrumental tonal art music since 1650, arguably forms a nonclassical, graded category that shows strong prototypicality effects. Just as Beethoven's Fifth Symphony is more prototypical than is Debussy's *La Mer*, Brahms's *Tragic* Overture is more prototypical than Scriabin's *Poem of Ecstasy*, Dvořák's Cello Concerto is more prototypical than Strauss's *Don Quixote*, and Tchaikovsky's Violin Concerto is more prototypical than Lalo's *Symphonie Español*. These are judgments of prototypicality, not artistic quality, despite the fact that Beethoven's symphonies (the first eight, at least), concertos, sonatas, and chamber music stand at the very center of this graded category. Cherubini's Symphony in D is also more prototypical than *La Mer*. *The more prototypical the musical work, the more, ceteris paribus, will the general conclusions reached in this book apply to it.*

These disclaimers having been made, put aside for the sake of present discussion the metrical, phrase-grouping, and prolongation reduction structures and consider the time-span reductions (see figure 2.3). Although the Lerdahl and Jackendoff theory bills itself as "generative" because it purports to supply rules and representations that can be applied recursively so as to yield well-formed musical strings of indeterminate length, its representational structures differ fundamentally from those of generative linguistics. Whereas the "trees" of generative linguistics represent grammatical categories, the musical time-span reduction trees[31] represent degrees of relative structural importance, the subordination and superordination of tones in musical episodes of different lengths. Still, there is a "deep parallel" between the time-span structure of music and the prosodic, or stress and intonation pattern of language (Lerdahl and Jackendoff 1983, 314ff). Time-span structure, to be sure, is a *syntactic* aspect of music whereas prosody is a *pragmatic* aspect of language. But as we shall see in the next chapter, this apparent discrepancy can be accounted for by hypothesizing common origins for language and music, an ancient "musilanguage" in which syntactic and pragmatic linguistic functions were not yet clearly separated. Prosody, however, is principally a matter of spoken language; only derivatively does it concern written language.

Patterns of prosodic production are *behavioral* patterns: they are the products of motor schemata in the brain areas that control speech: "at the phonological level of linguistic representation, we are dealing not only with linguistic information but also with its perceptual and motor organization" (ibid., 329). Prosodic speech patterns, it is clear, are closely allied with *gesture*, behavior patterns that involve principally the hands but also the whole body. As a matter of fact, the trees that Lerdahl and Jackendoff use to represent both the time-span and prolongation reductions are, as I am about to show, organized in the manner of motor control hierarchies and task-level action plans. But this should not be surprising:

it would be surprising if music and language were the only human abilities so structured. Rather, we should be led to look for something closely analogous to time-span structure in many human abilities under the rubric of "temporal patterning," from event perception to motor control to the planning of extended strategies of behavior. In particular, we should expect a hierarchically articulated notion of *head/elaboration* to figure prominently in psychological theories of temporal organization. (Ibid., 330)[32]

Koffka, one of the original gestalt psychologists, referred to any motor adaptation, the formation of any structured behavioral unit by a human being, as the "composition of a movement-melody" (Koffka 1924, 259). Writing in 1627, William Harvey referred to animal motion as "the silent music of the body" (quoted in Sacks 2004, 42n2). Eight years before Chomsky's celebrated critique of behaviorist approaches to language learning, Lashley (1951, 116) anticipated one of the fundamental insights of generative linguistics:

From such considerations, it is certain that any theory of grammatical form which ascribes it to direct associative linkage of the words of the sentence overlooks the essential structure of speech.

But he also went on to make the following telling observations:

This is true not only of language, but also of all skilled movements or successions of movement. The gaits of a horse, trotting, pacing, and single footing involve essentially the same pattern of muscular contraction in the individual legs. . . . The order in which the fingers of the musician fall on the keys or fingerboard is determined by the signature of the composition; this gives a set which is not inherent in the association of the individual movements. (Ibid.)

Consider, in light of Lerdahl and Jackendoff's references to the structure of human motor control, Jeannerod's account (1997, 164) of the structural properties of motor representations, representations that are similarly hierarchical and nested:

The neural layout of the representation can be figured out as a network where the goal information (the information about the action to be performed) appears as an array of enhanced activity. . . . This activated state will persist until completion of the action. For each individual unit of the network, however, the duration of the sustained activation will be determined by the hierarchical position of that unit in the network. A unit located upstream in the sequence of events that lead to the final goal will remain activated as long as the full action has not been completed. By contrast, a more local unit will remain activated only for a short time, that is the time to complete the intermediate step of the action encoded by that unit. In other words, the last unit to return to its resting state will be that with the highest hierarchical position.

Although much of Jeannerod's language suggests description at the neural or implementational level,[33] by "motor control hierarchies" I shall intend representational structures described at a level of functional abstraction above the neurological sub-strate, structures that are not necessarily conscious, though in some cases they may be-come conscious under conditions of attentional focus. At the neural level, the lowest layers of the motor system consist of reflex mechanisms, oscillators, and servomechan-isms of whose functions we are not conscious and *cannot become conscious*. These struc-tures organized into "lattice hierarchies," which are more loosely organized than strictly nested control hierarchies. As a result, they are subject to only limited top-down control and operate with a significant degree of local autonomy (Gallistel 1980, 1981). By "task-level action plans," on the other hand, I shall intend those conscious representations whose contents command attention at the personal level. (A "con-scious representation" is one whose *contents* are available to consciousness; we may not be, and normally are not, conscious of the representational vehicle itself.)

Any such functional account raises the difficult issues of psychological reality broached in the general introduction. What reason is there to think that these motor control hierarchies are psychologically real? The response is that there is experimental evidence that actions are hierarchically represented in the mind–brain:

Other experimenters, however, came to a similar conclusion concerning hierarchical organization, by studying discrete arm movements, and using motor reaction time (RT) as an index. By manip-ulating the advanced information provided to the subject, and by measuring the temporal costs or benefits of these manipulations, we can infer the structure of the preparatory mechanism. Rosen-baum (1980) found that cueing certain aspects of the response to be given (for example, the di-rection in which the target will appear) produces a greater benefit than cueing other aspects (for example, the target distance). Hence the logical conclusion is direction should be represented at a "higher" level than distance. (Jeannerod 1997, 129)

Any motor task will make use of both levels of structure, motor control hierarchies and task-level action plans. A goal is represented and a general plan for achieving that goal is implemented. But execution of the task will also require a range of muscular micro-movements that will go forward in a relatively unconscious, automated way and which will not be micromanaged, but only broadly supervised (Gallistel 1980, 1981; Jean-nerod 1994, 200; Gallese and Metzinger 2003). There will also be a constant transfer-ence of function from one domain to the other. A newly acquired set of organized movements may begin with a high degree of micromanagement, but then will be chunked into self-contained automated functional modules as familiarity grows (Edel-man and Tononi 2000, 186–188). If some problem of execution arises, micromanage-ment can then increase until the difficulty is smoothed out. As a matter of fact, a favored example of this phenomenon is learning to play a musical instrument (Jean-nerod 1994, 189; 1997, 95; 2006, 41). A novice pianist learning to play a scale will exert conscious control over each finger motion. The hands of the expert are able to execute entire scales and arpeggios without attentional control of details. In the case of musical *listening*, however, the division of labor between the two sorts of structures seems, when compared with instrumental execution, to be weighted in favor of the task-level structures: the listener tends to pay close attention to the unfolding *musical plan-in-progress*. Nevertheless, a similar chunking of low-level structures, especially when the listener is apprehending many notes of brief duration, also occurs; and with increased familiarity, more global organizational structures will command greater attention than they did on first hearing.

2.3.1 Mental Models and Analog Representations

Motor hierarchies and action plans also require additional representational structures. As an organism pursues a set of goal-oriented behaviors in its physical environment, it must constantly update the unfolding action plan by sampling the environment. It must construct an ongoing *internal* or *mental model* of its environment on the basis of these samplings and compare its contents with the contents of another mental model that represents its goal state.[34] As it detects discrepancies, it must modify its behavior accordingly. Models in general represent their target objects by exemplifying structural attributes they share with those target objects (Black 1962, 220, 230–232; Wartofsky 1979, 4, 142). To the extent this sharing of attributes is essential for the model's representational function, a model is an *analog* representation. A so-called *working model* is a special case that adds a simulational function. *Working* models bridge the gap between two distinct representational functions by doing both: standing *for* and standing *in for*.

The expression "analog representation" is notoriously multivalent and is used by various writers to mark at least three different distinctions. Since I shall be making rather heavy use of the notion of analog representation, we must now make some effort to sort them out. I shall emphasize the property-sharing aspect of analog representations, described by McGinn (1989, 178) as follows: "In analogue codes properties of the represented states of affairs are somehow reflected in features of the code itself; but in a digital code this is not so—here the representational relation is essentially arbitrary." McGinn is of the opinion that analog representations depend on "magnitude covariation" between representation and object. Because internal mental models are likely to exploit higher-order paramorphisms rather than first-order isomorphisms (see Shepard and Chipman 1970), I am inclined to construe the relationship more abstractly, as topological rather than metrical. A metrical relationship between an analog representation and what it represents preserves proportionality of magnitudes (magnitude covariation), as in the case of a map drawn to scale; but a topological one merely preserves order, as in the case of a diagram not drawn to scale.[35] A trajectory through the multidimensional activation space of a recurrent neural network, for example, might count as an analog representation of the behavior of an object. Yet such a representation is hardly isomorphic with the phenomena in physical space it represents.

The first distinction to be noted is that between analog *representation* and analog *content*. "The content possessed by experience," Peacocke (1992, 68) tells us,

has an analogue character and is unit-free.... To say that the type of content in question has an analogue character is to make the following point. There are many dimensions—hue, shape, size, direction—such that any value on that dimension may enter the fine-grained content of an experience. In particular, an experience is not restricted in its range of possible contents to those points or ranges picked out by concepts—*red, square, straight ahead*—possessed by the perceiver.

Peacocke's allusions to the fine-grained dimensions of analog content suggest consanguinity with two quite different notions of "analog" deriving (respectively) from Goodman and Dretske. I take these up in order.

In Goodman's theory of symbols, "analog" contrasts with "notational"; and he applies both terms to symbolic "schemes" and to symbolic "systems." A *scheme* is a syntax-governed class of symbol tokens; a *system* is a symbolic scheme that has been semantically interpreted, or "correlated with a field of reference." A notational scheme is one that is "disjoint" and not "dense." A scheme is disjoint if there is no overlap between "characters," or classes of tokens or "marks"; a scheme is finitely differentiated and not dense if there is a decision procedure to determine whether any given mark that does not belong to two different characters does not belong to one character or the other.[36] A scheme may also be merely locally dense or it may be "dense throughout," with no gaps between locally densely ordered classes of marks.[37] Whether locally dense or dense throughout, a dense scheme is analog.

A *system* is notational to the extent the extensions or "compliance classes" of the syntactic characters satisfy similar constraints. In addition, the characters of the system must be unambiguous: each character must have one and only one compliance class. If there is no decision procedure for determining whether some object not belonging to two compliance classes does not belong to one or to the other, the system is analog. The English language is a notational scheme but not a notational system, because the classes complying with its characters are neither unambiguous, nor disjoint, nor finitely differentiated. English contains many homonyms; the class of women intersects the class of physicians; and it may not be possible to determine whether a given individual is to be excluded from the class of attractive or the class of unattractive people. English is therefore semantically dense. Because of its fine-grained, unit-free character, Peacocke's analog *content* satisfies, at least in part, Goodman's criteria for *semantic* density. We shall take a closer look at Goodman's views in chapter 3 and at Peacocke's in chapter 5.

This brings us back to analog *representation*, where we find a second distinction. It is clear that a representation may be analog *in one sense* if it is a symbol that belongs to a *scheme* that is not disjoint and not finitely differentiated in Goodman's parlance. I do not mean to rule out this version of analog representation and am prepared to allow that it may be combined with the structural property-sharing version I favor.

A third distinction, one that involves yet a third version of analog representation, may be found by teasing out the Dretskean strand in Peacocke's notion of analog content, the strand discernible in the claim that the content of experience somehow outstrips the conceptual in its fine-grained detail. For Dretske, a representation is analog if it does not completely "digitalize" its informational content, that is, if the content carried by that representation is embedded in larger "informational shells." An informational content may be so embedded either nomically or analytically. If it is nomically embedded, the piece of information is derivable from the larger, embedding informational shell by way of some natural law, as the information that the pressure of a volume of gas is increasing is embedded in and derivable from the information that its temperature is increasing. If the information is analytically embedded, it is derivable by way of a logical relationship, as the information that an object is a quadrilateral is analytically embedded in the information that it is a square. In order to digitalize the former piece of embedded information, an information-processing system needs the concept *pressure*; to digitalize the latter, a system needs the concept *quadrilateral*.

It should, however, be noted that a "concept," for Dretske, is merely a representational structure-type whose function it is to be uniquely sensitive to the particular piece of information that constitutes its semantic content, to the exclusion of other pieces of information in which this content is embedded. On this view, "concepts" may be wielded by creatures as primitive as frogs (Dretske 1981, 175); and a representation that counts as "digital" for Dretske, because it succeeds in digitalizing a piece of information either partially or completely,[38] could be an analog representation in the sense I favor. I have no objection to regarding frogs as representational systems; but if they are, it is because they possess hard-wired eye-tongue coordinating motor schemata and (perhaps) primitive internal analog representations or mental models that are capable of digitalizing fly information *de re* present in the frog retina.[39] I shall, however, follow the early Millikan (1984) in terming any such analog internal representations "intentional icons," not full-blown, inferentially articulated conceptual vehicles, and shall follow Brandom, Andy Clark, Cussins, Evans, and McDowell in insisting that genuine concept possession requires inferential abilities lacking in a frog.

There is, finally, the following point to be made. Conceptual or propositional content may be represented analogically, as the frog represents the fact that there is a fly within reach; and nonconceptual content may be represented digitally, as a travelogue describes in words a visual scene. But in both cases, there is loss. Where the analog representation of conceptual content lacks inferential articulation, the digital propositional representation of analog content leaves out fine-grained detail.

With these three distinctions concerning the analog and the digital now in hand, let us consider mental models a little more closely. The notion originated with Craik (1943), but it has received much recent press in cognitive psychology (Pugh 1977; Johnson-Laird 1983, 1996; Arbib 1985; Jeannerod 1990; Rickheit and Habel 1999) and some in the philosophy of mind (Churchland 1979; McGinn 1989; Peacocke 1992; Braddon-Mitchell and Jackson 1996;[40] Bermudez 2003). Craik emphasized the predictive, anticipatory function of mental models: a cognizer predicts events in its environment by constructing a working model that simulates the relevant features of the situation and runs a scenario in its head, as a fleeing animal stops for a moment before a natural barrier to calculate whether it can make the required leap. Some animals, that is to say, are "Popperian," and not merely "Darwinian" (behaviorally hard-wired) or "Skinnerian" creatures susceptible to operant conditioning (Dennett 1995, 375ff). Popperian creatures are able to test possible courses of action by simulating, or running virtual scenarios in their heads, thereby avoiding the costs of actual operant testing. We humans are unique in being "Gregorians," capable of importing into our heads sophisticated "mind tools" like arithmetic numerals deriving from the cultural environment. These ideas will loom large in some of our later discussions.

Johnson-Laird has focused attention on the role of mental models in representing the truth conditions of propositions and the role of these models in the psychology of syllogistic inference. Experimental studies using various moods and figures of syllogisms suggest that humans do not carry out syllogistic inference by manipulating syntactic forms, but by juxtaposing mental models of arrays representing the extensions of the terms of the propositions involved. These arrays are not the mental models themselves, but internal images, which are "perceptual correlates of models from a particular point of view" (Johnson-Laird 1983, 165). These perceptual correlates, however, are subjective. An internal image, that is to say, is a construction by the mind–brain of a *virtual perceptual content* for a mental model. The mental model itself, on the other hand, is something like a Kantian schema[41] (ibid., 189–190), an abstract (paramorphic) analog representation that organizes temporal sequences of actual and virtual (imagistic) perceptual contents.

It is crucial, I believe, to maintain that the perception of distal objects is not mediated by these subjective images. Attributing any such function to them would make unavoidable the epistemologically self-defeating Cartesian view of representations as subjective mental contents. I am in no position to demonstrate this claim empirically, but in all likelihood perception of distal objects and the generation of subjective imagery are opponent neural processes. Imagery is suppressed by perceptual engagement with a distal object; and when the object of conscious awareness is an internal image, as in Shepard's rotational tasks or Johnson-Laird's syllogistic reasoning tasks, perceptual engagement with distal objects is suspended. "An image," says Prinz (2004, 214), "is just a state in a sensory system that has been generated from the top down rather than the bottom up." A percept, on the other hand, is generated from the bottom up: when we are imaging we are not perceiving, and vice versa.

This is not to say that internal images play *no* role in the perceptual process. Quite the contrary: there seems to be a complex, ongoing interplay between perception and

subjective imagery. Projections concerning the future behaviors, especially the imminent future behaviors, of objects currently perceived seem to be imagistic. This plays
an important role in the predictive, anticipatory role of mental models noted by Craik,
thereby contributing to the perception of affordances, of what can be done with
objects. A virtual *object* seen in an informationally structured surface, however, is
more than a mere subjective image. Such "seeing in" is a case of perception, albeit a
controlled *perceptual illusion*, the exploitation of an externally activated informational
system. A perceptual illusion, unlike an image, is generated from the "bottom up." To
the extent the informational system is externally activated, imagery is suppressed. The
same should be said about hearing musical virtual objects and scenarios in the informationally structured musical surface. But here, too, subjective imagery does play a
role. In the case of musical "hearing in," imagistic memories of what has transpired
and imagistic projections of what is to follow would seem to be particularly important.

Because of the structural affinities between the Lerdahl and Jackendoff trees and hierarchies of motor control and action planning, we are now able to characterize the
musical virtual object and explain how it might arise. The music is presented as a two-
dimensional surface, rather in the manner of a motion picture (though with some important differences), but a surface appealing to a haptic-style exploration rather than
the visual exploration of a field. Unlike the motion picture screen, the musical surface
consists of elements that are phenomenologically discrete. (We shall return to this
issue later in this chapter.) In addition, the attention of the musical listener is more
directed to the musical surface as an intentional object than is the attention of the
moviegoer to the cinematographic surface. In this way, the musical surface functions
more like a painting in which surface characteristics (e.g., brushstroke, impasto) enter
into awareness in aesthetically significant ways.[42] The internal representations employed in recovering the musical structure from the musical surface specify motor
hierarchies and action plans, which, in turn, *put the listener's body into off-line motor
states that specify virtual movements through a virtual terrain or a scenario possessing certain
features*. "This strong intertwining between music and action," say Besson and Schoen
(2003, 271), "is even reflected in language, the same word being used in several African
languages to refer to music and dance." If the specification of virtual scenarios by
bodily comportment seems questionable, think of the ability of a skilled mime to suggest by mere bodily movements a range of virtual situations. (This relationship between
musical representation and mime will turn out to be particularly important.) To understand a piece of music is to token the musical plan of the piece: composer, skilled performer, and comprehending listener produce representational tokens of the same
types. The musical "plan" of the piece may be identified with its version of the hier-
achically organized representational structures postulated by the Lerdahl and Jackendoff theory. The characters of the virtual movements specified by the action plans, slow/
fast, labored/easy, expansive/contracted, smooth/angular, and so on, limn in exquisite

detail the contours of this virtual layout by way of structural complementarity[43] and motivate the construction of appropriate analog representations, or mental models, which are constantly updated as the piece unfolds.[44] The virtual layouts and scenarios are the nonconceptual contents of the musical mental models.[45]

There is empirical evidence that similar cognitive principles govern both the organization of musical experience and the organization of wayfinding in physical space. After running a series of experiments using cinematic representations of travel through various scenes, the ecological psychologist Harry Heft (1996) and his colleagues discovered that human subjects tended to segment serially presented visual experiences in certain predictable ways. The major division employed was one that differentiated "vistas," relatively stable scenes in which only local changes of perspective occur, from "transitions," which include abrupt changes of scene. Subjects viewing these scenes were asked to rate various features or landmarks with regard to their relative significance for successful wayfinding through the depicted environment. Unsurprisingly, subjects tended to accord highest importance to features that marked transitions. In a separate test, the subjects were asked to segment the paths of travel into features that were relatively fine-grained and those that were relatively coarse-grained, the latter being "the largest meaningful and natural units" (ibid., 122). In both cases, feature representations were closely clustered (in time) around the transitions. But as familiarity with the paths of travel increased, the number of these clusters tended to decrease, while the responses coalesced around just a few salient transition points in the film.

These results indicate an increasingly effective cognitive economy, an ability to organize a larger number of less important features around a smaller number of important ones. The fine-grained features are, however, not entirely lost, but structurally subordinated as the significance of the salient transition features emerges. Heft argues (1996, 122) that this ability is best explained by attributing to the subjects a capacity to produce a nested organization of features. The idea is that with increased familiarity, subjects tend to organize features hierarchically. Any feature, except for the least important or noticeable ones, will nest subordinate features, and all but the most globally significant will be nested within superordinate ones; and even these will be subordinated to features of a more inclusive context that is implicit (see also Heft 2001, 186).

Although Heft, like Gibson, is suspicious of representation talk because of its Cartesian associations, I have already given reasons why we should not throw the representational baby out with the Cartesian bathwater. For us, the capacity to organize physical features hierarchically exploits plans and mental models that are paramorphic with the environment. Indeed, it is a little difficult to understand how a cognizer *could* organize perceptual experience, as Heft claims, both retrospectively and prospectively without relying on some variety of representational structures or schemata, for such organization involves some fairly elaborate conditional expectations:

Perceiving can be prospective when the individual is aware of what would be experienced in the environment with appropriate action; and it is retrospective when the individual is aware of what was already experienced in the environment, for example, if she retraced a prior set of actions. In both cases, it is awareness of what would accompany the pickup of information (i.e., it is awareness connected to the intention of information pickup). (Heft 2001, 181)

Significant for our purposes is Heft's assertion that the representation of *events* shows a similar segmentation and hierarchical organization *in time*, thereby demonstrating a marked similarity to hierarchical nesting relationships that have been found to be operative in musical listening (Jones and Boltz 1989), a result explicitly noted by Heft (2001, 119; see also Benzon 2001, 58). In fact, Heft's conception of hierarchical nesting of features was apparently inspired by and derived from Jones and Boltz's musical investigations (see Heft 2001, 185). The musical features that play the role of the "transitions" are, among others, phrase beginnings and endings, cadences, and large sectional divisions like those separating exposition from development in sonata movements. As in the case of wayfinding in physical space, one would expect an increase in familiarity with a musical piece to be accompanied by a decrease in the number of clusterings and the emergence of a few salient higher-order orientational points within which the less important musical events are nested.[46] This phenomenon is well represented in the hierarchically organized metrical-structure rules, phrase-grouping rules, time-span rules, and prolongation rules of the Lerdahl and Jackendoff theory.

2.4 Musical Motion and Musical Space

Motion pictures can suggest both object motion and observer motion depending on the placement and motion of the camera; and music can do the same thing. If you doubt this, compare Vaughan-Williams's *The Lark Ascending* (object motion) to the troika ride from Prokofiev's *Lieutenant Kije* (observer motion). If these examples seem tendentious because of reliance on verbal titles, compare the soaring violin solos in Rimsky-Korsakov's *Russian Easter* Overture (object motion) to the breakneck opening of the final movement of Bizet's Symphony in C (observer motion).

There is in fact a Gibsonian explanation of this phenomenon.[47] In the case of visual perception, an important component in distinguishing object motion from observer motion is "optical flow," the relative motions of near and far objects and the effects of these motions on the retina. If optical flow is such that all objects appear to be in motion relative to the observer, with those nearer by moving more quickly than those more distant, the observer feels himself to be in motion. If only one object appears to be in motion while the others remain stationary relative to the observer, the observer feels himself stationary. In real-world perception the ability to distinguish observer from object motion is enhanced by "corollary discharge"[48] as well as by proprioceptive feedback and input from the labyrinth, the organ of balance; but in motion pictures the effect is produced entirely visually. Something similar occurs in music: if one instrument is in "motion," an effect of object motion is produced, particularly if the lines of other instruments remain relatively "motionless"; if the entire ensemble is engaged in concerted, rhythmically coordinated "motion," an effect of observer motion is produced.

I have encased "motion" and "motionless" in quotation marks because these ideas only begin to explain the experience widely reported by musical listeners detecting movement in a virtual musical or "acousmatic"[49] space. Although this tendency to hear motion in music is central to the experience of the Western art music under discussion here, it remains a remarkable and puzzling phenomenon. After all, nothing in the musical surface really moves: discrete tones simply sound and cease to sound in specified sequences. Why should we find it so natural, indeed so irresistible, to interpret heard sequences of evanescent tones as *movement* through *space*? There is little doubt that the experience of motion in music is an illusion that bears *some* analogy to the illusion produced by motion pictures, where it is also the case that there is nothing literally in motion on the surface of the projection screen: regions of the screen are illuminated in various sequences. There may be no real motion in motion pictures; but the screen is, at least, a two-dimensional, apparently continuous, spatial surface. Why do we hear sequences of discrete tones as defining a space in which motion occurs?

Notice that in order to produce the cinematic effect of motion, the sequence of individual frames must be rapid enough to preclude their individual perception. Otherwise, the illusion of continuous motion is lost. Music is not like that. Individual tones, even ones of very brief duration, are easily identified and do not blend into apparently continuous motion. This suggests that the illusion of musical motion is produced in some other way, perhaps relying on motor representations in a way cinematic visual perception does not. There are, however, some interesting *visual* parallels where motor representations seem to play a more central role than they ordinarily do. Human visual perception, for example, is extremely sensitive to cues for recognizing human ambulatory motions. Miller and Johnson-Laird (1976, 95–96) point out that

The appreciation of dynamic relations can exploit extremely subtle clues. It is possible to make moving pictures of five lights placed on a person's body in such a way that all that is seen is one light at the hips, two lights on the knees, and two lights at the ankles....

Apparently the visual system can be exquisitely sensitive to components of motion that provide information about dynamic relations between moving objects. If the lights are placed between the walker's joints, however, their [apparent] motion does not create a perception of a person walking.

The fact that ambulatory motion can be picked up from cues this minimal and the fact that the ambulatory pattern suddenly evanesces when the lights are displaced to locations in between the joints suggest that such recognition, tied as it obviously is to certain orderly *sequences* of motion among the five separate lights, relies on the activation of motor schemata in the observer that control the concerted motions of limbs:

complex motion patterns produced by subjects (for example, dancing) can be recognized visually without difficulty, even if they are described in a very succinct way (for example by a few luminous dots placed at the level of the moving joints, on a dark background)....This very striking ability suggests a coupling between motor and perceptual processes, whereby certain properties of the motor system influence perceptual interpretation of a visual stimulus....It is tempting to generalize this statement, by saying that the properties of the motor representational system can determine the perceptual interpretation of motor patterns produced by other individuals. This interpretation would be the basis for understanding intentions. (Jeannerod 1997, 190)

Jeannerod reiterates the same points in his most recent book on motor cognition (2006, 103–105). The ease with which we visually pick up ambulatory movement, even from patterns of five luminous dots on a screen, does not, however, solve our present problem, which is to explain the equally strong tendency to hear spatial movement in music. There may be no real motion occurring on a projection screen; but again, the screen is, at least, a two-dimensional spatial surface. Why do we hear combinations of tones of set frequencies as defining a space at all? I propose a phylogenetic hypothesis, or, more accurately, a "how possible" evolutionary speculation of the kind Darwin himself, as we shall see in the next chapter, entertained with regard to the origins of music.

2.4.1   A Case of "Deep Homology"

But suppose that [a cognitive universal of human mentality] had a far more ancient, but still fully adaptational, origin in a distant ancestor of a very different form and neurological function, and also living in a very different environment—say, in the basal gnathostome fish of early Paleozoic times. Suppose also that this mental attribute has persisted ever since as a plesiomorphic aspect of the basic operation of the vertebrate brain....[A]s invariant and plesiomorphic traits of our entire clade (not only of hominids and primates, but of all mammals and tetrapods), [such features] operate as unchanging constraints upon any subsequent evolution of mental modes, despite their adaptational origin in such a distant ancestor of such different form and environment.
—Stephen Jay Gould (2002, 1265)

A look at the specialized human sensory systems shows that they share a remarkably common functional organization. They all code for stimulus modality, intensity, duration, and location (Kandel et al. 1991, 333). But they use three different modes of stimulus transduction: photoreception, chemoreception, and mechanoreception. Only two of these systems function by means of mechanoreception: the touch component of the sensory-somatic system (as opposed to the heat-sensitive, the nociceptive, and the proprioceptive components), and the auditory system. Musical sounds (considered as acoustic events) are periodic waveform phenomena; and the main aural transductional mechanisms in the inner ear are the motion-sensitive hair cells stretching between the basilar and tectorial membranes of the organ of Corti. The shape of the basilar membrane and its cross striations suggests, as Helmholtz noticed long ago, the organization

of the harp of a piano. This enables hair cells in different locations to respond strongly
to periodic waveforms of varying frequencies and amplitudes induced in the fluid of
the scala vestibuli and the scala media by the impact of the stapes on the oval window
of the cochlea, the movement of the stapes having been initiated by the sympathetic
vibration (caused by impinging air waves) of the tympanic membrane (eardrum).

All these are commonly known physiological facts. But less often remarked is the
close structural and functional relationship between the hair cells and their extended
flexible ciliae in the organ of Corti and the hair cells and ciliae in the vibration-
detecting lateral line organ of aquatic vertebrates (Matthews 1998, 437, 439). The lateral line, which extends bilaterally from head to tail along the length of the body, is a
device that enables fish to detect and locate moving objects, principally predators and
prey, in their spatial environments. The lateral line, that is to say, is particularly sensitive to the characteristic periodic rhythms of animate movement. Like the ciliae in the
organ of Corti, its flexible ciliae respond to disturbances in the surrounding fluid.

Evolutionary history tells us that the human cochlea developed from the lagena, a
bulging structure on the posterior section of the sacculus of fish (Sarnat and Netsky
1981, 165). The sacculus is a part of the labyrinth, the organ of balance in humans
and other mammals, but in fishes, which lack a cochlea, it is also a very primitive
organ of hearing (Sarnat and Netsky 1981, 165, 187; Todd 1999, 117). A sensitive area
inside the lagena known as the basilar papilla is the ancestor of the organ of Corti. The
cochlear homologue remains relatively straight in reptiles, birds, monotremes (e.g.,
the platypus), and marsupials, but takes on its characteristic coiled structure in placen-
tal mammals, including humans. In fishes, nerves from the labyrinth and the lateral
line innervate an area of the medulla known as the acousticolateral area, which is differentiated into dorsal, middle, and ventral nuclei. There is also considerable overlap
between lateral line and vestibular fibers, that is, those originating in the labyrinth
(Sarnat and Netsky 1981, 168–169).

What is significant is that these acousticolateral nuclei are the ancestral homologues
of the human cochlear nucleus, the first innervation point on the brainstem of the auditory fibers of the human vestibulocochlear (eighth cranial) nerve (Kandel et al. 1991,
495; Matthews 1998, 453). As living things adapted to conditions of hearing on land
by exploiting atmospheric pressure waves, the lateral line atrophied and its neural connections to the medulla were replaced by the vestibulocochlear nerve. This is in fact
what happens ontogenetically in tadpoles as they develop into frogs: "The lateral line
system is well developed in the tadpole or larval stage of frogs, but degenerates at the
time of metamorphosis and does not return. This system was lost in the evolution of
the earliest reptiles and has not reappeared in aquatic reptiles, birds, or mammals" (Sarnat and Netsky 1981, 162). There is, then, a genuinely homologous relationship both
between the acousticolateral nuclei of fishes and the human cochlear nucleus and between the acousticolateral nerve pathways of fishes and the human vestibulocochlear

nerve. The inferior colliculus and the lateral lemniscus, which are more recent structures of the mammalian auditory system, also developed from the acousticolateral nuclei (Sarnat and Netsky 1981, 170). Just as the human cochlear nucleus is organized to map the organ of Corti in the cochlea *tonotopically* (from high to low frequency), the acousticolateral nuclei map the lateral line *somatotopically* (according to location of hair cells on the body), thus allowing fish to determine the location (head to tail) of some stimulation of the lateral line, thereby determining the direction of the disturbance (Matthews 1998, 452; Sarnat and Netsky 1981, 168).

These facts, I suggest, illuminate a number of otherwise deeply puzzling features of musical experience. First, they help to explain why music is experienced as spatial at all. While any claims concerning "fish phenomenology" must remain highly questionable, the modality of the lateral line is thought to be more akin to touch than to hearing. The fish, that is, *feels* the presence of patterns of watery disturbance by way of the lateral line more than it *hears* it: "Lateral line organs are stimulated by vibrations of low frequency, but they are not sensitive to pressure waves, and therefore do not perceive sound" (Sarnat and Netsky 1981, 163). If this is right, and if this ancient tactual function is preserved in descendent structures, then it sheds some light on the puzzle of musical motion: sequential stimulations on the skin surface can easily suggest both object and observer motion.[50] The same could hold for sequential mechanical stimulations along the frequency-tuned length of the organ of Corti. After all, musical motion requires change of pitch, and change of pitch is mediated by just these sequential stimulations. Once the acousticolateral system was adapted to hearing in land-based creatures, the tactual aspect of its original function was suppressed. But the effects of touch in hearing never entirely disappeared, and remain a factor in all auditory experience.[51] Very low tones, for example, are felt nearly as much as they are heard. Katz (1989, 204) proposes that "the [tactual] vibration sense represents one step in the evolutionary sequence leading from touch to hearing."

These considerations also provide some explanation of the aspect of musical experience that is perhaps most puzzling of all: why higher-frequency tones tend to be heard as located higher in musical space. It is commonly observed that high-pitched sounds like the tone of a piccolo seem spatially smaller than do low-pitched contrabass sounds, probably because of the significantly longer wavelength of the latter. This is certainly true: witness Saint-Saens's elephant in *Carnival of the Animals*; but smaller is not necessarily higher. The acousticolateral-vestibulocochlear homology suggests an alternative explanation. The cochlea is coiled, snail-like; but were it to be uncoiled, the hair cells in the organ of Corti tuned to higher frequencies would be located closer in toward the brainstem, while those tuned to lower frequencies would be located farther out. Although the hair cells in the lateral line are not frequency-tuned in the same way, the remote tip of the cochlea corresponds structurally to the far end of the lateral line near the tail of the fish. As Gould suggests, preservation of function (in the form of constraint) is not uncommon in evolutionary "exaptation," the recruitment of existing structures for new functions. Bird feathers are aerodynamic; but they remain thermoregulatory. Assuming, as is reasonable, some preservation of ancient function between the somatotopical mapping in the acousticolateral nuclei of fishes and the tonotopical mapping in cochlear nucleus of humans, we might well expect a head-to-toe spatial orientation naturally built into musical pitch, with higher pitches heard "up" near the head and lower ones "down" toward the toe.[52] The reason for this is obvious: the human body, unlike the fish body, is normally oriented vertically with the head up relative to the terrestrial gravitational field.

In their recent discussions of the metaphorical bases of understanding, Lakoff and Johnson (1980, 1999) have argued that the human understanding of abstract concepts in general is "grounded" in "emergent concepts" of bodily orientation and movement, including *up/down*, *front/back*, *in/out*, *manipulative causality*, and *agency*. Emergent concepts are those that do not require metaphorical grounding in other concepts and that therefore ground the entire elaborate structure of metaphorical transference from more basic (more closely associated with bodily experience) to less basic and more abstract.[53] As Lakoff and Johnson repeatedly point out, human upright bodily orientation is of fundamental importance for the emergence of the *up/down* contrast. We shall return to these issues in chapter 3, where some of the promised philosophical dividends yielded by this descriptive sketch will be paid out.[54]

Interestingly, there is evidence that persons who are completely deaf are capable of sensing musically organized sound entirely by way of the tactual vibratory sense (see Katz 1989, 187–194). By placing her hand on the diaphragm of a radio speaker, she claimed, Helen Keller "could feel...the passion of the rhythm, the pulsation and swelling of music." She could "precisely distinguish between the cornet and the rolling of the drums, the deep tone of the cello and the singing of the violins" (quoted in Katz 1989, 193n9). Eugen Sutermeister, an elderly music lover deaf since age four from an attack of meningitis, claimed that he discovered at age fifty-nine that he was "good at discriminating the character of music, whether it is substantial or superficial, joyful or melancholy, solemn or thrilling, monotonous or colorful" by means of vibrational sensations located in his torso (ibid., 191). "In placing a hand on the body of a cello," Rousseau tells us,[55] "one can, without the aid of eyes or ears, distinguish solely by the way the wood vibrates and quivers whether the sound it produces is low or high [*grave ou aigu*], whether it comes from the A string or the C string."

While these testimonials underscore the strong affinity between the auditory and tactual senses, they also offer apparent counterexamples to the functional theory of musical space I have offered. How, on this theory, is it possible for someone to differentiate high and low locations in musical space without cochlear function, assuming that Keller and Sutermeister both suffered nerve deafness and not some dysfunction of the outer or middle ear (cf. Krueger 1982, 12–13)? Rousseau's claim can be explained by the strong association in a hearing person between high and low tones and the vibrational frequency constantly conjoined with them, as can the case of Sutermeister, who had cochlear function until he was four, long enough for some of these associations, especially those between very low tones and throbbing, low-frequency vibrations, to be established. The case of Helen Keller is more difficult, since she was deaf and mute from shortly after birth. There is no reason to doubt that she could distinguish by touch the characteristic tonal profile of the cello tone as she claimed, but there is room for skepticism that she actually *felt* the "deep tone of the cello" *as located low in musical space*. This description may, that is, have been linguistically motivated. Because hearing persons described the cello tone as low, Keller did too.

There is, however, another possibility (see Zbikowski 2002, 69, for a related suggestion). As the vocal cords tense to produce higher-pitched tones, the larynx moves upward in the throat; as the vocal cords relax to produce lower-pitched tones, the larynx moves downward. In subjects with normal hearing, there is an automatic adjustment of the tension of the vocal cords to cochlear frequency response in pitch matching. The spatial relationships that operate in both the cochlear and the laryngeal mechanisms (higher frequency = higher in the throat, lower frequency = lower in the throat) no doubt reinforce the association of higher frequency with higher spatial position in hearing persons. In deaf persons, the link between cochlear and vocal function is absent; but there is evidence that these persons can adjust the tension of their vocal cords by touching the vibrating larynx, and can thereby learn to match pitches by matching vibrational frequencies in this other way (see Katz 1989, 191; Krueger 1982, 13). The up-down position of the larynx in the throat and its association with different frequencies might thus provide, in a way still consistent with the Lakoff and Johnson "body-in-the-mind" theory, an alternative, if much less direct and probably considerably less effective, route to the perception of musical frequencies as spatially organized in those, like Helen Keller, who are deaf from very early childhood. But if so, this would do nothing to undermine the hypothesis I have offered concerning the structure of the cochlea and musical space. The positioning the larynx in the throat seems scarcely capable of accounting on its own for the robust phenomenology of the experience of movement in musical space.

2.4.2 Two Apparent Paradoxes

The structure of musical space does not, however, only reflect the frequency relationships of tones from low to high. For musical space has distinctive structural features that seem to be entirely missing from physical space. First, physical space is continuous, but the musical scale is discontinuous. The continuous flight of a numerically identical bumblebee somehow can be suggested by a sequence of discrete tones. Continuously flowing water[56] somehow can be suggested by sequences of discrete descending violin and viola thirds. How are such things possible? The standard account treats

Example 2.1
Beethoven, Quartet in E Minor, Op. 59, No. 2, *Molto adagio*.

this as an auditory version of the visual Phi phenomenon (see Sloboda 1985, 159; Clarke 2005, 70). Two lights flashing successively in a darkened room will appear as one moving light, if distance and frequency of flashing are properly coordinated. As distance increases, frequency must decrease for the illusion to be maintained. This inverse relationship between distance and frequency is thought to reflect a sensitivity of the visual system to the increased time interval required for an object to move between more distantly separated locations in space. The Phi phenomenon is, however, quite limited in scope, and only arises when frequency and distance remain within a fairly narrow range of distance/frequency values.

I certainly do not wish to rule out the possibility that there may be an aural analogue of the Phi phenomenon. But the experience of continuous movement between discrete tones in music is a far more ubiquitous and robust phenomenon. We experience continuous motion through musical space both in the case of slow-moving motifs consisting of small intervals, as in the opening of the slow movement of Beethoven's Quartet Op. 59, No. 2 (example 2.1), and in the case of quickly moving motifs containing rather large intervals, as in the lively violin tune in Weber's *Oberon* Overture (example 2.2). Continuous motion in musical space, as a result, seems to require some additional mode of explanation. I shall offer one below.

Second, whatever scale a particular musical style may favor, whether it be diatonic[57] (including the major, the minor, and the older modes), pentatonic (five-note), whole-tone, dodecaphonic (chromatic), microtonic (as in some music of India), or even one of a number of artificial scales invented by particular composers (octatonic, hexatonic), musical space is almost invariably[58] structured around the octave relationship. A tone separated from another tone by an octave sounds like "the same again" with regard to

Example 2.2
Weber, *Oberon* Overture.

its mate. This phenomenon is in one way not very puzzling; but in another way it is very puzzling indeed. The aspect that is not very puzzling concerns the fact that the frequency of any tone is related to its higher or lower octave by a factor of two. From a physical standpoint, therefore, tones separated by an octave are closely related because of similarity between their respective phase-frequency profiles. A curve representing one is easily superimposed on the curve representing the other using an amplitude-versus-time graph. The important point is that in terms of phase-frequency profile, two tones separated by an octave are more closely related acoustically than any other two tones except for those forming a unison: the frequency ratio of (the tones constituting) the unison is 1:1 and that of the octave is 2:1. On the other hand, the absolute frequency *difference* between tones separated by an octave is greater than the frequency difference between tones separated by smaller intervals: the frequency of the higher octave is twice that of the lower. This explains the greater distance heard between octaves in musical space. The octave sounds like the same again; but it also sounds further removed in musical space from its lower mate than do the intervening smaller intervals.

The puzzle arises when we attempt to put these two individually intelligible aspects of musical space together. Once we do, musical space exhibits a cyclical structure that is seemingly incoherent. When moving up or down an octave in musical space one seems to be moving farther away while still returning to the same again. Physical space is not like that. It is entirely homogeneous[59] and has no such cyclically articulated internal structure. But behavioral space does. Consider, once again, the evolutionary transformation of the lateral line into the organ of Corti. The lateral line responds strongly to waveforms in the aquatic environment that are periodic: "This encoding system [the lateral line] works best, however, for low-frequency vibrations produced by the swimming motions of a nearby fish (predator, prey, or mate)" (Matthews 1998, 437). Such vibrations tend to be periodic. This sensitivity to periodicity is preserved in the organ of Corti and underlies the marked phenomenological difference between the experience of pitched sounds, or tones, and the experience of unpitched sounds, or noises. As a result, the two organs share both discrimination and categorization capabilities, the ability to discriminate periodic from nonperiodic disturbances and the ability to group periodic vibration patterns on the basis of similarity of phase and frequency profile; and as we saw, the patterns of two tones separated by an octave are extremely similar. But unlike the lateral line, the organ of Corti is frequency tuned along its length. It is this function that actually creates musical space by supplying the frequency metric by which it is measured. In musical experience, the two functions, ancient and modern, coexist, but a little uneasily, for their coexistence combines two orthogonal metrics, the more recent one based on absolute frequency difference and the more ancient one based on similarity between phase-frequency profile; and it is this combination that gives rise to the apparently paradoxical structure of musical space.

The sensitivity to phase-frequency similarity in the organ of Corti (and, of course, the auditory cortex) is not, however, limited to the octave relationship, but extends to many of the relationships constituting the harmonic series. As is well known, all the tones of the diatonic scale stand in relationships determined by the harmonic series, which ranks the interval of the fifth just behind the unison and the octave with regard to similarity of phase-frequency profile: if the frequency ratio of the unison is 1:1 and that of the octave 2:1, the tones of the fifth are related by a proportion of 3:2, the fourth by a proportion of 4:3, the major third by 5:4, the minor third by 6:5, and the minor second by a proportion of 16:15. The smaller the common factors, respectively 1, 2, 6, 12, 20, 30, and 240, the more consonant the interval. Most distantly related in the diatonic scale, most "dissimilar" of all in terms of phase-frequency profile, are the pitches separated by an augmented fourth or diminished fifth (the tritone).

These are related by a proportion of 45:32[60] and the common factor is 1,440 (see Tramo et al. 2003, 132). According to the second, phase-frequency similarity metric, the pitches of the octave are the closest and those of the tritone the most distantly related members of the diatonic scale. Indeed, the tritone stands diametrically opposed to the tonic on the harmonic circle of fifths: the major key most distantly related to C major harmonically is F# major. According to the first (absolute frequency) metric, however, the pitches separated by an octave are more distant than those constituting a tritone.

How, then, do these two apparently orthogonal parameters of musical space cohere in the construction of musical space? I have argued that musical experience is fundamentally tactual and bodily, deriving from a mapping of the human body (as vertically oriented in the gravitational field) onto the tuned length of the organ of Corti, a mapping motivated by the deep homology of the organ of Corti with the lateral line. Now I ask: what aspects of bodily experience might these two orthogonal parameters naturally fit? Clearly, the frequency metric maps onto vertical motion in space. But what about the phase-frequency similarity metric? Here is my suggestion: *degree* of phase-frequency similarity maps inversely onto *degree* of deviation from the vertical of the center of gravity of the body moving in a gravitational field.[61] Why should this be so? Perhaps the harmonic stimulation of the organ of Corti affects the state of the labyrinth, the organ of balance, to which it is anatomically related and which is located right next door; perhaps, because pitch is already heard spatially, a high degree of phase-frequency dissimilarity in the stimulus pattern of the organ of Corti is interpreted by the brain as a "disturbance" in the scala vestibuli and the scala media, as something like a fluid disturbance or disequilibrium in the labyrinth, which would signal a deviation from the vertical in physical space.[62] These are empirical questions to which I do not have answers.

What is clear is that as we move in physical space, the bodily center of gravity constantly deviates from and returns to the vertical. But human anatomy, the distribution of body mass, and various human gaits dictate certain modes of deviation, that is, certain bodily postures and positioning of limbs, as preferred because they are more stable than others in certain terrains in the gravitational field. These map onto the steps of the musical scale that stand out vividly as islands of stability in the vast flux of audible frequencies, because we categorize pitched tones this scalar way based on their degree of phase-frequency similarity, something to which the human ear is extremely sensitive. Not all cultures use the same scales; but the recognition of the octave as a salient point of stability is nearly universal. It is certainly common to all standard Western scales. The fifth is scarcely less salient, the whole-tone scale most closely associated in Western music with the name of Debussy being an obvious exception.[63] While consonance and dissonance remain to some degree style-relative, consonant tones tend to have similar phase-frequency profiles and dissonant tones dissimilar profiles. Octaves and fifths, as a result, are highly stable, tritones highly unstable. In Western tonal music, pitches other than the twelve pitch classes dividing the octave are unavailable: they are simply categorized as out of tune pitches. Hearing the octave as the same again maps onto the bodily experience of regaining balance after having moved upward in space. Recall the paradox of musical space: because of absolute frequency difference, the octave sounds *further away* from the tonic in an upward direction than do the intervening intervals. Because of phase-frequency similarity, it sounds *the same again*. Momentary deviation from and then return to balance is a recurring aspect of gait; gait is therefore cyclical; hence, acousmatic space is cyclical.

In the special case of Western cadential-harmonic music, harmony plays an absolutely pivotal role with regard to the sense of stability in musical space by adding "mass" and "extension" to the "moving body" in musical space. Since the phase-frequency profiles of the tones constituting scalar intervals other than the octave are more dissimilar than are those constituting the octave, such intervals are more dissonant than the octave. As a result, the *simultaneous* sounding of such intervals in a chord produces some disturbance, some degree of imbalance and "torque" with regard to the "center of gravity" of the "moving body" in musical space. This claim rests on the following physical analogy. Torque is force applied so as to produce angular rotation. The attachment of a massive horizontal armature to one side of a rod placed upright in the gravitational field, for example, will increase torque on the rod, causing it to rotate at its base, or in plain English, to fall over. The addition of a horizontal extension in the opposite direction, however, will counteract this effect. The same principles apply to the physics of human bodily posture. Any unbalanced extension of the extremities, indeed any imbalance in horizontal distribution of body mass, will bring torque to bear on the vertically oriented body. This aspect of bodily experience shapes musical experience. The more consonant a chord is, the more balanced it is, the pure octave being the most balanced of all;[64] and the more thickly scored a chord is, the more tones within the octave it contains, the denser and more "horizontally extended" it is. The denser the chord, the more it is prone to instability and the greater are the forces of musical "torque" that bear on the moving body in musical space. The most massive and extended chords of all, both "vertically" and "horizontally," are thickly scored chords spanning many octaves, such as full orchestral or organ chords.

We are now in a position to address the paradox of the experience of continuous musical motion through discrete tones. Notice that the movements of ambulatory, terrestrial vertebrates like us are both discrete and continuous: the bodily movement through space is continuous, but the points of stable contact with the terrain are discrete. Hence the possibility of experiencing virtual continuous motion through a series of discrete tones. The recurrent *rhythmic* structure of music, which is also discrete, clearly plays an important role in the construction of the character of musical space, not least because of its affinity to gait. Compare Zbikowski (2002, 73n21):

Most of us find [musical] descent—especially scalar descent—well represented by the thought of walking down a staircase, but I think it could be argued that walking down a hillside works as well. The reason is that it is not so much the neat, two-dimensional image of stairs that is operative but the regular transfer of weight from one leg to another.

Musical acousmatic space is not, however, just cyclical. Like the ecological environment, it has features:[65] it is articulated into regions, media, layouts, and surfaces (Gibson 1986). It ranges from the cluttered to the uncluttered, from the dense to the rarified, and from the emotionally benignant to the threatening. But the account of musical space and its contents offered so far still remains too simple: there are complications.

2.4.3   Two Complications

The first complication is this: although musical experience is based on bodily experience, musical virtual spaces and objects are not subject to the limitations of the physical environment, and the subject of a musical experience (the listener) is not limited to the possibilities of physical motion that constrain the semirigid three-dimensional human body possessing head, trunk, four extremities, and twenty fingers and toes.[66] Consider Jeannerod's description of the structure of a typical action plan, or "source-schema" (1997, 160):

The notion of schema used here is broader than that of motor schemas already described in previous sections. It includes, not only the motor schemas themselves, but also less elementary representational units, which Shallice calls "source-schemas": those are structures which control complex actions, not simple movements. Using an everyday life example, a schema like "prepare breakfast" would be a typical source-schema. It would itself be composed of smaller component schemas (for example, "make coffee") and so on until the level of the motor schemas would be reached.

Suppose we were to construct a control-hierarchy tree representing the activity of preparing breakfast. It would no doubt be rather simple, lacking many low-level branches. The lowest level branches would represent hand movements like pourings, stirrings, breakings, beatings, spreadings, and the like. "We can think of the planning systems in the mind," says Prinz (2004, 187), "as a collection of hierarchically organized to-do lists." Suppose, though, we wanted (for theoretical purposes if not practical efficiency) to be very explicit, and attempted to extend the control-hierarchy tree down as far as possible to the level of the most basic actions. While this would add some lower branches to the tree, we would again quickly reach a limit, with the lowest branches of the tree representing the basic actions of individual digits, or perhaps of individual phalanges of the fingers. Even with this modification, our tree would remain relatively simple, for these basic actions are underlain by motor schemata governing muscle contractions of which we are not conscious and of which we could not become conscious.

Now compare this elaborated control hierarchy tree with a musical time-span reduction tree, the lowermost branches of which are available to consciousness. In a musical context of any complexity at all, particularly one with significant contrapuntal complexity, the musical trees will be far more elaborate than those representing physiologically feasible bodily movements in physical space.

The obvious counterexample is the performance of contrapuntal music on a keyboard, particularly performance on a pedal organ. Such performance does, after all, consist of movements in physical space, motions that conform to the plan of the musical trees. There are, however, two points to be made. First, keyboard performance is arguably the single most elaborately organized muscular activity engaged in by human beings, more elaborately organized than other exceptionally demanding muscular tasks like hitting a baseball, performing microsurgery, playing the violin, or even dancing ballet. (To say it is more elaborately organized is not to say it is necessarily more difficult.) But the second, more important point to be made is this: as elaborately organized a physical activity as keyboard performance is, the complexity of its organization reflects the musical surface only. Recall Gibson's distinction between informational structure and information "about." The musical surface *qua* informational structure has a certain complexity. But the information "about" in the musical surface (assuming there is such) is more complex yet. The physical actions of the keyboard performer produce the musical surface. But in order to coordinate the "actions" in musical *virtual* space mandated by the principle of psychophysical complementarity, one might well need capabilities that extend far beyond human physical limitations, the limitations of a middle-sized creature with a semirigid three-dimensional body with four extremities and twenty fingers and toes.

Consider, by way of illustration, the double *fugato* in six-four time that begins at bar 655 of the *Finale* of Beethoven's Ninth Symphony (example 2.3). The two principal subjects appear (respectively) in the sopranos and altos of the chorus, doubled by the flutes, oboes, clarinets, and second violins, while the first violins contribute a running accompaniment. As the *fugato* unfolds, the two subjects and the running accompaniment are passed around to various voices of the chorus and instruments in different registers. This episode *could* be reduced and played on the piano with considerable, but not totally debilitating, musical loss. During such a performance, the fingers of the player will execute real motions spanning inches in physical space. But if we acknowledge the phenomenology of virtual motion in musical or acousmatic space, these sweeping eighth notes and vaulting fugal subjects, all the while exchanging registral positions, do not sound as if they are traversing distances of mere *inches* in musical space: they sound as if the motions in question must be measured in *leagues*. Real motions in physical space of such speed, extending over such distances, and exhibiting such elaborate coordination and transfer of function (the physical analogue of the musical registral exchanges between the subjects and the running accompaniment) are

Example 2.3

Beethoven, Symphony No. 9 in D Minor, *Finale*.

not within the realm of physical possibility for the human organism. The brightly colored, high-register minor ninth chords gently pulsating over a deep pedal accompanying the words *"Über Sternen muss er wohnen* [Beyond the stars must He abide]" that
conclude the section immediately preceding the *fugato* suggest distances so vast as to
be measurable only in the musical equivalent of light-years.

These are artful illusions, made possible by the structure of musical space. But how
do they arise? The answer is that the structure of virtual musical space, unlike that of
real physical space, is entirely determined by the acoustics of sound and by human
physiology and aural phenomenology. However musical space may be defined, even
taking into account the related spatial "regions" of different keys (see Lerdahl 2001),
this space is bounded by the highest and lowest musically usable audible frequencies.
It is possible, therefore, that a musical episode should put the listener into direct and
instantaneous contact with the limits of musical space, or at least come near to doing
this. The octave As that open Mahler's First Symphony, ranging from the A below the
bass staff in the contrabasses to stratospheric violin harmonics, seem to mark the very
limits of musical space and thus set the parameters of the musical experience that is to
follow (example 2.4). Comparably subliminal are Richard Strauss's deliberately dissonant superimposition of ethereal B major chords in the violins and high winds over
chthonian *pizzicato* low Cs in the cellos and basses at the close of *Also Sprach Zarathustra*, and the eerie, widely separated trombone and flute sequences in the *Hostias* and
the *Agnus Dei* of the Berlioz *Requiem* (examples 2.5 and 2.6). As already suggested, the
Mahler in particular suggests direct and instantaneous contact with spatial limits. But
no physical being *could* be in direct and instantaneous contact with the limits of *physical* space. For one thing, human sensory acquaintance with the distant regions of the
universe is limited to indirect contact with the *visible* universe because of the indispensable reliance on electromagnetic radiation as the medium for information transfer;
for another, the contact could not be instantaneous because of the physical constraints
on information transfer (information transfer even at the speed of light takes time);
and for a third, physical space is unbounded and has no limits. These are issues to
which we shall return in chapter 6.

The second complication concerns the nature of the musical virtual objects themselves. As suggested earlier, and as we shall see in the next section, the musical virtual
object presents itself as an animate object[67] that is to be understood empathetically via
simulation: like the world of the poet,[68] the acousmatic realm of the composer is an
animistic realm.[69] The brook or the storm representations in Beethoven's *Pastoral* Symphony, the sea representations in Debussy's *La Mer*, the windmill representations in
Strauss's *Don Quixote* represent their objects by inviting, indeed compelling the listener
to simulate the *behaviors* of these objects *as if* they were intentional beings animated by
an action plan.[70] To hear the brook, the storm, the waves, or the windmills in the

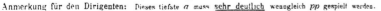

Example 2.4

Mahler, Symphony No. 1 in D, *Langsam, schleppend.* © 1927 Universal Edition (London), Ltd., London. © renewed. All rights reserved. Used by permission of European American Music Distributors LLC, U.S. and Canadian agent for Universal Edition (London), Ltd., London.

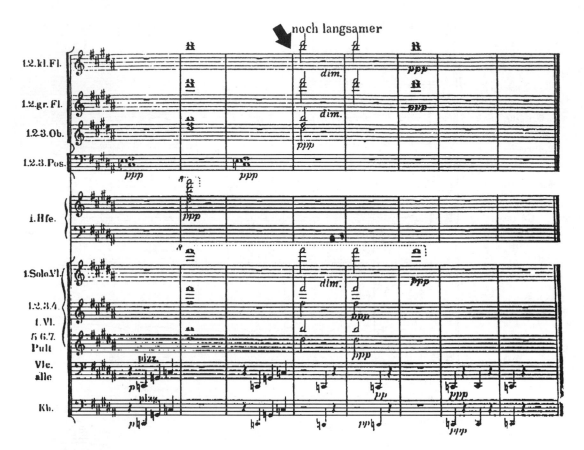

Example 2.5

Strauss, *Also Sprach Zarathustra*. Copyright © 1932 by Peters Edition Ltd. C. F. Peters sole selling
agent. Used by permission. All rights reserved.

music is to engage (off-line) in charade-like bodily displays.[71] We shall take up the
topic of animism in later chapters. For now, let us now take a closer look at the issue
of simulation.

2.5   Simulation, Neurophysiology, and Musical Experience

*Motor imagery departs from other types of mental imagery. Visual images, for example, are experienced
by the self in the same way as a spectator who watches a scene.... Motor images, by contrast, are experienced from within, as the result of a "first person" process where the self feels like an actor rather than a
spectator.*

—Marc Jeannerod (1997, 95)

Example 2.6
Berlioz, *Requiem.*

It is known that blood flow to the supplementary motor area of the brain increases when a subject simulates in imagination but does not perform a complex sequence of actions. Blood flow to the primary motor cortex, on the other hand, increases only during actual execution (Kandel et al. 1991, 619–620; Jeannerod 1994, 192; Jeannerod 1997, 115). PET and fMRI studies have yielded similar results, although some fMRI studies indicate limited primary motor cortical activity during simulation (Jeannerod 1994, 235). Other studies (Rizzolati and Arbib 1998, 190; see also Gallese and Goldman 1998) have established a link between observational simulation of action and activity in the premotor cortices of humans and monkeys.[72] Using PET scan, Halpern (2003) found clear evidence of increased blood flow to the right supplementary motor area in eight musically trained college-age adult subjects, both during musical listening and while carrying out a task involving musical imagery. Because the supplementary motor area activity was even higher during the imagery task than it was during listening, Halpern hypothesizes (2003, 229) that the motor planning in question concerned some manner of "internal humming" used to maintain the auditory image in imagination over time. This may or may not be the case; but notice that supplementary area activity was present during the ordinary listening test as well.[73]

There is also evidence of heightened beta activity in the supplementary motor area and related cortical areas under conditions of musical listening. Nakamura et al. (1999) carried out experiments that showed correlation between music listening and activity in the motor system in the brain, including the premotor cortex and the adjacent prefontal cortices bilaterally, the anterior region of the precuneus (a parietal area close to the parietal/occipital sulcus and identified by the authors with Brodmann area 7), the anterior cingulate cortex (part of the old mammalian cortex associated with emotional arousal), and the posterior portion of the precuneus. The premotor cortex, we should note, receives its principal input from the posterior parietal cortex (areas 5 and 7) by way of the basal ganglia, the centromedial and ventral lateral nuclei of the thalamus, the supplementary motor area, and the prefrontal cortex, which together constitute the motor control system (Kandel et al. 1991, 613, 620, 651). During the experiment, which was carried out with the cooperation of eight right-handed normal volunteers, electroencephalogram (EEG) electrodes were placed on twelve carefully chosen scalp sites from which seven were selected, and regional cerebral blood flow (rCBF) in the specified areas of the brain was measured using positron emission tomography (PET). Positive correlation between beta activity as recorded via EEG and rCBF in the motor areas was established during both the listening and the rest conditions. The exception was rCBF in the posterior precuneus, which was activated only during the listening condition. However, during the listening condition beta activity generally was significantly higher than it was during the rest condition: that is, "the regression line of the rCBF on the beta power in these regions was significantly steeper in the music condition than in the rest condition," indicating a significant increase in functional neural synchrony in these regions during listening.[74] The authors of the study point out that "in non-human primates, the premotor cortex and posterior parietal lobe (especially area 7b) appear to form a system for the coding of near-extrapersonal space for guidance of movement within that space" and that "exchange of information between the premotor and parietal areas appears to be necessary *when the visuo-spatial stimulus is processed even only mentally and hence, without the execution of motor activity and independent of perceptual modalities*" (ibid., 225, emphasis mine). These findings, I suggest, provide empirical support for the account of musical experience I have sketched. Located in the premotor cortex which, as we just saw, has been found to be implicated in action simulation, are so-called *mirror neurons* (Rizzolatti and Arbib 1998; Gallese and Goldman 1998), which are thought to enable "mind-reading" through simulation of another's actions.[75] If music activates the same system, as it seems to do, this would provide some empirical support for the thesis advanced above that music invites simulation of virtual animate objects.[76] But there is an additional source of empirical evidence.

Proponents of the simulation theory and proponents of the theory-theory of folk-psychological understanding have both given considerable attention to the phenomenon of autistic spectrum disorders (ASD) in their ongoing dispute. The issue between the two approaches is this. When normal humans predict the actions of others, are they applying an implicit folk-psychological theory using psychological generalizations, as the proponents of the theory-theory hold? Or are they running simulations on themselves off-line, determining what they themselves would do under a similar set of circumstances, and then basing their expectations concerning others on these results? The simulation theory/theory-theory dispute concerns the nature of the relevant predictive strategies and, as a consequence, the nature of the lack in social intelligence displayed by children with ASD. (See the essays collected in Davies and Stone 1995a,b.)

Music has been enlisted therapeutically for the treatment of ASD, and there are some clinical results that bear significantly on the simulation theory/theory-theory dispute, as well as on the theory of musical representation I have advanced. This is not the place to attempt to adjudicate in any definitive way the issue between the simulationists and the theory-theorists, but some music-therapeutic results suggest that the simulationists may have gotten something important right, concerning both the strategy employed by human beings when predicting the actions of human agents and the nature of the autistic deficit. These same results can also be seen to provide additional empirical evidence for the account of musical representation I have offered.

In general, autistic children relate better to machines than they do to people (Alvin and Warwick 1991, 13): they are "good at controlling them and do not seem to be afraid of them" (ibid., 41); autistic children "treat people as if they were objects" (Davies and Stone 1995a, 39); "children with autism as a group have 'difficulty in taking another person's point of view'" (Tomasello 1999, 77). These tendencies can be accounted for by both approaches: the autistic child can be said to lack the ability to simulate, or instead to lack an adequate theory of mind. But the fact that music therapy has markedly beneficial effects on these children seems to favor the simulation approach. For although there is no reason to expect that exposure to music would enhance folk-psychological *theorizing*, there is every reason to think that such exposure might enhance simulational ability, given the neuro-functional results reported by Nakamura et al. (1999). Relying (in part) on these results, I have argued that music encourages a simulational animism regarding all objects, not just animate ones; but it does so by engaging the motor system and nonconceptual, procedural or "pragmatic" (Jeannerod 1994, 198–201, 233; 2006, 15) representations rather than "semantic" or declarative representations.

Some of the accounts that have emerged from the music-therapeutic context may be taken to support this interpretation. In music, we are told, "we seem to return to a magic conception of sound *expressing life and giving life to an object*—a conception which may easily be a part of the world of the autistic child" (Alvin and Warwick 1991, 25, emphasis mine). These therapists produce a passage from Lorna Wing's *Early Childhood Autism* suggesting a deficit in the autistic child's ability to interpret intentional action, one that can be overcome through motor experience: "'an autistic child finds it difficult to watch other people perform and translate the movements onto his own body; he cannot understand verbal instruction, but can learn through feeling his own muscles move'" (quoted in Alvin and Warwick 1991, 90–91). This is learning by simulating, and in the music-therapeutic context, simulating *facilitated by* musical experience.

Here is Adam Smith's description of normal, nonautistic human observation of action (quoted in Goldman 1995, 196, a leading proponent of the simulation theory of folk-psychological understanding):

When we see a stroke aimed, and just ready to fall upon the leg or arm of another person, we naturally shrink and draw back our leg or our own arm.... The mob, when they are gazing at a dancer on the slack rope, naturally writhe and twist and balance their own bodies, as they see him do.

This is just what autistic children have difficulty doing without the aid of music. One child under music-therapeutic treatment "seemed to lack imagination, but given a theme or a picture suitable to the music he could function better and expand more. He began to move and mime a sea bird to one of his favorite tunes, 'L'Amour est bleu' which provided all the requisites for inspiration and freedom" (Alvin and Warwick 1991, 94). Of course, these episodes involved mimetic activity on-line and not off-line; but it is surely reasonable to expect a linkage that would allow facilitation of on-line simulation via music to carry over to off-line simulation, thereby improving, on the simulation theory, the understanding of animate beings by the child with ASD.

2.6 Musical Representation and Mental Modularity

Music as such knows only the tones or notes, not the causes that produce them.
—Schopenhauer (1844/1966, II, 448)

Having argued that musical experience is haptic, kinesthetic, and spatial, I attempted to make a case for the psychological reality of the Lerdahl and Jackendoff internal musical tree representations by pointing to their structural similarities to better-established motor representations and to the importance of the cognitive science of action in any attempt to explain the phenomenon of musical experience. But the generative approach has not gone unchallenged.[77] The "implication-realization" theory of musical understanding first developed by Leonard B. Meyer and more recently elaborated by Eugene Narmour (1990) is generally thought, not least by the theories' respective proponents themselves, to be the chief cognitivist competitor of the Lerdahl and Jackendoff theory, that is, to be the major theoretical alternative for the explanation of musical understanding that posits internal representations.[78] According to this theory, as musical sequences unfold, they engender expectations on the part of listeners. When these expectations are not fulfilled, uncertainty ensues. This produces mainly negative emotional arousal (frustration, dissatisfaction). Positive emotion ultimately prevails when uncertainty is resolved. Whereas the Lerdahl and Jackendoff hierarchical trees are procedural representations, Narmour dispenses with any such procedural representations and relies entirely on declarative inferential rules encoded in a language of thought. I do not wish to deny the competitive relationship between the two approaches, but its significance should not be exaggerated, since there seems to be at least one point of rapprochement between them, a point that is deeper than the mere fact that both theories make heavy use of ideas from gestalt psychology. As we shall see, this point of rapprochement may be able to fill a lacuna in the Lerdahl and Jackendoff theory, which has been charged with a serious neglect of melody (Narmour 1990, 4n1).

Narmour's version of the implication-realization theory derives considerable support from a reformed gestalt theory, holding that the mental processing of what he calls "parametric melodic style shapes," or scalar pitch structures organized with regard to parameters of registral direction (up and down) and size of successive intervals (ranging from the unison to the octave and beyond),[79] is subject to "bottom-up" gestalt "laws" of similarity, proximity, and common fate. These laws hold that perceivers tend to group arrays of objects by similarity, by proximity in space, and by direction of motion. In the musical case, the listener expects an ascending melody consisting of small intervals to continue that way. The melody is expected to continue with tones similar in duration, intensity, and instrumental color, to continue to move by small intervals, and to continue in the same direction. These allegedly innate, universal and invariant "bottom-up" laws are, however, hedged by "top-down" constraints associated with intra- and extra-opus musical styles that are culturally variable and learned. Like many contemporary cognitive psychologists,[80] Narmour accepts the psychological reality of the gestalt principles while he rejects the holistic neurobiological explanations offered by the original gestalt psychologists.[81] For these contemporary cognitive psychologists, as for Narmour, gestalt phenomena result from unconscious "inferences" carried out by the sort of modular input systems hypothesized by Fodor (1983). The gestalt rule of *Prägnanz*, for example, which includes principles of closure, "good" continuation, simplicity, symmetry, and regularity, is implemented by way of ongoing if-then inferences. In the case of visual perception, for example, *if* an apparently occluding object is opaque, *then* the apparently occluded object is seen as incomplete; otherwise there is no occlusion but mere contiguity (see Bregman 1981, 108).

One important component of contemporary thinking about gestalt phenomena, however, is curiously missing from Narmour's discussions. Current thinking suggests that gestalt principles are evolutionarily adaptive heuristics implemented by modular mechanisms that enable organisms to interpret proximate sensory arrays so as to arrive at interpretations of distal three-dimensional spatial layouts swiftly and accurately. The gestalt law of similarity, for example, is effective in determining object identity; the rules of *Prägnanz* help make quick sense of cluttered, occluded environments. The law of common fate is especially effective in individuating and tracking rigid and semi-rigid bodies with definite surfaces and edges. As Fodor says (1983, 47), modules "are highly specialized computational mechanisms in the business of generating hypotheses about the distal sources of proximal stimulations."

It is a salient, widely acknowledged fact that such gestalt principles operate strongly in the musical context. But *why* do they? That is, what "distal sources," what invariants, what objects are Narmour's auditory modules designed by natural selection to track? There seem to be only three possibilities, not all mutually exclusive. (1) The modules in question are dedicated to tracking the musical melodic and rhythmic structures themselves, much as the so-called language module is dedicated to tracking phonetic and grammatical structures in spoken language. (2) The modules are dedicated to tracking patterns of sound in general in the physical environment, to extracting and isolating sounds that belong together from the confusing ambient flux of auditory stimuli. On this second hypothesis, musical tracking would be merely a special case of this more general auditory tracking process. (3) The modules in question are designed to generate hypotheses concerning the distal sources of sounds, the objects causally responsible for producing them.

The third hypothesis can, I think, be immediately dismissed. Although there may be auditory modules designed to generate hypotheses concerning the spatial *location* of these causally responsible objects in space, such objects themselves generally are *not* disclosed to human perception by modular input systems performing unconscious automatic inferences, but by way of higher-level (i.e., centrally processed) conscious inferences that depend heavily on associative learning: specific sounds are associated with specific objects. Moreover, even granting modular spatial-location function, such modules would have no essential connection with musical experience, since in musical experience the listener abstracts from the location in physical space of the causal sources of musical tones. Notice that the claim is not that we *must* abstract from the spatial location of causal sources in musical experience, only that we *may* so abstract, that we *need not* take account of them to achieve musical understanding. If this were not so, monaural recordings would be irredeemably musically unsuccessful. But they are remarkably successful. The reason for this is simple: spatial location, as we saw, is not indispensable for the individuation of musical tones; only pitch and time are.

Scruton (1997, 3), like Schopenhauer before him, has discerned something important in musical experience:

Imagine a room (call it the "music room"), in which sounds are heard; any normal person entering the room is presented with sounds which are audible only there, but which can be traced to no specific source. For instance, you may hear a disembodied voice, or the pure note of a clarinet. Notice that I have described these sounds in terms of their characteristic causes: but I do not *have* to describe them in that way.... The one who hears these sounds experiences all that he needs, if he is to understand them as music. He does not have to identify their cause in order to hear them as they should be heard.

If the musical surface functions in the Gibsonian way as a two-dimensional informationally structured representation, abstraction from the locations of the causal sources of musical sound in physical space would be called for. In musical experience, "location" in acousmatic space supersedes location in physical space. In the middle section of Debussy's *Fêtes*, for example, the illusion of an approaching parade is achieved by means of skillful manipulation of orchestration and dynamics. The physical locations of the instruments are irrelevant to the effect. Where Scruton and Schopenhauer go wrong, I believe, is in extending abstraction from the location of the causal sources of sound in physical space to abstraction from *causal sources entirely*.

Pitch is known to have risen by nearly a half step over the last two centuries,[82] yet the colors of the various keys seem to have remained the same. E-flat major sounds just as muscular and regal today as it (appears to have) sounded in 1804. The distinctive qualities of the major and minor keys must, therefore, be a function of their mutual relations and of the acoustics of our modern, post-seventeenth-century Western musical instruments, particularly the stringed and wind instruments, rather than a function of absolute pitch location. When the open strings on a modern violin are tuned to G, D, A, and E, the major keys based on these tones take on their characteristic colors, wherever the pitches happen to be placed (within certain limits). As a matter of fact, orchestras throughout the twentieth century have used significantly different tuning for As, ranging in frequency from 435 to 455 Hz. Mahler's tuned-up solo violin in the *Scherzo* of his Fourth Symphony does sound as if it is playing a slightly strange C minor, rather than the B-flat minor in which its part is written, because the ear accepts the tuning of the surrounding orchestra. Mahler in effect makes his violin a "transposing instrument."[83] Nevertheless, I predict that if an entire string orchestra were to be tuned, like Mahler's violin, up a whole step, its performance of a work written in C minor, say Mozart's *Adagio and Fugue* K. 546, would retain much of the work's characteristic key coloring. Because of the physical properties of the instruments, the work would not sound as if it had been transposed and played in D minor. The open cello "C" strings would be a dead giveaway, and one reason a passage in C minor played on the violin sounds as it does is that the open A and E strings cannot be used without accidentals. Any passage in the Neapolitan key of D-flat major would use *none* of the open violin strings. Those with perfect pitch would, of course, notice the change in absolute pitch. Perfect pitch, however, is merely an unusually accurate and retentive pitch memory, which can be calibrated to alternative tunings.

This issue could perhaps be dealt with by rejecting "pure sonicism" in favor of "timbral sonicism," the view that what counts for the musical effect is the sounded outcome, including the full range of instrumental timbral qualities, regardless of how the sound was produced (see Davies 2001, 64). On this view, if the sound has the right quality, its source could just as well be an electronic synthesizer as a violin. The problem with timbral sonicism is this. An awareness of how musical sounds are produced is part of the background knowledge the enculturated listener brings to the musical experience, thereby shaping the total musical effect, just as the viewer of an oil painting on canvas understands the impasto he sees to be the result of the artist's brushwork.[84] Both sorts of background knowledge are required for the "hearing-in" and "seeing-in" experiences central to the experience of musical and pictorial art. We shall return to the notions of hearing- and seeing-in in chapter 5.

Rejecting hypothesis (3), we are left with hypotheses (1) and (2). In favor of hypothesis (2) are pitch-streaming phenomena, the automatic tendency we have to group high-pitched (but not necessarily acoustically periodic) sounds with other similar, spatiotemporally proximate high-pitched sounds and low-pitched (but also not necessarily acoustically periodic) sounds with similar, spatiotemporally proximate low-pitched sounds. Pitch-streaming phenomena are salient in both nonmusical and musical contexts, as, for example, when we group the partially overlapping low barking sounds of dogs and high snarling sounds of cats during a neighborhood territorial dispute, or when we momentarily hear a solo cello performing a passage that contains repeated large register skips in a Bach suite as two separate instruments, one playing high notes and the other low notes. Pitch streaming is also subject to strong gestalt effects of grouping and common fate. Although the importance of pitch streaming in musical experience should not be underestimated (see below), hypothesis (2) is vitiated or at least weakened by the issue of "indispensable attributes" considered earlier (see section

2.3). Any modules dedicated to generating hypotheses about sounds as acoustic phenomena *in physical space* will be strongly biased to compute direction and location and to individuate on those bases. As a result, they will involve motor commands to change the orientation of the head so as to maximize the effects of asynchronous onset. But this just does *not* occur in musical listening, for, as I have argued, the location of sounds in physical space plays no important role in musical experience, even if stereophonic sound reproduction may have the enhancing effect of simulating the live performance situation. Musical tones are individuated not like sounds in physical space, but on the bases of pitch and timbre. As a matter of fact, in the musical context, melodic grouping will actually *trump* spatial location, a remarkable phenomenon that composers have exploited.[85] The actual scoring of the first and second violin parts in the opening of the final movement of Tchaikovsky's *Pathetique* Symphony is shown in example 2.7; but they sound as if example 2.8 were the correct scoring, even if the

Example 2.7
Tchaikovsky, Symphony No. 6 in B Minor, *Pathetique, Adagio lamentoso*, first and second violins as written. Reprinted by permission of Oxford University Press/Oxford University Press, Inc.

Example 2.8
Tchaikovsky, Symphony No. 6 in B Minor, Pathetique, *Adagio lamentoso*, first and second violins as heard. Reprinted by permission of Oxford University Press/Oxford University Press, Inc.

second violins are seated, in the traditional manner, opposite the first violins. As Sloboda points out (1985, 157), it is something of a shock for someone who knows the work only by ear to see the score: people have even been known to suspect that it might be a misprint. Finally, what is perhaps most damaging to the spatial tracking hypothesis is that it cannot explain the expectations of intervallic and registral continuation and reversal hypothesized by Narmour.

That leaves hypothesis (1). As it happens, Fodor (1983, 47) allows that there may be dedicated modules consisting of "computational systems that detect the melodic or rhythmic structure of acoustic arrays"; and Mithen (2005, 36–40) presents clinical evidence concerning cognitive deficit due to neural insult demonstrating that the neural systems activated when tracking environmental sounds function *independently* of those activated when processing musical sounds. So let us, for the sake of present discussion, grant Narmour his musical modules. Our task now is to try to make evolutionary sense of them. Complex, dedicated mechanisms do not arise from nothing. They must, that is, have homologues in evolutionary ancestors. The most promising candidate for *recent* homology, I suggest, are modules dedicated to the production and interpretation of gesture, mime, and, most especially, prosodic vocalization involving pitch and rhythm in prelinguistic hominids, all three closely allied, and all three important for the simulational and mimetic aspect of musical experience we recognized earlier (see Schwartz et al. 2003). Humans effortlessly interpret gesture and prosodic pattern as intentionally significant. Moreover, a convincing adaptive story concerning early prelinguistic hominid communication by way of mimetic representation using the voice and the body can be told. Indeed, versions of such a story have been told by Donald (1991) and Mithen (2005), a story we shall be taking up in the next chapter.

But even this does not by itself explain the strong intervallic and registral biases emphasized by Narmour. Why *should* the musical listener expect (if he does) registral and intervallic continuation when successive intervals are smaller than a fourth, but expect reversal of direction and intervallic size after larger intervals? Assuming that these "unconscious inferences" are built into the musical input systems, *why* are they? Why, in particular, is the *reversal* expectation so salient?[86] Narmour is forced to concede that in his theory, these expectations of registral and intervallic reversal merely have the status of a "symmetrical construct" (1990, 150): that is, they merely satisfy a general requirement of opposition. The only justification he offers for this is to suggest that the opposition between continuation ("process") and reversal might be a special case of the principle of binary opposition, which, in turn, is deeply ingrained in human mental function. This last claim is certainly correct (see Ogden 1932). But once again, the principle of opposition does not by itself offer any satisfying explanation of the specific details of the intervallic and registral expectations to which Narmour draws attention. Why do reversal of registral direction and reduction of intervallic size strongly suggest closure, whereas continuation of registral direction and expansion of intervallic size strongly suggest nonclosure? I suggest an alternative hypothesis, one, again, for which there is some empirical evidence.

That the mammalian organs of hearing originated in the acousticolateral system of fishes is an uncontested fact. There is also agreement that the lateral line is a tactual rather than an auditory sensory organ. These facts, as I have argued, contribute strongly to the spatial and tactual character of musical experience, both of which are very difficult to account for in any other way. Consider now the haptic exploration of objects and surfaces by humans. There is experimental evidence showing that continuous tactual exploration of an object by adult subjects tends to continue without change of direction until an edge or a corner is reached (Gibson 1962). At that point the direction of exploration reverses, and scanning range tightens, pending a new phase of exploration. There is further evidence suggesting that the longer an episode of tactile exploration of a textured surface proceeds in a uniform direction, the more likely it is to undergo change in direction (Katz 1989, 153–160). These behavioral patterns have the hallmarks of innate tendencies: Piaget claimed three ontogenetically fixed stages in the development of the capacity for haptic exploration. Stage I (2–4 years) shows an absence of regular exploratory technique of any kind. In Stage II (4–6 years), exploration proceeds serially, but without systematic operational guidance. But in the "mature" Stage III that begins after year 6, "operational direction," which includes *reversibility*, emerges: "an operation is 'an action which can return to its starting point, and which can be integrated with other actions also possessing this feature of reversibility.' The operational method involves 'grouping the elements perceived in terms of a general plan, and starting from a fixed point of reference to which the child can always return'" (quoted in Warren 1982, 98).[87]

We have already noted that both haptic exploration and musical processing are serially organized, and we have emphasized the consequent importance of reversibility in haptic exploration and in the delineation of melodic structure.[88] Each cycle of haptic exploration, moreover, has its natural limit: the full extension of the hands, arms, and ultimately, of the body. At this point, reversal ("closure") is all but required. As Gibson (1962, 488) says, "[t]he visible array of surfaces extends for miles of course, and the tangible array only to the length of man's arm." These restrictions on limb extension during exploratory movements, we should also note, apply equally to gestural and mimetic movement. Gesture and mimesis track the configurations of the mental models engaged in the mind of the communicator: mental models of extensive objects call for extensive expressive gestures.[89] The best candidates for the evolutionary homologues of Narmour's musical modules, I submit, are mechanisms for haptic exploration and mimetic gesture, since they are the ones that best explain the genesis of the melodic intervallic and registral (directional) implications.

The close connection between invariance tracking and the disclosure of affordances, and the correlation between affordances and action, both recognized by the original

Example 2.9
Brahms, Symphony No. 2 in D, *Allegro non troppo.*

Example 2.9
(continued)

Example 2.9
(continued)

gestalt theorists, serve to make clear the rapprochement between the generative theory of Lerdahl and Jackendoff and Narmour's version of the implication-realization theory to which I alluded earlier. There is no need at all for the generative theorist to deny a modular, bottom-up, automatic, relatively encapsulated[90] level in musical processing, should such a hypothesis be empirically supported, since the motor system is itself organized that way, with lower-level neuro-muscular assemblies functioning relatively automatically and independently of high-level supervision. And there does seem to be some empirical support for the modular hypothesis with regard to musical processing: once they are familiar with Western tonal-musical style, normal human beings do effortlessly parse simple melodic and rhythmic shapes, imposing (in effect) time signature, bar lines, and pitch groupings that show some definite cognitive impenetrability (without necessarily possessing these *concepts*). One may know that the motif introduced by Brahms in bar 136 of the first movement of his Second Symphony (example 2.9) starts on the second beat of the bar in three-quarter time; but it is very difficult to resist hearing each pitch grouping returning to the downbeat. As a result, this particular passage gives rise to a certain tension between a partially encapsulated input system and more global musical central processing, a mildly disorienting effect that Brahms seems to have especially favored[91] and that appeals strongly to some listeners (though I do not count myself among them). Any expectancies or "implications" will have to be represented procedurally, not declaratively, on the Lerdahl and Jackendoff nested tree model; but that is all to the good, given the procedural, nonpropositional nature of musical representation and understanding and its deep connection with the motor system and with simulated action, as well as the mental modeling required in the representation of musical virtual scenarios. (Recall the predictive capacities of Craik's mental models.)

Thus the implication-realization theory, in my view, is far too narrowly informational in its conception and insufficiently action-oriented to make sense of musical experience and musical emotion, especially the continued enjoyment of musical works intimately known to their listeners. In musical experience, to *understand* is to *undertake*. This is a topic to which we shall return in chapter 5. The Lerdahl and Jackendoff theory has a great deal to say about relative structural importance of pitches, but it has very little to say about melodic shape. Interpreting the reduction trees in the light of motor plans and bodily gesture, I propose, enhances the plausibility of the Lerdahl and Jackendoff theory by facilitating its application to the issue of melodic shape.

2.7 Summary and Conclusion

What, then, is the primary musical representation? Is it the musical surface, the primarily external representation? Is it the primarily internal representation? The answer is that both are implicated. The musical surface fulfills a symbolic function to the extent that it is informationally structured, and is *produced* and *used* to carry such information. This, we recall, was one of the two aspects that Gibson accorded external representations. To the extent that the informational structure in a representation discloses invariants to appropriately equipped perceivers, it can be said to represent its virtual objects successfully. A picture manages to represent virtual objects because of the effect of its reflecting surface on the human visual system. I have suggested that artfully contrived musical patterns, including symmetry, parallelism, contrast, and large-scale formal structure function as invariants. The extraction of these invariants simulates the perception of virtual layouts and scenarios, by means of an analogy between musical perception and the haptic exploration of surfaces, areas, and volumes occupied by media of differing densities. But in addition, two varieties of *internal* musical representations have emerged. Internal representations of the first kind (the Lerdahl and Jackendoff metric structures, grouping structures, and trees) are used to recover the informational structure from the musical surface. Representations of the second kind are mental models whose nonconceptual contents are the musical virtual scenarios that the informational structure is "about." They are used to update the evolving musical plans.

In supplying plans of action, music puts the listener's body into states that would fit with or be appropriate to interacting with and simulating scenarios and terrains with certain features and with varying emotional valence. The affinity between Lerdahl and Jackendoff's time-span and prolongation reduction trees and control hierarchies and action plans makes it possible for musical organization to suggest movements in a virtual space. This, in turn, motivates the construction of internal representations (musical mental models) that represent the features of the layouts and scenarios in which these virtual movements occur. The ultimate source of our ability to find in music the significance we do is, then, as unexpected as the ability itself is remarkable: it is to be found in the phylogenetic origin of the brain as the organ of motor control.[92]

In this chapter, our approach to the varieties of musical representation has been primarily descriptive, with only an occasional glance (e.g., the discussion in section 2.3.1 of analog representation and content) toward normative issues of syntax, semantics, and pragmatics. It is to these issues that we now turn.

2.8   Appendix: Does Cognitive Psychology Need Mental Representations?

By countenancing representations internal to the mind–brain, I have assumed the fundamental correctness of what is at present the dominant explanatory paradigm in cognitive psychology, the representational theory of mind (RTM). In doing so, I have signaled agreement with Johnson-Laird, Marr, Shepard, and others who hold, against traditional ecological psychology, that invariance detection requires representational function. Acceptance of RTM, it should be noted, need not amount to an endorsement of classical computationalism or of any version of the language of thought hypothesis that requires the psychological reality of programmable, representation-level rules.

A more serious challenge to RTM, however, issues from a different quarter. In a provocative essay, Keijzer (2001) has argued that the psychology of *behavior* does not require representations (in any of the currently accepted versions) as theoretical posits at all. In his view, the motor system consists of multiple levels of hierarchically organized neural oscillators. These neural mechanisms, which engage in mutual interlevel modulations, enter into chaotic, but parametrically constrained, limit cycles over widely varying periods. The varying time scales are supposed to do the work of representations of distant goal states: neural oscillators that cycle over longer time scales function proleptically relative to those that cycle over shorter ones. At the most basic organic level, the ongoing depolarization and repolarization of a neuron displays a cyclical profile. But so do long-term behaviors like mating and hibernation and the neural and hormonal dynamics that control them. This mode of organization, Keijzer argues, explains the flexibility of the behaviors of organic systems as (relatively) unsophisticated as insects, as compared with the rigidity of the behaviors of even the most sophisticated computerized robots. In the course of his argument, Keijzer draws attention to impressive existence proofs from robotics that suggest the superiority of "behavioral systems theory" (BST), the nonrepresentational, multilevel oscillator model, over "agent theory" (AT), the standard input, central processing, and output model of computational robotics.

Conceptually, BST relies on an analogy between behavior and embryology. Just as the expression of a gene is not a strictly programmed phenomenon but rather a multilevel affair involving complex interaction and feedback loops between genes and cellular cytoplasm, so the expression of plans in the behavior of an organism is the result of multilevel interactions between neural structures, musculo-skeletal system, and environment. Borrowing from the biologist Jacob von Uexküll, BST emphasizes the fit between an organism and the specific "Umwelt" or surround in which it is equipped to function. As a result, BST has much in common with ecological psychology. Despite the powerful analogy between behavior and embryological development, however, BST is far from settled doctrine. Keijzer admits this, pleading growing pains of a youthful or even newly nascent research program. Although it is clear that the lowest levels of the motor systems of organisms are constituted of hierarchically organized reflexes, oscillators, and servomechanisms, it is less than obvious that cascading levels of oscillators will take us all the way even to sophisticated cerebral motor function without motor representations described at levels higher than the neural substrate.

While I cannot do full justice here to Keijzer's rich discussion, three responses are available to deflect his challenge to RTM. First, his topic is deliberately circumscribed. Keijzer treats only "behavior," defined as autonomous movement that is goal-directed but *subpersonally organized*. He deliberately excludes purposive "action" at the agent level. Much less does he attempt to extend his conclusions to cognition in general. His main concern is the entirely laudable aim of ridding the psychological explanation of behavior of all covert reliance on undischarged intentional notions, that is, of eliminating the "theoretical hitchhiking" that, in his view, infects AT. For Keijzer, as for others (e.g., McGinn 1989), classical computationalism merely displaces the problem of intentionality without solving it: strings of symbols or "syntactical shapes" inside the head are as much in need of intentional interpretation as are strings of symbols outside the head. (We shall engage this issue briefly when discussing mental models and nonconceptual content in chapter 5.) Unlike the Churchlands and other psychological eliminativists, however, Keijzer has no quarrel with the explanatory adequacy or with the psychological reality of folk-psychological categories of representations for the explanation of *action* at the *agent level*. He even takes Dennett to task for the "instrumentalism" of the intentional stance: "beliefs and desires can be as real as atoms and stones are" (2001, 37). Does Keijzer mean, then, to suggest that there are no intermediate levels in functional abstraction between the neural and task levels, and that folk-psychological internal representations suddenly appear in the head? As we are about see, he does not.

Second, Keijzer suggests that the distributed representations of a neural network may not count as representations at all (ibid., 98). This in effect pushes representationalism in the direction of its classical computational version, thereby making it more vulnerable to criticism.[93] Recurrent neural networks handle limit cycles very well (Churchland 1995, 101), and a trajectory in the activation space of a recurrent neural net is reasonably regarded as a representation that can function as an internal model of a sequence of events or states of an object (Churchland 1995, 103).

Third, Keijzer claims that the nervous system "changes its internal states under the influence of external perterbations" (2001, 157). While this "internal structure may not 'reflect' reality," he admits that "it is far from arbitrary either ... most nervous systems that will be encountered in life have a strong *structural congruency* to a particular environment" (ibid., 162, emphasis mine). Surely the nervous system, the neural wetware *itself*, is not structurally congruent with an environment: its functional states are. But what states, and at what level of functional abstraction? "Structural congruency," I submit, is just a terminological variant of isomorphism or paramorphism, the structural similarity between mental models and their objects. Keijzer denies that nervous systems engage in information processing. Yet there is a systematic correlation between changes in internal states and external perterbations; and internal token states need only correlate reliably with the external events to function as informational vehicles. As we saw early in this chapter, the nomic correlations that underlie "hard" information are not required: "soft" information will do. In the end, Keijzer comes to accept "representation-like" entities in the mind–brain, if not "traditional" representations (ibid., 243). He is as dismissive of behaviorism as is the most dedicated cognitivist.

For our purposes, Keijzer's most important point is this: the "traditional image" of a representational structure, he maintains, "turns up as a coarse view on the nested set of dynamical structures" that constitutes a nervous system of even minimal complexity (ibid., 223). Unlike a digital computer or even a simple (uncoupled)[94] neural net, an organic nervous system is a hierarchically layered "subsumption architecture": "Every behavioral capacity involves sensing, control, and behavior" (169). "[a]ll behavior," he concludes, including the behavior of unicellular organisms, "is anticipatory behavior. If there is cognition involved here, then it is a form of cognition shared by humans and animals alike" (234). If these conclusions are correct, they would make representations doubly "distributed." Not only would a representation (or a representation-like state) be distributed throughout an activation space; it would be distributed across multiple layers of activation spaces.[95] This may well turn out to be right.

3   The Musical Utterance: How Music Means

To make music possible as a separate art, a number of senses, especially the muscle sense, have been immobilized (at least relatively, for to a certain degree all rhythm still appeals to our muscles), so that man no longer bodily imitates and represents everything he feels.... The actor, the mime, the dancer, the musician, and the lyric poet are basically related in their instincts and, at bottom, one—but gradually they have become specialized and separated from each other, even to the point of mutual opposition. The lyric poet remained united with the musician for the longest time; the actor with the dancer.
—Nietzsche (1889/1954, 520)

3.1   Introduction and Chapter Conspectus

In the previous chapter we isolated three varieties of musical representation, one external and two internal: (1) the structured musical surface; (2) the hierarchically organized, planlike internal representations that enable the listener to parse the musical surface and to construct the musical virtual scenarios in virtual musical space; and (3) the mental models that represent these virtual scenarios and are used to update the evolving musical plans. The listener was said to perceive virtual scenarios in musical space and to act (off-line) in that virtual space. To this point, however, the account has been largely descriptive and empirical, relying on results from cognitive science and biology to develop the relevant classes of representations for reflexive metainterpretation. Reflexive metainterpretation, recall, attempts to establish relatively wide reflective equilibrium between normative principles and judgments of cases, including the judgments of the interpreter himself. Since it is representations that are in question, the principles in question will be syntactic, semantic, and pragmatic; and the relevant judgments will be the intuitions of competent listeners concerning their musical experience.

At this point a series of leading questions naturally arise. Is the musical surface syntactically organized at all? How is the listener motivated to construct the internal hierarchical structures and mental models? Can we say more about the semiotic function of these mental models, the rules according to which they represent? To what extent is music capable of carrying extramusical meaning? What are the details of the application to music of the Lakoff and Johnson "body-in-the-mind" theory of metaphor and what is its impact on the issue of musical meaning? These questions will dictate the present chapter's order of exposition.

Section 3.2 begins the reflexive metainterpretation of the musical surface by making some requisite distinctions between representations, signs, and symbols. Like signs, symbols are external or public representations, but they have distinctive properties and are subject to normative constraints that do not apply to all signs. Symbols are external representations that are either syntactically organized, or whose referents may be widely separated in space and time from the occasions of their use, or both. Traffic lights, for example, are signs, not symbols, because their syntactic organization is minimal, consisting of a green-yellow-red sequence with no possibility of combination or recursion, and because their meanings (Go! Prepare to Stop! Stop!) are primarily directed to events at their occasions of use. Syntactically organized symbols are not only type-classed, but are governed by concatenation rules. By these syntactic and semantic criteria, the musical surface is symbolic, and section 3.3 takes up its syntactic and semantic properties. Following Lerdahl and Jackendoff, I argue that the syntax of the musical surface is generative; and following Goodman, that its semantics is exemplificational. Section 3.4 then addresses the pragmatics of the musical surface, arguing that the musical performance functions as an external "pushmi-pullyu" representation, which is an utterance carrying both indicative and imperative force. Section 3.5 establishes important relations between hierarchical plans, categorization, and semantic fields. The introduction of the idea of semantic fields lays the groundwork for the attribution in section 3.6 of "field structure" to the musical surface. Because this *musical* field structure is capable of modeling the structure of *semantic* fields, the organization of music models a dimension of conceptual organization without being itself conceptual. Since only the structure, not the content, of semantic fields is modeled, I term this aspect of musical meaning "extramusical *form*." But there is a second aspect of extramusical meaning that models extramusical conceptual *content*. This variety of meaning involves the models of scenarios in virtual musical space mentioned above and anticipated in chapter 2. Section 3.7 interprets this variety of musical meaning by applying the Lakoff and Johnson "body-in-the-mind" theory of metaphorical understanding. Section 3.8 outlines an existence proof for the Lerdahl and Jackendoff generative theory of tonal music. Finally, section 3.9 provides a summary of conclusions reached in the chapter.

3.2   Representations, Signs, and Symbols

As we observed in chapter 2, the musical surface is not only an informationally structured event; it is an external representation produced by performers for the consumption of listeners. Since an external representation is a sign or sign token, this will now require us to turn our attention to issues of semiotic, or the general theory of signs. In the taxonomy here adopted, representations constitute the most general case of semiosis or signification: even a mere informational vehicle may be regarded as a representation if it is used as such. As I argued in chapter 2, an informational vehicle becomes representational when it is used by an interpreter to derive information or to direct action. Symbols, on the other hand, constitute a special case of representation: they are external representations that are organized according to some combination of syntactic, semantic, and pragmatic rules that can in principle be explicitly stated by the user of the symbol.[1] Animals represent and use signs; but only humans symbolize.

The most thorough philosophical treatment of issues of musical semiosis known to me, and one that includes an exhaustive examination of existing theories, is that of Davies (1994). Building on (but also modifying) H. P. Grice's classic account (1957), Davies distinguishes five varieties of meaning (1994, 29–36):

Meaning A: Natural, unintended meaning
Meaning B: The intentional use of natural significance
Meaning C: Systematized, intentional use of natural elements
Meaning D: Intentional, arbitrary stipulation of stand-alone meaning
Meaning E: Arbitrary meaning generated within a symbol system

These five classifications might be perspicuously regrouped into the following three categories:

Unintended meaning (meaning A)
Intentional but nonarbitrary meaning (meanings B and C)
Intentional but arbitrary meaning (meanings D and E)

Davies's meaning A partially coincides with what I described in chapter 2 as *de re* informational content. The coincidence is only partial for two reasons. First, like Dretske in his better moments and unlike both Grice and Davies, I hold that *de re* informational content is a nonintentional, physical phenomenon and deny that it is a variety of meaning or signification at all. Meaning is carried by representational vehicles only, and, as I argued in chapter 2, an informational vehicle becomes representational, and therefore normatively evaluable according to correctness conditions, only when it is used as a representation by an interpreter. So there is, in my view, no uninterpreted "natural meaning." For me, if not for Davies, if music is meaningful[2] at all, then it is representational.

But second, Davies also allows that in addition to the natural relations of nomological dependency and reliable correlation, a "natural relation" of resemblance is also capable of securing meaning A. "Natural" here merely means "not arbitrarily stipulated from within a cultural setting." But in order to get a notion of natural *meaning* even from this, use by an interpreter must be brought in. As Davies (1994, 30) himself admits:

resemblance, as an absolute relation, lacks the selectivity and directionality on which meaning depends; resemblance is a symmetrical, reciprocal relation. Moreover anything may resemble any other in some respect.... That two things resemble each other is not, therefore, a reason for treating either as signifying the other. Nevertheless, resemblance is standardly relativized to our interests.

Because interests are intentional, it is difficult to see how their introduction does not collapse meaning A based on natural resemblance into meaning B, the intentional use of natural significance. Because anything may resemble any other in some respect, there is some question whether the notion of "natural" (i.e., non-interest-relative) resemblance is useful at all. Goodman (1972), for one, thought that it was not. Consider one of Davies's own examples. An orange, he points out, "naturally" resembles the sun more closely than does a paperclip with regard to color and (approximate) sphericity. But a paperclip also resembles the sun more closely than does an orange: the orange is a food source, but the sun and the paperclip are not. A paperclip, however, also resembles an orange more closely than it resembles the sun: the sun is a light source, but the orange and the paperclip are not. It seems that there is no escaping the conclusion that meaningful judgments of resemblance are interest relative.

Still, this remains a relatively small point in the present context, for we can identify meaning A, or natural unintended meaning, with *de re* informational content, though once again, I deny that uninterpreted informational vehicles are, as such, meaningful. That leaves the remaining groups of two, meanings B and C and meanings C and D. Their differences capture an important distinction we shall need. Meanings B and C require some point or points of resemblance between sign and signified, with resemblance, of course, relativized to the interests of the sign user. Meanings D and E, on the other hand, do not: the association between sign and signified may be entirely arbitrary and conventional. Linguistic types and tokens carry meaning E and the noon whistle carries meaning D. Into which category does the musical surface fall? I shall be arguing that its primary mode of signification requires both syntactic organization and resemblance between sign and signified. In Davies's terms, the meaning of the musical surface is *primarily* a case of the systematized, intentional use of natural elements, or meaning C—primarily, but not exclusively.

First, I agree with Davies that musical elements *may* function both in B and D modes, that is, as signs, both nonconventional and conventional, with stand-alone meaning. As examples of the former, consider the instrumental birdcalls introduced by composers into musical compositions; as examples of the latter, consider the traditional bugle calls of the United States Cavalry. Second, I also agree that the organization of the surface of musical works has a significant conventional component that has to do with its belonging to a style whose implicit rules must be mastered in order to understand it. To insist, as I just have done, on systematized musical symbols as the primary vehicles of musical meaning, however, is to stake out common ground with Nelson Goodman, the author of what is perhaps the most influential purely conventionalist account of music as symbol. For Goodman, musical meaning, and indeed the meanings of all artistic products, is exclusively a case of meaning E. It is to his views that we now turn.

3.3   Goodman on Symbol, Syntax, and Exemplification

Toward the end of *Languages of Art*, Goodman (1976, 254) allows that four symptoms of the aesthetic—syntactic density, semantic density, syntactic repleteness, and exemplification—"may be conjunctively sufficient and disjunctively necessary" for "aesthetic experience."[3] Having identified these four symptoms, Goodman goes on to say something he probably should not say: "perhaps, that is, an experience is aesthetic if it has all these attributes and only if it has at least one of them." This claim is questionable because syntactic and semantic attributes[4] can belong only to symbolic schemes and systems, and not to experiences.[5] Dense schemes and systems, recall, do not allow for finite differentiation. In a dense *scheme*, there is no finite decision procedure to determine whether a "mark" (or token) that does not belong to both of two "characters" (or types) does not belong to one or to the other. In a dense *system* (which is an interpreted scheme), there is no finite decision procedure to determine whether an object that does not belong to two "compliance classes" does not belong to one class or the other. Having already discussed density in chapter 2, let us direct some attention to repleteness, attenuation, and exemplification. A scheme is syntactically replete to the extent all aspects of the scheme are symbolically significant, that is, realize a symbolic function. A scheme is attenuated to the extent aspects of the symbolic scheme are not significant. Goodman offers the following illustration of this last distinction (ibid., 229): The color and thickness of a line in an artistic drawing are symbolically significant, whereas those of an electrocardiogram tracing most likely are not. To the extent this is the case, the drawing is syntactically replete and the line graph is syntactically attenuated. Finally, exemplification is a *referential* function in which the standard "downward" referential direction from "label" (predicate or nonlinguistic symbol) to object or reference class is reversed: an object or a member of the reference class may, if used as a symbol, exemplify or refer "upward" to the label or labels that denote it.

Rather than saying what he does about an *experience* being aesthetic, what Goodman should say, I suggest, is that a *symbol* may achieve *aesthetic significance* if it has all these attributes and only if it has at least one of them. It is to symbols, not to experiences, that these four attributes—syntactic density, semantic density, syntactic repleteness, and exemplification—properly apply. Once we have noticed this, an intriguing issue concerning musical symbolism arises. The musical score does not possess any of the four attributes. The score itself, as a symbol in a notational system (the score without verbal directions, implicit rules of performance practice, etc.), is syntactically and semantically disjoint, it is syntactically attenuated, it is semantically unambiguous, and it is denotational and nonexemplificational.[6] The score, therefore, is not by itself an aesthetically significant symbol. And in fact, Goodman (1976, 255) says as much: "A score and its mere reading are devoid of aesthetic aspects."[7] The compliant performance, on the other hand, is not syntactically dense, since its sound events must, in order to be heard as music at all, be grouped into disjoint classes of tones. But the performance *is* exemplificational and semantically dense, for it exemplifies densely ordered nuance properties.[8] Finally, because every musically relevant aspect of the performance is symbolically significant, it is (arguably) syntactically replete as well. To the extent the performance possesses these attributes, it displays three of Goodman's four symptoms of the aesthetic. This, however, seems merely to tell us something concerning Goodman's musical ontology that we already knew: for him, the musical work is the class of compliant performances, not the musical score.[9] But if the compliant musical performance is semantically dense, syntactically replete, and exemplificational, while the score is none of these, the musical performance, in addition to complying with the score and inheriting its syntax from the score, has symbolic attributes the score does *not* have. Therefore, it must function as a symbolic token in its own right belonging to a distinguishable symbolic system. Semantic density, syntactic repleteness, and exemplification are attributes of symbolic systems exclusively.

The musical performance, then, is denoted and prescribed by the score, yet is itself a distinct symbolic token that possesses symbolic attributes not possessed by the score. But what sort of symbolic token is it? To what manner of symbolic system does it belong? We can answer the first question with some confidence. As a symbolic token, a musical performance would have to be a nonpropositional utterance of some kind. It is clearly not an inscription, nor is it a natural sign (like the smoke caused by a forest fire), nor is it a nonverbal conventional sign (like a traffic sign), nor is it (strictly speaking) a gesture, that is, a communicative bodily movement. And these seem to exhaust the possibilities. The second question requires a more elaborate answer. If the musical performance is a symbolic token that has conventional and rule-governed aspects (as it clearly does), it must belong to a symbolic scheme. But any symbolic scheme must possess rules of formation or a syntax. Yet this syntax cannot (merely) be the inherited syntax of the score: since the performance has specifically *symbolic* attributes the score lacks, it must belong to a distinguishable symbolic scheme, which will require for its definition different (or additional) formal properties.[10] We need a source of musical syntax that goes beyond the syntax of the score.

It might be thought that the performance inherits whatever additional formal properties it needs from the supplementary instructions in the score, the verbal instructions concerning tempi and dynamics and the nonverbal directives (like hairpin dynamic indicators) that do not belong to the score as a notational system. A performance complying with these instructions can be said to exemplify a semantically dense range of labels in Goodman's sense. But directions of this sort, "play loudly/play softly," "become louder here/become softer there," "play at a fast/moderate/slow tempo," "speed up here/slow down there," are surely much too coarse-grained and vague to come close to specifying the grammar of what might be thought of as a "well-formed" performance, one that can carry the right exemplificational significance, most especially, the right *expressive* or *metaphorically exemplificational* significance. We shall return to Goodman's notion of expression or aesthetic metaphorical exemplification presently. For now, let us consider exemplification itself.

Goodman's version of exemplification presents two related difficulties. The first is his extreme nominalism, his insistence that objects exemplify only "labels," including, but not limited to, descriptive labels or predicates. This ontological program, if consistently carried out, precludes the possibility of all talk of attributes or properties considered as universals, a Spartan regime to which Goodman himself does not always adhere. Such lapses, however, are deliberate and are explicitly tagged as mere shorthand for more rigorously formulated, if also more unwieldy, locutions. This is not the place to attempt any full-blown defense of the propriety of property talk. I shall follow Levinson (1978) in regarding properties as "ways-of-being-a-certain-way," for example, being red or being square, or as ways of being determinate; and I shall regard the exemplification of a property as a state of affairs. To the extent Goodman's extreme nominalism is not simply an expression of philosophical taste, the taste for desert landscapes he shared with Quine, it appears to arise from an excessive distrust of all forms of essentialism, of modal locutions, of counterfactuals, and even of disposition talk, and from a corresponding commitment to strictly extensionalist approaches to theoretical languages. The difficulties of carrying through in any consistent way such a purified extensionalist program even with regard to the language of the basic sciences have been well documented, in part by Goodman himself; and since the 1970s, versions of realist metaphysics have been sufficiently rehabilitated, albeit in suitably chastened forms, for me to feel little compunction in helping myself to property talk, as does nearly everyone else these days.

The second, and graver difficulty is Goodman's insistence that exemplification is directly *referential*, that the exemplifying symbol invariably *refers* to the label it exemplifies. Indeed, this commitment has a subversive effect on Goodman's account of musical exemplificational reference. If not all labels are verbal, what nonverbal label does a painting or a musical composition exemplify? The response is that it exemplifies itself (see Elgin 1983, 78). "The still life" or "the sonata," therefore, also (qua exemplified label) *denotes* itself, along with "the other things that match it." This, in my view, threatens a reductio of Goodman's version of musical exemplification. He may, perhaps, get by with the counterintuitive claim that portraits, diagrams, and maps are all self-referential and denote themselves. After all, these are items that carry out the more usual referential function of denoting objects and places. To tag something as counterintuitive is not to provide a counterargument. But claiming that a performance of a sonata denotes itself or any other performances of the piece seems patently ad hoc. With the exception of musical quotation, a relatively rare phenomenon in Western tonal art music (see the discussion in section 3.6 below), musical performances, as opposed to musical scores, are normally not in the business of denoting at all, and musical works can hardly be said generally to quote themselves. (Recall that for Goodman, a musical work is the class of performances compliant with the score.) A performance, say one exemplifying a particular interpretive approach, may, however, "allude to" or exemplify "indirectly" other performances with which it shares *properties* ("that match it"): "Exemplification relates the symbol to a label that denotes it [in our idiolect, to a property it instantiates], and hence indirectly to the things (including the symbol itself) in the range of that label" (Goodman 1976, 92). I suppose the performance may even allude to itself. But if so, the shared properties are being "used," not "mentioned" or referred to.

By allowing property talk, we can, I believe, make a much more powerful case for indirect musical exemplification, extending it well beyond Goodman's allusion. In some of Goodman's central cases, for example, the celebrated paint chip or tailor's swatch, no doubt the exemplifying symbols may be said to refer directly to their properties: given their respective uses, the chip refers to its color, the swatch to its pattern and texture. But in musical aesthetic contexts, the symbolic function seems generally not directly referential, for such objects do not function as samples or even as exemplars: their properties, as I shall argue, are used, not mentioned.[11] If we wish to retain exemplification as a symptom of the musically aesthetic, as I think we should, we shall need a different account of what manner of representational[12] function musical exemplification and musical expression are. Here is my suggestion: musical exemplification is nothing other than the modeling function we considered in the previous chapter. A model, as we saw, models its target object by using structural properties it shares with that target object. The musical performance, I propose, is a nonpropositional symbolic utterance that motivates the construction of mental models by the comprehending listener, models that carry out the indirect exemplificational functions. But to consolidate this case, a richer version of musical syntax than that provided by Goodman must be found. Because it is performances that display the symptoms of the aesthetic, what is needed is an elaborated syntax of musical *performance*. Given results reached in the previous chapter, I propose the well-formedness rules, preference rules, and hierarchical representations of Lerdahl and Jackendoff (1983) as the most credible and developed version of such an elaborated syntax.

With these considerations in mind we may return to our two questions: what sort of a symbolic token is a musical performance, and to what manner of symbol system does it belong? We answered the first question by characterizing the musical performance as a nonpropositional utterance; and we now have provisionally identified the syntax of the symbol system to which the musical performance belongs with some version[13] of the well-formedness rules, preference rules, and hierarchical representations of the Lerdahl and Jackendoff theory. The answer given to the first question was admirably decisive, but disturbingly vague. There are many kinds of nonpropositional representations. Which should we intend?

3.4   Music and Mimesis

I propose a specific class of representations as particularly appropriate for our present purposes, those dubbed by Millikan (1996, 2004) "pushmi-pullyu representations." (In Millikan's usage, "representation" refers both to internal and to external representational vehicles.) She characterizes pushmi-pullyus as double-aspect representations (hence "pushmi-pullyu") possessing both descriptive and prescriptive pragmatic force. Although pushmi-pullyu representations may be propositional,[14] let us now consider representations that are logically (and evolutionarily) "more primitive" than either the beliefs or desires of folk psychology. Beliefs and desires have propositional contents expressed by "that" clauses which enable them to enter into the inferential relationships of practical reasoning. Millikan's pushmi-pullyu representations possess at once both descriptive and prescriptive significance, but need not be propositional, for the descriptive and prescriptive functions of primitive versions of these representations have not yet been drawn apart and assigned to different representational types.[15] In the more technical language of her (1984) book they are "intentional icons," and not (strictly speaking) representations at all, not only because they are, as nonpropositional, incapable of entering into inferentially articulated relations with other representations, but also because they cannot be used to refer to particulars in the manner of proper names, definite descriptions, or the bound variables of quantification. Examples of very primitive nonpropositional—indeed, nonsymbolic—pushmi-pullyu representations offered by Millikan are a mother hen's calls to her chicks, animal signals like the alarm calls of vervet monkeys and rabbit danger thumps, and the celebrated figure-eight nectar-locating dances of honeybees. Such pushmi-pullyu representations indicate how things stand (Danger there! Nectar in that direction!); but they also either enjoin an appropriate action or express an intention to engage in such an action (Away quickly! Now heading that way!). This dual imperative and intentional expressive function constitutes a second dimension of double aspectuality in these representations: pushmi (intention to engage), pullyu (imperative).

Darwin (1871/1962, 463) was one of the first to speculate that "language owes its origins to the imitation and modification of various natural sounds, the voices of other animals, and man's own instinctive cries, aided by signs and gestures." In recent times, Merlin Donald (1991) has taken up "Darwin's thesis," suggesting a possible common origin for language and music. According to Donald, both language and music arose from what he calls "rudimentary song," and thereafter went their separate ways. In this case, the rudimentary song would have been some manner of "song without words": "In effect, rudimentary song would have been the precursor of both the prosodic envelope surrounding speech and the rhythmic, melodic, and harmonic aspects of song—that is, everything but the lyrics" (Donald 1991, 39). This primitive version of song need not even have consisted of pitched tones, and may have consisted of rhythmic shouting, as Maori *haka* do even today (ibid.). Whether pitched or non-pitched, the rudimentary song hypothesis explains the presence of prosody in modern speech as a vestigial inheritance reaching back two million years to *Homo habilis* and the most ancient stratum of the Paleolithic era.

In a similar vein, Brown (2000, 279) argues that both language and music evolved from "musilanguage," which he differentiates into three successive stages: (1) the use of isolated discrete pitches to convey semantic meaning; (2) the syntactic or rule-governed combination of these lexical-tonal elements into melodic and rhythmic units; and (3) introduction of expressive modulation of these combinatorial items by means of expressive phrasing at both local and global levels. Brown contends that musilanguage, in turn, descended from emotionally expressive but also referential animal calls, like those of vervet monkeys that signify three different predator types: eagle, snake, and leopard. Interestingly, each call elicits a distinctive pattern of evasive behavior on the part of the monkeys. Such calls are, as we saw, pushmi-pullyus.[16] If the rudimentary song/musilanguage hypothesis is empirically supported, then not only is there the "deep parallel" between music and language suggested by Lerdahl and Jackendoff; there may also be a relation of evolutionary homology. Brown points out (ibid., 281) that "the majority of the world's languages are tonal," that is, most of the world's languages use lexical tone as a suprasegmental device, as do Asian languages, and not only for prosodic function, as do English and other Indo-European languages. Language, Brown hypothesizes, originally was tonal. "The roots of music and language," says Lerdahl (2003, 427),

are the same, in the form of premusical and prelinguisitic communicative and expressive auditory gestures involving shapes of duration, stress, contour, timbre, and grouping. We still communicate with infants and higher mammals in this manner.... With evolution came specialization: music and language diverged in their most characteristic features, pitch organization in music and sentence meaning in language. Poetry straddles this evolutionary divergence by projecting, through the addition to ordinary speech of metrical and timbral patterning, its common heritage with music.

As a matter of fact, "Darwin's thesis" is a little more radical than Donald's paraphrase would lead us to believe. For Darwin not only speculates that singing, or the production of "true musical cadences," was the primordial use of the human voice. He also holds that human singing is a result of sexual selection, that it evolved during the "courtship of the sexes," when it served to attract mates, to express various emotions such as sexual love, jealousy, and triumph, and to challenge rivals. Darwin (1871/1962, 875) even goes further and suggests a sweeping adaptationist hypothesis:

> Although the sounds emitted by animals of all kinds may serve many purposes, a strong case can be made out, that the vocal organs were primarily used and perfected in relation to the propagation of the species.... The chief and, in some cases, exclusive purpose seems to be either to call or charm the opposite sex.

If we look carefully at what Donald calls "Darwin's thesis," we see that it really consists of two parts and that it makes two distinct claims concerning what I have termed the "musical surface." One claim concerns the musical surface as such, the second concerns its representational function. The first part of the hypothesis highlights the sheer attractiveness of the musical sound as such, holding that all vocalization was originally "musical" and served as a sexual lure. This aspect of animal vocalization or, more generally, musical sound making applies to phenomena as diverse as birdsong and the chirping of crickets.[17] The second part of the hypothesis then postulates a new *mimetic* representational function for vocalization in some more advanced species, including our own immediate ancestors. Once this mimetic function is in place it extends vocalization to communicative functions not directly tied to sexual selection:

> The strong tendency in our nearest allies, the monkeys, in microcephalous idiots, and in the barbarous races of mankind, to imitate whatever they hear deserves notice, as bearing on the subject of imitation.[18] Since monkeys certainly understand much that is said to them by man, and when wild, utter signal-cries of danger to their fellows; and since fowls give distinct warnings for danger on the ground, or in the sky from hawks (both, as well as a third cry, intelligible to dogs), may not some unusually wise ape-like animal have imitated the growl of a beast of prey, and thus told his fellow monkeys the nature of the expected danger? This would have been a first step in the formation of a language. (Darwin 1871/1962, 463, Darwin's notes deleted)

Disentangling these two strands of "Darwin's thesis" enables us to see how music and language might have developed from "rudimentary song" and then gone in separate directions: as the representational function gained ascendancy, vocalization moved toward discursive language, while music, poetry, and even oratory, concerned as they are with emotional impact, continued to retain vestiges of their ancient origins in sexual communication, "the use of the vocal organs," as Darwin says (1872/1965), having "become associated with the anticipation of the strongest pleasure which animals are capable" (1871/1962, 880):

We must suppose that the rhythms and cadences of oratory are derived from previously developed musical powers. We can thus understand how it is that music, dancing, song, and poetry are such very ancient arts. We may go even further than this, and . . . believe that musical sounds afforded one of the bases for the development of language.

As we shall see in chapter 5, Gurney (1880/1966) builds an entire philosophy of music on the Darwinian account of the origins of musical vocalization in sexual selection.[19] Because Donald ignores this first strand in Darwin's thesis, let us postpone further discussion of it here and direct our attention to the second strand, the one that concerns imitation or mimesis. Donald has gone on to develop this aspect of Darwin's speculations concerning the origins of language into an evolutionary account of the emergence of the modern mind, postulating a "mimetic" stage of representation standing between modes of representation exploited by the "episodic" mentality, which *Australopithecine* hominids shared with their apelike ancestors and modes of representation exploited by the "mythic" mentality, the linguistically mediated mentality of *Homo sapiens*, the species to which we belong. Although a primate with episodic mentality is capable of associative learning, holding sequences of events in memory, and using available signs (both natural signs and artificial signs taught via operant conditioning), such a creature is incapable of semiotic invention because it lacks a certain level of intentional awareness. That is, the creature with episodic consciousness cannot press a sign into service with the intention of affecting another intentional being as he himself is affected by it. In the terminology of G. H. Mead, the "significant symbol" is unavailable to the episodic mentality (see Tomasello 1999 for extended discussion of this issue). The significant symbol is available to the mimetic mentality, but only in a *nonpropositional* form, the form of gesture and mime. An intentional vocal imitation of the growl of a predator, Donald suggests (1991, 41), would "communicate the specific nature of a threat and allow a specific response on the part of a tribal group." Not only, we might add, would such an imitation *allow* the response; it would *prescribe* it. *The mimetic vocal gesture would function, that is, as a pushmi-pullyu representation.*

Conformity and coordination of group behavior are major accomplishments of mimetic culture.[20] It is easy to imagine a tribal group of *Homo erectus* sitting around the communal fire, revisiting events of the day, or planning those for the next, while communicating by way of a mixture of gesture, pantomime, and songlike vocalizations.[21] The quasi-spatial organization of musical pitches would enhance the gestural aspect of these vocalizations. Donald suggests that the traditional game of charades (a phenomenon whose musical significance we briefly noted in the previous chapter) exploits the considerable mimetic abilities still extant in modern humans, young and old, abilities that are a holdover from these ancient lower Paleolithic communicative practices. The structure of mimetic symbolism, moreover, seems to display some compositional properties: certain standardized elements such as stylized hand motions (beckoning and distancing), bodily postures (confident/vigorous or wilting/moribund), and pancultural emotionally expressive facial configuration, Donald claims (ibid., 171–172), can be combined and recombined so as to yield varying narrative sequences. Music displays a much higher degree of syntactic organization and is more complexly generative than any such mimetic symbolism.[22] Still, there is good reason to regard the musical surface produced by a performer as a descendant of rudimentary song, and therefore as a mimetic utterance, an external pushmi-pullyu representation. According to this proposal, a musical performance—the presentation of the musical surface—is a nonpropositional intentional icon that indicates to the listener how things stand by communicating the musical plan, the hierarchical representations whose content is the organized musical surface. Normally, neither performer nor listener is aware of the representations themselves; rather, he is aware of their contents, the organized musical surface. After all, the generative theory of tonal music, as a piece of metainterpretation, indeed of (narrow) *reflexive* metainterpretation, is required to make these representations explicit.[23] The intentional icon, however, also functions as an imperative (Implement this musical plan!) and expresses an intention (Now implementing this musical plan!). The occurrent mental entity constructed by the listener is also a pushmi-pullyu representational token: an internal one expressing that same intention. During a musical experience a performer sends a pushmi-pullyu representation the listener's way that both communicates this plan structure and enjoins him to implement it and to construct an appropriate set of mental models in his own head, models which are themselves action-oriented.[24] "Perhaps," Millikan (2004, 160) speculates, "the neural representation produced in the bee watching the dance is similarly articulated."

It may be objected that talk of implementing a plan may make sense with regard to the composer or the performer, but not with regard to the listener. In what sense can the listener be said to be able to implement such a plan? And if the listener (in principle) cannot do so, he cannot be enjoined to do so. The mentally constructed representation, the objection would conclude, therefore cannot be a pushmi-pullyu representation. But such an objection would miss the important distinction already established in chapter 2 between action taken and action simulated, or action "online" and "off-line." In order to understand the musical performance, the listener must feel it correctly. And to feel it correctly, he must make its plan his own: certain bodily sets must be adopted, and motor areas of the brain activated, even as their signals are inhibited. The listener must act the music out, play it or, more likely, sing it. If the conclusions of the previous chapter are correct, he must also move through its virtual tonal space in imagination and simulate the virtual entities contained in this space.[25] Naive listeners tap their feet or move their legs in rhythmic synchronization with the music. More sophisticated listeners engage in a significantly more varied repertoire of tiny, often barely detectable, whole-body movements, especially movements of the head, the seat of the mind–brain and the exclusive location of all the peripheral sense receptors except those of touch-temperature. Naive listeners merely emulate the rhythmic and melodic surface of the music via sympathetic activation of low-level neuro-muscular mechanisms, and tend to prefer music with minimal hierarchical organization; more sophisticated listeners token an unfolding multileveled musical plan-in-process.

Plan representations themselves, however, can have pushi-pullyu characteristics. An everyday contemporary example of an external pushmi-pullyu of this type might be a flowchart-style schematic drawing (without any verbal instructions) of the separate parts-in-proper-relation of a piece of furniture that requires assembly. In this case we are aware of the plan representation itself (the flowchart drawing), not just of its contents (the parts in proper relations). Such a drawing tells you both how the assembled piece you saw at the store is put together and how you are to go about assembling the one you have. Musical experience can often be compared to assembling a complex structure by moving elements and their combinations around in the virtual acousmatic space discussed in the previous chapter. Examples of *internal* pushmi-pullyu representations offered by Millikan are perceptual representations of Gibsonian environmental affordances as well as motor control schemata (see her reference to Jeannerod 1994; see also Jeannerod 1990 and Arbib 1985). In light of conclusions reached in the previous chapter, both allusions are significant. An equally good example of an internal pushmi-pullyu representation would be a hierarchically organized action plan at the psychological task level, something like the control hierarchies discussed in the last chapter.

It is to these task-level hierarchically organized plans of action that I wish to redirect attention here. We have already seen that the tree structures on which Lerdahl and Jackendoff rely for representing time-span and prolongation reductions share formal properties with action plans, but we also saw that such hierarchical organization is fundamental not only to musical understanding in particular but to human planning in general. In fact, this kind of hierarchical organization, as Scruton (1997, 312) observes, "is characteristic of all serious reasoned action, whether or not it has an aesthetic goal." How plans are carried out, with what speeds, bodily sets, and emotional tones, will vary greatly with the subject domain. Plans undertaken with regard to the items on a menu at a leisurely dinner will differ in feeling from those undertaken in amatory circumstances, which will differ from those undertaken in a harrowing life-or-death situation. Such considerations are important, for they yield a promising line of approach regarding two vexed issues in musical aesthetics: musical meaning and musical emotional response. The issue of musical meaning we shall take up now; we shall consider emotional response in later chapters. Since the mental tokening of the plan of a musical piece exhibits the structure of a control hierarchy, it can, as a pushmi-pullyu, *motivate the construction of mental models that share structural attributes with models that are not musical.*[26] This, I shall argue, forms the basis of music's ability to carry extramusical meaning.

3.5 Plans, Categorization, and Semantic Fields

It is not only English grammar that is built around hierarchical Plans and their various transformations—the grammar of every language is constructed in that way, so a speaker's thought processes cannot be in any way unique on that account. Moreover, nearly all of man's behavior is similarly organized. We might speak metaphorically of a general grammar of behavior, meaning that the grammar of a language was only one example of a general pattern of control that could be exemplified in many other realms of behavior.
—G. Miller, G. E. Galanter, and K. Pribram (1960, 155)[27]

The basic hierarchical "plan" unit or atom, according to Miller et al., is the test-operate-test-exit (TOTE) schema controlling goal-seeking behavior (see figure 3.1). The simple TOTE can be recursively embedded, TOTEs within TOTEs, and iterated, thereby generating an elaborate nested plan structure. Although the Miller et al. quotation above clearly refers to the nested trees of generative grammar, it is to specifically semantic issues that I now wish to direct attention. An important example of an abstract venue in which hierarchically structured plans play an important role is the organization of what have been termed "semantic fields."

Semantic field theory is a holistic theory of lexical term meaning deriving originally from Saussure, but recently influential in linguistics, psychology, and, to a somewhat lesser extent, philosophy. One need not subscribe to Saussurian structuralist linguistics to find the notion of a semantic field a very valuable one. Various versions of semantic field theory have been put forward since Saussure (for review and discussion see Lehrer 1974; Miller and Johnson-Laird 1976; Lyons 1977, vol. 1; Johnson-Laird 1983; Kittay 1987; McNeill 1987, 1992; Grandy 1987, 1992; Holdcroft 1991; Lehrer and Kittay 1992). In philosophy, recent mainstream holistic theories of meaning, even those proffered by those who, like Brandom and the Churchlands, reject causal-informational semantics, have tended to emphasize inferential relations between concepts: the holistic

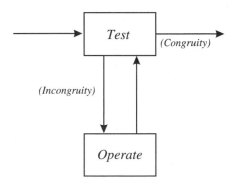

Figure 3.1
The basic TOTE schema. (From Miller et al. 1960, reprinted by permission of the author.)

meanings of terms are constituted by the inferential roles of the concepts they express. The semantic field theorist does not deny the importance of this, but holds that over-emphasizing the inferential aspect of term meaning underplays what philosopher Eva Kittay (1987, 123ff) has designated the "expressive" aspect of language, the way in which linguistic terms serve simply to mark things off from one another within fields of opposition. "A contrast," says psycholinguist David McNeill (1992, 252), "can only be understood as pertaining to a certain field of oppositions. Without this field no contrast is possible. (An electron and a syllogism are different but they do not contrast because there is no sensible field of oppositions.)" This expressive, or, as it might also be termed, contrastive or "feature-placing" linguistic function is, by all accounts, its most primitive linguistic stratum, for it precedes the fundamental differentiation between logical subject and predicate.[28] Compare Miller and Johnson-Laird's suggestion that feature contrast and discrimination form the basis of the negation, disjunction, and conjunction operators, as well as the distinction between subject and predicate in language (1976, 266):

One can conceive of a language that would make no use of synonymy; it is hard to imagine how a language in which contrastive and hierarchical field properties played no part could function at all. Viewed psychologically, these field properties are closely related to processes of attention and discrimination. Viewed formally, they provide a cognitive basis for logical operators and *perhaps for predication itself* [emphasis mine].

We shall take up the notion of feature-placing language in more detail in chapter 5. For now, let us look a little more closely at the role of this expressive aspect of language in linguistic metaphor.

Kittay (1987, 15) has argued that lexical concepts emerge from this more primitive, expressive stratum of affinities and contrasts. Whatever one may think of this emergence story,[29] she is surely right that the expressive function of language is crucial to the construction of linguistic metaphor, since linguistic metaphor requires the unexpected juxtaposition of terms belonging to apparently unrelated semantic fields. When we compress the already ambiguous sentence "The whole town was populated by old men and women" by ellipsis into "The whole town was old men and women," we do achieve, as Bernstein (1976, 122) claims, a heightened poetic effect. But this effect is not due to an increase of ambiguity alone, as Bernstein seems to suggest, although this is certainly a factor. It is due to the new and unexpected juxtaposition in a predication of two different semantic fields: the semantic field of population centers and the semantic field of human beings.

This view finds a certain resonance in Goodman (1976), who holds that metaphor arises when a label that belongs to one "schema" of symbols, say emotion terms, is applied to or is "expressed by" an object to which these labels are not, by way of custom or habit, standardly applied. For example, the predicate "is sad," which is normally applied to the "realm" of emotional beings and to the "range" of sad beings, may be expressed by or *aesthetically metaphorically exemplified* by a blue harlequin painting by Picasso, which literally exemplifies the label "is blue." A realm is something like a semantic field, or a semantic field considered in extension. Unfortunately, Goodman's indefatigable nominalism and antipsychologism create considerable difficulties for his theory of metaphor, because he has no principled grounds for distinguishing between successful and unsuccessful metaphors. That is, he cannot explain why applying a label belonging to a foreign schema sometimes achieves expression or aesthetic metaphorical exemplification and sometimes does not. All he can say is that when successful, the expressed label "fits" or is somehow "right." But we are left in the dark as to why it fits, or in what its rightness consists.

To answer this question, we must have recourse to talk of properties shared by mental models that are constructed in the minds of readers or hearers. A metaphor works when mental models, constructed for the concepts that hail from foreign semantic fields, mesh or achieve an unexpected but compelling fit *that is grounded ultimately in bodily experience.*[30] The success of Wallace Stevens's arresting metaphor "The garden was a slum of bloom" (see Kittay 1987, 65) might be explained by the unexpected fit between mental models of repulsively unkempt profusions of organic matter, whether they be models of heaps of steaming trash in a slum or models of nauseatingly luxuriant and fragrant plant growth in a neglected garden. One suspects that Sartre's Roquentin, about whom more anon (chapter 6), might have especially appreciated Stevens's metaphor. The fundamental idea behind semantic field theory is that groups of terms are related by meaning relations often weaker than formal negation, indeed even weaker than material incompatibility and material implication, and are organized into fields in certain determinate ways, including affinity and contrast, hyponymy and superordination, cyclical relations, kinship relations, partonymy, observer-relative and object-relative motion, and ownership relations, to name the most important. Such groups of related terms define semantic fields. "Physician" and "lawyer" contrast within the semantic field of occupations, and "punch" and "kick" within the semantic field of aggressive acts. But "X is a physician" does not imply "X is not a lawyer," any more than "X punched Y" implies "X did not kick Y." Keil's (1979) investigations into the abilities of children to categorize demonstrate an apparently innate *semantic* bias in favor of nested relationships of hyponomy and superordination in categorization tasks, a semantic bias that affects language acquisition by children and thus does not simply arise *from* language, indicating that categorization emerges from a more primitive, prelinguistic practical ability to sort and categorize.

In *Language and Perception*, Miller and Johnson-Laird (1976) proposed a procedural account that stands as one of the earliest attempts to adopt a computational approach to semantics and the psychology of linguistic understanding. But their work repays close study even today. Although Miller and Johnson-Laird's computational model is classically implemented, they allow for graded category membership and prototypical-ity effects (ibid., 225), both staples of contemporary semantic field theory (cf. Grandy 1992). This so-called *procedural semantics*, it should be noted, is intended to relate lan-guage to mental models, not language to the world (see Johnson-Laird 1983, 248). Since mental models are representations, procedural semantics is really *a syntax of mental models*.[31] How to understand the language–world relation is a highly contested philosophical issue that cannot, in my view, be captured by an exclusively procedural-semantic approach; nor do Miller and Johnson-Laird claim that it can. As an account of the language–world relation, procedural semantics, like pragmatist accounts of mean-ing and meaningfulness, is prone to slide into verificationism, operationalism, or some other form of semantic antirealism, a consequence to be avoided if at all possible.

Any detailed treatment of these issues would require a separate monograph and is out of place in a discussion of musical representation. Briefly, the view I favor is a modified version of McGinn (1989, 209; see figure 3.2). Sentential inscriptions and utterances, which are worldly entities and events, instantiate propositional contents. These propositional contents may be understood as quasi-Platonic abstract objects, as neo-Fregeans are inclined to do (see, e.g., Peacocke 1992); or they may be understood as mappings from possible worlds to truth values, as possible-world semanticists are inclined to do (see, e.g., Chalmers 1996); or they may be understood as a variety of abstracta, or rule-constituted entities (i.e., meanings), that emerge within norm-governed linguistic practice, as I would prefer to construe them. Inscriptions and utter-ances (i.e., linguistic tokens) stand in bidirectional causal relations with the brain as inputs and outputs by way of the sense receptors and motor systems of the body. The mental models, the analog representations in the mind–brain, do not instantiate prop-ositions, they are indexed by them; and propositions stand to the world in semantic and metaphysical relations of description, reference, individuation, and truth-making. Whereas the semantic relations of description and reference run from proposition to world, the metaphysical relations of individuation and truth-making run in the "oppo-site" direction, from world to proposition. For the sake of present discussion, the world may be said to consist of states of affairs: objects possessing properties and standing in various relations. Finally, the mental models do not *describe* states of affairs in the world; they *model*, or, as McGinn says, they "simulate" them by way of shared struc-tural properties.[32] A standard glass thermometer may serve as an illustration of these ideas. The length of the mercury column in the thermometer varies causally with the temperature of the atmospheric surround, thereby modeling temperature change ana-logically. The numbers on the glass tube are abbreviated sentential tokens expressing propositions, say the proposition that the ambient temperature is 33° Fahrenheit. These propositions *describe* atmospheric states of affairs in the world, not the states of the column of mercury, which they *index*.

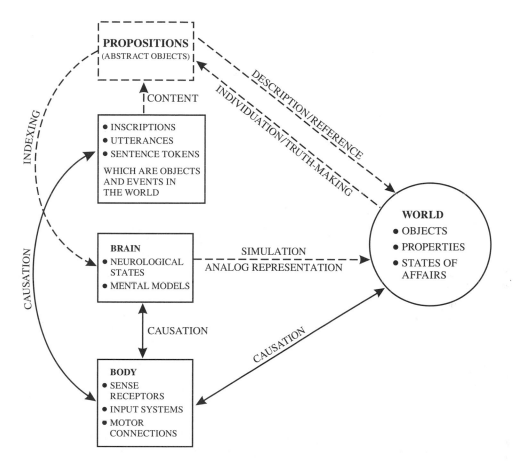

Figure 3.2
Propositions, sentential tokens, brain, body, and world. Solid arrows represent causal relations, dashed arrows represent relations, including intentional relations, that are not causal. (Adapted from McGinn 1989, 209, by permission of Blackwell Press.)

Broadly speaking, Miller and Johnson-Laird's semantic procedures serve to update the mental models that represent (model) the truth conditions of sentences *as understood* in discourse. In a nearly contemporaneous paper, Johnson-Laird (1977, 207) specifically characterized the procedures in question as "plans" in the sense established by Miller, Galanter, and Pribram (1960). In addition, Miller and Johnson-Laird (1976) contains much of the theoretical background for Johnson-Laird's (1983) later theory of mental models, which, I have argued, are the prime candidates for the internal representational vehicles of musical meaning. For Miller and Johnson-Laird, to grasp the meaning of a lexical item is to follow a computational decision table (or a hierarchically

X.

   A.

      a.

      b.

   B.

      c.

      d.

      e.

Figure 3.3
A plan in outline form. (From Miller et al. 1960, reprinted by permission of the author.)

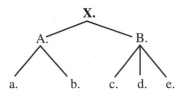

Figure 3.4
The same plan in hierarchical tree form.

nested set of decision tables) or, equivalently, a decision tree. Miller, Galanter, and Pribram (1960, 15) treat trees, outlines, and decision tables as alternative, formally equivalent versions of the same procedural structures.[33]

But what exactly is a plan? Figure 3.3, which actually appears in the work of Miller et al. (1960), represents a plan in outline form, where X is the goal, A and B are sub-goals, and a, b, and c are sub-subgoals; figure 3.4 is exactly the same plan, but translated into tree form. For a concrete application, consider the following well-known puzzle: How does a ferryman get a wolf, a goat, and a cabbage from one side of a river to the other without leaving either the wolf and the goat, or the goat and the cabbage alone together, assuming he can fit only one of these items into his boat at a time? Figure 3.5 represents the solution as a tree plan.

A decision table represents a plan that provides a list of features against which objects, events, and actions can be systematically checked, thereby determining the organization of the various important perceptual and conceptual semantic fields, including the ones adverted to above. A decision table, that is, functions as a "key" to a semantic field. But a semantic field is easily represented by a mental model comprising mental models of its separate subfields considered as field-related *categories* of

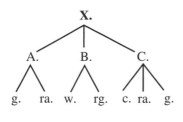

g = take goat across
ra = return alone
w = take wolf across
rg = return with goat
c = take cabbage across

Figure 3.5
The solution to the goat problem as a hierarchical tree plan.

entities, and mental models are naturally suited to carry content with field structure. Compare Johnson-Laird (1983, 414):

> Semantic fields provide us with our conception of the furniture of the world—of what exists—and the semantic operators [i.e., concepts of time, space, possibility, permissibility, causation, intention] provide us with our concept of the various relations that may inhere between these objects. Time and space are primitives that are merely simulated in mental models. Possibility and permissibility depend on our capacity to construct models of situations that are alternatives to reality and to evaluate them with respect to our knowledge of the "laws" of nature or morality.... Causality and intentionality can be analyzed into more basic concepts...but they lie at the right descriptive level for formulating the main domains of mental models.

By way of illustration, Johnson-Laird (1983, 202) supplies a decision table "capturing the interrelations between the spatial concepts corresponding to *in*, *on*, *at*, and *with*," which define a semantic field of spatial relationships between objects (figure 3.6). In order for *x* to be in *y*, for example, the answer to the question, "Is *x* (or part of *x*) included in *y*?" must be "yes"; but in order for *x* to be at *y*, the answer to this question must be "no." If I am at the table, I am not in the table.

Perhaps a more straightforward example is the following case, adapted from Miller and Johnson-Laird (1976, 281ff). Imagine a simple decision table for categorizing a piece of furniture, expressed as a series of questions, strictly binary answers, and categorial decisions. Question: Does it have a backrest? Answer: Yes. Does it have a seat? Yes. One or more? More. Two or three? Two. Classify as a loveseat. End. It is quite easy to conceive an entire taxonomy of furniture types, for which the decision table provides the key, established in this way: furniture types constitute a hierarchically structured semantic field. But the same can be done for a semantic field like cooking,

Semantic Conditions

1 x (or part of x) included in y	+	+	+	+	−	−	−	−
2 x is included in the region of the surface of y & y supports x	−	−	+	+	+	+	−	−
3 x is included in the region of y	+	+	+	+	+	+	+	+
4 y is included in the region of x			+	−	+	−	+	−

Expressions

1 x is in y	+	+	+	+				
2 x is on y				+	+	+		+
3 x is at y					+			+
4 x is with y					+		+	

Figure 3.6

A decision table representing the semantic conditions for the concepts corresponding to the prepositions *in*, *on*, *at*, and *with*. Each column shows which conditions obtain for each expression (+), which do not obtain (−), and which may or may not obtain (blank). Looking, for example, at row 1 under Semantic conditions and row 1 under Expressions, whenever x or part of x is included in y, conditions for "x is in y" are satisfied, whereas conditions for "x is at y" and "x is with y" are not satisfied. (From Johnson-Laird 1983, 202, after Miller and Johnson-Laird 1976; reprinted by permission of Harvard University Press.)

to take a fairly well worn but clear example (Kittay 1987, 249; Lehrer 1974, 69). Problem: classify a cooking method. Question: Dry or wet heat? Answer: Dry. Contact with heating element or no contact? No contact. Roasting or broiling? Roasting. End. The decision table used to classify cooking methods could also be represented in outline form, as in figure 3.7, or in tree form, as in figure 3.8.[34] It may, however, also be represented by a different sort of tree, one that is strictly nested, as in figure 3.9, where dominant branches mark affirmative decisions and subordinate branches negative ones. ("Y" might represent raw food preparation.) The tree in figure 3.9, notice, structurally resembles Lerdahl and Jackendoff's (1983) time-span reduction (TSR) and prolongation reduction (PR) trees.

Just as the tree in figure 3.9 provides a key to the semantic field of cooking methods, the TSR and PR trees could be said to provide "keys" to what might be thought of as musical "fields." The Lerdahl and Jackendoff trees, I propose, parse the musical surface into nested field relationships of affinity/contrast and superordination/subordination. Whereas individual musical notes must (with one exception)[35] either be superordinate or subordinate to other notes, musical field relationships emerge only at a higher level of organization, in the first instance at the level of the smallest recognizable motifs or phrases. Affinity and contrast, in the guise of gestalt principles of good form, play an important role in Lerdahl and Jackendoff's preference rules, and contrast sets, cyclical

X.
    A. Dry Heat
        a. Contact (Grill)
        b. No Contact
            1. Roast
            2. Broil
    B. Wet Heat
        c. Boil (poach, stew, etc.)
        d. Fry (saute, etc.)

Figure 3.7
A decision outline as a key to the semantic field of cooking.

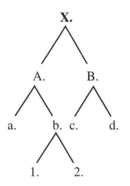

Figure 3.8
The key in decision tree form.

and otherwise, are ubiquitous in tonal, cadential-harmonic music, from the scale, to the circle of fifths, to thematic and contrapuntal contrast and parallelism, to large-scale formal organization. As for subordination and superordination, the Lerdahl and Jackendoff trees are strictly nested structures. The musical surface, that is to say, contains an elaborate *field structure*—not, to be sure, a *semantic* field structure organized according to semantic contrasts or contrasts of *meaning*, but a field structure rich enough to *model* a semantic field structure, or, considered in extension, a semantic *category* structure. With regard to every note of a musical performance, the comprehending performer and the comprehending listener must "answer" (albeit only implicitly) the following "questions" regarding time-span and prolongation reductions: Is this note subordinated or subordinating (placed higher or lower in the hierarchical musical plan)? Is it subordinated or subordinating to the previous note or to the ensuing note? Is it subordinated (subordinating) to the previous (ensuing) note or to the previous

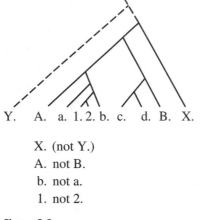

X. (not Y.)
A. not B.
b. not a.
1. not 2.

Figure 3.9
The key in strictly nested decision tree form.

(ensuing) *group* of notes? To a group of this size, or of that size? Is this note subordinating to an entire phrase or melodic grouping or not? Is it subordinate to it or not? Is a note terminal, that is, located at the bottom of the hierarchy, or not? These decisions, moreover, must constantly be updated according to the evolving grasp of the musical plan.

The questions and answers need not, however, be represented declaratively, nor need the listener possess any of these *concepts* in order to make these decisions and parse the musical surface.[36] Indeed, decision-tree representations may be employed for all manner of categorization tasks without awareness of their underlying bivalent logic, as they are, on some tellings, even by young children and infrahuman animals (Aunger 2002, 38; see also Bermudez 2003, 136):

In the case of animals, figuring out the category in which to place the animal might run through a branching decision structure mirroring the nested hierarchy into which scientists have organized the "tree" of life-forms. The individual would then check off, say, "long," "no legs," and head-with-hood-shape." The conclusion might be, say, "It's a cobra!"

In the musical context, the conclusion might be "It's that pattern again!" To the extent a categorization process such as the hierarchical organization of musical events by a listener goes forward with little effort or instruction, there is reason to suspect the involvement of a dedicated mental module:

Such modules develop reliably in human beings without effort or formal instruction and they can be applied without conscious awareness of their underlying logic. The processing of information by such instincts is effortless, automatic, reliable,[37] and fast precisely because we have all this complicated machinery dedicated to the task. (Aunger 2002, 38)

Recall that in the previous chapter we took note of independent reasons for thinking that musical representation by the competent listener, particularly on the local level, is to some degree modular.

3.6   The Field Structure in the Musical Surface: Musical Meaning as Extramusical Form

Musical semantics is of a similar type to poetic semantics.
—J. A. Sloboda (1985, 64)

Saussurian theory of semantic fields distinguishes between two interrelated systems: signifiers and signifieds. The signifiers, or linguistic "sound images," are conventionally correlated with the signifieds, or the system of concepts that constitute the contents of the signifiers, which are the "positive values" of the signifiers. The sign is the unified whole of signifier and signified (Saussure 1915/1959, 66–67).[38] Both systems (signifiers and signifieds) are internally articulated by "differences," or contrasts, which also determine two additional sets of "negative values": the identity (or "value") of a signifier is determined by way of its contrasts with other signifiers; the identity (or "value") of a concept (a signified) is determined by its contrast with other concepts (see Holdcroft 1991, 120–121; Saussure 1915/1959, 115). The holistic implications of all this should be obvious.[39]

The theory makes use of three fundamental axes of contrast: phonological, syntagmatic, and paradigmatic (or "associative"). Consider phonological contrast first. Languages obviously differ with regard to which phonological contrasts they exploit, and this will determine what sounds are functionally available. In English, for example, the soft "g," which is phonologically type-identical to the "j," contrasts with the "ch" diphthong. In German, "cz" is phonologically type-identical to the English "ch." But the English contrast with "g" is lacking: there is in German no soft "g" sound at all, and the German "j" is phonologically type-identical with the English "y." German, however, has available the German "ch" by way of contrast with "k." English does not have this contrast, so the German "ch" sound is unavailable in English, and is assimilated to "k." (Witness the tendency of English speakers to pronounce the name of the composer of the *St. Matthew Passion* as "Bock.") The German umlaut affords a range of systematic vowel-sound displacements and contrasts that are unavailable in English. Hence, while the umlaut "a" may be identified phonologically with either the English short "e" or the long "a," which contrast with the short "a," the umlaut "o" are "u" are unavailable in English phonology.

More central to Saussurian theory than phonological contrast, however, are the two axes of syntagmatic and paradigmatic contrast (see McNeill 1987). The former concerns contrasts between *different* grammatical roles, whereas the latter concerns contrasts within semantic fields between words that may play the *same* grammatical roles. For example, "red" and "apple" contrast syntagmatically insofar as they fill the different grammatical roles of modifier and noun within the noun phrase "red apple"; "red" contrasts with "green" and "yellow" paradigmatically within the semantic field of color terms; "apple" contrasts paradigmatically with "pear" and "banana" within the semantic field of fruit terms; and all of them can fill the same grammatical slot. Whereas syntagmatic contrast is grammatical, paradigmatic contrast is semantic.

In the previous chapter we took note of the fact that the Lerdahl and Jackendoff trees differ from linguistic trees in one significant respect: the nodes and endpoints of the branchings are not occupied by anything like grammatical categories. That is, the musical surface displays, strictly speaking, *no syntagmatic organization*. Because syntagmatic contrast and paradigmatic contrast in language are sometimes thought of respectively as "linear" and "vertical" axes of organization (Ross 1981, 54),[40] and because music, on the Lerdahl and Jackendoff account, is organized in a "linear" fashion according to syntactic well-formedness and preference rules, it might seem as though music is also subject to syntagmatic contrast. But musical syntactic structure does not achieve genuine syntagmatic organization, for it does not contain grammatical categories and has no analogue to the subject-predicate-modifier structure. Because it lacks grammatical categories and therefore lacks true syntagmatic organization, the structure of music (according to the Lerdahl and Jackendoff theory) is less strictly "generative" (organized from the "top down") and more "cumulative" (organized from the "bottom up") than is linguistic generative grammar, a distinction pressed by Scruton (1997, 311ff). Why is this? Any sentence is analyzable into specific grammatical components, which are further analyzable in specifiable ways; and new sentences can be generated simply by filling in the grammatical slots appropriately. All of these grammatical categories can be expanded indefinitely in a rule-governed way "from the inside": noun phrases can be expanded by adding adjectives, relative clauses, or participial or prepositional phrases, verb phrases by adding adverbs, adverbial clauses, and prepositional phrases. There is no analogue in music to this strictly category-governed generative process. Nonetheless, a melody can also be expanded "from the inside" by adding more and more properly nested subordinate tree branches, as occurs perhaps most commonly in variation and in ornamentation. Whether Schenker-inspired theory is right that *all* musical structures, or at least the structures of all bona fide *Meisterwerke*, are elaborated ("generated") in this way, indeed generated from a fundamental tonic–dominant–tonic cadence, is, to say the least, debatable.

Still, because it is recursively organized, musical syntax does seem generative to some degree; and it may be appropriate to regard the generative/cumulative distinction as not absolute but relative. Even the rules of generative grammar have important limitations. Contrary to some popular misconceptions, these rules do not provide recipes for the creation of new sentences, nor would they, if computationally implemented, allow the construction of a "speaking machine." Universal grammar, Chomsky (1980, 220) tells us, "strongly generates" structural descriptions, but only "weakly generates" sentences themselves, meaning that any well-formed sentence must not violate certain structural constraints that rule out grammatically deviant sentences. Nevertheless, sentential syntax, because it specifies the combination of grammatical categories, is more strongly generative than musical syntax. But as we saw, even mimetic representation can be seen to possess *some* generative characteristics. The hierarchies of action plans generally are more cumulative and less generative than those of musical syntax. Many a tree-structured action plan will lack rules governing the generation of lower-level branches entirely, leaving these aspects of the plan flexible and determinable by exigent circumstance.

Although the musical surface may lack syntagmatic contrast, it is, however, exceptionally rich in a musical version of paradigmatic contrast; and it is paradigmatic contrast that grounds semantic field structure. But it also constitutes the first aspect of musical meaning, because it resides in the categorial organization of the musical surface itself. It is present in all tonal, cadential-harmonic music, regardless of any additional scenario content the music may or may not have. In tonal, cadential-harmonic music, individual tones contrast with other tones in the scale of the key. Chords contrast with other chords, phrases and motifs with other phrases and motifs, rhythms with other rhythms, sections with other sections, keys with other keys. As a tonal, cadential-harmonic piece progresses, tones, phrases, and motifs constantly shift in their significance because they are simultaneously and sequentially drawn into varying fields of affinity (parallelism) and contrast. What affinities and contrasts are actually available in a particular piece will, of course, be strongly determined by musical style. As Bernstein (1976, 130) says,

The constant rearrangement and transformation of these "letters" [i.e., the twelve pitch classes of the chromatic scale] is made particularly rich by the combined possibilities of horizontal and vertical structures—melodic, harmonic, and contrapuntal anagrams—which of course language cannot do, even with twenty-six letters. Music is further enriched by the extension of these possibilities to near-infinity, through the extraordinary variety of high and low registers, durations, dynamics, meters, rhythms, tempi, colorations. It's as if all music were one supergame of anagrams.

Except for the anagram analogy, this, in my view, is exactly right. (An anagram is just a scrambled word. It has no interesting structure, nor does it contrast with other anagrams. It is merely a puzzle to be solved.) Consider, by way of illustration, the following musical example. In the first movement of Beethoven's Violin Concerto, bar 207 (example 3.1), the unexpected low F in the cellos and basses is heard as (i.e., understood as) a lowered sixth in A major by the comprehending listener, even if that listener has neither absolute pitch nor even the concept *lowered sixth*. The listener will hear it as a lowered (minor) sixth (though not necessarily under that description) in

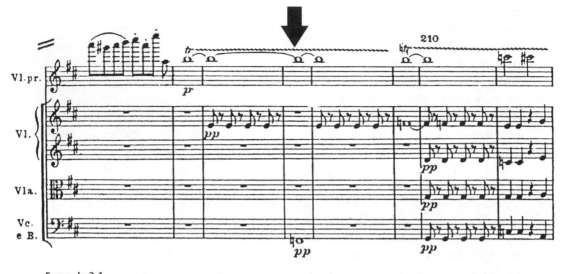

Example 3.1
Beethoven, Violin Concerto in D, *Allegro, ma non troppo.*

the current home key, which happens to be A major at this point in the piece. Two bars later the same absolute chroma (now sounding two octaves above in the first violins) is heard as the seventh of a dominant G7 chord, effecting a momentary modulation to a moderately distantly related major key (C major) before the return to A major. The fact that the chroma is heard as changing field location, moving from one pair of melodic and harmonic contrast sets, those belonging to A major, to another pair of sets, those belonging to C major, and the fact that it is also heard as changing functional significance from lowered sixth (in A) to fourth (in C), alterations that are enhanced by the change in register and instrumental color, suggest movement between semantic fields. It can also suggest (model) anaphoric reference: Something is this (belongs to this category), but *it* is also that (belongs to that category). (The parallel passage in D major in the recapitulation occurs between bars 481 and 483 where the pivotal tone is B-flat.) Just as the F pivots between two harmonic contrast sets, the same lexical item will often belong to more than one contrast set and more than one semantic field. "Ice," for example, contrasts on the one hand with "water," "vapor," and "steam," and on the other with "snow," "sleet," and "slush."

Ross (1981) makes a related, if more limited, point. In any given major key, he observes, each note of the diatonic scale is a member of three different "shadow" (or implicit) triads (three-note chords, with each note separated from the next by an interval of a third), depending on whether the note in question is the root, the third, or the fifth of the triad. For example, the note G in a C major scale is a member of three shadow triads: it is the root of the dominant chord, the third of the mediant (the triad built on E), and the fifth of the tonic chord. "Since any given word," says Ross (1981, 70–73),

like any given note sign, can in distinct contexts belong to distinct predicate schemes (like sets of shadow triads), the meaning of any given word can, in a given context, be represented as a certain class of meaning-relevant words. Distinct predicate schemes for equivocal occurrences of the same word represent differences in their meanings, just as different triple triads for the same note sign represent different harmonic identities for that note.

Ross's direct move from "predicate schemes" to "triple triads" is perhaps a trifle abrupt. Still, the idea, is fundamentally correct: it is this ability to model semantic field relations[41] that enables music to give the strong, but also puzzling, sense of good (or bad) musical "logic" so often remarked on by performers and listeners, and so clearly evident in the excerpt from the Beethoven Violin Concerto. Music cannot literally express logical relations because it is nonconceptual. But it can model them nonsententially. Bermudez (2003, ch. 7) presents arguments, both conceptual and empirical, that nonlinguistic creatures are capable of modes of protoinference that exploit sensitivity to feature contrariety. Where formal negation (contradiction) operates on sententially vehicled, structured propositional contents, feature contrariety supports "protonegation," which would be expressed propositionally as Aristotelian *predicate* negation (ibid., 142ff). A land-based animal sensitive to affordances can represent its immediate surround as solid or liquid, rugged or smooth, open or cluttered, and can take appropriate action based on rejection of one of the contraries. Such a creature can represent a conspecific as sexually receptive or indifferent, as dominant or submissive, as kin or intruder. It can represent an object as edible or nonedible, nutritious or nonnutritious, delectable or nondelectable. By representing the presence of gazelles or lions at the watering hole as mutually exclusive, such a creature may also (by means of "protologic") infer from the presence of gazelles that it is safe to approach (cf. Bermudez 2003, 143–144).

Notice that all these oppositions are *oppositions within fields*: they are not mere unrelated differences like McNeill's syllogism and electron. But the oppositions also derive from different fields: the field of environments, the field of conspecific and kinship relations, the field of food sources. Constructing these fields of contrast and affinity as genuine semantic fields and establishing systematic relations between them that support more sophisticated inferences is most likely dependent on linguistic ability, as is the capacity to evaluate these inferences at the metalevel; and it is plausible that musical mental modeling exploits this systematic organization of semantic fields that is the product of linguistic ability. But it can do so while still remaining fundamentally nonconceptual. We shall take up the issue of nonconceptual content in more detail in chapter 5.

Even in the case of human, linguistically mediated reasoning, the psychology of inference or "mental logic" seems not to proceed by computing syntax alone. Experimental evidence concerning the relative difficulty in working various syllogistic figures and moods suggests that human beings make these inferences by constructing and juxtaposing mental models of arrays that stand for the *extensions* of the syllogistic terms (see Johnson-Laird 1983, chaps. 4 and 5). A "Barbara" syllogism (first figure, first mood) is the simplest syllogistic form. Most subjects can process syllogisms of this form in their heads because there is only one consistent way to model the premises. One need only construct a single mental model of three arrays or "tableaus" of elements, the first less extensive than or equal to the second, and the second less extensive than or equal to the third. The content of an "individual" mental model consists of an array that can be held in its entirety in working memory without storage of any of its parts in short-term memory (see Johnson-Laird 1983, 115). Some figures and moods require two models; some require three. Consider, for example, the following conditionally valid fourth-figure syllogism: No C are B; all B are A; therefore some A are not C. Because there are three consistent ways to integrate the premises, this syllogism requires three models. Either the Cs are excluded from the As, or the Cs and the As intersect, or the Cs are included in the As. Holding these models distinct in working memory is difficult. The larger the number of mental models required to compute a syllogism of a given figure and mood, the more difficult it is for subjects to judge the validity or invalidity of the syllogistic inference and the more time is required to make the inference, if it can be made in the head at all.

Empirical evidence suggests, then, that semantic, not syntactic, considerations are fundamental in the *psychology*, if not the formal logic, of syllogistic inference. It may be the case that syllogistic inference is psychologically, if not logically, more basic than formal propositional inference. After all, the logical dependence of syllogistic on propositional inference had to wait more than two thousand years for its discovery. Because syllogistic inference is a mode of formal inference, valid syllogistic inferences can, however, be represented purely syntactically, as they are in first-order predicate logic. Valid *material* inferences, on the other hand, cannot be represented by syntax alone. As a result, there is no reason whatever to suspect that the psychology of material inference is less semantically driven than is the psychology of formal syllogistic inference. The psychology of material inference, however, requires more than models of extensional arrays of elements. To understand that from "*X* is jaundiced," both "*X* is disillusioned" and "*X* is ill" can be validly inferred, requires representations (models) of the semantic fields of psychological and physiological terms. Judgments of Gricean implicature (see further discussion below), a relation weaker than implication, require the construction of models of more than one semantic field. If music is able, as I have claimed, to model semantic field structure by way of its rich structure of paradigmatic contrast, its ability to suggest good and bad inference (i.e., the failure of a phrase to "follow" musically) becomes understandable. "Good musical inference" requires that the composer establish contrastive and affinitive relations within and between musical fields that seem "right" or somehow convincing.[42]

Once the musical surface is understood to contain a complex field structure, musical passages become capable of suggesting movements of thought, the introduction of "psychological predicates." A psychological predicate is not a grammatical predicate but a "carrier of topical emphasis" (Vygotsky 1986, 221), a "formation of contrasts from the preceding context" (McNeill 1992, 127–128). A "psychological predicate" in Vygotsky's sense seems to be something like the placement of a topical presupposition, as a lawyer in a courtroom lays a "predicate" or a foundation for subsequent argumentation. What makes the musical suggestion of movement between semantic fields possible is that semantic fields are organized as contrast sets: *red* contrasts with other colors; *triangular* with other geometrical shapes. Types may be similarly organized: chess pieces (*qua* types) are distinguished from other chess pieces by their shapes and their repertoires of legal moves, just as chess pieces as such contrast with checkers pieces in the semantic field of checkerboard games. But a field is itself an analog model: a field is a physically structured layout. Ross (1992, 145), for example, goes so far as to claim that lexical organization exhibits a field structure that "follows principles of 'general relativity,' by analogy with the physics of general relativity." Moreover, he continues, "the analogy with physics holds for a considerable depth, even to the component forces (of meaning contrast) and the roles they play.... Furthermore, like physical relativity, lexical organization is dynamic." Although music is presented as a two-dimensional surface defined by axes of pitch and time, the contents of the listener-constructed mental models of the field structure *contained in* the musical surface are similarly multidimensional and *dynamic*, for musical meaning remains gestural and mimetic. The parsing of the musical surface, as I argued in chapter 2, recruits the motor systems and is analogous to *haptic exploration of surfaces in three dimensions*. If, as Ross suggests, the dynamics of physical space can model semantic field structure, so can the dynamics of musical or acousmatic space.

Interestingly, it is when introducing psychological predicates or new movements of thought that speakers rely most heavily on gesture. On the basis of extensive empirical studies of gesture use by speakers, McNeill (1992) established four fundamental categories of gesture: iconix, metaphorix, beats, and deictics. Iconix and metaphorix are essentially externalized mental models. Whereas iconix model concrete objects and events that are the referents of discourse, metaphorix model abstractions, and are often used at the metanarrative level to indicate the structure of the ongoing narrative itself. Where a set of iconic hand motions might model the motion of a character moving through a large pipe, a metaphoric will model a salient portion of narrative by means of a presenting gesture, as one might present a container, say a box or a basket, with contents. Beats, on the other hand, indicate episodic boundaries or changes in topic during discourse; and deictics point to individuals, places, and times in the story. Deictics might be used when a speaker, in recounting a narrative, says "Just then, a specter appeared" (pointing up), or "While this was occurring over here, similar events were unfolding over there" (pointing down and then to the right), or "Danglars discovered, to his horror, that the Count of Monte Cristo and Edmond Dantes were the same person" (the speaker putting both hands together). Like prosody, gesture harks back to the origins of language in the song without words of mimetic culture (see Donald 1991, 220ff). In fact, we might say that *gesture is the expression of the common mimetic ground where linguistic and musical mental models originate.*

Do we have, then, in music anything that comports with Saussure's signifier/ signified distinction? Not really. For one thing, Saussure's signifieds are concepts, not mental models. For another, the correlation between linguistic signifier and signified is conventional. That a certain lexical item, say "dog," signifies the concept it does is arbitrary. Musical "signification" is not like that, but more like picturing: just as virtual physical space is "seen in" pictures, musical space is "heard in" music. *Pace* Goodman, seeing something in a picture is not simply a matter of familiarity, habit, and convention (though these are not irrelevant either); rather it invokes innate functions of the visual system.[43] To hear something extramusical in a piece of music is more like pictorial seeing-in than it is like the interpretation of a conventional, arbitrary symbol. When he hears-in, the listener constructs mental models of the musical field as he parses the musical surface. Both the system of linguistic signifiers and the musical surface carry information and motivate the construction of mental models. But they do so in entirely different ways. Language is conceptually structured, but it presents no informationally structured surface from which invariants must be perceptually extracted. In the case of language, mental models represent truth conditions for sentential representations. In the case of music, the models are constructed according to the musical plan and are gestural and mimetic in significance. The musical surface has no grammatical categories and therefore has no syntagmatic contrasts in Saussure's sense.

It is the richly articulated paradigmatic or field structure contained in the musical surface that some theorists have mistaken for "internal" or "congeneric" musical meaning (see Coker 1972), the idea that musical meaning involves some mode of self-reference, that parts of a work "signify" other parts.[44] For Saussure, once again, "signification" is not reference, but the correlation of lexemes with conceptual contents.[45] Coker, however, follows more standard semiotic usage, which identifies the signifying function with reference. I shall do the same, unless otherwise indicated.[46] On Coker's view, the exceptionally strong thematic and rhythmic affinities between various statements of the "fate" motif in the first twenty-one bars of the first movement of Beethoven's Fifth Symphony establish internal iconic significations. It would perhaps be peremptory to dismiss this view as untenable; but in my view it confuses musical signification with affinities within a field of signifiers. Indeed, on Saussurian principles, it would be a category mistake to see relations within a field as iconically signifying at all, for one part of a field of signifiers cannot *signify* another part of the field. Signification depends on distinguishing signifier from signified, but this cannot be done *within* the musical surface. Signification is an "extra-field" relation, a relation between signifiers and signifieds. Whether Saussure's particular version of field theory is accepted or not, surely we do not want every case of *similarity* of theme or motif to count as a case of congeneric iconic *signification*.[47]

Coker's view leads him to make some additional, questionable moves. "This grounding for artistic truth of congeneric [musical] statements," we are told, "is patently tautologous in the sense that most statements of mathematics are. To a considerable extent congeneric truth depends upon the syntactic relation of gestural statements by equality or equivalence" (1972, 196). It is clear what analogy is driving this comparison between music and mathematics: "congeneric" musical meaning is to "extrageneric" musical meaning (i.e., musical signification of nonmusical entities) as the logical truth of tautologous material equivalences or of mathematical equations is to empirical truth. What Coker probably means to say is not that the *grounding of* the "artistic truth of [musical] statements" is "tautologous," but that it is *grounded in* tautology. It is the statements themselves that are tautologous or logically true, not what "grounds" them, namely, that they remain true under all possible consistent assignments of values for nonlogical terms. But the underlying analogy is still misconceived, for it requires us to assimilate the relation of congeneric *signification* to the relation of *logical equivalence*. Aside from the strain resulting from the assimilation of musical syntax, which lacks grammatical categories, to logical syntax, the analogy is guilty of a basic confusion. Logically equivalent statements do not signify (i.e., refer to) each other, precisely because they are located at the same level of language. At best, they paraphrase each other. And some analogue of paraphrase does seem to be what Coker has in mind regarding congeneric "truth." Only a metalinguistic statement can refer to another statement, and this requires quotation, direct or indirect, of the statement being referred to.

I do not deny that musical quotation does occur, as Beethoven (arguably) quotes seriatim each of the main themes of the first three movements of his Ninth Symphony and then "comments" on them during the cello and bass recitatives in the *Finale* (cf. Davies 1994, 41n43).[48] But such intraopus quotation, I submit, is a relatively rare occurrence in Western tonal art music, the style of music that is our main concern here. Similarly, despite cases like Tchaikovsky's quotation of *La Marseillaise* in the 1812 Overture, Mozart's quotation of *The Marriage of Figaro* in the climactic scene of *Don Giovanni*, or Bartók's quotation of (and unflattering "comment" on) a vulgarized Shostakovich tune in the fourth movement of the *Concerto for Orchestra* (example 3.2), extraopus quotation is nearly as rare. Not just any return or reappearance of a musical theme constitutes a *quotation* of that theme. The return in the *Finale* of Franck's

Example 3.2

Bartók, *Concerto for Orchestra. Intermezzo Interrotto.* Copyright 1946 by Boosey and Hawkes (London) Ltd. Copyright Renewed. Reprinted by permission of Boosey and Hawkes, Inc.

Symphony in D Minor of the principal theme of the second movement, for example, is not, in my view, a quotation of that theme; nor does Beethoven's reuse of (what came to be known as) the "Eroica" theme in various works constitute quotation of the theme.

In Western tonal art music, quotation occurs only in the context of certain recognizable musical "framing" gestures, which include, but are not limited to, the disruption or momentary suspension of ongoing musical sequence. These gestures mark the insertion of an element so as to render it available for "comment"; they might be said to function like the insertion of quotation marks or the expressions of indirect discourse, as a speaker might attempt to indicate quotation by tone, pacing, and gesture without resorting to explicit locutions like "I quote," or "he said that," or "we are told that." Musical quotation must rely on analogues of such pragmatic devices because semantic ascent and the distinction between object language and metalanguage are not available.[49] *Perhaps* the inclusion by Mahler of Klezmer-style music in the third movement of his First Symphony counts as extraopus quotation, since he seems to present it as an element for comment. But perhaps not: perhaps it is more like the appearance of folk material in the music of Dvořák, Smetana, and Bartók, material that is *used*, not *mentioned*.

The employment of an existing theme as a subject of variation in Western tonal art music, on the other hand, is not quotation. Brahms does not, as it were, *mention* the *St. Anthony Chorale* in his *Variations on a Theme of Haydn*, he *uses* it (incorporates it into a new piece); nor does he mention the student songs he incorporated into the *Academic Festival* Overture.[50] Similarly, Beethoven does not mention Diabelli's theme in his variation work of that name, nor does he mention the two Russian themes that appear in the first two *Rasoumovsky* quartets: he uses them. If, in the interest of driving this point home, we push the linguistic analogy—probably a little farther than we should— Mozart's quotation of the *Figaro* theme in the penultimate scene of *Don Giovanni* might be seen as part of a piece of gently self-mocking commentary, part of a second-order musical "statement" in the "metalanguage" (recall that Leporello refers to it disparagingly in Italian), while Brahms's use of the *St. Anthony Chorale* theme might be seen as a first-order "statement." Of course, none of these musical episodes is really a statement at all.

I do not wish to deny that there are musical styles in which something like the parody and metalevel comment that occur in Bartók's *Concerto for Orchestra* may, owing to existing conventions, take on a more central role than they have in Western art music. I say "may" because the musical idioms in which this is alleged to occur fall outside my knowledge and expertise. Following Henry Louis Gates, Zbikowski argues that "Signifyin(g)," a trope of African-American rhetorical practice that makes use of parody to critique the voice of the oppressor (among other things), is an integral part of certain jazz styles. "A stellar example of this," says Gates (1987, 243), and one specifically noted by Zbikowski (2002, 224), "is John Coltrane's rendition of 'My Favorite Things' compared to Julie Andrews's vapid original" (see also Gates 1988, 104). Another case, according to Zbikowski (2002, 223–224), is Miles Davis and Coltrane's 1956 recording of the song "Bye Bye Blackbird." The performance, he says, "makes a mockery of the simplistic messages of the song," which by that time was loaded with racist associations. What seems to be occurring in both recorded performances is something akin to the Bartók/Shostakovich case, but more subtle. If Gates and Zbikowski are right, Davis's interpretation of "Bye Bye Blackbird" and Coltrane's interpretation of "My Favorite Things" proceed simultaneously on two levels: that of *using* the original tune and that of *mentioning* it in a commentary, something like using a sentence and commenting on its content by uttering it in a tone expressive of an attitude taken toward that content. It is not easy to come up with examples of this sort of "double voicing"[51] in the Western art-music repertoire. The ghostly appearance of tonal waltz strains in Berg's dodecaphonic Violin Concerto is a possible case, though the "metalevel voice" seems to express more a melancholy attitude of loss than one of mockery. Perhaps Prokofiev's *Classical* Symphony, with its deliberate air of parody, is another. Stravinsky's *Pulcinella* may be a third. Notice, though, that neither Berg's waltz nor Prokofiev's symphony uses any previously existing tune or musical work.

Davis's and Coltrane's performances of "Bye Bye Blackbird" and "My Favorite Things," however, are special cases of a more general phenomenon that Gates terms "Signifyin(g) *on*," which comprises an exceedingly wide range of expressive and communicative behaviors, from jesting and competitive wordplays on the remarks of interlocutors to creative reactions to traditional artistic corpora. Many examples of Signifyin(g) on seem to involve something like Goodman's "allusion," or indirect reference by way of shared properties; but few engage in quotation. The motion picture *Roxanne* is a *version* of Rostand's *Cyrano de Bergerac*; it does not quote it. Yet *Roxanne* Signifies on *Cyrano* and alludes to it. Someone who quips "The unlived life is not worth examining" is Signifyin(g) on and alluding to a Socratic (or Platonic) maxim, just as Bernstein and Sondheim are Signifyin(g) on and alluding to Shakespeare's *Romeo and Juliet* in *West Side Story*. Beethoven may, then, as Zbikowski (2002, 224n47) claims, be said to be Signifyin(g) on Diabelli, just as Schubert may be said to be Signifyin(g) on Beethoven in the *Finale* of his "Great" C Major Symphony (cf. Elgin 1983, 134). It is far from clear, however, that Beethoven is even alluding musically to Diabelli, much less quoting him. He is just *using* the waltz tune based on its musical potential. For reasons already given, it is a mistake to maintain that allusion (indirect reference) occurs with any and every occurrence of musical similarity, either within or between works. In the end Zbikowski (2002, 224) is forced to admit that the performance practice of producing alternative versions of existing tunes "is so common in jazz...that Signifyin(g), present everywhere, would seem to signify nothing."

While Coker also wishes to allow for the possibility of extramusical (extrageneric) signification, many theorists in the formalist tradition that derives from Hanslick reject it, or are at least suspicious of it, insisting that all legitimate musical meaning is internal. Bernstein's (1976) Chomsky-inspired theory falls into this category,[52] but his account of internal musical meaning is quite different from Coker's. For him, internal musical meaning consists entirely of "metaphors," comparable "analogically" (1976, 131–132) to metaphorical statements of the form "This is that." In my view, Bernstein, like Coker, is mistaking the field structure of the musical surface for something else, in this case, a musical analogue to metaphorical, as opposed to logical or formal, statement. His analysis of the first two bars of Brahms's Fourth Symphony (ibid., 126–127) suggests this (example 3.3). The falling thirds followed by rising sixths, the harmonic progression from tonic to subdominant and then from dominant to tonic do indeed constitute, as he says, "a beautiful parallelism"; but they are less a "luminous example of this-is-that" than luminous examples of affinities and contrasts within a field. Musical phrases are no more comparable to metaphorical statements than they are to mathematical formulas: musical phrases don't say anything, for they have no conceptual content. Still, there is something about Bernstein's view that seems right, for as we saw, linguistic metaphor requires the juxtaposition of terms that belong to different semantic fields; and the musical surface does contain field structure, and therefore, can *model* this sort of juxtaposition of semantic fields, as, for example, in the Beethoven Violin Concerto excerpt we considered: the F is both a lowered sixth in A major and a dominant seventh in C major—this is that.

The metaphorical significance of music rests, however, on a very different basis than that identified by Bernstein. I agree that music is metaphorically more direct than language, even than poetic language, because it is not burdened with "literal semantic weights," and I agree that "music *already exists in the poetic sense*" and is "all art from the first note on" (ibid., 127–128). But this is because all successful metaphor, whether musical or poetic, depends on the mesh or "invariance" of mental models; and music, unlike language, has no literal meanings that mediate the construction of these models. It is these mental models, constructed by the listener and not the musical surface by itself, that carry out the exemplificational modeling function and that are, as a result, *the primary vehicles of musical meaning.* Even the field structure in the musical surface must be modeled in the mind of the listener by invoking the appropriate rules and representations. But as we are about to see, musical mental modeling is not limited to modeling musical field structure; it extends to scenarios, objects, and events in virtual musical space. This is important because musical field structure only models the *form* of semantic fields, the fact that they are structured by relations of affinity, contrast, cycles, hyponomy, and superordination. As I now shall argue, the reach of musical semantics reaches beyond this merely formal modeling. Music is capable of modeling

Example 3.3

Brahms, Symphony No. 4 in E Minor, *Allegro non troppo*.

semantic *content* as well by motivating the construction of scenarios in musical space that model conceptual content itself, *while remaining nonconceptual.*

Because conversational implicature is a weaker relation than logical implication, and because relevance is highly sensitive to semantic field relations (recall McNeill's syllogism and electron comparison), semantic fields also play a crucial role in Gricean conversational pragmatics. Gricean implicature, that is to say, relies heavily on semantic field relations of affinity and contrast, which provide the contrast sets that affect conversational relevance, an important Gricean concept (cf. Grandy 1987, 262).[53] Someone who answers the question "Is today Tuesday?" by answering (however truly), "No, it's our anniversary," would violate the Gricean maxim of relevance by going outside the cyclically ordered contrast set (days of the week) implicated in the question. Yet while the contrast set of days of the week is implicated by the questioner, it is not *implied.* If the respondent happened to be a neglected spouse, the response might accord with the maxim of relevance after all. The field structure contained in the musical surface makes possible the musical modeling of topical relevance.

Consider another example from Beethoven, whose music seems to me to be exceptionally vigorous in its tendency toward extramusical modeling, usually without being explicitly programmatic.[54] The second movement of the Fourth Piano Concerto has suggested to many a listener a conversation, or at least an extended confrontation, between two agents, one adamantine, the other conciliatory.[55] How is this possible? The mental model generated by the plan of the music models the structure of a conversation, which mandates a temporally nested organization of stages, including initiation, interaction, and resolution, and is subject to Gricean pragmatic rules of informativeness, concision, relevance, and clarity. Musical "irrelevance," whether thematic, harmonic, or formal, is something we all have encountered. Mozart's *Musical Joke*, K. 522 makes a study of it. The Beethoven movement models conversational structure while emptying it of all propositional content. Yet no creature incapable of taking on conversational roles could so understand it, for such a creature would lack the appropriate mental models and concepts. The fact that musical structure can carry out this sort of modeling function can explain the extramusical meanings that human beings seem to find in music, without imputing to it the sort of propositional content it clearly cannot have. Pure musical performance is "exemplificational," not descriptive or denotational, just as Goodman claimed it was—but exemplificational in our reformed sense, of modeling by means of shared attributes.

Notice, though, that with this musical example we have gone beyond the modeling of semantic field structure to the modeling of an unfolding conversational *scenario*, a scenario that incorporates bodily sets and sequenced behaviors of two imagined *antagonists* that are simulated off-line during the musical experience. It is to this second aspect of musical modeling, the modeling of scenario content, that we now turn.

3.7 Musical Metaphor and "The Body in the Mind": Musical Meaning as Extramusical Content

As it turns out, the conception of physical force and causation, as well as that of the resistance or the acquiescence of one object to force applied by another object, finds parallels in such domains as social coercion and resistance and in logical and moral necessity.

—Ray Jackendoff (1987, 157)

"This modeling story is most dubious; and to the extent it is not, it applies only to mere program music," the musical purist will say. But I am prepared to argue the rather unfashionable claim[56] that *all* Western tonal art music since 1650, including so-called pure music, is program music, if by program music we mean music which does not necessarily tell a story or depict specific scenes, but which has extramusical significance because the contents of the mental models it motivates are layouts and scenarios in which the listener acts off-line. It is just that some programs are explicitly identified via verbal descriptions and titles; some programs that are not explicitly identified are more obvious than others; and still other programs can be verbally expressed hardly or not at all. Depending on its style, a musical work will emphasize the modeling of semantic field structure, or extramusical form, as does much Baroque and early Classical music; or it will emphasize the modeling of extramusical content, as does music that is Romantic or overtly programmatic. All the music under consideration here will, however, do some of both. There is, moreover, a theoretical route to a psychological explanation of how the musical modeling of conceptual content, particularly the musical modeling of *abstract* conceptual content, might be achieved. Let us now attempt to navigate that route.

We noted in the previous chapter that Lakoff and Johnson (1980, 1999; Johnson 1987) have argued that all human conceptual understanding, including the understanding of highly abstract concepts, is "metaphorically grounded" in so-called emergent concepts of human kinesthetic and motor experience, including the concepts *up/down, front/back, inside/outside, manipulative causality*, and *agency*. Movement itself, however, is hierarchically organized, from the partonymic relations of body, limbs, and smaller body parts to hierarchically organized plan structures themselves. These facts enable us to understand how hierarchical musical structures that are partonymic (metrical and grouping structures) and those that are treelike (time-span and prolongation reductions) could generate mental models that model (by exemplified properties) the domains of a range of hierarchically organized *nonmusical* human actions, extending from quotidian movement in physical space, to agency and social interaction, and even, via "the body in the mind," to the content of highly abstract concepts, including metaphysical concepts.

Of first importance in the Lakoff and Johnson account of metaphorical understanding is a certain asymmetry of mapping direction. The *structuring* concept (or "vehicle") invariably derives from a stratum of experience that strongly involves the body, while the *structured* concept (the "topic") is more "abstract" and further removed from bodily, that is, somatosensory, kinesthetic experience. All the empirical evidence presented for this asymmetry thesis in their (1980) book was linguistic: the authors scoured ordinary language for expressions that betrayed some systematic underlying metaphorical transference in the "metaphors we live by," e.g., *time is money* or *argument is war*. When we say "You are wasting my time," or "I must budget my time better," or "I have no more time to spend on this," it is *money* that structures *time*, not the other way around. Similarly, in such expressions as "He blew his opponent's arguments out of the water," or "He shot those arguments full or holes," or "He defended his position," it is *war* that structures *argument*. In both cases—*time is money, argument is war*—the second concept is the structuring one (or vehicle), the first the structured (or target); and in both cases the structuring concept is more closely allied with bodily experience and action. Whereas the notion of time is abstract and metaphysically elusive, there is nothing elusive about money in its most familiar forms and uses: it is a socially constructed entity that is tangible, fungible, and easily quantified. An argument is a rather abstract entity. The concept of war, on the other hand, is well defined and evokes strong visceral reactions and bodily images. Notice also that although sense experience is metaphorically more basic than thought, certain sense modalities are more basic than other sense modalities. So while seeing structures understanding ("I see what you mean") via the *understanding is seeing* metaphor, touching structures seeing ("The scene grabbed my attention") via a more basic *seeing is touching* metaphor, not the other way around. Given results from the previous chapter concerning the haptic quality of musical experience, we might well expect this asymmetry or inequality among the senses to have some special significance for musical meaning.[57]

While Lakoff and Johnson reprise much of this linguistic evidence in their more recent joint effort (1999), they also adduce some evidence of a different kind by means of what they call "existence proofs." An existence proof in their sense is a computational simulation showing that a biologically plausible computational architecture programmed or trained up to represent bodily action plans can perform certain inferential tasks. Lakoff and Johnson supply almost no detail concerning the organization of these systems, descriptions of which are mostly to be found in unpublished material, as well as in a small number of recent publications by other authors. What may be gathered, however, is that these systems are able to compute logical inferences by following plans for bodily actions, provided that a mapping from the domain of the actions encoded in the plans, say actions of stumbling and falling, to the domains of abstract concepts, say events belonging to economics, can also be established. By implementing appropriate *action schemata*, these systems can make cognitive transitions into states that can be mapped onto *logical consequences* of statements. Narayanan (1999, 121) supplies the following example (without necessarily endorsing the political position expressed):

In 1991, in response to World Bank pressure, India boldly set out on a path of liberation. The government loosened its strangle-hold on business, and removed obstacles to international trade. While great strides were made in the first few years, the government is currently stumbling in its effort to implement the liberalization plan. (See also Feldman and Narayanan 2004)

According to standard Lakoff and Johnson lore, in order to understand this newspaper snippet it is necessary to conceptualize countries and institutions as physical agents. By metaphorically mapping the experiential domain of agents and forces onto the more abstract domain of economic causes and events, it is possible to draw appropriate inferences: because stumbling leads to falling, and because *falling* can be mapped onto *failing*, one can infer that governmental economic policies are likely to fail. But a simulation of bodily experience is necessary to make this inference. "The central idea behind our model," Narayanan explains, "is that the reader interpreting a phrase that corresponds to a motion term is in fact performing a *mental simulation* of the *entailed event* in the current context" (1999, 122, emphasis mine). Narayanan's achievement was to produce a computational design that was able to infer that the economic policy of the Indian government was failing without explicitly representing this inference sententially.

To see in a little more detail how Narayanan's computational model works, consider the logic of verbal "aspect." Some languages supply grammatical forms for coding the distinction between actions that are ongoing and those that are completed. For example, available in English (though not in German) are the progressive forms "is walking" and "was walking." "Is walking" implies that an activity is ongoing, not yet completed, and contrasts with the perfective forms "walked" and "has walked," which imply that an action has been completed. In another published piece, Narayanan (1997) shows how the semantics of these aspectual forms can be represented by way of computer-simulated action plans, which he terms "X-schemas." X-schemas employ formal systems known as Petri nets, which consist of nodes made up of "conditions" or "places," represented by circles, and "events" or "transitions," represented by boxes. These nodes are connected by arrows (see figure 3.10 below). Petri nets, we should note, are not computational *architectures* but abstract formal systems that may be variously implemented. While they definitely fall within the category of software and not hardware, they are not the themselves task-level X-schemas (see figure 3.11 below). Nonetheless, they constitute yet another formalism capable of representing plans. The solution to the ferryman problem we considered earlier, for example, can also be represented by a Petri net as in figure 3.10. Notice that four of the circles (the "conditions") contain dots ("tokens"). Each dot represents one item in the story: ferryman, wolf, goat, and cabbage. To follow the plan, begin with the dotted circle labeled "ferryman alone" and move the tokens appropriately by way of the arrows.

It is clear that a Petri net is capable of modeling any plan-structured action. There are X-schemas for various ongoing activities, like walking or applying an ointment, and

The problem is solved by taking the goat back across the river at one point.

Other Side

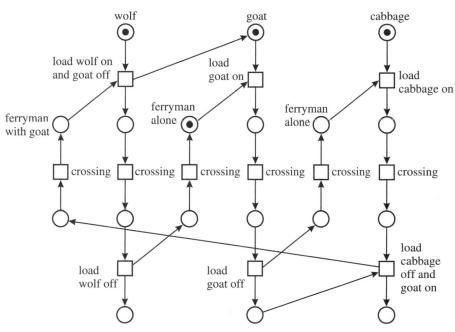

This Side

Figure 3.10
The solution to the goat problem in the form of a Petri net. (From Reisig 1992, reprinted by permission of Springer Verlag.)

there are controller schemas, themselves X-schemas, that can assume a higher-level monitoring or supervisory role over a variety of lower-level schemas. According to Narayanan, the English progressive would be modeled by activating an iteration X-schema, while the perfective would be modeled by activating termination (figure 3.11). The X-schematic representation of "Jack has walked to the store" sanctions the inference that Jack is at the store because his walking schema includes a termination state (Narayanan 1997, 551). Looking at the top diagram in figure 3.11, the loop including "visual coordination," "take step," "test footing," and "move test foot" is iterated until the walker arrives at his destination and is "done." The bottom diagram provides a more general version of the schema with the iteration loop represented by the arrow at the top and "cancel" and "suspend" loops (along with a "failure" place at the lower right) represented below. Such X-schemas, Narayanan proposes, are also

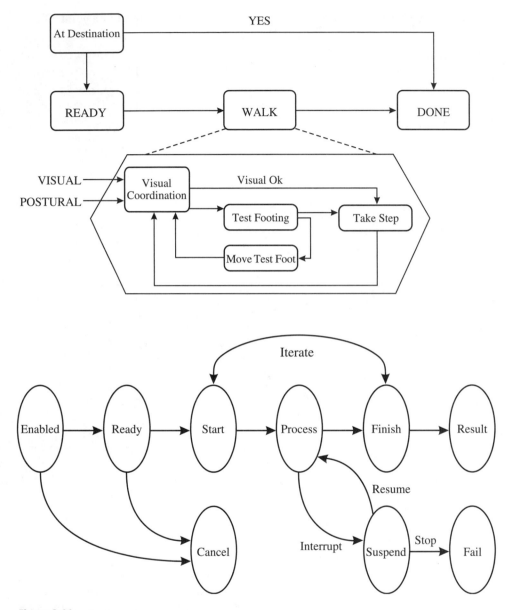

Figure 3.11
Two X-schemas. The top figure represents a schema for walking, the bottom a more general action schema. Notice the structural similarity between the walking schema and the basic TOTE schema. (From Narayanan 1997, 549, reprinted by permission of Lawrence Erlbaum Associates.)

capable of modeling metaphorical understanding of abstract concepts and of sanctioning appropriate inferences, provided the metaphorical transference is appropriately mapped. For example, a neurologically implemented version of the walking X-schema would be activated in a hearer when someone makes the claim that a business is approaching a financial goal, so as to infer that it has not yet reached it. The activation of a walking X-schema requires construction of a mental model of the context of walking, minimally including a starting point, a path, and a goal. *If simulated action plans can generate mental models of conceptual contents, and if musical plans can generate models of action in musical space that model actions in physical space,[58] then, by transitivity, musical models can model conceptual contents, assuming that the relation "is paramorphic with" can be transitive.*

To be sure, musical experience *invites* the deployment of concepts; but in this case, the musical models drive the concepts, rather than the other way around as in the processing of propositional content. The models, moreover, exceed the *expressive range* of the concepts, a topic to which we shall return in chapter 5. Musical meaning, then, can be seen to depend on the varieties of musical models, which model a significant range of mental models that pertain to a variety of human nonmusical experiential domains.

3.8   An Existence Proof for the Generative Theory of Tonal Music

To my knowledge, Petri nets have not been used to represent musical plans. But they probably could be. Parallel distributed processing (PDP) networks, on the other hand, have yielded biologically plausible computational simulations of musical representation. A biologically plausible computational model (see the general introduction, section 1.3) may be said to provide an existence proof for a theory of representation. Unlike Petri nets, however, which, as we saw, are abstract formal systems, PDP networks are computational architectures consisting of nodes and connections. They possess a layered structure such that every node in each processing layer, whether "visible" (input or output) or "hidden" (located in between), has a weighted connection to every node in subsequent and previous layers. The nodes of a standard PDP network, moreover, have activation levels determined by the values of their weighted input connections. Unfortunately, PDP networks generally have difficulty carrying out recursive, iterative operations.

Recursive, auto-associative memory (RAAM) networks, however, have had some success in surmounting these difficulties. A RAAM network is a species of recurrent network, but with some special characteristics. First, the standard RAAM network consists of five layers: input, encoder, hidden, decoder, and output layers. Second, instead of passing contextual information exclusively from *output layer* back to its *hidden layer* by way of descending connections, as in standard recurrent networks (see Churchland

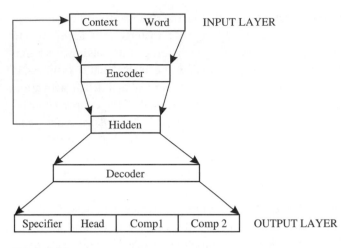

Figure 3.12
The functional organization of a recursive auto-associative memory (RAAM) sentence parser network. (From Horgan and Tienson 1996, 58, reprinted by permission of MIT Press.)

1995, 100), the RAAM network passes information from its *hidden layer* back to its *input nodes*, thereby reprocessing cyclically a constantly updated input as a "moving target" in iterative fashion (figure 3.12; see Horgan and Tienson 1996, 58). Third, the input layer of the RAAM architecture is divided into "buffers" so as to encode information in binary or ternary chunks. These buffers are banks of contiguous input units that are wired so as to function as structural units. The input layer of Berg's and Pollack's RAAM sentence parser, for example, is buffered in binary fashion into a "word pool" and a "context pool." A representation of each word of a sentence ('The boy with a dog ate spaghetti with a fork') is successively activated in the word pool of the input layer, the context layer then receiving the "tentative, partial parse representation" (Horgan and Tienson 1996, 58) so far present in the hidden layer. From there, the process goes on iteratively until all the words of the sentence have been passed through the word pool and all the updated contexts have passed through the context pool. At that point, the parsing of the sentence is complete, and if the network has been properly trained (normally using a backpropagation[59] learning regimen) on a corpus of representative English sentences, the RAAM parser yields accurate grammatical parsings of English sentences, including parsings of new well-formed sentences that were not present in the training set.

Large et al. (1999) were able to train two modularly connected RAAM networks to compress and then reconstruct simple melodies. To "compress" is to encode information in the hidden layer or layers of a connectionist network. In the case of the RAAM sentence parser, for example, information concerning the structure of English sentences was present in compressed form in the network's hidden layer after successful training. With two modularly connected networks, one module of the network takes the output of the other module as input. Large et al. adopted this modular strategy because a single network with a reasonable number of hidden units was not capable of coding a sufficient number (i.e., 6 to 7) of levels of hierarchical organization required even by simple melodies (ibid., 296). Coding the seven pitch classes of the major diatonic scale, plus two additional units for melodic contour (one ON for a change up, the other ON for a change down, both OFF for no change in melodic direction) strictly required only nine input units (7 + 2), assuming octave equivalence. But in the interest of achieving higher-dimensional activation spaces, each module was provided with an input layer of 140 units (divided into 4 separate input buffers of 35 units each),[60] a middle layer of 35 units, and an output layer of 148.

Large et al. used a twenty-five-member training set containing eighteen melodies ranging in length from four to twelve measures and with time signatures of 2/4, 3/4, 4/4, 6/8, or 12/8, plus variations on five of these melodies. These were variations that had been improvised on the piano by *human* musicians (example 3.4). Three of these improvised variations had already been examined and found to agree closely with the Lerdahl and Jackendoff theory's predictions concerning which notes of the original melodies would be retained as most important (Large et al. 1999, 290–292, a fairly significant bit of empirical support, by the way, for the generative theory and for the psychological reality of the time-span reduction representations). The fact that the melodies were single-voice lines without any accompaniment minimized the importance of the prolongation reductions, which track harmonic significance.

Large et al. employed the following training and testing procedures. During the training phase, four melodies randomly chosen from the training set of twenty-five were presented to the network as time-span segmentations. A time-span *segmentation* (as opposed to a time-span *reduction*) of a melody is a structured set of pitch groupings, with each smaller or lower-level group metrically nested within a larger or higher-level group. Group size is determined by metrical value of the constituent notes. The pitches in a time-span segmentation have determinate duration, for example, sixteenth-note value, eighth-note value, quarter-note value, and are temporally ordered. But a time-span segmentation lacks any information concerning the structural importance of the various pitches in a melody, the information that is represented by time-span reductions. At the lowest levels, the time-span segmentations generally follow rhythmic structure within the bar, that is, they consist of groups of two and four in the case of duple meters, groups of three in the case of triple meter, and of combinations of triple and duple, as in 6/8 and 12/8 meters.

As with Berg and Pollack's sentence parser, input was coded in simple binary, and in the case of triple meters, simple ternary form. The 140 input units of each module were assigned to four input buffers of the compressor (cf. the "pools" of the Berg/Pollack

Example 3.4
From Large et al. 1999, musical network training set. (Reprinted by permission of Elsevier Publishers.)

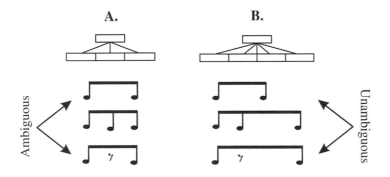

Proposed buffering for encoding duple and triple grouping structures.

(a) Three buffers cannot discriminate between a group of two events and a
    group of three events in which the middle event is a rest.

(b) Four input buffers can make the discrimination.

Figure 3.13
The organization of the input layer of the musical memory network. (From Large et al. 1999, reprinted by permission of Elsevier Publishers.)

sentence parser) so as to be able to distinguish between duplet rhythms, triplet rhythms with a missing second note, and triplet rhythms with all three notes present (see figure 3.13). The first buffer represented the first event of any group, the third buffer the second note of a group of two, the second buffer the second note of a group of three, and the fourth buffer the third note of a group of three. The network achieved compression by combining (in groups of two or three) the notes of lowest metrical value (sixteenth notes) into vectors (ordered sets of activation values in the output layer), and then combining these output vectors with notes at the next-higher level of metrical value (eighth notes), then combining these vectors with notes at the next-higher level (quarter notes or dotted quarters), then (in the case of 4/4 and 12/8 meters) combining vectors representing half-bars (the half-note or dotted-half-note level) into vectors representing whole bars until the melody was completely compressed (figures 3.14 and 3.15).[61] The proper order of musical events in each melody was invariably preserved in each training cycle. The network functioned recursively because, as in the case of the sentence parser, information from the hidden layers was fed back into input layers: previous, metrically lower-level vectors were combined with new, metrically higher-level tones to produce new vectors. The network was then trained by backpropagation to reconstruct the four melodies with as much accuracy as possible.[62] The goal was to make output match the original melodies as closely as possible.

A. Encoding (Compressor)

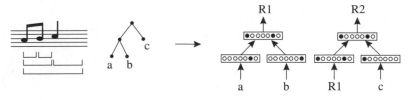

B. Decoding (Reconstruction)

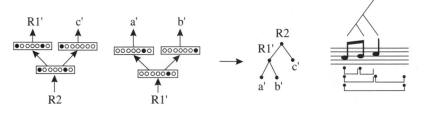

Encoding and Decoding of a musical sequence by a RAAM network.

(a) Based on a vector representation for each event and a constituent structure analysis, the compressor combines the group (ab) into a single vector, R1, and the combines (R1c) into a single vector R2.

(b) The reconstructor decodes the vector R2 to produce the facsimile (R1'c'). It then decodes R1' into (a'b').

Figure 3.14
Encoding (compression) and decoding (reconstruction) by a RAAM musical network. (From Large et al. 1999, reprinted by permission of Elsevier Publishers.)

Once the training phase was completed, the networks were given a sort of "memory" test. They were tested on three melodies, the same three that had been examined in the human improvisation test. One of these three was present in the set of four melodies that had actually been used to train the networks; one was not present in that set of four but was a variant of four melodies in the original set of twenty-five; and one was completely novel and unrelated to the twenty-five test melodies. Unsurprisingly, the network was able to produce a very accurate version of the melody on which it had been trained. The network's version of the variant melody had more errors, but these errors, including deletions, additions, and incorrect pitches and rhythms, tended to concern the *structurally* less important melodic events, as the theory of time-span reductions would predict. This was taken as evidence that the network had constructed internal time-span reduction representations (Large et al. 1999, 287, emphasis mine):

A. Encoding (Compression)

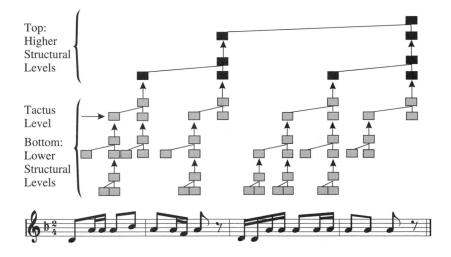

B. Decoding (Reconstruction)

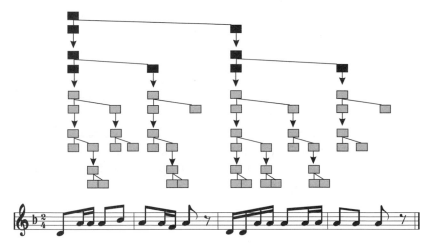

Simplified Schematic of the modular RAAM used in the network experiment

(a) In the encoding diagram, time flows from left to right and bottom to top.

(b) In the decoding diagram, time flows from top to bottom and left to right.

Figure 3.15

The encoding and decoding of "Hush Little Baby" represented on a two-dimensional time grid. (From Large et al. 1999, reprinted by permission of Elsevier Publishers.)

If, in the compression/reconstruction process, the network consistently loses information pertaining to less important events and retains information about more important events (i.e. as predicted by the [Lerdahl and Jackendoff] music-theoretic analyses), then the network has also captured *information that extends beyond pitch and time-span segmentation.* The test is whether or not the network training procedure discovers the relative importance of events corresponding to metrical accent and time-span reduction.

With the novel melody, where neither it nor anything closely similar to it was present in the training set of twenty-five, the network did reasonably well with the rhythms, but relatively poorly with pitches. Still, the network did much better than chance. Large et al. were also able to formulate an algorithm that expressed the degree of similarity of each reconstructed pitch event to the original. This was interpreted as a measure of probability of error for each reconstructed pitch event. In the case of the familiar and variant melodies, but not the novel one, the probability of error was lowest for pitches of the highest structural importance. In the case of the novel melody, however, probability of error was lowest for pitches at lower, more intermediate levels of structural importance. The network, therefore, had missed the events of highest structural importance in the novel melody. Nevertheless, these results were judged significant enough to have led Large et al. to conclude that a version of TSR representations (one of our two varieties, recall, of internal musical representation) was distributed in the weights of the network. Given these results, the Large et al. model might be said to constitute a Lakoff and Johnson–style "existence proof" for a part of a generative musical grammar (time-span reduction rules and representations) constructed according to the Lerdahl and Jackendoff theory. Equally important, the RAAM compressor-reconstructor network seems capable of implementing a connectionist version of the classical recursive TOTE procedural schema and of constructing a "key" to the field or paradigmatic structure of the musical surface.

Despite these encouraging results, I wish to stop short of an unqualified endorsement of the Lerdahl and Jackendoff account of musical understanding in all its details. Musical structure, especially large-scale structure, may be more heterarchical than Lerdahl and Jackendoff's Schenker-inspired theory allows. Pursuing the linguistic analogy, large-scale musical structure seems to be far more like *discourse structure* than it is like *sentence structure.* It is just implausible to think that a large symphonic movement would (or even could) be represented in the mind of a listener, or even in the mind of a compositional genius,[63] by one immense, fully nested time-span or prolongation reduction tree unified under a single dominant branch, as would be required by the Lerdahl and Jackendoff tree structure. Discourse structure, however, is a pragmatic, not a syntactic or even a semantic aspect of language.[64] But discourse structure is certainly amenable to mental modeling and plan-structuring, as we saw in the earlier discussion of Beethoven's Fourth Piano Concerto.[65]

Recall once again the deep parallel between musical tree organization and prosody noted by Lerdahl and Jackendoff. McNeill (1992, 84–85) draws attention to an equally striking parallel between prosody and the gestures of speakers: the two hierarchies of sound and gesture correspond closely. The "phonological hierarchy" rises from most prominent *syllable*, to the phonological peak within a clause, to the *tone unit*, a syllabic grouping that contains a complete "intonation tune" or rise-fall, to the *locution*, which maps onto complete sentences, to the *locution group*, and finally to the *locution cluster*, which maps onto the paragraph and is marked by altered pitch and/or tone quality and thematic shift of content. In closely parallel fashion, the "gestural hierarchy" rises from *stroke*, to the *gesture phrase* consisting of one or more movement phases (strokes), to the *gesture unit*, the period of time between successive moments of rest, to consistent *head movements*, to *arm use and body posture*, which correspond to a *paragraph*. Each such paragraph constitutes a relatively complete cycle of thought. Thereafter, a new thought movement begins with the construction of a new mental model or with new additions to the existing one, which is then constituted into sentences and a paragraph, and "so forth endlessly" (McNeill 1992, 237). I suspect that the largest psychologically graspable unified and detailed TSR or PR reduction tree would correspond to the musical equivalent of a paragraph, that is, a relatively complete musical gesture.[66] Whatever that may be, it is almost certainly a musical unit smaller than a movement or even a major movement-section, *pace* Bernstein (1976, 58), who pairs the sentence, the smallest complete meaningful linguistic unit, with the entire musical movement.

The smallest complete meaningful *musical* unit, on the other hand, is most likely the motif, as Zbikowski (2002, 26ff) suggests. As I have already indicated, Zbikowski's theory has much in common with my own. One of his core ideas is that musical structures, from the small to the large, are grouped by both composer and listener into graded, nonclassical categories that show strong typicality effects. The musical motif, the basic unit of musical significance, constitutes the basic-level musical category. According to Lakoff, Rosch, and other theorists (see Lakoff 1987, 46ff), terms designating basic-level categories are located in the middle of the abstraction hierarchy: "chair" designates such a category, while "rocker" and "piece of furniture" respectively designate subordinate and superordinate categories. Basic-level category terms tend to be lexical items that are comparatively short and easily handled. Most significantly, they mark aspects of objects that are *practically* salient. Objects falling within basic-level categories tend to be those "closest to hand," those most suitable for characteristic forms of manipulation, and mental representations of these categories, on the Lakoff and Johnson view, have the most richly articulated nonpropositional structure involving "motor program schemata" (Johnson 1987, 189), the representations I have termed "motor plans."

I do not deny that the musical surface presents the listener with a non-classical categorization task. That was one of the lessons of our discussion of musical field structure and hierarchical decision trees. For Zbilowski, as for me, the categorization of the musical surface is just the beginning of the process of musical understanding, which exploits Lakoff and Johnson-style metaphorical transferences. Zbikowski's handling of the Lakoff and Johnson material, however, differs from mine in a fundamental respect. For him, music functions principally as the *target* of these metaphorical transferences: (Zbikowski 2002) "For an element to count as musical, it must be able to serve as a target for the cross-domain mappings that guide our discourse about music" (76); "in each case, the basic mapping relies on embodied knowledge and on the correlation of the musical domain with a more concrete domain" (72). To paraphrase Zbikowski's argument: just as the metaphor *argument is war* structures our thinking about argument, the metaphor *music is spatial* structures our thinking about music and, consequently, structures musical experience itself. A number of other metaphors do so as well, including *music is an organism* (ibid., 302) and *music is a mechanical clockwork* (ibid., 313). I have no quarrel with the idea that music may assume the target role in metaphorical transferences. But this handling of the Lakoff and Johnson theory has its limitations, which emerge when Zbikowski proffers *music is a metaphysical hierarchy* as a structuring metaphor (ibid., 314ff).[67] Here the vehicle (*metaphysical hierarchy*) is arguably more abstract and more distant from bodily experience than the target (*music*). But this is problematic from the standpoint of the Lakoff and Johnson theory. For them, the vehicle or structuring concept is invariably more concrete and intimately related to bodily experience than is the target or structured concept. The same goes for other structuring metaphors we have discussed, including *music is a semantic field* and *music is a conversation*. Something seems to have gone awry.

What has gone awry is that music's gestural, mimetic function has gone missing in Zbikowski's account. Nor has Zbikowski explained how "conceptual blends" between musical and nonmusical domains are achieved. Music, once again, consists just of organized sequences of tones. Once acknowledged, musical mimesis can accommodate mapping between the metaphysical and musical domains, while respecting Lakoff and Johnson's principle of asymmetry of metaphorical transference. We construct mental models of the truth conditions of metaphysical sentences, as we do for all sentences we can understand. Mental models, however, are, as we have seen, simulational and action oriented. On the basis of the plan of a musical work, the listener constructs musical mental models whose contents are the virtual scenarios in which the listener acts off-line. If the musical plan generates appropriate mental models and puts the listener's body into appropriate motor states off-line, the musical mental models can then model the metaphysical mental models and, by the transitivity relation discussed above, can model the metaphysical conceptual content itself, albeit nonconceptually. Once the musical and metaphysical models mesh, once "invariance" between their contents is achieved, *then* "cross-domain mapping" from the metaphysical back onto the musical domain can and does occur; and no doubt such cross-domain mapping strongly affects the manner in which a culture conceptualizes and experiences its music. Zbikowski does grant that "our experiences with music allow us, on occasion, to map from the musical domain onto other domains" (ibid., 327). Perhaps he has in mind occasional metaphors like *cosmic order is musical harmony* or *praise is music to the ears*. Musical modeling of nonmusical domains, however, is hardly the occasional occurrence Zbikowski represents it to be. If I am right, it is pervasive, because musical experience is fundamentally bodily, gestural, and simulational in significance. In chapter 5, I shall argue that emotional response to Western tonal art music, a topic Zbikowski does not entirely ignore but also does not explore in any depth,[68] arises out of simulated action in acousmatic space.

3.9   Summary and Conclusion

This chapter began with a review of the semiotic of signs and symbols. I proposed that musical meaning is primarily a case of Stephen Davies's meaning C, the systematized, intentional use of "natural," that is, iconic, elements. This variety of meaning is carried by syntactically organized symbols and is to some degree nonconventional. We then considered Goodman's conventionalist theory of musical meaning in conjunction with his four symptoms of the aesthetic: syntactic density, semantic density, exemplification, and syntactic repleteness. While the musical score, we saw, had none of these attributes, the performance had three of them: semantic density, exemplification, and repleteness. Since these are properties of symbolic systems, I argued that the musical performance must be regarded as a symbol that belongs to a symbolic system, or, as I shall argue in the next chapter, a token of a symbolic type. A symbolic system, however, requires a syntax; and I suggested the Lerdahl and Jackendoff generative theory as offering the best candidate for such a syntax. We then approached the issue of musical meaning by construing the performance as a pushmi-pullyu representation, which made it possible to develop further the notions of mimesis and mental modeling introduced in the previous chapter, and then to connect these up with issues of meaning. I argued that the musical surface contained field structure and that this allowed for the modeling of the structure of semantic fields, with the hierarchical TSR and PR trees playing the role of a "key," a formal variant of a decision table. This yielded musical meaning as extramusical form. Finally, I argued that mental models of actions, events, and objects in musical virtual space model conceptual content by way of the Lakoff and Johnson body-in-the-mind theory of metaphorical transference from bodily experience to the contents of concepts distantly removed from that experience.

Having discussed the varieties of musical representation and the nature of musical meaning, we now have the appropriate theoretical apparatus in place to allow us to confront another set of issues, those concerning the ontology of the musical work. Taking exception to Goodman's identification of the musical work with the class of performances compliant with the score, Lerdahl and Jackendoff (1983, 2) identify the work with "a mentally constructed entity, of which scores and performances are partial representations by which the piece is transmitted." But which "mentally constructed entity," and in whose mind, is *"the piece"* to be? The piece, as opposed to some individual's mentally constructed version of it, seems to have an independent status of some kind. But of what kind? Whatever it is, the musical work is no material particular as is a painting or a sculpture. Is it, then, an abstract object of some sort? If so, of what sort? Is Goodman right that the work is the class of performances compliant with the score? And if he is, is he also right that this class of performances is limited to those performances that are perfectly compliant, or may they be partially compliant? And if they may be noncompliant, just how noncompliant may they be? Are musical works created, or might they be invented or even discovered by their composers? How one answers the questions of the immediately preceding sentence will depend strongly on how one answers the others. Let us now try to find some of these answers.

4 The Musical Work

4.1 Introduction and Chapter Conspectus

In the general introduction, I distinguished between internal and external representational functional kinds, designating the former "natural representation" and the latter "artifactual representation." Following Sperber (1996, 83), I maintained that these kinds are instantiated not by individual tokens of representational types, but by "strains or families of concrete representations related both by causal relationships and by similarity of content." I also drew attention to a parallel between this ontology of representation and the ontology of biological species. Just as families of representational tokens instantiate these high-level functional representational kinds (natural representation and artifactual representation), I proposed, species are families of organisms that instantiate high-level biological functional kinds (e.g., *predator* and *prey*, *parasite* and *host*, *peripheral isolate*, or *polytypic species*). The aim of the present chapter[1] is to develop this parallel with respect to *musical* representations. I shall be arguing that musical works may be regarded as species-like entities, as families of causally-historically connected particulars, namely performances (or performance events). Does Sperber's "similarity of content" requirement undermine the alleged parallel between the ontologies of representation and biological species, since no such requirement applies to families of organisms? This is a question we shall address later on in the chapter.

To my knowledge, only one writer has attempted to base a musical ontology on an explicit comparison between musical works and biological species. In an influential article, Nicholas Wolterstorff (1975, 115–142) makes the following three claims concerning musical works:

1. Musical works are norm-kinds (129).
2. Musical works display many close similarities to natural kinds (127).
3. Biological taxa (e.g., categories picked out by folk-biological species-terms like "the grizzly") are natural norm-kinds (127).

Wolterstorff does (in effect) distinguish natural from nominal kinds. *The grizzly* is an example of the former and *red thing* is an example of the latter, though he does not, for all that, wish to deny that *red thing* names a "genuine kind." Although he does not do so explicitly, Wolterstorff also means to distinguish between natural kinds that are norm-kinds and those that are not. Just as any "properly formed" grizzly must share certain predicates "analogically" with *the grizzly*, he proposes, so must any properly formed instance[2] of a musical work share predicates analogically with the work itself.[3] But norm-kinds are just those kinds that may have "improperly formed examples" (ibid., 129), and there can be no improperly formed examples of water or gold any more than there can be an improperly formed electron or quark. Yet these are surely natural kinds if anything is. It is clear that musical works "display many close similarities" only to natural *norm*-kinds, and that all of Wolterstorff's natural norm-kinds are biological entities, that is, species or their traits.

To evaluate a similarity claim, we must inquire into the basis of the comparison, since any two things are similar in some way or other. In this case, the claim is that musical works and biological species are similar with respect to norm-kindhood. But as we shall see, the notion that species are kinds at all is a contested one; and if species are not kinds, they are also not norm-kinds. If the claim that species are norm-kinds collapses, so will Wolterstorff's basis of comparison. And even if species may be construed as natural kinds, the comparison with musical works as norm-kinds is, as we shall see, more problematic than it might at first appear. There are also, as I hope to show, independent reasons for resisting entirely the assimilation of musical works to kinds. Still, species and musical works may, as I have already indicated, be usefully compared. But to make the case for similarity, a different basis of comparison must be found. I shall offer one in the next section. In section 4.3 I shall introduce a naturalized version of normativity, namely proper function, that differs sharply from Wolterstorff's, but which does some of the work of his norm-kinds. In section 4.4 I shall attempt to determine what musical works are. In section 4.5 I shall put some of these conclusions to work in an attempt to determine whether musical works are discovered, invented, or created. Section 4.6 provides a summary and conclusion. Although this chapter and the following ones are mainly interpretive, we shall on occasion move back to the descriptive mode, shifting from the vocabulary metavocabulary to the causal metavocabulary, as in the discussion of meme theory below. Generally, I shall not stop to indicate these shifts, unless required for clarity.

4.2   Biological Species, Musical Works, and Reproductively Established Families

It is difficult these days to find any reputable philosopher of biology willing to countenance species essentialism,[4] the view that species are kinds whose memberships are determined by satisfaction of some set of necessary and sufficient conditions, even genotypical necessary and sufficient conditions. Genotype varies too much between individuals constituting a species, and genotypical considerations can be trumped by historical phylogenetic considerations, or by considerations of reproductive and ecological isolation in determining species identity. Genetic similarity between members of a species is a *result* of species membership, not *determinative* of species membership. As a matter of fact, many philosophers of biology are prepared to deny that biological species are natural kinds at all, holding instead that they are ontological individuals, that is, mereological sums of distributed biomass.[5] According to this view, species are contingently arising and evolving historical lineages of organisms. The fact that species are spatially and temporally restricted individuals, these philosophers claim, explains why names of species do not appear in any biological laws. Because species are individuals, they *instantiate* various biological natural kinds, for example, *predator, prey, parasite, host, lineage, Darwinian clan, Darwinian subclan, Darwinian subcland*,[6] which, according to some,[7] are the subjects of genuine (i.e., universal, unrestricted) evolutionary laws. Other biological natural kinds, for example, *interactor* or *replicator*, which figure in laws of evolutionary biology and genetics, may be instantiated, respectively, by the individual organisms constituting a sexually reproducing species or by their genes. Another view of species ontology agrees that species are individuals, but insists that they are *natural kind–like* to the extent they ground reliable inductions: knowing that an organism belongs to a biological taxon makes it possible to make reliable predictions about it, say, predictions about its metabolic processes and learning capacities (Griffiths 1997, 213). Natural kinds are those kinds traditionally held to ground reliable inductions. Still another view denies that species are individuals and regards them as *sets* of organisms that constitute natural kinds because they figure in legitimate scientific explanations, even if they are not mentioned by name in universal laws (Kitcher 1984). A corollary of this last view is that not all scientific explanation need be nomological in character.

None of this affords much comfort to one who would compare musical works to species construed as natural norm-kinds. Either biological species are individuals (mereological sums of parts) and therefore not kinds at all, natural or otherwise; or they are spatiotemporally restricted sets of organisms whose members are historically, reproductively, and ecologically related, not norm-kinds that must themselves share properties with their properly formed instances. This is not to deny that categories of organisms that play scientific explanatory roles may (with certain caveats) be regarded as natural kinds, or to deny that judgments of "proper formation" may be made regarding them. But it is to assert that judgments of proper formation would be of more use to a health professional (a medical doctor or a veterinarian) than to a biological taxonomist, since they are easily trumped by historical, reproductive, and ecological considerations, and therefore relatively unimportant in developing an adequate species concept or in the determination of species identity.[8] Yet the concerns of musical ontology are the same as those of biological taxonomy: we want both an adequate concept of the musical work and adequate criteria of musical work identity. Once we look a little more carefully at the biological situation, the comparison with biological species as norm-kinds appears to fall well short of its original promise.

Still, the idea that musical works display some important similarities to biological species is a valuable one that can and should be salvaged. To accomplish this we shall need a different basis of comparison, a notion that carves out a category capable of comprising both biological species and musical works. But there is such a notion, namely that of a *reproductively established family* (hereafter "REF"). Ignoring for the moment the important distinction between first- and higher-order REFs, we may define a REF as follows (Millikan 1984, 23):

Any set of entities having the same or similar reproductively established characters derived by repetitive reproductions from the same character of the same model or models form a *first-order reproductively established family*.[9]

This idea is useful on a number of fronts. (1) Both the performances of a musical work and the individual organisms that make up a species collectively constitute, as I shall argue, REFs. (2) A REF may (though it need not) be regarded as natural kind–like. (3) The notion of a REF is neutral between the two competing views of species as mereological sums of biomass and as sets of historically connected organisms. (4) Although not all REFs are subject to normative constraints, many are, including biological species and musical works, because issues of proper function come into play. (The notion of "proper function" will be explained presently.) Organisms (and, as I shall argue, musical performances) proliferate differentially because of selection pressures, and selection pressures are normative constraints because they play a central role in determining which organic functions are proper functions. (5) The REF notion makes perspicuous connection with an approach to musical ontology that has recently become quite popular, namely the construal of musical works as types and their performances as tokens (Bachrach 1971; Harrison 1975; Margolis 1977, 1980; Scruton 1997; Sharpe 1979; Wollheim 1970).[10] Whatever else performances as tokens of a musical type may be, it is difficult to deny that they are reproductively established families of events. (6) The notion of a REF is ontologically parsimonious: it remains uncommitted to the existence of abstract entities. A REF of tokens may be held to instantiate a type *qua* abstract object; or it may be regarded merely as a causally-historically ordered collection of entities (cf. Hull 1986, 221). If the claim that the "sound structure" of a musical work is an "abstract particular" is intelligible at all (see Davies 2001, 38–40, 97), such an entity is a type.[11] On the second, more nominalistic interpretation, there are no abstract types, only tokens-of-a-type (see Margolis 1977). (7) The causal-historical identity conditions that apply to REFs reinforce the conception of musical works as types and lend support to the strong intuition that musical works are particulars that are created by composers, because types exhibit characteristics of particulars.

Types have been considered to be particulars for at least two reasons. First, names of types function naturally as singular logical subjects: we tend to use the definite article when referring to them in ordinary language, for example, "the letter 'a,'" "the violin," "the Model T Ford." We do, it is true, also say "the great white shark"; but this, I submit, points to the fact that biological species possess type characteristics (as they must if they are to be considered REFs). We are much less inclined to say "the quark" or "the electron"—which is not to claim we do not say such things at all: witness the relative familiarity of the expression "the atom." This may tell us something already fairly obvious, namely that the distinction between kind and type is not demarcated with perfect clarity in ordinary language. My suggested principle of demarcation is that types must involve a process of historical reproduction of tokens and the transmission of reproductively established characters,[12] whereas kinds need not. It is frequently acknowledged that the contemporary type–token distinction is due to C. S. Peirce. What is less frequently noticed is that he specifically refers to tokens as "replicas" (1932, 2.247). Regarding sets of tokens as REFs is therefore consistent with, perhaps even mandated by, Peirce's original usage. Interestingly, the Greek root (in its verbal infinitive form) of the English word *type* (*typtein*) means "to strike," and the corresponding substantive term (*typos*) means "blow that is struck." Both Peirce's original usage and these etymological considerations suggest a factor of causal reproduction. Though a replica is a copy, it need not be a *direct* copy.

Second, it is sometimes claimed that types, as opposed to kinds and universals, may be created and destroyed (Margolis 1980, 75). Such a claim would be vindicated if types required the production and reproduction of tokens: any such historical process would constitute a unique, causally linked chain that is initiated at one point in time and comes to an end at another. Do such requirements mandate the nominalistic interpretation of types as tokens-of-a-type, rather than as abstract objects that may or may not be instanced? We shall address this question in section 4 below. Without the requirements of reproduction and historical uniqueness, however, the reasonable claim that types, unlike kinds and universals, "straddle the ontological divide between particular and general"[13] remains unsupported. Wolterstorff, for one, and Kivy (1983a,b, 1988), for another, do not feel the need to distinguish explicitly between "kind," "type," "sort," and "universal" in their discussions.

As REFs, biological species constitute higher-order, and not first-order REFs, in Millikan's terminology. An organism's genes are direct copies of the genes contributed by its immediate ancestors, but the organism itself is not a *direct* copy of anything. It is constructed according to its genotypical plan, and the resulting phenotypical expression is the joint product of its genotype and its environment. Any set of entities so produced according to plan, but not directly copied from any model or prototype, constitutes a higher-order REF. A set of buildings constructed according to a single architectural plan, for example, would also constitute a higher-order reproductively established family. Performances of scored music, interestingly enough, constitute *both* first- and higher-order REFs. Insofar as a musical performance is produced by following a score, it will be a member of a higher-order REF, since (*qua* compliant performance) it was not directly copied from another performance.[14] Still, the performance is a copy, albeit an indirect copy mediated by the score. But the compliant performance will also be a member of at least one *first-order* REF, namely a REF of interpretations. As an interpretation, the performance will be modeled on earlier performances, most likely those emanating from the school of interpretation to which the performer belongs; or it will be modeled on interpretations the performer admires. Interpretations do not arise in a cultural vacuum, but emanate from schools or traditions of performance. This suggests that although Sharpe may overstate the case in arguing that the musical types of which performances are tokens just *are* interpretations and not works at all, he is onto something important. Copies of scores themselves also constitute first- and higher-order REFs. They are either copies printed from a single master template which itself is a copy of the original autograph score or of earlier master templates, thereby constituting a higher-order REF;[15] or they are direct copies of the autograph score or of copies of these copies, thereby constituting a first-order REF; or, in the absence of an autograph score, they are copies of some version held to be authoritative. Performances of musical works that are not scored, that belong to a performance tradition lacking musical notation, on the other hand, will constitute first-order REFs exclusively. Since buildings and musical performances, given Millikan's definitions, constitute perfectly acceptable REFs, REFs, it is clear, need not be natural kinds or even natural kind–like.

4.3   Reproductively Established Families, Co-evolution, and Memes

Not every REF is subject to selection pressures. A set of footprints constitutes a REF that is not so constrained. Biological REFs, however, are subject to selection pressures because they proliferate or do not proliferate in a competitive environment depending on the adaptations of their members. There is also a normative requirement of fidelity of replication at work, namely fidelity to the sequence of nucleotides that constitutes the gene; but this requirement is importantly limited. Every biological replication event produces small variations;[16] and those genetic variations that code for phenotypic traits of increased adaptation will, leaving aside contingent factors like genetic drift or environmental cataclysms, crowd out the original forms. Millikan terms the capacities of organic traits and mechanisms that enable their possessors to proliferate successfully "proper functions."

It is important to bear in mind that though Millikan's theory of REFs and proper functions is inspired by evolutionary biology, it is not intended as a contribution to the philosophy of biology. It is a theory of signs, and as such a contribution to philosophical semiotic and to the philosophies of language and mind. Millikan's principal concern is the development of a naturalistic account both of intentionality and of content for mental and linguistic representations ("intentional icons," as she calls them in the general case). Of particular concern to her are those public representations that carry propositional content, namely, declarative sentences. Tokens of declarative sentences proliferate, form continuing REFs, to the extent they serve "adapted" proper functions: they are produced and consumed by mechanisms present in the brains of speakers and hearers because declarative sentences have historically adapted speakers and hearers to their environments by mapping those environments frequently enough with a degree of accuracy sufficient to satisfy the standard evolutionary tradeoff between cost and benefit. The intentionality of representations depends on their derived[17] proper functions, what they are supposed to be doing according to natural design. If declarative sentences did not realize these functions, then speakers would stop producing them and hearers would stop responding to them. And if declarative sentences hadn't satisfied these constraints historically, the neural mechanisms for producing and using them would not have proliferated.

I do not endorse without qualification Millikan's original and challenging evolutionary account of mental content and sentence meaning. As already indicated in the general introduction, a strongly externalist account of meaning like Millikan's does not, in my view, exhaust everything we wish to say about issues of meaning, which include normative issues. In particular, although the evolutionary approach to meaning and intentionality does to some extent succeed in naturalizing their normative aspects, it does not adequately address the interpretive side of meaning and the issue of the achievement of reflective equilibrium regarding the normative commitments of speakers. In addition, principles of natural selection cannot, without supplementation, account for the proliferation of cultural items. Let me explain why.

To use Sperber's (1996, 134ff) terminology: a mental module possesses a proper domain, the environment in which it was designed to function, and an actual domain, a possibly different environment in which it presently does function. The proper domain of the human visual apparatus was the African savanna containing landmarks, dangerous nonhuman predators, and no dangerous artifacts other than primitive weapons. Its actual domain now includes the urban and suburban environments containing landmarks, dangerous human predators, and dangerous artifacts including weapons and nonweapons. Still, the proper function of the visual module translates smoothly to its contemporary actual domain. A human mental module may, however, also operate in a cultural domain. That is, humans may turn a naturally designed neural mechanism, say the auditory system, to novel uses by way of a "cultural exaptation"[18] in an "artificial" (i.e., humanly designed) cultural environment. Such novel uses initially cannot be proper functions of the neural mechanism because these uses are not the result of the application of natural selective forces, since the existence of the cultural domain depends on the prior existence of the neural mechanism:

> Note that the very existence of a cultural domain is an effect of the existence of a module. Therefore, initially at least, a module cannot be an adaptation to its own cultural domain. It must have been selected because of a pre-existing proper domain. In principle, it might become a function of the module to handle its own cultural domain. This would be the case when the ability of the module to handle its cultural domain contributed to its remaining a permanent feature of a viable species. The only clear case of an adaptation of a module to its own effects is that of the linguistic faculty. (Sperber 1996, 145)

The anatomy and physiology of Beethoven's auditory apparatus were basically the same as those of the apparatus possessed by our Upper Paleolithic ancestors 30,000 years ago. But 30,000 years is a "blink of an eyelid" in evolutionary terms (Pfeiffer 1982, 13).[19] Could it really be the case that the proper functions of musical utterances like Beethoven's are derived from the proper function of the auditory system and that musical art is that system's proper domain? (I doubt it.) Or must we tell a more complicated tale that loops through cultural exaptation? (I think so.) Still, the new use of the biological device must exploit *some* proper function, either of the device itself, or *perhaps the proper function of one of its homologous ancestors*. In chapter 2, recall, I proposed that musical audition exploited the proper function of the lateral line, the homologous ancestor of the organ of Corti. Interestingly, Sperber (1996, 141–142) offers musical art, a sophisticated, normatively governed cultural practice, as an example of a cultural domain. We shall return to the issue of cultural exaptation in chapter 6.

But similar points can be made regarding Millikan's representations of choice, namely declarative sentences. It may be, as Sperber seems prepared to allow, that the biological proper function of the language module, assuming there is one, is to produce declarative sentences that are true and mutually consistent. But producing *science*—a body of sententially expressed doctrine that is not only true and consistent, but also (ideally) maximally comprehensive and systematic—surely is not one of its proper functions, nor is it a proper function of the naive or folk physics module, assuming humans have one of these. Science, like music, is a cultural domain; and just as humans have performed a cultural exaptation of the proper functions of the auditory system and have acquired a taste for musical art, so have they culturally exapted the language module, the folk physics module, and perhaps the subitizing arithmetic module as well, thereby *indulging an acquired taste for comprehensive, systematically organized scientific truth*. As a result, if we are to take a Darwininian approach to culture, it must not only be evolutionary: it must be *co-evolutionary*. The cultural domain, that is, constitutes a new competitive environment that has achieved some independence of biological evolution by breaking loose of, indeed even on occasion by subverting, the biological purposes from which it originally arose. Artificial sweeteners and birth control devices, for example, are cultural artifacts that allow us to exploit, but also to subvert, the biological purposes of sweet tastes and sexual pleasure.[20] Although Millikan's notion of proper function is clearly evolutionary, it is not so clearly co-evolutionary, for she ties the proper functions of all representations directly to the naturally designed mechanisms that produce them, and she does not make Sperber's distinction between proper and cultural domains. Indeed, this is indicated in the very title of her book, *Language, Thought, and Other Biological Categories* (1984). Still, her theory of representation can be accommodated to a genuinely co-evolutionary approach if we recognize the possibility of cultural exaptation of biological proper functions.

In the context of Millikan's theory, families of representations, both public and internal ("in the head"), are important examples of types that have both derived and direct proper functions. Concerning aesthetic symbolism Millikan has little to say, and what she does say, relegating aesthetic objects exclusively to the realm of nonconventional improvised signs (1984, 123), is, by her own admission,[21] in some error. A nonconventional improvised sign (e.g., a charade-like bodily display used to communicate with someone with whom one does not share any language) will not be a member of a REF, since its production will tend to be a one-time affair tailored to some uniquely occurring set of circumstances. It will not be copied directly from any previous models, nor will it serve as a model for any subsequent signs. In chapters 2 and 3 I argued that music is representational and bears nonconceptual content. I argued in chapter 3 that music is symbolic, that is, that it consists of conventional symbols subject to syntactic or quasi-syntactic formation rules. To the extent musical symbols are conventional, they form REFs. And to the extent they are produced and consumed, their proliferation (or lack thereof) is subject to some set of normative constraints, albeit not the environment-mapping constraints to which declarative sentences are subject. In chapter 6 I shall propose an account of what these constraints are and an account of what the (culturally exaptational) "direct proper function" of musical performances might be. Performances (now including recorded performances[22]) of certain musical works have proliferated massively, judging by frequency of their appearance on concert programs and recordings, and have crowded out performances of other works, as have performances that exemplify certain *interpretive approaches* to these works. Consider the amazing fecundity of the "faithfulness to the composer's intentions" tradition of orchestral performance initiated by Toscanini. Like declarative sentences, if musical symbols ceased doing whatever it is they do for producers and users, if they ceased to fulfill their proper functions, they would not continue to be produced and so would stop proliferating.

Considerations such as these bring us into the vicinity of so-called *meme* theory, a family of selectionist accounts of the proliferation of cultural items. Although memes are, as I shall be arguing later, a subcategory of REFs, the meme notion is less useful than the notion of a REF because it suffers from serious vagueness and is understood by various theorists in manifold and conflicting ways. Although Dawkins originally defined the meme as a "unit of imitation" (1976, 206), his later formulation as "unit of information" (1982, 109) seems to have gained some degree of acceptance. Durham (1991, 421–422) uses the term "to represent the variable unit of transmission in cultural evolution" and suggests that "the meme [*sic.*] should refer to any kind, amount, and configuration of information in culture that shows both variation and coherent transmission." Dennett (1995, 353–354) tells us that "what is preserved and transmitted in cultural evolution is *information*—in a media-neutral, language-neutral sense." Blackmore (1999, 66) proposes to "use the term 'meme' indiscriminately to refer to memetic information in any of its many forms; including ideas, the brain structures that instantiate those ideas, the behaviors these brain structures produce, and their versions in books, recipes, maps and written music. As long as that information can be copied by a process we may broadly call 'imitation,' then it counts as a meme."

The problem with these characterizations is that the expression "information" serves as a catch-all for any and every variety of content, including, but not limited to, representational content both conceptual and nonconceptual, and clearly goes well beyond the information-theoretic conception of uncertainty reduction, as well as the notion of informational structure discussed in chapter 2. In the information-theoretic sense, recall, information, unlike conceptual content, is neither true nor false, accurate nor inaccurate; and the same goes for the information contained in an informational structure until that structure is used as a representation by an interpreter. "Both genes and memes," Durham (1991, 422) tells us, "are units of information (though of different kinds)." A gene, understood as a segment of DNA (including regulatory sequences) that is transcribed into molecules of mRNA encoding polypeptides, is clearly an informational structure as we have defined it; but it is not at all clear what a meme or its informational content is, nor whether memes should be individuated by historical descent, by representational content, or some combination of both.[23] As we shall see in the next section, this has the potential to cause conceptual difficulties for meme theory. But for now, let us ask a more basic question. Should a co-evolutionary approach to culture rely on *selectionist* principles at all? Sperber thinks not (see also Boyer 2001, 38–40). For him, an epidemiological model is more appropriate than a selectionist one. Let us now attempt to determine whether he is right about this.

Although it is the first objection that gets top billing, Sperber (1996, 104) in fact lodges three distinct objections against selectionist models of cultural proliferation:

1. A Darwinian selectionist process requires high-fidelity replication if adaptive mutational features are to be preserved between generations. The proliferation of cultural representations involves their communication from mind to mind. But communica-

tion requires reconstruction on the part of a receiver, and is not simply the result of a process of extracting a pre-packaged semantic content. What a receiver derives from a communication will depend on context and will exploit pragmatic principles of implicature, especially the principle of relevance, which, for Sperber, motivates a variety of inferences on the part of the receiver. If someone tells me that Tom is in trouble, I may, depending on context and conversational cues, infer that evil events have befallen a close friend or that they have befallen a prominent political figure. Context and cues will also shape the inferences I make regarding the nature of the evil events that have transpired. Because of this aspect of reconstruction, Sperber claims, exact or nearly exact replication is the exception or limiting case with regard to the communication of cultural representations, rather than the rule, as it is in genetic replication. Representations are almost invariably transformed when communicated, not almost invariably faithfully replicated as genes are.

2. In the cultural context, degree of influence counts more than sheer differential rate of reproduction. Replicated tokens of printed junk surely outnumber tokens, both internal and public, of difficult, but highly influential, cultural items like relativity theory or Gödel's proof, cultural items that few people are able to represent mentally.

3. A cultural item like a token of the song "Yankee Doodle" or a particular clay pot has an indeterminate number of immediate "ascendants" on which it was modeled. A gene at a particular locus on a chromosome, on the other hand, has just one immediate ascendant. The genotype of an organism that belongs to a sexually reproducing species has just two.[24]

Let us grant these points. It does not follow that the epidemiological model is superior to a selectionist one.

As to objection (1): Universal Darwinism is a highly abstract selectionist schema that requires reliable *heritability*, not replication that is both direct and faithful. "Just because replicator theory has its origins in biological theory, where the archetypal replicators, genes, have astonishingly high copying fidelity," Plotkin (2003, 155) points out, "is no reason to suppose that similar fidelity is necessary when applying replicator theory in other realms." Even biological natural selection requires the high fidelity of direct genetic replication only on the Dawkins view of gene selectionism, the view that genes are the *sole units of biological selection* and that all other biological levels, cell, organism, deme, species, and clade are gene "vehicles," or aspects of the "extended phenotype." I do not claim that this view is obviously wrong; but it is controversial. Even Dawkins's ally G. C. Williams, the only other biologist to whom Sperber (1996) refers,[25] has in recent years moderated his commitment to it (see Gould 2002, 641).[26] According to Darwinian orthodoxy, the organism, not the gene, is the unit of selection. According to Dawkins's antipode Gould, "individuals" on all biological levels, including species and clades, are units of selection.[27] I also do not claim that the Gould view is obviously right, for it, too, is controversial. What this dispute shows is that the question as to what the biological unit or units of selection are remains a contested one. It is also one that I am not competent to address, much less to resolve in any conclusive way. All that is required to counter Sperber's first objection, however, is the entirely reasonable assumption that genes need not be regarded as the only units of biological natural selection. This assumption will allow us to deny the claim that natural selection is the wrong model for cultural transmission because the replication of representations does not achieve the high level of fidelity achieved by gene replication. Compare Gould (2002, 622): "faithful replication is not—and never was—the defining characteristic (or even a necessary property) of a unit of selection."

That Sperber should have focused his attention on Dawkins, the originator of meme theory, the dominant cultural selectionist model, is quite understandable. But a cultural selectionist theory need not follow principles of gene selectionism. For the opponent of gene selectionism, all that is required for biological selection to go forward on some level is that fidelity be high *enough* for a significant rate of *inheritance* relative to variation of traits across generations of biological entities. Replication, moreover, need not be direct copying, as it is not in the case of the production of higher-order REFs. But how similar do cultural replicas have to be to meet standards of fidelity? The answer: it depends on the cultural item in question. As we shall see, in the special case of scored music, requirements of fidelity of replication may, under some conditions, meet or even exceed genetic standards.

As to objections (2) and (3): An epidemic is just a Darwinian parasite/host phenomenon as seen from the perspective of the host rather than the parasite. Biologically speaking, *parasite* and *host* constitute competing populations of organisms. Using contagion language, therefore, does not really buy us any new purchase on either the influence or the multiple ascendants problem, especially if we are to take seriously the kind of anthropological materialism Sperber recommends, namely, a nominalism that regards cultural types as tokens-of-a-type. When we use the language of contagion we are still talking about the proliferation of genes and organisms with small numbers of ascendants, namely the proliferation of organisms that belong to the parasite species and the "plurification" (Gould 2002) of their genes. The contagion language does not buy us anything—that is, *unless* we shift the analogy between biology and culture from a *species/organism ontology* to a *disease/case ontology* along with a disease/case *symptomology* (see Boyer 2001, 46). If we do, *then* we may be able to talk with greater ease about strength of influence (*spread* of the disease, stronger and weaker *cases* of the disease) and multiple ascendants (multiple exposures, multiple pathogens?). This will also encourage us to direct our attention to mental functions, especially strongly modular ones, which facilitate proliferation of some cultural "parasites" as opposed to others. It would be foolish to deny that making this shift is useful, indeed indispensable, for the notion of cultural exaptation depends on it. But we should not imagine that this somehow disqualifies the selectionist model.

In fact, Sperber exploits both approaches by trading on a process–product ambiguity in the notion of "representation." Representation (i.e., representing) is something a mind does; and a representation is the product of such activity. To exploit the epidemiological contagion analogy, a representation must be regarded as a *state* into which the mind enters (like a disease state) when it represents. But Sperber also wants, as well he should, to hold on to the organism analogy and regard representations as products, for he countenances public representational tokens, and any such a token is a product, not a state of anyone's mind. He wants, that is, to see a representational token as a material particular, not a state, that carries out a representational function (Sperber 1996, 25):

Just as one can say that a human population is inhabited by a much larger population of viruses, so one can say that it is inhabited by a much larger population of mental representations.

Notice, by the way, that the analogy here is between representations and organisms, not, as with Dawkins, between memes and genes.

The epidemiological model of cultural transmission, I conclude, demonstrates no obvious advantage over the selectionist model because either it assumes gene selectionism; or it is just a selectionist story told from the host point of view (i.e., an epidemic is the spread of a parasite in a host population); or it trades on an ambiguity between species/organism and disease/case ontologies. Still, the three challenges to selectionist accounts of culture posed by Sperber remain. Can a *co-evolutionary* selectionist account that takes something from Hull and Millikan on the one side and Sperber on the other, specifically a selectionist account of *musical* representation, meet them? I believe it can.

(1) As to the fidelity issue: Let me begin on an irenic note. There are aspects of the story I have told about musical representation that fit very well with Sperber's reconstruction model of transmission. The musical performance, I proposed, is a pushmi-pullyu representation that motivates the hearer to construct the musical plan of the piece. The musical plan, recall, is an instantiation of the nested hierarchical structures and rules of the Lerdahl and Jackendoff theory which constitute the syntax of the musical performance. The syntax of the musical performance, recall, goes beyond the syntax of the notational score. Public musical representations consist of printed scores and performances; and we saw that the notational score does not fully specify the syntax of the performance. The musical plan, then, is one variety of musical representation that is not copied at all but constructed by the listener from the musical surface. This fits Sperber's reconstruction model very well, which is not surprising given the influence Chomsky's generative theory of language has had on his thinking about these issues.

But the musical plan constructed in the mind of the listener is *not* the unit of cultural selection: the performance token is; and the proliferation of these cultural representations can be explained perfectly well using selectionist principles. Hull (1982, 311), with whose view I have already expressed some solidarity (see note 12 above), is of the opinion that both contagion critics and other critics who hold that culture cannot be explained on selectionist principles because the transmission of cultural representations is allegedly Lamarckian trade on a trait–replicator ambiguity, a close relative of the process–product ambiguity noted above. Like a disease *state* (the state of infection), a Lamarckian acquired *trait* can be passed from one organism to another. Culture may then look Lamarckian if "ideas" (i.e., representations) are regarded as acquired traits (characteristics) of organisms; but it looks Darwinian if they are regarded as replicators (individuals), the view Hull recommends. Similarly, the spread of representations in a culture may look like a contagion if representations are regarded as mental states; but it looks like proliferation by natural selection if they are regarded as replicators. Accepting a version of meme theory, Hull, like Dawkins, regards genes as the only *biological* replicators. But unlike Dawkins, he is not a gene selectionist, regarding this view as "overly parsimonious" (Hull 1982, 277), and prefers to see organisms as interactors, rather than as gene "vehicles" in the Dawkins sense. It is the interactors, not the replicators, that are the units of selection. But for Hull, memes, unlike genes, are "naked": they are not housed in interactors but are themselves interactors, as well as being replicators (ibid., 307):

The chief difference which I see between biological and sociocultural evolution is that genes play two roles in biological evolution (autocatalysis and heterocatalysis), while memes perform only one (autocatalysis). Genes not only produce other genes, they also produce organisms of which they are a part.[28]

I have advocated a view of cultural replication that is relaxed enough to recognize the members of both first- and higher-order REFs as *replicas*, even if not necessarily as *replicators* (though members of biological first-order REFs *may* be replicators). But nowhere does Hull suggest, nor should he suggest, that in order to function as his cultural replicator-interactors, memes must achieve genetic standards of fidelity. Once again, all that is required is a standard high enough to ensure reliable inheritance of features relative to rate of variation; and once again, the standard in force will depend on the cultural item in question. If cultural representations are construed both as replicas and as interactors, the selectionist model of cultural transmission faces no in-principle difficulty.

(2) As to the influence issue: The proper functions of representations include influencing the behaviors of representation users. If declarative sentences did not adapt speakers and hearers to their environments, recall, speakers would stop uttering them, hearers would stop responding to them, and they would cease to proliferate. If hearers

stopped complying with imperatives, speakers would stop uttering them, and they would cease to proliferate. If musical representations stopped doing whatever it is their proper function to do, even assuming, as I shall argue in chapter 6, that this function is the result of cultural exaptation and not of natural selection, musicians would stop producing them, audiences would stop listening to them, and they would cease to proliferate. One measure of influence is effect on behavior; and in all cases, influence on behavior is part of the proper function of representations. Unlike bins of useless photocopies, representations must, in order to proliferate, get into and remain in the minds of users. Useless photocopies are likely to fail any reasonable longevity requirement and, as a result, to fail the fecundity requirement over time.

(3) As to the many ascendants issue: This is a problem only if the co-evolutionist ties the selection of representations needlessly closely to biological evolution. If genes, species, and representations are all regarded as varieties of REFs, *both first-order and higher-order*, with representational tokens regarded both as replicas and interactors, there is no reason to insist that every representational token must, like biological ones, have only one or two immediate ascendants. All that is required is that the representations have some definite ascendants, whatever their number. Because the reliably inherited environment of representations includes the minds of users, this reliably inherited environment is quite different from the physical environment of any species. Representations can be stored in the suspended animation of memory, while remaining available for replication throughout the lifetime of the organism. Exosomatic storage of representations extends this availability even further: representations may stay dormant without replication for long periods of time but still remain available, as was the case, for example, with Mendel's published results. But once these admittedly significant differences between biology and culture are recognized, there is no reason to conclude that they debilitate the selectionist paradigm.

4.4   The Identity of the Musical Work

In sections 4.1 and 4.2 I proposed acceptance of the Wolterstorff comparison of the ontology of musical works with the ontology of biological species, while shifting the basis of comparison from the norm-kind to the REF. This shift brought into focus a host of issues concerning the reproduction and transmission of tokens of cultural types that were sorted out in section 4.3. Let us now retrieve the main thread of argument and attempt to develop the reformed biological analogy in some detail. Earlier on, I suggested that certain musical contexts impose standards of fidelity even more stringent than those operative in the case of gene replication. In the case of scored musical works there seems to be a standard that is prima facie even more stringent than the one operative in the case of gene replication: performances, including performances from memory, it is thought, ideally should comply exactly with the notational aspects of the score. This introduces an apparent strong essentialist element into the determination of the identity of a scored musical work that has no place in contemporary conceptions of species identity. Noncompliance with the score in musical performance is strongly discouraged, indeed is considered so serious a threat to the identity of the work as to have moved some theorists to deny that a performance with even one noncompliant note (or sound event) counts as an instance of the work. The concern here involves a variety of sorites paradox: how many wrong notes does it take to change the identity of the work? Without a principled answer, the opening motif of Beethoven's Fifth Symphony, Goodman (1976, 187) notoriously warns, could quickly morph into "Three Blind Mice."

Levinson (1990a, 87n34) has attempted to finesse this issue by distinguishing between instances and performances: an *instance* of a work must exhibit perfect fidelity to the notational score, but a *performance* of it need not. We may, that is, be offered a performance of a work, "possibly a great one," that is not an instance of it. But this just postpones the difficulty, for what work is this possibly great performance a performance of? For Levinson, it is the one the performer intended to perform, but failed to instance (ibid., 86). In order to have provided a performance of the work, he says, the performer must succeed "to a reasonable degree" (ibid., n33): "what differentiates poor or marginal performance from nonperformance, is for many compositions perhaps marked by the ability of an informed and sensitive listener to grasp, at least roughly, what S/PM [sound/performing-means] structure is struggling to be presented." But what is it to "grasp" an S/PM structure? Absent some mysterious act of intuition, surely it is to take the performance to be trying to instantiate the abstract S/PM structure, which just is to take it as a near instance of the S/PM structure. But this just lands us back in Goodman's sorites paradox: how similar to a genuine instance must the attempted performance be in order to achieve performance of that work? And why is the defective performance not an instance of another work?

The REF notion may be of some help here. A scored musical work, I have suggested, is a REF of scores and performances. Compliance with the score certainly serves as one important epistemological criterion of musical work identity, perhaps even, for scored music, the most important one: compliance is good, indeed very strong, *evidence* that a given performance is a token of a certain work. But as a metaphysical identity condition, perfect or even close compliance with the score is, as I now shall be arguing, neither necessary nor sufficient. The principal *determiner* of musical identity for scored music, I propose, is the fact that a performance arises causally from a performer's visual interaction with a token of the score, and not from its compliance with the score. A performance of a work could also derive causally from a performer's aural interaction with an earlier performance of that work; but this is unusual with scored music. In either case, the question we should be asking is not how compliant with the score must an attempted performance be to be a performance of a particular work, but rather, *how noncompliant must it be to trump its causal provenance.*

Levinson (1980a, 105) takes an opposing view:

The identity of a performance, say, is more a matter of what work the performer has in mind, of how the performer conceives of what he or she is doing than of what work is the causal source of the score or memory which directly guides the performer in producing the appropriate sound event.

This approach, however, will spike any attempt to gain leverage from the biological analogy in dealing with the metaphysical problem of musical work identity. It also generates counterintuitive consequences. Suppose, says Levinson (1980a, 99n23), that

I intend to play a famous waltz by Y I have not heard and have never seen the score of. Someone devilishly gives me a score of the Dadaistic composer Z's recent waltz, which strangely enough has the same S/PM structure as Y's waltz. I think that the sound event I produce is a performance of Y's waltz, not of Z's waltz. Yet there is no continuous causal chain running from Y's creative act of indication to my performance of Y's waltz. . . . I am inclined to believe that where intentional and causal criteria conflict, the former will generally determine the identity of the performance.

But why should we accept this? Either Z's waltz was lifted from Y's score or it wasn't. If it was, then there *is* a "continuous causal chain" running from Y's creative act of indication to Levinson's performance of Y's waltz. If it wasn't, then why the reference to Dada?[29] But what support is there for Levinson's claim that intentional criteria trump causal criteria regarding identity determination?

Assume, per hypothesis, that there is *not* a causal connection between Levinson's performance and Y's creative act of indication. Suppose the waltz is scored for piano, four hands. Suppose, moreover, that it is none other than Levinson's performing partner, devil of a fellow that he is, who has perpetrated the hoax. In this case, Levinson and his mischievous colleague would be simultaneously engaged in performances of two different pieces while reading the same printed score, a result which, while not beyond all conceivability, strains credulity.[30] Better, I think, just to say that Levinson thought he was performing Y's waltz but wasn't. If, contrary to hypothesis, Levinson is already acquainted with Y's score and with earlier performances of it, his own or others, the identity conditions of his performance are considerably murkier, for now there is an alternative reproductive causal chain extending back to Y's score and its performances. As a result, Levinson's present effort might be claimed by three different REFs: a higher-order REF of performances of Z's waltz, a higher-order REF of performances of Y's waltz, and a first-order REF of *interpretations* of Y's waltz. Still, unless Levinson has the piece committed to memory and is using the substituted score little or not at all, we should say (I maintain) that the causal provenance of the score read in the present performance trumps the alternative causal path, and that it is Z's waltz he is performing.

Levinson's view, however, might be defended in the following way. The required intentional connection between performer and what is performed may be considerably weaker than Levinson claims, because "it focuses on the score in hand" and "is not directly aimed at a particular composer or work." Nevertheless, in order to perform a score the performer must identify "the musico-historical context relevant to interpreting the notation" (Davies 2001, 165). If the respective musico-historical contexts of the two waltzes are as different as nineteenth-century Vienna and twentieth-century Paris, then perhaps Levinson is *not* performing Z's waltz after all, despite the use of Z's score. Following a score is certainly an intentional act, and interpreting any score presupposes performance practices not explicitly specified in the notation. In this case, however, the contextual differences would not, in my view, rise to work-constitutive status and trump causal provenance. If Levinson is using a score that derives from Z's creative act of indication, I claim he is performing Z's waltz, even if misinterpreting it.

Although Davies rejects Levinson's view that intentions generally trump causal provenance, he agrees that Levinson succeeds in performing Y's waltz, but only because the trickster *knew* the respective scores of the two waltzes to be notationally identical. This conclusion is based on a counterfactual analysis, the strategy Davies employs to deal with a variety of such thought experiments: if Z's score had not matched Y's exactly, the diabolical substitution would not have been made and Levinson would have played from Y's score. Therefore, it is Y's score, and not Z's, that is determinative of Levinson's performance. If Y's score had been different, Levinson's performance would have been different, whereas Levinson's performance would not have been affected by any change in Z's score. Yet, Davies concludes, if the substitution is entirely accidental and unrecognized, it is Z's waltz that is performed, because the counterfactuals come out differently: it cannot be said that the substitution would not have occurred (ibid., 173).

There is nothing objectionable per se about this analysis. How the intuitions fall out will depend on how much weight is accorded the counterfactuals concerning the matching process and how much weight is accorded the performance's actual reproductive history. Note that Davies (2001, 79, 169) thinks that two composers, working *independently* in the same musico-historical situation, who pen notationally indistinguishable scores have composed the same work. Presumably, the reasoning is once again counterfactual: which score is used would not materially affect the character of a performance of the work. But Davies also endorses, or seems sympathetic to, the analogy between musical works and biological species I have suggested: "A male lion that cannot roar is a lion because it came from a lion zygote. Like me, Fisher thinks instances of musical works, especially malformed ones, must stand in an appropriate causal relation to the composer's creation of the work" (ibid., 176n14). Yet as we shall see, two independently originating lineages would not count biologically as the same species, whatever the phenotypic similarity between the organisms they comprise.

A determination to take seriously an informed comparison between biological species and musical works recommends that we assume that only a performance with the right reproductive history qualifies as a token of that particular work. An important corollary is that if a performance lacks the right reproductive history, *no degree of compliance with the score*, even perfect compliance, will suffice to make it an instance of a given work. This makes causal history a metaphysically necessary condition for musical work identity.[31] As we shall see, however, it is not a sufficient condition, for there are requirements of structural affinity that must be satisfied or, perhaps better said, must not be violated. Considered in this way, the musical case does display some interesting similarities to the biological one, if we take, as many do these days, either a strict cladist view or an "evolutionary" view (which combines cladist and pheneticist elements) of species identity (Ridley 1986, 6ff).

Pheneticism, which in its pure form is now widely discredited, was an attempt to determine taxonomy by applying mathematical similarity metrics to a large number of *equally weighted* phenotypical characters of organisms without invoking phylogenetic history at all. The organisms that come out closest in multidimensional similarity space after the calculations are completed are grouped together into taxa at various levels. The problem is that equally valid bases for clustering in similarity space yield incompatible results. Each dimension of similarity space is correlated with a specific character. As the clusters form in multidimensional similarity space, it can happen that a given organism[32] will be claimed by two different clusters, depending on what principles are employed. For example, if the *nearest* organism of one cluster is nearer to a given organism than the *nearest* of a second cluster, but the *farthest* organism of the second cluster is nearer than the *farthest* of the first cluster, to which group should the given organism belong? Or should the organism's distance from an *average* of the positions of the organisms forming the two competing clusters count? There is no way to resolve such ambiguities in an objective, nonarbitrary way. Assuming similarity space to be Euclidean, there is also more than one mathematical metrical technique that can be used to calculate distance, with different techniques yielding different results. For the sake of simplicity, consider two organisms located in a two-dimensional similarity space. Will the distance between them be the hypotenuse of the right triangle whose sides are their distances from each other along each of the two dimensions? Or will the distance between them be the *average* of the distances along each of the two dimensions? Pheneticists were unable to supply a principled defense of one technique over the other. Even the decision on the part of pheneticists to weight all characters equally has been criticized as arbitrary and a priori. As a result of these difficulties, the pheneticist account of species identity collapsed into subjectivity.[33]

Cladism (called "phylogenetic systematics" by its originator Willi Hennig) began as an attempt to provide objective conditions of species identity. On the strict cladist view, what counts for species membership is exclusively phylogenetic history:

speciation occurs at the branching points in the unique phylogenetic treelike pattern that has been traced out by life on the planet, *and only at such points*. Only monophyletic groups (lineages with neither gaps nor branching events that postdate a most recent common ancestor) count as species. Structural similarities and differences may be indicators of these causal-historical relations, but they are not determiners of species identity; only the causal-historical relations are. Moreover, a lineage structurally similar to an already existing species that came into existence at a later time but is not causally connected to the existing species would not, according to a strict cladist, constitute a continuation of the existing species. It would be a new species, whatever its structural or morphological similarity (Hull 1978). Such considerations cohere nicely with Levinson's reasonable insistence that a musical work is not merely an abstract sound/performing-means structure, but such a structure "indicated" by an individual (the composer) at a definite time and place within a musical context that has a history.

   Levinson (1980b, 81) briefly considers the evolutionary comparison himself. But he is suspicious of Wolterstorff's assimilation of musical works to biological norm-kinds, and rightly so. For one thing, Wolterstorff's essentialist conception of species membership is crude and outdated: there just is no set of "features which a thing cannot lack if it is to be a properly formed example" (Wolterstorff 1975, 128) of a biological species, since the "proper form" of a species, assuming such a notion is even intelligible from an evolutionary point of view, is not static but varies historically.[34] For another, Wolterstorff is not sufficiently sensitive to the important differences between the biological and musical cases. Levinson (1990a, 260n193) observes that musical works possess no causally relevant inner constitution that plays a role analogous to that of the genotype of an organism; and he doubts that the notion of "natural function" has any application in the musical sphere. Both points are well taken. As to the first, biological species may qualify as natural kinds (or as natural kind–like) to the extent they ground reliable inductions and figure in scientific explanations. But this depends on the presence of underlying causal mechanisms that maintain the rich cluster of projectable properties that natural kinds have and that nominal kinds lack. We can, to be sure, make reliable predictions about current performances of musical works based on past ones. But insofar as these are *causally* grounded and explanatory, the relevant causal mechanisms in question are to be found in the brains, bodies, and instruments of the performers, and not in the musical work, if by "causal mechanisms" we mean (as I think we should mean) "physical causal mechanisms." Yet the musical work is supposedly the norm-kind. As to the second point, though we might agree that Levinson's notion of "natural function" (were we able to render it precise) might well have no application to musical works, a more careful handling of the many varieties of REFs and the varieties of *proper functions* appropriate to their members would, I think, be capable of muting such concerns. Levinson also doubts that S/PM structures, as opposed to biological species, can have properly and improperly formed instances: they are either perfectly instanced or not instanced at all. But this, I have argued, is dubious.

Although essentialism may be a discredited view in biology, the essentialist element we have discerned in the determination of the identity of scored musical works is too obvious to be ignored. This, as we saw, is an important point of disanalogy between the biological and musical cases. Indeed, on a strict cladist view of species, *no degree of dissimilarity*, even significant genetic divergence (should it occur), is sufficient to trump species identity. Strict cladists, that is, do not recognize speciation by anagenesis, speciation within a single phylogenetic branch in the absence of a new branching event. Without a branching event, a historically connected group of organisms remains the species it is regardless of structural or morphological alterations. A branching event begins with the isolation, initially effected through mere physical separation, of a subgroup belonging to a population of interbreeding organisms. This separation blocks gene flow, and as the Darwinian processes of mutation, selection, and inheritance go forward, interbreeding between the two groups that produce fecund offspring eventually ceases to be possible. At this point a speciation event is consummated; but its inception is identified with the original isolation event. Cladistic speciation, therefore, has a mildly counterintuitive retroactive aspect to it. Nor will a strict cladist countenance as a taxon anything other than a monophyletic group, whatever degree of similarity, genetic or morphological, happens to obtain between organisms.

Biologists who reject strict cladism in favor of what sometimes is referred to as the "evolutionary" view of species identity also emphasize phylogenetic provenance (see Ridley 1986). But these biologists are willing to let structural considerations trump causal provenance if they are significant enough. So, for example, whereas evolutionary taxonomists class the *crocodilia* with lizards as *reptilia* on the basis of robust phenotypical similarities, and do not classify *aves* with the *crocodilia* because of rapid and extreme phenotypical divergence, cladists refuse to do the former, because crocodiles and birds have a more recent common ancestor than do crocodiles and lizards, and happily do the latter. For the cladists, the *reptilia* simply do not constitute a well-formed monophyletic group. Other biologists regard capacity and opportunity for interbreeding as primary, which creates notorious difficulties regarding the identities of nonsexually reproducing species; still others emphasize ecological considerations. The last two views are for fairly obvious reasons irrelevant to the musical case. The evolutionary view, however, is not: if musical works are to be compared to species, an approach like the evolutionary one seems to fit best, since there clearly comes a point at which a noncompliant performance will no longer count as a performance of a work, whatever its causal provenance.[35]

Unfortunately, there seems to be little consensus, either within biological science or in the philosophy of biology, concerning which account of species identity is the right one. (Kitcher [1984], for example, is a pluralist who countenances nine distinct varieties of approach, three structural and six historical or phylogenetic.) Against the evolutionary view, the pure cladist will argue that the inclusion of a pheneticist element (judgment of morphological similarity) reintroduces a subjective factor that is unacceptable in a science (evolutionary biology) that, according to the title of its own founding text, purports to explain the origin of *species*; but cladists do not always recognize their own dependence on considerations of gene flow and ecological isolation to determine the genuine branching events. However this may be, there is at work in the cladist argument an underlying realist metaphysical assumption, namely that there is a fact of the matter concerning the identity of species which it is the business of biological science to ferret out. At least one reputable philosopher of science convinced of the need for a pluralistic approach to species identity has grasped the nettle and embraced an antirealism regarding species. In Stanford's (1995) estimation, whatever species-concept furthers the aims of biological science at a particular historical juncture, be it evolutionary biology, comparative anatomy, functional physiology, or paleontology, is, in the context of the science in question, legitimate. There need be no one-size-fits-all species concept. Sometimes historical considerations will be paramount, sometimes structural ones will be; sometimes historical continuity will bear emphasis, sometimes historical discontinuity. If the various species-concepts are mutually incompatible, as Stanford thinks they are, so much the worse for realism concerning species. Kitcher, on the other hand, who stoutly maintains that his nine species-concepts can be coherently combined, is unwilling to forgo realism.

Is there a metaphysical fact of the matter concerning the identity of musical works as there is concerning species for the biological realist? We need not attempt to answer definitively here. Whatever we say, antirealism concerning musical-work identity is at least no *more* problematic than antirealism concerning biological-species identity, if both are regarded as REFs. Indeed, considered in a certain way, it seems considerably less problematic. While species *may* be natural kinds or natural kind–like, musical works most assuredly are neither. (The question of whether musical works are abstract Platonic entities will be taken up in section 4.5 below.) I hold no brief for an unqualified antirealism concerning musical-work identity, much less for an antirealism concerning species identity, but the claim that the identity of the products of human culture like musical works may be sensitive to our similarity judgments and so infected with subjectivity in a way the identity of natural products like biological species should *not* be has a prima facie plausibility. A performance, *provided it has the right causal provenance*, is an instance of a work if performers and listeners, who are participants in an ongoing musical practice, are prepared *to regard it as* an instance of that work. Here the sort of prototypicality effects emphasized by Zbikowski (2002, 36ff) could well come into play: some performances will be judged more "typical" and more centrally located in a graded category than others. Leaving aside for the present the musical Platonism to be discussed below, there just is no reason to demand that musical works should be amenable to stricter metaphysical identity conditions than are biological species. Like species, musical works are historical entities, and construing a musical work as a causal-historical REF gives us a leg up on solving the sorites paradox of musical identity. Similarity judgments, however, play an important role as well; indeed, they seem to play a more significant role in the musical context than they do in the biological one. We may not be able to say in the case of musical works exactly how much structural divergence is enough to trump causal-historical provenance; but at least we can *deny* that complete compliance with a score is metaphysically either necessary or sufficient to maintain work identity. It is not necessary because given the right causal provenance, a performance that is not completely compliant may still be counted a performance of a given work. Complete compliance is not sufficient because even a totally compliant performance will not, absent the right causal provenance, count as a performance of that very work. If a pluralism that recognizes the importance of structural similarity along with causal history is an option in the case of species identity (the evolutionary approach), it is also available in the case of the identity of musical works. Again, this should not be taken as an endorsement of metaphysical antirealism in either case, but merely as an attempt to loosen the grip of the Goodman worries concerning the identity of musical works.

There is, moreover, a further consideration. It will be recalled that compliance with the score is relevant only to higher-order REF membership. But a performance also belongs, as we saw, to a first-order REF of *interpretations*. In the case of nonscored music, say music belonging to folk traditions or improvisational jazz, this distinction collapses: various REFs of interpretations just are the work. Since the work is now a variety of REFs all deriving from a common ancestor, our grip on the identity of nonscored musical works is significantly more tenuous than our grip on works of scored music.[36] But this is not to say we have no grip at all. The effective principle seems to be the one I have recommended: what should be fundamental for identity is causal provenance or the replication of tokens; but at some point (which we cannot specify precisely) structural divergence will trump causal provenance. If a performance diverges too much from earlier tokens of a work, it will not be regarded as a token of that work. If sufficiently numerous and sufficiently divergent or degraded contemporary performances of a work were to crowd out more compliant ones—if all that remained, in some future world, of Beethoven's Ninth Symphony were repetitions of the recorded signature theme of the MSNBC television news show *The Countdown with Keith Olbermann* and performances of a caroling tune based on the *Ode to Joy* theme, or if all that remained of Dvořák's *New World* Symphony were performances of *Goin' Home*—those particular symphonic "species" could be said to have undergone "extinction," assuming the scores and/or the performing practices that went with them were no longer recoverable.

Now if, as I have argued, the performances of a musical work constitute a REF of tokens, and if a REF of tokens constitutes a type, then the performances of a musical work constitute a type. But if the performances of a musical work constitute a type, then, I propose, the musical work itself is a type. And if the musical work is a type, the claim that the work is a particular is now well grounded, or at least better grounded. A reproductively established family of replicas is a historical, spatiotemporally restricted particular that can come into and go out of existence. Once it disappears, that very particular, that causally connected family of replicas, cannot be recreated. Kinds, and natural kinds in particular, are different. Water exists wherever and whenever hydrogen hydroxide shows up in this or any possible world. The history of water instances is not important as regards their identities; their microstructure is. No instance of water, moreover, need be a copy or a replica of anything in order to *be* water.

Objection: surely an artifact like the incandescent lightbulb is a type, and surely individual lightbulbs are tokens that constitute a higher-order REF. Suppose Earth is destroyed along with all existing lightbulbs. Do we really want to say that if some future race of intelligent beings reinvented the lightbulb and started producing tokens having no historical connection to the prototype originated in Edison's workshop, then these objects would not be lightbulbs? Reply: No, that would be absurd. What this shows is a certain overdetermination in the application of the kind–type distinction. Lightbulbs are indeed tokens that form REFs; but the incandescent lightbulb also possesses a causal-functional essence, an essence that would also belong to anything that produced light by exploiting the same physical principles, whatever its causal ancestry. In this case, we would be inclined to regard the lightbulb as also a *functional kind*, and, in the case of conflict, to let functional essence trump causal provenance. Because they all derive historically from Edison's prototype, incandescent lightbulbs are type-identical; but because they are all similarly functionally organized, they are also (functionally) kind-identical.

Objection: What, then, do we say about the organ systems of living things? Eyes have originated multiple times in evolutionary history because of their functional virtues for locomoting creatures in transparent media, and because differing designs were accessible given light-sensitive organic structures "on hand." This is why the eyes of vertebrates, arthropods, and cephalopods are analogous but not homologous: they do not all derive from one set of primordial structures.[37] Must we regard them as belonging to different types because they do not share a common causal origin? They are all *eyes*, are they not? Reply: This is also a case of overdetermination involving a functional essence. But because of the hold of cladist principle in biological taxonomy, we may be rather less inclined here to let functional essence trump causal ancestry. Even the evolutionary taxonomist, to say nothing of the pure cladist, will deny trait identity based on mere functional convergence. We might just have to adopt a pluralism like Kitcher's or Stanford's and allow the two identity criteria an uneasy coexistence.

When we wish to refer to all these structures as "eyes," we will favor functional essence and regard them as a *kind*. When we are engaged in biological classification we will regard them as analogues, and therefore as different *types*. Notice, though, that *individual species* do not possess functional essences in the way eyes do. Only the natural kinds *instantiated by* species, kinds like *prey* or *predator*, could be said to possess such essences, and then only at a high level of functional description. As a result, the same sorts of pressures do not arise with regard to species, or at least do not arise with the same intensity. Now one may quibble in one way or another with the celebrated Kantian dictum that works of art evince "the form of purposiveness without representation of a purpose"; but whatever musical works are, surely they possess, *qua* individual works, no functional essences. They are therefore more unambiguously typelike than lightbulbs or eyes, and, as I have argued, in this regard they are similar to species.

4.4.1   Cultural Evolution and Authenticity of Performance

What is *an appropriate Mozart style for the 21st Century?*[38]
—Scott Cantrell

Toward the end of chapter 2, we briefly considered pure and timbral sonicism, two versions of the thesis that what matters in a musical performance are the sounds that reach the listener, not how they are produced. At that juncture, we saw that there are reasons for resisting either view in any unqualified form. Like Davies, Levinson (1990c, 404) rejects the thesis in both its versions, holding that an "authentic performance should seek to present a piece's aesthetic substance as it *is*, to present the expressive gestures that really belong to the piece—and not a mere simulacrum of that substance and those gestures." For him, as for Davies (2001, 217), only a performance using appropriate period instruments can be a maximally authentic performance of musical works from the past. Davies, in particular, is impatient with the more extreme claims of the new musicology, most especially with the thesis that "there are no old musical works as such, only reconstructions shaped in the present" (2001, 95).[39]

In my view, there is something to be said for and against both the philosophers and the new musicologists. For the philosophers and against the new musicologists, there *are* old musical works: they are REFs of tokens of scores and performances produced at specific times and places. Musical works have as great (or nearly as great) a claim on historical actuality as species. But for the new musicologists and against the philosophers, musical works no more possess unchanging essences than do species, assuming that the "aesthetic substance of a piece as it *is*" is something essential. Davies's musical works considered as "abstract particulars" presumably also possess timeless essences. I have agreed with Davies that some scores are "thicker" (more detail-determining) than others. But I will also agree that no score of a piece that belongs to the tradition of Western tonal art music is as thick as a performance, and that performers must rely on performance practices to interpret any such score, however thick, including its work-determining properties. Performance practices, however, evolve, which is not to say, here any more than in biology, that they steadily improve toward some goal. But interpretations do compete in a cultural struggle for existence. What was considered tasteful interpretation of Classical or Baroque scores in the nineteenth and early-to-mid-twentieth centuries, say Beecham's interpretations of Mozart or Casals's interpretations of Bach, is generally not preferred now.

Even contemporary performances on period instruments will be influenced by other contemporary performance practices. Roger Norrington's disciplined recorded performances of Beethoven's symphonies on period instruments bear the stamp of George Szell's Cleveland Orchestra, which, depending on one's point of view, set either a new standard of precision or one of frigid detachment in orchestral performance. Norrington's performances, in turn, have also influenced performance on modern instruments. Norrington's performances doubtless are sonically closer to what Beethoven's contemporaries heard than are contemporary performances on modern instruments, but it is not at all clear that they are necessarily more authentic *sans phrase*. Is not overwhelming, elemental force a feature that belongs to the opening movements of Beethoven's Fifth and Ninth Symphonies "as they are," if anything does? Who has realized this feature more authentically than Karajan in his final recordings with the Berlin Philharmonic? Does not the Fifth Symphony's first-movement oboe cadenza constitute an all-too-fleeting moment of pathos in that inexorable *Allegro con brio* "as it is"? Who has realized this moment more authentically than the Cleveland Orchestra's Marc Lifschey on his modern Lorée instrument and sophisticated modern reed?

By no means do I seek to minimize Norrington's accomplishment. Only a stopped natural horn could produce the deliberately clumsy *ostinato* that he achieves in the trio of the *Scherzo* of Beethoven's Seventh Symphony, a genuinely authentic touch. "The apotheosis of the dance"[40] this symphony may be, but it is also a study in wildly improbable *ostinato* effects.[41] The point, however, is that Norrington's "authenticist" performance belongs to a REF of *interpretations* of the symphony, which must compete with other interpretations. Only time will tell how well his approach will fare. What counts for validation of an interpretation is the extent to which it realizes the spirit of a work. But what is that, exactly? It is, I maintain, no unchanging essence, but something affected by the contemporary state of the performing art. The work's spirit, however, is not *just* contemporary: it is also historical. It is realized by interpreters who belong to a tradition, who make something of a score that is convincing to audiences and to other practitioners belonging to the tradition. An interpretation should not depart from the work-specifying properties of the score so as to produce a new version of the work, rather than an interpretation of it. But what is work-specifying and how much departure is too much are issues on which those who conserve and renew the art must needs have their say.

4.4.2   Memes, Once Again

In the introduction to this chapter, I deferred discussion of the implications for musical ontology of Sperber's claim of "similarity of content" for historical strains of representations; and in the previous section I promised some further discussion of meme theory. It is now high time to discharge both these obligations. Hull, an avowed meme theorist, flatly rejects the similarity of content condition, arguing for a causal-historical account of the identity of conceptual systems and theories, for example, the identity of the theory of evolution itself. On Hull's view, two representational tokens, *even if they carry the same semantic content*, are not tokens of the same theory if they lack a common ancestor (1982, 290–291):

> Evolutionary theory is not a type with numerous tokens, but a "population" with different "versions."...Two [historical conceptual lineages] could be identical in assertive content and belong to two different, possibly even competing, conceptual systems. Conversely, two quite different [assertive contents] could be part of the same conceptual lineage....One can certainly group individual propositions and even entire conceptual systems into kinds on the basis of shared assertive content. There may even be reasons for doing so. However, these kinds are not the kinds relevant to evolutionary development. If conceptual systems evolve in anything like the way that species do, then they must be treated as historical entities related by descent and not as timeless sets of similar ideas.

I have recommended a view of type identity very close to Hull's. But his account of theory identity is more extreme than my account of musical work identity. For Hull, the burden of argument is significantly heavier because of the great significance for us in standard usage of the same (or similar) propositional content in the determination of theory identity, a burden my cognate account of musical work identity does not bear, since music, even if it is representational, is not conceptual. In the case of theory identity, on analogy with the musical case, some degree of semantic divergence will trump common ancestry in the determination of theory identity. Against Hull's causal-historical account of theory identity, however, we surely wish to allow for the possibility of convergence, since we recognize the independent discovery of the same theory or theoretical content.[42] With regard to music, all we need say is what has already been said: historical provenance is a necessary but not a sufficient condition of musical work identity. Some standard of structural similarity between tokens must not be violated. Although structural similarity is more a syntactic than a semantic condition, it is this nonviolation of structural similarity requirement that plays the role of Sperber's requirement of similarity of content in my account of musical ontology. To say that a REF of tokens complies with a similarity of structure requirement, however, is just to say that the tokens in question share certain reproductively established characters.

Like Hull, Dennett identifies the cultural replicators with memes. Unlike Hull, however, Dennett (1995, 354) is committed to a strong version of the similarity of content condition for meme identity, holding that the meme is primarily a semantic classification. But is he right about this? Notice that there is a subtle equivocation in Dennett's account. For he wishes to regard memes both as cultural items ("The first four notes of Beethoven's Fifth Symphony are clearly a meme, replicating all by themselves, detached from the rest of the symphony" [344]) and as *ideas of* cultural items, such as "the idea of 'Greensleeves'" (344). A cultural replicator and the idea of a cultural replicator do not necessarily come to the same thing. Is the "idea" of "Greensleeves" a concept of the song? Is it a mental capacity to token the song? Is it a mental tokening of the song? In this case, the cultural replicator, I submit, is the song itself, the REF of its tokens. The cultural replicator is not the idea, which is most plausibly glossed as the capacity to produce or to recognize tokens of the song. It is the tune itself that gets into people's heads by having its tokens copied. Compare Dawkins (1976, 208): "The copy of 'Auld Lang Syne' which exists in my brain will last only for the rest of my life. The copy of the same tune which is printed in my volume of *The Scottish Student's Song Book* is unlikely to last much longer. But I expect there will be copies of the same tune on paper and in peoples' brains for centuries to come." At least one of these copies (the printed one), notice, is unambiguously a member of a higher-order REF. The "copy" in Dawkins's brain, on the other hand, is the capacity to generate a higher-order REF of mental tokens of the song, and so is not really a *copy* of the song at all.

In the case of evolution by natural selection, another of Dennett's meme examples, meme and idea are not so easily distinguished, for, absent a causal-historical account of theory identity like Hull's, that meme is naturally identified with that very semantic content. But on any view, that semantic content becomes a meme, or a cultural replicator, only when tokens carrying it are replicated and form causal-historical lineages. The case of the *Odyssey*, a third of Dennett's examples, seems to fall in between "Greensleeves" and evolution by natural selection. Its meme is an idea that shares semantic content with the artifact: the idea must contain the story of Odysseus and his ten-year quest to return home. But in order to be that meme, it must also be descended from the artifact, the text, and ultimately the performances attributed to Homer. In the case of Homer himself, however, the meme just is the text itself repeatedly tokened in his mind. Consider, finally, an example not deriving from Dennett. The *Mona Lisa* is not a meme: *it* cannot, strictly speaking, be replicated, since it is a unique individual. But its "idea," especially the idea of the famous smile, is a meme. The content of this "idea," however, is principally, even if not entirely, imagistic. Like the idea of "Greensleves," this idea is most plausibly glossed as the ability to produce a mental token of that image or to recognize tokens of it. Someone who has the concept, but cannot token or recognize the image, does not have the idea. And once again, the *Mona Lisa* meme, like the *Odyssey* meme, must be descended from the artifact.

Where does this leave us? In view of the musical and (to a lesser extent) the painting cases, identification of a meme with a semantic content seems too narrow a construal.

"A popular tune," says Plotkin (2003, 288), "is not the same thing as a belief in God. If they are both memes, they are memes of such great difference that little is gained by giving them the same tag." Surely he is right. Musical memes are musical artifacts themselves, even if generally not, though they may be, entire pieces or extended works. The *Mona Lisa* meme is not the artifact; but it is an "idea" whose content is imagistic and that derives from the artifact. Any meme, however, even the evolution-by-natural-selection meme, indeed even the "calculus meme" (Dennett 1995, 344), seems subject to some conditions of causal provenance: tokens carrying those semantic contents must replicate in order to be memetic. Finally, as in the case of the *Odyssey*, the meme may be the work itself, but more often will be a sketchy semantic content deriving from the work, sketchy because it will emphasize the salient events of the story and leave out any number of details.

Let us, then, say this: a meme is a type whose tokens may, but need not, carry semantic content; it is a type that must allow itself to be mentally tokened but that also may be tokened by external artifacts; and it is a type that requires minds for the replication of its tokens. This definition makes memes a subcategory of REFs that share reproductively established characters, as, I have argued, are both musical works and species. It seems clear, however, that the identity conditions for memes are rather looser than the identity conditions for works like Beethoven's Fifth Symphony or the *Odyssey*. How much of the symphony a musical snippet must include to be a Beethoven's-Fifth meme, or how much and how many details of the story of Odysseus an idea must contain to be an *Odyssey*-meme, is highly indeterminate. Both memes must, however, descend from the works in question, just as all tokens of the "Auld Lang Syne" meme (or at least all tokens of the poem) must descend from Robert Burns's original manuscript.

Memeticist Robert Aunger takes a view fundamentally opposed to Dennett's. For him, neither an artifactual type nor an idea qualifies as memetic. The artifactual type is not memetic because "artifacts don't have the requisite qualities of causation, similarity, information transfer, and duplication" (2002, 164). But the idea of an artifact is also not memetic, for "memes don't mean, they just are. Memes are states of being" (221). So the idea of a wagon with spoked wheels is not, contrary to Dennett (1995, 348), a meme: an artifactual token cannot be memetic, and memes are not ideas because they are "states of being" that don't mean. And what states of being are they? They are states of the brain: all memes are neuromemes. Artifacts, on the other hand, are simply "signal templates," entities that facilitate the transmission of the interpersonal signals on the basis of which receiver brains then construct memes. Since I have not hung my account on the meme idea, but rather on the more general notion of a REF (of which, I now have proposed, memes are a special case), it is not necessary, strictly speaking, for me to subject this or any particular theory of memes to critical scrutiny.[43] Nonetheless, Aunger's view would, if correct, constitute a serious challenge to the account of the ontology of the musical work I have offered. If musical scores are merely signal templates and if public performances are merely signals, public performances are not tokens of musical works.

Fortunately for the view of musical ontology I have recommended, the neuromeme view faces considerable conceptual difficulties. When we ask what prevents artifacts from having the "requisite quality" of duplication, we are told that "one car does not play any role in generating the next; computer programs direct the machines that perform that job" (Aunger 2002, 165). Since cars of a certain model (type) rolling off an assembly line constitute a paradigmatic case of a higher-order REF, the difficulty seems to be that each car is neither a causal product nor a direct duplicate of the preceding one. Once again, this is a case of tying cultural replication too closely to genetic replication and demanding that all replicas of cultural items be self-replicating members of first-order REFs, a demand that is, as I have argued, misplaced. But there is worse to come. For when examined more closely, the neuromeme theory is doubtfully coherent.

Clearly conceiving the brain as a connectionist architecture, Aunger (2002) characterizes neuromemes in (at least) four ways: memes are "attractor[s]" (196), they are "nodes" (196), they are "states of being" (221), and they are "physical things" (221). Unfortunately, these descriptors are not mutually consistent. Taking the second pair first, a physical thing, on the most standard interpretation, is a particular that *enters into* states (of being). Memes, therefore, cannot both be physical things *and* states of being, though a meme could be a physical thing (a brain or a brain region) *in* a certain state. But this is not what Aunger intends. For him, "physical thing" means "physical propensity": memes "are, in fact, *electrical* things—propensities to fire—tied to the special kind of cells called neurons (but are not the neurons themselves)" (196–197). This, however, remains problematical, for propensities are dispositions; and because dispositions are not token states or events, but universals, they cannot be *duplicated*, but only *expressed* or *occurrently tokened* by one or more neurons, although a thing *with* a certain disposition certainly may be duplicated. So construing memes as propensities fails Aunger's own duplication requirement. The "propensity" is not itself copied, it is repeatedly tokened; and each token is not a direct copy of the previous token, but an occurrent expression of the underlying dispositional state of the neuron. The dispositional state is not copied; and the occurrent tokenings are members of a higher-order, not a first-order, REF.

Perhaps, though, we are looking at this at the wrong level of abstraction.[44] Consider copying a document onto a digital computer using a standard word-processing program. This seems to accord with Aunger's construal of memes as physical propensities. During the copying event, the document is input by being newly tokened, either by way of a series of keyboard strokes or by reading an inserted portable disc. This tokening causes a change in the state of the machine, a change in the distribution of charges, positive or negative, on or off, in the computer's circuitry. Once input, the new "copy" is nothing other than the newly acquired states of these circuits, their propensity or disposition to cause a token of the document to be displayed or printed on command. But again, these dispositional *states* have not been duplicated. *They* have been newly instantiated. The machine has been put into physical states that it shares with the machine from which the document was derived, assuming it is a machine of the same model, using the same operating system and running the same program. The new document may, then, be a propensity. But it cannot both be a propensity and be duplicated. With brains, the situation is considerably more problematic, since two copies of the same document in two brains, even assuming causal provenance of one from the other, are almost certainly *not* realized by the same neuronal propensities to fire.

Perhaps the assertion that propensities are dispositions, dispositions are states, and states are universals begs the question against nominalist views of dispositions and properties. On both accounts, there are no universals. According to the nominalist, a thing has a disposition if and only if a subjunctive conditional is true of it: an object is brittle if it would shatter when dropped under certain conditions. But then, there is no disposition to be duplicated. Properties, on the other hand, are abstract individuals, some of which are multiply repeatable *in re*, like a specific shade of color. A shade of color can be construed as a disposition to look a certain way to normal perceivers under standard conditions. One may well wonder whether these repeatable individuals are *duplicates* of one another. But no matter: whether they are or not, such abstract individuals are not physical things.

Aunger's first pair of characterizations is no better off. An attractor is an abstract entity, a location in the multidimensional activation space of a connectionist network, whereas a node, even if it is a node cluster and not necessarily an individual node, is a processing unit with weighted connections to other units. The activation levels of processing units (resulting from their summed inputs) in various layers constitute vectors (ordered sets of activation values) whose members vary along dimensions that define the abstract activation space in which the attractors are located. A neuromeme, then, cannot be both a node and an attractor, for these terms designate entirely different functional aspects of the neural net.

I conclude that neuromemetics poses no threat to my proposed account of the ontology of the musical work. Musical works are types: they are REFs of performances, whether public or inside the head. But in order to make it plausible to construe musical works as types, must we be ontologically parsimonious? Must we regard the musical type merely as the historically connected set of performances, or tokens-of-a-type? Or can the musical type be an abstract object? This will be a topic of the next section.

4.5   Discovery, Invention, and Creation

Like the space of possible five-hundred-page novels, or fifty-minute symphonies, or five-thousand-line poems, the space of megabyte-long programs will only ever get occupied by the slenderest threads of actuality, no matter how hard we work.

—Daniel Dennett (1995, 450)

Are musical works discovered by their composers? One who adopted the ontologically parsimonious interpretation of musical works as REFs of tokens would quickly answer no, for the work does not exist before its first tokening, whether autograph score, first performance, or perhaps first complete mental tokening by the composer. The more Platonically inclined theorist who is committed to the proposition that musical works are (or may be) discovered might reasonably object that the parsimonious interpretation begs the question. Such a theorist, moreover, will not rest satisfied with Levinson's (1980b, 66ff) asseveration that the discovery view offends against a deeply entrenched intuition of a creatability requirement for musical works, and rightly so (cf. Cox 1985). Although such an intuition should not be cavalierly dismissed, the fact that it is deeply entrenched, if it is,[45] does not make it right. Any such intuition must remain sensitive to requirements of reflective equilibrium with normative principle. Let us, then, address and not beg the question of a creatability requirement by assuming the ontologically more profligate interpretation of the musical work as a type that is an abstract object that might be discoverable. In this section, I shall attempt to show that the intuition behind Levinson's creatability requirement is defensible after all.

In order to proceed, I require an assumption that I do not know how to argue for, but one that might be considered a postulate of realism. The assumption is that discovery, as opposed to invention and creation, affects only the epistemological modality and not the ontological modality of an object *already actual*. A discovered object, that is to say, is one that is (or once was) already *there*. It either is actual, or it once was actual. It is not actualized by its discovery; rather, what changes are its epistemic relations to those who have come know it, in some acceptable sense of "know." (Let us ignore here as irrelevant revelations from quantum mechanics, on some interpretations, concerning the effects that acts of observation may have on the states of subatomic particles, given the inverse relation between degree of uncertainty regarding position and degree of uncertainty regarding momentum established by the Heisenberg uncertainty principle.) Invention and creation, on the other hand, actualize *possibilia*. I shall assume for the sake of present discussion that collapsing the distinction between the actual and the possible is not an option. I shall proceed, that is, on the assumption that "actualism," the metaphysical doctrine that only the actual is possible, is false at some level of description (cf. Dennett 1995, 106). Establishing the falsity of actualism, or even delimiting the proper application of the concept (if it has application at all), would be a task extending far beyond the scope of this book.

Now it might hastily be assumed by one who took a conventionalist line regarding abstract objects that the only objects that are properly discoverable are objects of empirical knowledge. But this once again would beg the question against the Platonist, for mathematical objects provide prima facie compelling examples of objects of discovery.[46] Pythagoras (or some other pre-Socratic thinker), it is perfectly reasonable to claim, discovered a geometrical fact concerning Euclidean plane right triangles, just as Cantor discovered that the power set of a set (the set of all the subsets of a set) always has a greater cardinality than the set itself whether that set is infinite or finite, and Gödel discovered the incompleteness of all consistent finitary[47] first-order axiomatizations of arithmetic. If Pythagoras, Cantor, and Gödel made these discoveries, may not the musical Platonist justifiably claim that Wagner discovered the "*Tristan* chord" as a musical type, an abstract musical-combinatorial object (Kivy 1983a, 46)? And if he may say that, may he not also claim with equal justification that Wagner discovered *Tristan und Isolde* itself? Unfortunately, no, for there are some important features to notice about the mathematical cases that ultimately work to the detriment of the musical Platonist.

The feature to notice first is that the discoveries of Pythagoras, Cantor, and Gödel all were demonstrated by way of chains of deductive reasoning; and deductive connections, whatever else they may be, are atemporal. Valid deductive inferences are timelessly valid. Should a mathematical intuitionist/constructivist demur, we at least have reason not to expect such an objection from the consistent musical Platonist. This, however, allows us to say the following about the mathematical cases. If deductive relations (expressed as truths of logic and set theory) are timelessly valid, then the Pythagorean theorem always has been true and the abstract mathematical objects of which it is true (Euclidean plane right triangles) have always existed, *if they exist at all*. Similarly, it always has been the case that the power set of the set of natural numbers is uncountable and that these abstract objects (numbers and their sets) have always existed, just as it always has been the case that no consistent finitary axiomatization of arithmetic in first-order logic can be complete. Moreover, Gödel's incompleteness theorems, as well as the natural numbers and the infinite number of finitary first-order axiomatizations of arithmetic, have always existed. Indeed, a strong case can be made for the claim that such objects, as the referents of necessary truths, exist necessarily if they exist at all, that is, in all logically possible worlds, or at least in all nonempty logically possible worlds.[48] It may be that no one before the twentieth century could have been in a position to arrive at Gödel's results, just as no one before the nineteenth could have been in a position to arrive at Cantor's. Indeed, how *could* anyone have done Gödel's work before the appearance of *Principia Mathematica*? But these are epistemological points, which, on a Platonic interpretation of mathematics, are completely irrelevant to the ontological status of its objects.

In order to make the case that musical works are discovered, the musical Platonist must take a similar line regarding musical works. But can he? I think not. Since there

are no timelessly valid deductive routes to specific musical works in the space of musical possibility, as there are to specific formal results in logical space, there are no similar
grounds for regarding these works as actual before they were composed.[49] Although
musical terms may be substituted in logically true expressions, they do not appear in
any of the definitions or the theorems of pure set theory, as mathematical terms (or
their set-theoretical equivalents) do.[50] Musical works, therefore, are not actual before
their composition in the way mathematical entities, *qua* necessarily existing abstract
objects, (arguably) are actual before their discovery; musical works not yet composed
are mere *possibilia*. And if they are not actual before their composition, they cannot
be discovered by their composers, if my original assumption be agreed to. This *is* an
ontological point: *pace* Kivy (1983b, 70), the reason Beethoven's Seventh Symphony
was not "discovered" before the second decade of the nineteenth century was not
because no one was in a position to discover it before that time. It is because, the symphony not being actual, there was nothing to discover.

Objection: On a modal realist view, *possibilia* exist. Reply: This is just a terminological variant of the view I am urging, for the modal realist exploits a distinction between
the actual and the existent. All possible worlds exist; but actuality is an indexical notion.[51] A world is actual only from the standpoint of beings at that world. (Does this
entail that possible worlds lacking intentional beings exist but remain nonactual?) *We*
do not discover actuals in other possible worlds; our counterparts do. We may know
that the Pythagorean theorem is true in all possible worlds, or that water is hydrogen
hydroxide in all possible worlds,[52] but that is because we have discovered these things
to be the case in our world.

Objection: Modal realism and issues of cross-world discovery aside, can't we discover
possibilia? Reply: This is just a misleading way of speaking. We may discover that something is possible. But such a discovery consists in actualizing some as yet nonexistent
object, process, or state of affairs, or in determining (in imagination) how these might
be actualized.[53] Such cases are more properly seen as cases of invention (compare: Eli
Whitney discovered the possibility of constructing interchangeable parts and, consequently, of mass production by actualizing them, or by constructing in imagination
a procedure whereby they could be actualized). Alternatively, the discovery of a possibility may consist in demonstrating that the *concept* of some nonexisting thing is not
logically incoherent or inconsistent with established physical law or other relevant
standing principles (compare: physicist X claims to have discovered the possibility
of a time machine). None of these seems to be what the musical Platonist has in
mind.

A possibility space allowing a limited number of combinatorial possibilities that
could be exhaustively searched by way of a brute procedure, say the space of all the
possible four-note seventh chords in root position, may give rise to an illusion of discovery, since the *Tristan* chord seems already to be "there" in this space waiting to be

found. But it is only "there" as a possible, not an actual, because it is still a member of a possibility space, albeit one that happens in this case to be small enough to be searched by a brute procedure. Because it remains a possible, not an actual, it is not discovered but actualized when tokened. This illusion of discovery is aided and abetted by a conflation of musical sets with mathematical objects. Mathematical objects, on a Platonist telling, may be said to be actual; but, contrary to Levinson (1980b, 66), a sequence of sets of "sonic elements" is not itself a "mathematical object," unless one means by this merely an object of applied set theory, a claim far too weak to support musical Platonism. To be sure, any set of elements, considered as an object of second-order quantification, is an abstract object that is not identical with any or all of its members.[54] But that does not make it a mathematical object, for a set is defined by its membership, and sets of *sonic* elements are contingent entities: sonic elements, unlike mathematical objects, do not exist in all possible worlds. A natural number, surely a mathematical object if anything is, is (set-theoretically) either a property of sets or a set of sets. So the set of sonic elements constituting the *Tristan* chord, considered either as a token or a type, has the property of fourness or, following Frege, is a member of the set of all quadruples. Whichever we say, it is the property or the set of sets that is the mathematical object, not the set of sonic elements that merely instantiates the property. In order for a musical work, considered as a sequence of sets of sonic elements, to be a discoverable mathematical object, it had better be a finite connected sequence, which is a finite class of connected ordered pairs that is defined by some recursive function (see Quine 1969b, 80). A familiar example is the sequence of a person and his ancestors, defined by recursive application of the relation "is a parent of." A musical work or a sequence of biological ancestors are at best *instantiations* of abstract mathematical objects, not the objects themselves. But it is doubtful that most musical sequences even instantiate a finite connected sequence. Leaving aside possible exceptions like scales and a few other highly regular musical progressions, most musical sequences seem not to be recursively definable. It is, of course, important not to confuse Platonic mathematical objects with the symbolic systems that represent them. The latter do consist of types and tokens that are historically actualized, for example, Roman and Arabic notations for numbers.

Objection:[55] Why are *possibilia* not universals that can be discovered? And why, then, are pure sound structures not discoverable as universals? Reply: As already agreed, to discover is to come to know, and knowledge is either a posteriori or a priori. Pure sound structures considered as universals cannot be discovered a posteriori, for knowledge a posteriori requires sense experience, internal or external, of particulars. But pure sound structures also cannot be discovered a priori, for a priori knowledge of universals includes knowledge of necessary relations between them.[56] Yet we have established that there are no formal necessary relations between sets of musical elements in sequences; and even if we waive for the sake of argument naturalist objections to necessary material truth a priori, whether analytic or synthetic, there are no necessary relations between them that are informal either.

Objection: There are twenty-four possible different ordered sets of any four elements ($4 \times 3 \times 2 \times 1$). This is a necessary truth of mathematical combinatorics. As the object (or objects) of this necessary truth, therefore, all twenty-four possibilities are actuals (on a Platonic construal of mathematics). Assuming octave equivalences, Wagner's first statement of the *Tristan* chord is one of twenty-four possible orderings of four sonic elements (F, B, D# and G#). The *Tristan* chord, therefore, was actual before Wagner discovered it (on a musical-Platonic construal). Reply: Mathematical combinatorics gives us the *number* of different ordered sets of any four elements, but it neither specifies the elements of the sets nor any necessary ordering or relations between these sets as, for example, number theory specifies the natural numbers and their necessary ordering, and set theory demonstrates (by the "diagonal method" of proof) the existence of the first transfinite cardinal ($\aleph_0$) as a necessary consequence of the existence of the power set of the infinite set of natural numbers as well as the existence of an unending series of higher-order transfinite cardinals. The relations between the sonic elements are established music-theoretically, not set-theoretically; and music theory has empirical content. Despite the appearance of necessity given by mathematical combinatorics, therefore, the space of twenty-four ordered sets of elements remains an unstructured possibility space that mandates no internal forced moves and whose contents can be exhaustively determined by brute search alone.

Objection: Don't composers find solutions to compositional problems, and isn't finding just discovering? (Compare Kivy's [1983b, 69] example of "finding" a third species of counterpoint to a *cantus firmus*.) Reply: A problem situation requiring a solution may indeed arise during the composition of a work. (Compare: Beethoven found a solution to the problem of recapitulating the triumphant opening theme of the *Finale* of his Fifth Symphony by reintroducing the pianissimo version of the second motif from the *Scherzo*.) But since the *work* did not exist (was not actual) before its composition, the exigent problem situation and its solution also could not have antedated composition of the work. Similarly, Kivy's third species of counterpoint did not exist before the *cantus firmus* did. But solutions do not suddenly pop into existence once a problem situation arises, either, and then wait to be found. The fact that the composition of a work will often produce a relatively determinate problem situation (determinate, that is, compared to the problem situation of writing the work itself) creates the illusion that the solution is "there to be found," for once composition has begun, the range of possibilities that a composer will take seriously is significantly narrowed. Kivy's counterpoint example may constitute a limiting case because of the extremely narrow range of possible solutions in this tightly rule-bound musical context. No doubt this is why he chose it. Yet even here, the solutions are *possibilia*, and not actuals, because they cannot be actualized before the *cantus firmus* is, and because they are generally not strictly predetermined even once the *cantus firmus* is in place. One can perhaps imagine a situation where the choice is so narrow that there is only one thing to be done that remains in accordance with the rules of counterpoint. Perhaps we must grant that in this extreme case, the problem situation and its solution come into existence together, and that in this limited sense, the solution may be there to be "discovered," *given the actuality of the cantus firmus and the strict rules of the Gradus ad Parnassum.* But this extreme case is hardly representative of what generally occurs in musical composition.

Objection: Just as inventing is not all making, discovery is not all finding. Just as Edison had to discover the properties of tungsten in order to invent the lightbulb, Michelson had to invent the inferometer to discover the constant speed of light. Invention, therefore, is also part discovery and discovery is also part invention. An inventive feat like Michelson's, however, is also creative. Discovery, therefore, can also be part creation and creation part discovery. If Mozart created his works, then he also discovered them (cf. Kivy 1983a, 39–40). First reply: The first conclusion does not follow and is just false. The invention of the lightbulb may have *required* discovery, and the discovery of the constant speed of light may have *required* invention. But it does not follow and it is false that discovery *is* (in part) invention or that invention *is* (in part) discovery. The ontological requirements of the two cognitive operations are entirely different. Second reply: The argument equivocates on "creative," which can mean "exceptionally imaginative or resourceful" as Michelson and any number of other scientists certainly were; or it can mean "capable of generating products no one else is likely to have generated." As we are now about to see, these are two very different things.

Invention, as I have argued, differs from discovery precisely with regard to changes wrought in the ontological modality of the objects in question: *possibilia* are rendered actual. Invention brings something into existence; discovery does not. If this is right, then creation differs a fortiori from discovery. Like invention, creation also carries implications concerning a change in the ontological modality of the created object. But creation also differs significantly from invention. Here, though, we shall be able to recognize only a difference of degree, not an absolute difference like the modal difference distinguishing discovery from invention, thus ruling creation *ex nihilo* out of consideration and respecting Kivy's puckish observation that "in one sense of 'creator,' there has never been one at all except the Lord God Jehovah himself" (1983a, 40). Compare Archimedes' invention of the water screw or Edison's invention of the incandescent lightbulb with Shakespeare's creation of *Hamlet* or Beethoven's creation of the *Eroica*. All were *possibilia* before they were actualized. But there is a difference: if Archimedes had not invented the water screw, or if Edison had not invented the lightbulb, others probably would have. But if Shakespeare or Beethoven had never lived, or if these individuals had been born under less fortunate circumstances (less fortunate for art, that is), the chances these works would ever have come into existence are next to nil (cf. Dennett 1995, 139–140). Is this because Shakespeare and Beethoven, as Kivy (1983b, 72ff) would have it, were uniquely qualified to make "discoveries" that no one else could have made, before or since? Not if it is correct to deny that such works were actual before they were written or composed, and therefore to deny that they could have been discovered. But did Shakespeare and Beethoven create? Or did they merely invent?

The inferences of Cantor and Gödel, however penetrating the insight required to make them before anyone else did, were what Dennett has called "deep forced moves" because they instantiate truths of logic, set theory, and arithmetic.[57] Edison's inventions were not forced moves. But they were, again following Dennett, "Good Tricks," functionally superior locations in a space of design possibilities that was "Vast" (huge albeit finite), but which were reasonably accessible, given the materials and the technology on hand. If one wanted to construct an incandescent lightbulb in late nineteenth-century America, there were only so many ways[58] to skin that particular cat. A similar phenomenon can be observed in the case of natural (evolutionary) design. Just as eyes were invented (not discovered!) by evolution more than once, the incandescent lightbulb could also have been and probably would have been. They are both Good Tricks. Notice that reinvention requires that causal-functional essence trump historical provenance in determining the identity conditions on an invented type. Otherwise, the new invention would not be a *reinvention* of the same type.[59]

Other Vast design spaces include the space of possible five-hundred-page books using Roman letters (Dennett's "Library of Babel"), the space of possible genomes of finite length ("The Library of Mendel"), and the space of possible computer programs (relativized to a particular language) up to the length of one megabyte that can be run on a computer with a twenty-megabyte hard disk ("The Library of Toshiba"). The Library of Babel contains 100 to the power of 1,000,000 volumes,[60] compared with an estimated 10 to the power of 70 atoms in the visible universe. Considering a (permutationally) possible genome to be a string of the four nucleotides adenine, cytosine, guanine, and thymine (ACGT) that is approximately 3×10 to the 9th power long, the length (in base pairs) of the human genome,[61] it would take a set of 6,000 500-page volumes in the Library of Babel *containing only the letters ACTG* to represent it. So the Library of Babel contains *all* the 6,000 volume sets that represent all the possible genomes of that length. The design space of fifty-minute symphonies, while a Vanishingly small subspace of the design space of all musical compositions of finite length is also, I hope to show, Vast.

Let us call this musical design space the Library of Orpheus. A performance of Beethoven's *Eroica* will take about fifty minutes. The nature of musical notation and scoring makes it impossible to give a precise specification of number of lines and character-spaces per page as Dennett does for the books in the Library of Babel. Nevertheless, some useful, if artificial, approximations can be made. The *Eroica* is scored for pairs of flutes, oboes, clarinets, bassoons, and trumpets; three horns and tympani; and the usual string complement of first and second violins, violas, cellos, and basses. This yields nineteen potentially independent lines. My pocket score of the work is 174 pages long. Score-printing conventions, however, are such that when fewer than the full complement of instruments are engaged, rests are not printed out. The staves belonging to the resting instruments are simply not printed, and the staves belonging to the remaining instrumental combinations are doubled or tripled up on the same page. So by all rights, the score is really quite a bit longer than 174 pages, since rests are possible notational items. But let us ignore this wrinkle, since doing so will not work in my favor. To keep things manageable, let us take the *Scherzo* as our base case, where the meter is three-quarter time and the rhythms are relatively simple and uniform, and let us assume that these conditions apply throughout. This assumption also does not work to my favor. Let us simplify even further and pretend that the only permissible notational variants are quarter notes and quarter rests, and that these constraints apply throughout the length of every one of the fifty-minute symphonies. (This would, of course, require making appropriate adjustments of tempo to maintain the fifty-minute length.) Let us give each line a conservative two-octave (twenty-five-note) chromatic range. (This will grossly overestimate the pitch range of the tympani and will ignore the limitations of Beethoven's natural trumpets and horns; but it will also underestimate the ranges of some of the other instruments.) Finally, let us stipulate that each line of staff contains ten bars, a round, but not wildly inaccurate estimate. Given these highly artificial limitations, how many fifty-minute symphonies are there in the Library of Orpheus? With nineteen lines per page, ten bars per line, and three "character-spaces" per bar, this will give us nineteen times ten times three or 570 character-spaces per page. Each character-space will contain a quarter rest or a quarter note from the two-octave range. (We are ignoring the fact that given the different ranges of the instruments, these two octaves will not always be the same. But this is just another artificial simplification that does not work to my advantage.) Multiplying 174 pages times 570 characters per page gives 99,180 character spaces per score, so there are 26 (25 notes plus the quarter rest) to the 99,180th power number of fifty-minute symphonies in the Library of Orpheus, a number perhaps not as large as the number of five-hundred-page books in the Library of Babel, but still (even with the considerable simplifications we made) significantly greater than the number of atoms in the observable universe. The design space of fifty-minute symphonies is Vast.

When the space of possibilities is Vast, and the locations in this space are not accessible as Good Tricks or forced moves, *then*, it would seem, the language of creation as opposed to that of invention is in order. Levinson's creatability intuition, therefore, is vindicated: musical works are neither the results of forced moves nor Good Tricks. The foregoing considerations also suggest that even when considered as abstract objects and not merely as tokens-of-a-type, types are mere *possibilia*, not actuals like mathematical objects (on the Platonic interpretation of such objects). But if an abstract type is merely a possible, then its actualization *requires the production of tokens of the type*.

Now it is certainly fair to object that no composer enters the Library of Orpheus entirely unconstrained. (Of course, no writer enters the Library of Babel entirely unconstrained either. For one thing, only a small subset of these books can be semantically interpreted.) When Beethoven composed the *Eroica*, only a small subset of the permutationally possible combinations of notes and rests were live options, given standing music-theoretical requirements, the state of symphonic art in his time, and constraints of musical taste. These points may be granted. Still, none of the really distinctive compositional decisions that make the *Eroica* the *Eroica*, one small but significant example being the still shocking introduction of four bars of *alla breve* in the reprise of the *Scherzo*, come close to implementing Good Tricks that someone else is likely to have arrived at independently (example 4.1); much less are they forced moves, deep or shallow. The *Tristan* chord, by contrast, could perhaps be considered an invention. If so, it would be a particularly impressive Good Trick, and not a creation, according to the proposal of the previous paragraph. *Tristan und Isolde* itself, on the other hand, is, as I now shall argue, most certainly a creation and no mere Good Trick.

Recall that between invention and creation we have been able to recognize no absolute difference, just one of degree; that is the price of "naturalizing possibility" using the notion of natural design space in the Dennett way. But by invoking just this difference of degree we also block Kivy's slippery slope argument from the *Tristan* chord to *Tristan und Isolde*. We recognize the slope, all right; but we have principled grounds for denying that it is all that slippery. An item like the *Tristan* chord seems to lie close to where invention goes over into creation. This, no doubt, is what lends Kivy's argument some of its plausibility. It would not, indeed, be surprising if another composer had incorporated, independently of Wagner, a half-diminished seventh chord into a composition somewhere. Indeed, Ridley (1995, 17) informs us that Chopin did just that; and the chord does, after all, have a generic music-theoretical designation. What would be surprising, though, is the independent incorporation of a half-diminished seventh chord with Wagner's distinctive voicing: the root and diminished fifth in the bass and tenor, the seventh in the alto, and the third in the soprano, as the chord is voiced in the bassoons, English horn, and oboe in the opening of the *Prelude* to the opera (see example 4.3). More surprising still would be its appearance as the very first chord of an independently composed piece. Downright astounding would be the independent invention of Wagner's unexpected resolution to an unresolved dominant seventh chord rooted one half-step below the initial half-diminished seventh chord. This begins to appear creative, and not merely inventive; and at this point we are barely into the opera. Incredible would be the independent decision by another composer to use the very same (structurally kind-identical) half-diminished seventh chord (with a

Example 4.1
Beethoven, Symphony No. 3 in E-Flat, *Eroica. Scherzo.*

few enharmonic notational replacements) as Wagner does at the climax of the *Prelude*, now *fortissimo* in full orchestral voicing (example 4.2). This, like Beethoven's four bars of cut time in the *Scherzo* of the *Eroica*, is the sort of thing we are accustomed to call a "stroke of genius," a genuinely creative move that is neither forced nor a Good Trick. If Wagner hadn't done it, it is unlikely that anyone else would have.

Objection: On your view, the half-diminished seventh chord is, then, not a single type or REF of tokens at all. For if it were, *it* could not have been *independently* introduced by Chopin or anyone else. From this it follows that there is no chord properly called "the half-diminished seventh chord"; there are only various REFs of chords that bear close structural resemblances to one another. Is this not a reductio of the REF view? Reply: The objection has merit, but the conclusion is overstated, for we have a case of conflict not unlike ones faced by evolutionary biologists and other life scientists who must reconcile historical and structural/functional considerations in the study of life forms, a conflict like ones that drove Stanford to species antirealism. The music-theoretic expression, "half-diminished seventh chord," designates any four-note chord whose members stand in certain relations, whatever its key, position/inversion, or voicing. In this case, we may be prepared to let structural considerations trump historical ones, as we do when we designate groups of animals bipeds, including certain dinosaurs, birds, and primates. Dinosaurs and birds are closely related according to cladistic principle. Primate bipedalism, on the other hand, is not directly related historically to the other two at all. If it were historically related, it would have to rest on a far deeper homology, reaching back to a common ancestor among the cotylosaurs or primitive reptiles that gave rise to such biologically diverse groups as lizards, snakes, and turtles, as well as to the archosaurs that gave rise to primitive birds, crocodilians, and dinosaurs (cf. Sarnat and Netsky 1981, 5).

I don't know whether there were any biped cotylosaurs (it seems unlikely). But suppose there weren't, and that dinosaurs, birds, and primates have no common biped ancestor. Grouping dinosaurs, birds, and primates together as bipeds might be perfectly acceptable for certain ethological purposes, say studying characteristic hunting and foraging behavior, while remaining unacceptable for purposes of biological classification. Even Gould, who is more sympathetic than most contemporary biologists to traditional structuralist/formalist tendencies in biological classification, tends to construe structural principles historically as constraints due to deep homology and to insist, with the cladists, that "if all peacocks die, the species-individual *Pavo cristatus* disappears forever. Even if some human engineer retained an electronic record of the entire *Pavo cristatus* genome, and future technology permitted chemical reconstitution from nucleotides, we wouldn't call the resurrected creature a member of *Pavo cristatus*, even if the reconstituted object looked and acted like an extinct peacock of old" (Gould 2002, 602–603). This, I have argued, is just what we should say about musical works, and probably also about the *Tristan* chord, Wagner's distinctive version of the half-

Example 4.2

Wagner, *Prelude* to *Tristan und Isolde*.

diminished seventh chord, as well.[62] The half-diminished seventh chord may rest on a "deep homology": assuming no direct influence of Chopin on Wagner, the two employments of the chord could have a common ancestor. But this is unlikely. And even if there is no one common ancestor to all uses of the chord, at this point structure is capable of trumping history: all instances of half-diminished seventh chords may be grouped into a structural artifactual kind for music-theoretic purposes.

4.6   Summary and Conclusion: Cranes, Skyhooks, and the Musical Imagination

I began this chapter by arguing that the Wolterstorff strategy of comparing musical works with biological species remains a useful one. But its proper deployment yields a number of conclusions that depart fairly radically from his. These include the following. Musical works are types, not kinds, because they are historically produced first- and higher-order REFs of tokens, that is, performances, including realizations "in the head." *Qua* REFs, musical works and biological species do, as Wolterstorff claims, display certain "close similarities." Like biological species on the evolutionary interpretation, the principal determiner of the identity of musical works is historical provenance; but with musical works, as with biological species (again on the evolutionary interpretation), historical provenance can be trumped by structural divergence. Construing musical works as REFs supports a principled distinction between types and kinds, allowing us to explain, or at least to begin to explain, why types seem to function as particulars and why they might be held to differ from kinds and universals with respect to the possibility of their creation and destruction.

These conclusions yielded some grounds in support of Levinson's "creatability requirement" for musical works. Adducing these grounds required recognition of an absolute difference of ontological modality separating discovery from invention, but only a relative one separating invention from creation. The distinction between invention and creation turned out to be a difference in degree but not in kind, and to depend on the accessibility of a design product in natural design space. By invoking this distinction of degree we were able to halt the slide down Kivy's slippery slope from invention to creation; but invoking it also required us to place creativity on a continuum that includes undirected evolutionary design. Although such an approach may demystify musical creativity by bringing it within the ambit of natural design, it need not disenchant it. The musical imagination that has, over time, established the slender threads of actuality in musical design space may be a crane (or a cascade of cranes) and not a skyhook,[63] firmly anchored, like natural selection itself, to the terrestrial surface whence it arose. But it constitutes what is arguably the most directly accessible and compelling skyhook simulacrum encountered in human experience, framing design products so nearly immaterial and yet so dense with intentionality that they seem to slip the bonds of natural necessity.

Because scores and performances are artifactual and representational items, they may be expected to be intentional. But how does the musical imagination constitute a sky-hook simulacrum, and how do its products achieve the illusion of immateriality? To answer these questions, we must now turn our attention to the emotional aspects of musical experience. One final question: Is musical ontology, as Ridley (2003) claims, utterly pointless? I shall leave that for the reader to decide when we come to the end of these inquiries.

5 From Musical Representation to Musical Emotion

Which various emotions humans or animals can have—the various action readiness modes they may experience or show—depends upon what action programs, behavior systems, and activation or deactivation mechanisms the organism has at its disposal.

—N. Frijda (1986, 469)

5.1 Introduction and Chapter Conspectus

In chapter 3 I argued that the musical performance is a pushmi-pullyu representation, a nonpropositional intentional icon that has both indicative and imperative functions. Pushmi-pullyu representations like Millikan's mother hen calls and animal danger signals have an immediate emotional salience for the interpreting organism, as do the representations of Gibsonian affordances she specifically mentions. Considered as a pushmi-pullyu representation, the musical utterance carries a similar emotional salience. Indeed, as we soon shall see, the well-executed musical utterance affects the listener immediately with the emotional impact of a friendly touch. But our consideration of the musical utterance will also disclose a far more profound mode of musical emotional response, more profound because unlike mother hen calls, danger signals, or even what I shall be calling "the musical touch effect," this mode of affective response is bound up with the mental processing required for the off-line implementation of sophisticated musical plans.

Section 5.2 opens with a discussion of arousal and formalist theories of musical experience. While rejecting formalism and accepting a version of the arousal theory, I argue that musical experience does have important cognitive components. Section 5.3 provides some requisite biological and psychological background detail concerning the complex phenomena that are termed "emotions." Particularly important, as we shall see, is the claim that emotions involve action tendencies or changes in action readiness. Once section 5.4 has developed the idea of the musical touch effect broached in the preceding paragraph, the stage is set for section 5.5, the heart of the chapter.

After drawing a brief contrast with Leonard B. Meyer's implication-realization theory (subsection 5.5.1), subsection 5.5.2 introduces the idea of nonconceptual content. Drawing on this idea and on the notion of the Gibsonian musical affordances introduced in chapter 2, I argue in the ensuing subsections that music arouses emotion by motivating virtual (off-line) actions *afforded* in musical space. The egocentric and nonconceptual organization of musical space activates (off-line) in the brain of the listener relatively primitive modes of spatial orientation and motor guidance, which, as section 5.6 then explains, allow the musical environment to take on a subjective, intensely emotionally charged quality that is normally muted in human experience by the objectifying goals of conceptual cognitive functions. Section 5.7 recapitulates this extended argument and concludes with a discussion of Sartre's theory of the emotions, a discussion that serves to clarify the concerns of this chapter and to link them with those of the next.

5.2   Arousal and Formalist Theories of Musical Experience

Arousal and formalist theories of musical experience are generally regarded as incompatible rivals. The first theory, whose provenance extends back to Descartes and even beyond to Plato, construes the musical experience as fundamentally an emotional one. It explains the significance of music in terms of its capacity to arouse in the listener various standard or so-called garden variety emotions like anger, sadness, fear, or joy. The second theory, which is of more recent vintage, received its classic nineteenth-century formulation in Eduard Hanslick's *On the Musically Beautiful*. It construes the musical experience as fundamentally a cognitive one. Music possesses certain formal/structural properties, and the musical experience requires that the listener recover these from the musical surface. The emotional aspect of musical experience is then traced to the satisfaction that attends achieving an understanding of a complex, intentionally constructed object. In recent years formalism has forged a natural alliance with the cognitivist revolution in psychology that has occurred over the last three decades and on which I have relied in previous chapters.

The theory I have presented to this point in the book is a cognitivist one, but it is not formalist, because it imputes an extramusical representational function to the musical surface and to the musical mental models constructed on its basis. Whatever one wants to say about formalism, I believe that it would be a mistake to regard cognitivist and arousal approaches as incompatible. In this chapter I shall try to show that the arousal theory has gotten important things right and that it can be combined coherently with cognitivism. I shall then offer an arousal theory, but one that avoids what Budd (1985, 125) and, following him, Ridley (1995, 38) have termed "the heresy of the separable experience": the idea that a musical work gives the listener an experience that can be fully characterized apart from the work itself and could in principle be elicited by other means, say, by a drug with some remarkable properties. The arousal theory I shall be offering will be what Ridley (1995, 128) terms a "weak" arousal theory, holding that in order to experience emotions appropriate to (as opposed to merely contingently associated with) a musical work, that is, in order to experience the emotions of which a musical work is really expressive, the listener must adopt and act out, albeit off-line, the plan of that very musical work. But I shall also argue that principles like the ones I propose are required even by a strong arousal theory like that of Matravers (1998) if such a theory is to retain any plausibility.

5.3   Emotions, Affective Feelings, Moods, and Passions

The question, What is an emotion?, has elicited a bewildering variety of answers. It is widely, though not universally, agreed that emotions are complex, intentional (occurrent) states and (dispositional) traits involving some combination of cognition, valent appraisal, motivation, autonomic arousal, and bodily action tendency or change in action readiness. But which of these components (if any) constitute necessary constituents and which do not remains controversial.[1] Indeed, at least one theorist (Griffiths 1997) doubts that emotions comprise a scientifically respectable natural biological- or psychological-kind category at all. Even the question concerning the nature of a theory of the emotions is a vexed one. Is the question of what an emotion is likely to yield to philosophical conceptual analysis? Or is it a question for an empirical, in this case a psychological *cum* biological, theory to answer?

A second vexed question concerns the role of cognition. While no one these days considers an emotion a reflexive, involuntary episode like a sneeze or a merely subjective sensation like a sinking feeling in the gut, theorists differ widely concerning the nature and degree of involvement of cognition in emotions. On one extreme are arrayed those, for the most part philosophers pursuing some version of a conceptual analysis approach, who consider emotions to be evaluative judgments (Nussbaum 2001;[2] Solomon 1980) or to require the formation of evaluative judgments or other beliefs as causally necessary conditions (Gordon 1987; Kenny 1963; Lyons 1980). On the other extreme are those, generally psychologists, neuroscientists, and naturalistically oriented philosophers pursuing an empirical-theoretical approach (e.g., Damasio 1994, 1999; Griffiths 1997; Prinz 2004; Zajonc 1980), who contend that emotional states require little or nothing in the way of full-fledged judgment or propositional cognition. Others, including both philosophers and psychologists (de Sousa 1987; Frijda 1986; Greenspan 1988; Lazarus 1991; Oatley 1992; Ortony et al. 1988; Robinson 2005), hold various intermediate positions. It hardly needs emphasizing that when arousal theorists and cognitivists enter into disputes concerning music and the emotions, what theory of the emotions happens to be in play becomes a critical issue.

The position I shall be adopting on the cognitive issue falls between the extremes outlined above. I endorse a view of emotion that is perhaps closest to Frijda's, holding occurrent emotions to be intentional, but not necessarily propositional, states with both mental and bodily aspects.[3] According to Frijda (1986, 256–257), an emotional experience (emotion "from the inside") is a valent *perception* or *perceptual taking* of a situation as "relevant, urgent, and meaningful with respect to ways of dealing with it."[4] Although it is emotional *experience* that Frijda characterizes as perceptual, perception, emotional or otherwise, need not be conscious. An emotion considered "from the outside" is a bodily action tendency or change in action readiness that is generally (but not invariably) accompanied by arousal on one or more of four different axes (autonomic arousal, attentional arousal, behavioral activation, and electrocortical arousal). Emotions are therefore motivational, a point insisted on by Lazarus, even if they are not, strictly speaking, motivations, since the tie between motivations and actions is tighter than the tie between emotions and actions (see Prinz 2004, 191ff).

Nonetheless, although action tendencies or changes in action readiness merely prime the organism for imminent action, emotions may also motivate. To say that emotion involves appraisal is to say that it is concerned with the bearing of some situation on the perceiver's weal or woe. To say emotions are valent is to say that they are evaluative: they evaluate the positive or negative impact of a situation on the self or others. Something is "at stake" for the perceiver because a "core relational theme" is engaged (Lazarus 1991, 59). The core relational theme of anger, for example, is "a demeaning offense against me or mine" (Lazarus 1991, 222). To say that emotions involve arousal is to say that emotions have a "temperature": they are hot or cold, or at least they involve some *change* in temperature. The emotional experience of fear, for example, is a hot, negatively charged perception of something as threatening to you or yours, a perception accompanied by one or more modes of arousal that engage the tendency to freeze or to take flight. Last, and very important, emotions are not mere subjective feelings. "Emotional experience," says Frijda (1986, 188),

in its more direct manifestations, is not conscious of itself. It is not a "subjective state." It is, as Sartre argues, primarily a perception: a mode of appearance of the situation, whether truly perceived or merely thought. Emotional experience is a perception of a certain kind. . . . Emotional experience is "objective," in the sense that it grasps and asserts objects with given properties. . . . The properties are out there. These properties contain the relationship to the subject: Emotional experience is perception of horrible objects, insupportable people, oppressive events. They contain that relationship implicitly: the "to me" or "for me" dissolves into the property.

Although Prinz defends a perceptual theory of emotion, he rejects Frijda's "objectivist" version of emotional experience:

there is an important difference between fear experiences and color experiences. The conscious feelings associated with mental states that represent colors are projected out into the world.

When we experience redness, we experience it as if it were out there on the surfaces of objects. Not so with emotions. The feeling of rage, for example, is not projected onto the object of rage; it is experienced as a state within us. (Prinz 2004, 61)

Like Frijda and like Sartre before him, I think this description of the phenomenology of emotional experience is just mistaken. Rage is not experienced as a state within us, but is projected onto the offending object, which is perceived as hateful. A root problem in Prinz's account lies, I believe, in assuming as paradigmatic the cognitively most sophisticated mode of human perception. Like many a philosopher, Prinz takes vision as the standard case. This motivates his basic model of emotion, in which an antecedent, nonvalent perception causes a subsequent change in the state of bodily arousal, which then gives rise to an emotion.

Prinz's theory seems to be what he calls a "precondition multicomponent" theory. The antecedent perception of the object or event is a necessary causal precondition for the emotion, but it is not part of the emotion process, which consists of only two components: an embodied appraisal (something bears on my well being) and a valence marker (that something is good or bad). While a perception of the bodily state is part of the emotion process, the bodily state is merely the emotion's "nominal object." Its "real object" is not the original object of perception, but a "formal object," the relational *property* of the perceived object whereby it engages a core relational theme for the perceiver. To take one of Prinz's favored examples, the visual perception of a snake in the immediate vicinity causes a bodily reaction. The danger posed by the snake (the emotion's formal object) is then perceived by way of a perception of the bodily state (the emotion's nominal object). The threat of imminent physical harm is the core relational theme (cf. Lazarus 1991, 235), which Prinz identifies with the emotion's formal object.

Although this story is most plausible in the case of visual perception, it is less so with regard to cognitively more primitive human perceptual systems. The disgust aroused by a revolting taste, texture, or smell is not consequent upon perception, but is inseparable from the perceptual experience itself. The object of disgust is no formal object perceived by way of a perceived bodily reaction; it just *is* the offending object or stuff itself, perceived *as disgusting*. The same, I maintain, is true of all the human perceptual modes, despite the fact that vision, and to a lesser extent hearing, have achieved greater perspectival independence than have the other sense modalities.[5] The object of fear *looks* fearsome; the object of rage *looks* hateful. This view of emotional experience is not only more faithful to its phenomenology. As we shall see, it also bears significantly on the issue, broached in chapter 2, of musical experience as tactual.

Moreover, Prinz (2004) appears to contradict himself. On page 62, he says that "emotions represent their formal objects, not their particular objects. An episode of sadness may concern any number of distinct particular objects, but the sadness in each represents loss." But on page 185, he says that "one can be both sad and depressed about the same particular object. The difference is that sadness represents its object as an isolated loss, while depression represents its object as bearing on one's general position in life." In the first quotation, sadness represents *loss* (or *being a loss*), a relational property. In the second, sadness represents a particular object, in this case a failing relationship, *as a loss*. Prinz does introduce the expression "ontic object" (185) to designate the class of things possessing the property that serves as the formal object of an emotion. The ontic object of sadness, for example, is the class of things irrevocably lost. But that does not help resolve the apparent contradiction, for sadness is still said both to represent and not to represent particular objects.

It is possible that in the second instance, Prinz is speaking of a composite whole consisting of a representation of a particular object *along with* the consequent emotional response, something he terms an "attitudinal" as opposed to a "state" emotion (179– 182). A state emotion is an occurrent embodied valent appraisal that represents a formal object, whereas an attitudinal emotion is a state emotion "bound together" with a representation of the particular object whose relational property supplies the state emotion with its formal object. The representation in question, however, seems to be a thought (hence the label "attitudinal"), not a percept. I contend that emotional perception of an object requires no propositional representation, and that denial of this encourages the faulty subjectivist picture of emotional experience. Emotional states perceptually represent objects, events, or stuffs as valent with regard to core relational themes.

Kenny (1963, 56–57), from whose discussion Prinz's notion of the formal object of emotion derives, rejects the perception view of emotion entirely. For him, "emotions, unlike perceptions, do not give us any information about the external world." He supports this claim by looking to "what we can say," that is, to linguistic conceptual analysis: "We can say 'I know there was a policeman there, because I saw a flash of blue,' but not 'I know there was a policeman there, because I felt a wave of hatred.'" Notice that he has begged the question by construing an emotion as a subjective feeling, a felt "wave of hatred." He does, however, also cite some empirical evidence:

But the dissimilarities between emotions and perceptions are more significant than the similarities. There are not organs of emotion as there are organs of perception. We see with our eyes, smell with our noses, hear with our ears; there are no parts of our bodies with which we fear or hope or feel jealous or excited. (Kenny 1963, 56)

Kenny recognizes that "not every part of the body which is necessary for a particular mode of perception is an organ of perception" (57). However, these parts of the body that are necessary for perception but are not organs of perception are not sufficient, for without organs of perception, that is, organs of the special senses, perception is not possible. This conclusion is based, once again, on an analysis of concepts of specialized modes of *human perception and human organs of perception* that by definition, as it were, excludes perception by organisms lacking such specialized sensory systems:

What then is an organ of perception? The concept is not entirely precise; but it seems that we shall not be far wrong if we say that an organ of perception is a part of the body which can be moved at will in ways which affect the efficiency of the sense in question. Thus, part of what is involved in the concept of sense-organ is expressed in such remarks as "You can see it if you look through this crack." "You can hear them if you put your ear to the wall." "If you don't like the smell, then hold your nose." (Ibid., 57)

It is clear that there is a major disagreement here over whether emotions are or are not perceptions, as well as disagreement concerning the intension and the extension of the concepts *emotion* and *perception* themselves. Perhaps most important, there is a profound *methodological* disagreement over how one goes about determining the intensions and the extensions of such concepts. Kenny, we just saw, relies on analysis of emotion talk and perception talk, along with a brief glance in the direction of human anatomy and physiology. Frijda's approach is quite different. His strategy is to approach human emotion as a psychobiological phenomenon and determine what emotions are by grouping them, if possible by homology, with related traits in other species that may lack, in one way or another, characteristics that apply in the human case—say, certain anatomical structures, or certain cognitive abilities, or the experience of affective qualia, or the capacity to undergo certain modes of arousal, or the ability to engage in certain modes of action. According to Frijda (1986, 474–475), this family of related traits forms a continuum:

There is no sharp dividing line between "reflexive" or "instinctive" behavior and emotion; behavior organizations can be ordered on a continuum in this regard. Hence the possibility of differing in opinion as to whether, say, disgust, is or is not an emotion; and hence the possibility of differing in opinion as to where, in evolution, emotion begins: with the worm, or the lizard, or the mouse, the chimpanzee, or the human animal.

For Frijda, the question of whether emotions are perceptual and the question of determining the contents of the relevant concepts are empirical-theoretical questions. For answers, we look not to conceptual analysis but to the appropriate sciences, in this case evolutionary biology, physiology, and psychology. If the concepts in question are construed as empirical-theoretical, they will not be immune to the pressure of empirical evidence. This, in turn, requires that we be prepared to alter the intensions and the extensions of our concepts as the theories in which they are embedded evolve.

As a psychologist, Frijda has not troubled to make the logical and methodological commitments of this approach to the emotions explicit. But philosopher Paul Griffiths (1997) has. For Griffiths, the problem with any approach that relies heavily on linguistic analysis is that even if it yielded an explication of "the" concept of *emotion* on which there is wide agreement, it would not necessarily tell us what emotions are. At best, it would tell us what some group of language users *think* emotions are (cf. Griffiths 1997, 39; Zajonc 1984). Just as painstaking analysis of concepts of *water* current before 1750 or concepts of *light* current before 1850 could not have sufficed to disclose the nature of water or of light, a careful analysis of a folk concept of *emotion* cannot be expected to disclose the nature of emotion. Water and light are natural kinds, and as such may be said to possess essences. But these are empirically discovered, causally efficacious physical microstructures that ground reliable inductions, not definitional essences accessible by way of an a priori analytical method. Although species, as we saw in chapter 4, are widely considered to be historically extended individuals and not kinds at all, they are, according to Griffiths, natural kind–*like* because they ground reliable inductions (1997, 213). Their essences, however, are historical, and not, as in the cases of water or gold, microstructural. Emotions, considered as dispositions and not as occurrent states, are properly seen as species-specific traits, species-specific because different species possess variant repertoires of emotions. As species-specific traits, some emotions, Griffiths argues, are likely to turn out to be innate behavioral programs that depend on selected-for internal mechanisms in humans (and nonhuman animals) that are found by biological and psychological science to cause the cluster of behaviors and subjective experiences that induced application of the concept in the first place.

Once exposed to empirical pressure, the folk concept of *emotion* could turn out to lack theoretical integrity and could, in the extreme case, even become a candidate for outright elimination, for the conceptual analysis approach to the emotions tends to place under one vernacular concept a variety of traits, thereby carving out a gerrymandered class that includes so-called basic emotions like fear, anger, joy, and sadness. Although some are skeptical of the very idea of basic emotions (see Ortony et al. 1988), Ekman (1984, 1992) and Griffiths (1997) have argued that there is a small set of emotions that can be considered "affect programs" because they display modular, reflexive characteristics, because they are pan-culturally recognizable on the basis of facial expression and bodily comportment, and because they display some clear physiological and behavioral homologues, for such programs can be found in some infrahuman nonlinguistic species. As modular, these programs tend to remain *relatively* insulated from propositional processing. We shall return to these affect programs in the next section. But this gerrymandered class of emotions also comprises some very different traits that are not obviously affect programs, including the higher-level, distinctively human emotions like pride, shame, and jealousy that seem to require beliefs as well as higher-order intentionality, and that are significantly less modular because they appear to be subject to social constructionist forces. (Compare the incidences of and varying attitudes to *crime passionnel* in various locales.) The required beliefs and higher-order intentional states may be part of the emotion process; or they may be causal preconditions that "recalibrate" the emotion process (Prinz 2004, 99). None of Griffiths's arguments claim to demonstrate in any conclusive way that "emotion" is ripe for elimination as a legitimate scientific term, and some (Prinz 2004; Robinson 2005) remain skeptical of Griffiths's disunity thesis. Nevertheless, what these considerations show is that it may be unwise to permit a particular folk concept of emotion yielded by linguistic analysis to rule a priori on the nature of emotion, since, in the end, any such concept may break up under the strain of having attempted to unify phenomena that turn out to be significantly divergent in nature.

Understanding emotional experience as perceptual in Frijda's way will prove important for pursuing the connection between musical representation and musical emotion, and his method is more in accord than is Kenny's conceptual analysis approach with the naturalistic approach to musical representation I have advocated. As already suggested, the notion of perception in question is a broad one, certainly not limited to human perception mediated by highly differentiated special senses. Minimally, perception requires the registration of information. But it also requires something more, for the registration of information is not necessarily intentional. Information concerning past geological eras, for example, is registered in various strata of the earth's crust, and environmental information is registered in the rings of trees. Neither the earth's crust nor a tree, I argued in chapter 2, is properly regarded as an intentional system. Perception, however, also requires categorization. But even this may not be enough, for categorization could be construed as a matter of causal response. "Iron," Brandom points out (1994, 33), "rusts in some environments and not others, and so can be interpreted as classifying its environments into two sorts.... Such responsive classification is a primitive kind of practical taking *of* something *as* something." A piece of iron, I contend, does no "taking" at all because it cannot mis-take. As Dennett (1996, 37) says, "there is no *taking* without the possibility of *mistaking*." In my terms, a piece of rusted iron is an informational vehicle, but not an intentional system and therefore not a perceiver. Perception is "taking truly," *Wahrnehmung*, as the Germans say. It is categorization subject to normative evaluation, categorization that could go wrong. This categorization need not be conceptual, as it is not (on most tellings) in nonlinguistic animals. It also need not be conscious. In principle, it could involve nothing more sophisticated than the assimilation of an input vector to a location (or an attractor) in the activation space of a simple (i.e., low-dimensional) connectionist-style network. Categorization may not even exploit computations so sophisticated as these. A perceiver could be a device as simple as a thermostat at a specific setting which places ambient temperature information (accurately or inaccurately) into three categories: too hot, too cold, and acceptable.[6]

While a standard[7] connectionist network or a thermostat may be counted a perceiver, neither is an *emotional* perceiver. Because they are products of human and not natural design, they have totally different developmental histories, and as a result of these developmental histories, they lack the appropriate functional organization. Before there were any vertebrate brains, before there were central nervous systems or sophisticated representational capacities in organisms at all, there were multicellular creatures that operated by means of a single division within a simply defined neurally implemented activation space, a division establishing the original evaluative behavioral dichotomy of approach and avoidance or, perhaps better, acceptance and rejection, the most primitive form of emotional appraisal.[8] Predating in evolutionary history the emergence of special sensory systems and the perceptual qualia they support, there were such valent appraisals of the environment and the primitive motor guidance systems that made the appropriate acceptance-rejection responses possible. These were then taken up and incorporated into newer neural structures, for their homologues are present in the brainstems and spinal ganglia of modern animals. As a result, the twin afferent and efferent dimensions of appraisal and valent action tendency configure all terrestrial mental life. Vestiges of appraisal and valence persist in the opponent processing and feature detection so basic to the design of vertebrate sensory systems, for example the red-green and blue-yellow opponent systems and the edge detectors in the human visual system. Opponent processing requires that neurons and neuronal assemblies be sensitive to preferred inputs. Even a sensory transducer is tuned to "shriek with joy" (Clark 2000, 23) when provided with its optimal stimulus.

A series of experiments have lent support to an opponent-processing theory of "affective changes" (R. L. Solomon 1980, 693–694).[9] Dogs placed in a Pavlovian harness were administered a frightening 10-second shock to their hind feet. Heart rate, which varied directly with amperage of the shock, increased sharply from a baseline of 100 to about 200 beats per minute, peaked at about 5 seconds, and then declined to baseline. Interestingly, after the shock, heart rate then *decreased* significantly *below* baseline to 80 beats per minute, before finally returning to baseline. Reasonably enough, Solomon interprets the first phase as negatively valent (fear) and the second as positively valent (relief), and takes heart rate, which varied with the amperage of the shock, to be a reliable indicator of intensity of emotional experience. At first, increase and decrease of heart rate were more or less symmetrical, although the negative phase was more sluggish and took five times as long (50 seconds) to complete. After habituation to electric shock in "veteran" laboratory dogs, however, positive increase in heart rate declined, but the negative phase remained as before. Other experiments with different animals showed the same pattern, but with the valence signs reversed: When the initial stimulus was positive or "hedonic," the secondary phase was affectively negative. In a similar fashion, humans have been observed to go through the positive–negative sequence in drug habituation and subsequent withdrawal, and through the negative–positive sequence with fear-inducing activity (e.g., skydiving) and subsequent euphoria. Solomon (1980, 694) draws the parallel with color vision:

Turn on a relatively pure red light and keep it on for 30 seconds. At first the red appears to the observer to be rich and saturated. As the seconds go by, however, the redness seems to decrease, as though one had mixed white light with the red. Now turn the red light off. The observer experiences a green afterimage that peaks in saturation immediately and then slowly dies away until the greenness is undetectable. Many data sources suggest that there is probably a similar or analogous pattern of affective dynamics for hedonic stimuli.[10]

According to Damasio's (1994, 173ff) "somatic marker hypothesis," a version of which I endorse,[11] organic systems designed by natural selection process *all* environmental input by way of cortical monitoring of bodily states. Characteristic of these systems is an evolved multilevel brain with recurrent pathways arranged to allow sensory and association areas of the cerebral cortex to monitor, modulate, and inhibit the more automatic and reflex-like responses of the diencephalon (thalamus and hypothalamus), the brainstem, the lateral areas of the cerebellar cortex, and even ganglia in the spinal cord (via the corticospinal tract), and to integrate and categorize the sensory information that is delivered to the primary sensory areas of the cortex via these more primitive structures by way of the limbic system. The limbic system is a ring of phylogenetically primitive cortical structures encircling the diencephalon that is believed to support emotional function in mammals. In humans, it includes the parahippocampal gyrus, the cingulate gyrus, the subcallosal gyrus, and the underlying cortex of the hippocampal formation. This last structure comprises the hippocampus proper (implicated in primitive olfaction and memory), the dentate gyrus, and the subiculum. The septal area of the hypothalamus, the nucleus accumbens, and two neocortical areas, the orbitofrontal cortex and the amygdala, are customarily also included within the limbic system (Kandel et al. 1991, 736–737). The limbic system is the principal mechanism for behavior modulation and control in the ancient mammalian cortex. This coheres with Frijda's notion of emotions as action tendencies or changes in action readiness.

Because they involve action tendencies, human (and many animal) emotional states have been said to involve perception of Gibsonian affordances:

Roughly speaking, emotional experience corresponds to a mode of appearance involving "demand characteristics."...We will refer to such a mode of appearance of situations as *situational meaning structures*. (Frijda 1986, 189–190, emphasis in original)

Context components are those features of situational meaning structures that determine the nature of the emotion. They pertain to what the subject feels he can or cannot do with respect to the situation and are in fact action relevance components...their contents [correspond] with "affordances" in the Gibsonian sense. (Ibid., 204–205)

The relevance of these claims to issues of musical representation and musical emotional arousal should be obvious, given our discussion of the musical affordance in chapter 2.[12] We shall take up this topic in more detail later in this chapter.

It has become customary to distinguish between emotions, affective feelings, moods, and passions. An emotion, according to the view I have proposed, is a valent perception of an object, situation, or event relating to a core relational theme and accompanied by one or more modes of arousal as well as a change in action readiness. Taking emotion as our base case, we can define the others in terms of their deviation from it.

(1) Affective feelings If an emotion is a valent perception of an identifiable object, an affective feeling is whatever is left over when a definite object of the emotion is lacking. Writers are not always clear regarding the question of whether the object of an emotion must be a so-called material object (cf. Ridley 1995), that is, an existing particular to which the subject of emotion is causally related, or whether it may be an intentional object that is known not to exist. There is a third case as well, in which the object of an emotion is fictional but not thought to be fictional, as is the case, on some tellings, with religious emotions. In the last two cases, there can be genuine emotion that includes action tendencies, despite the fact that a material object may be lacking. Where the object of emotion is intentional but known to be fictional, the action tendency or change in action readiness will be suppressed, since the subject will not be prepared to take real action. But on the first interpretation of "object" as "material object," emotions regarding fictional objects are not aroused at all. Only affective feelings are, since the objects of the putative emotions do not exist. On the second interpretation of "object" as "intentional object," emotions regarding fictional situations may be aroused, but only "off-line," that is, with action tendency *inhibited* (see Currie 1995). On this interpretation, Richard III's malevolent intentions regarding the princes in the Tower may cause us to fear Richard or fear for the princes; but the emotion does not fit the standard case, the sort of thing that would arise were the staged events actually to be occurring.[13] As is often pointed out, if such negative emotion were the genuine article, few would willingly subject themselves to an aesthetic experience. Moreover, ordinarily appropriate behaviors like trying to intercede or warn the victims are not engaged. On either account of the nature of the object of an emotion, however, the state of arousal attributable to a musical listener would be one of affective feeling, not emotion, since music depicts no identifiable objects, not even fictional ones.

(2) Moods Since emotions require identifiable objects, moods must be classed either as affective feelings or as emotions that take objects that are indefinite or global, as "bearing on one's general position in life" (Prinz 2004, 185). I shall follow what I take to be a growing consensus in favor of the second interpretation. If music is capable of giving rise to moods, then it may also be capable of arousing emotions, that is, mood-like emotions, after all.

(3) Passions Although passions have traditionally been regarded as emotions that are particularly intense, persistent, and centrally important to a particular person, not everyone so construes them. Ridley (1995), for example, appropriates "passion" to serve as the genus-word under which he subsumes emotions, affective feelings, and moods. Since I shall not be using this term in my discussion, I shall not take a stand regarding its proper use. Ridley (or anyone else) may appropriate a common term as a term of art provided he is clear about how it is to be used.

While I shall be agreeing with the general consensus that musical scenarios do not contain identifiable intentional objects and that, as a result, central cases of arousal in musical contexts strictly speaking are cases of the production of affective feelings and not full-blown emotions, I shall be arguing that inhibited action tendencies play an important role in the musical arousal of feelings, and to this extent these musical affective feelings bear a strong analogy to the off-line emotions that, on one interpretation, may arise in fictional situations. After all, musical scenarios provide the musical affordances that, as I argued in chapter 2, motivate virtual (off-line) actions. But this agreement comes with three provisos. First, even if musical scenarios contain no identifiable objects, music may give rise to moods, that is, emotions with indeterminate or global objects. Second, musical scenarios may contain musical virtual objects, that is, the objects of representations with nonconceptual content. As I shall argue in later sections of this chapter, musical space has the character of an egocentric, and not a public or objective, space. As a result, musical objects are identifiable only by way of a variety of indexical reference, or a musical analogue of indexical reference. Nonconceptual content, as we shall see, may be protopropositional, thereby allowing a minimalist version of indexical reference.[14] The objects of such reference are not identifiable in the way virtual objects of literary and cinematic fiction are, for the latter are understood to occupy locations in public space; but objects "tracked" in musical, egocentric space still may engage emotion. Indeed, the egocentric nature of musical space, as we shall see, enhances the emotional response to musical virtual scenarios.

In the discussion of nonconceptual content to follow, I shall be agreeing with Strawson and a number of his Oxonian followers that individuation and recognition of objects in public space requires conceptual representation, which, in turn, requires linguistic vehicles. Because musical scenarios may contain virtual objects, musical *affective feelings* can, under some circumstances, at least approximate the off-line *emotions* that arise in fictional contexts after all. And third, as we are about to see in the next section, musical performance does give rise to at least one bona fide emotion whose object is the musical surface itself as an event or series of events, an emotion, moreover, that is *not* aroused off-line but that elicits real action tendencies and changes in action readiness. Because of these cross-cutting complexities, I shall on occasion allow myself to talk generally of the arousal of musical emotions, while asking the reader to keep in mind my overall agreement with conventional wisdom concerning emotions and affective feelings along with the relevant provisos.

5.4 The Musical Touch Effect

Anterior to its status as a sign, music is an action on and of the body.
—D. Lidov (1987, 69)

Hearing is a form of touch.[15]
—Evelyn Glennie

For the formalist musical aesthetician (see Kivy 1989, 1990), arousal theories, even weak arousal theories, suffer from a number of flaws.[16] But one flaw in particular is fatal. According to most versions of the arousal theory, the emotions aroused include the so-called garden variety emotions, and such emotions require an intentional object. On some tellings, as we saw, this intentional object must be an existing material particular; on others, it may be a nonexistent object. But in either case, if I am angry, not only am I angry at someone or about some circumstance, but I must be aware of just who it is I am angry at and what it is that I am angry about. If I am dejected, I am dejected about something, and I must be aware of what it is I am dejected about. As we saw, an emotional state requires an intentional object in order to *be* an emotional state.

Although pure music (i.e., music that is not explicitly programmatic and that lacks text or contingent memory associations) can be said to possess a syntactic (or quasi-syntactic) structure, it (says the formalist) can carry no semantic content and, a fortiori, no propositional content. It therefore cannot supply the sort of intentional object required by the standard emotions. Nor does the music itself seem capable of serving as the intentional object of such an emotion: how sensible would it be to say that a listener is *angry at* the first *allegro* of Beethoven's *Grosse Fuge* or *sad about* the *Marcia funebre* from the *Eroica* or *triumphant concerning* the *Finale* of the Fifth Symphony? Surely it is some kind of purported content of these works that is supposed to supply the intentional objects for the emotions in question, as Ivan's description in *The Brothers Karamazov* of a child torn to pieces by a nobleman's dogs may supply the object of the reader's anger, or Marlow's description of Jim's death in Conrad's novel may supply the object of the reader's sadness. But pure music has no such content and can supply no such objects. Therefore, the music is incapable of arousing any emotions of this kind.[17] The sensible formalist will allow that pure music can arouse emotions of some kind: listeners, after all, are often visibly moved by music. But here the music itself will serve as the intentional object; and these emotions will not be of the garden variety, but will be highly specialized: either a distinctive musical emotion (see the discussion of Gurney later in this section), or if not this, emotions like the awe and wonder that *follow upon* prior cognitive apprehension, indeed upon the apprehension *under a potentially statable verbal description* of the *structural-organizational properties of the music*. Even a listener untutored in music theory must be able to *say* what it is about the music that moves him. Such a listener may know nothing of the old modes, but if he is moved by the strains of "Greensleeves" he must be able to apply some appropriate description, say, that he finds the tune's "sort of old-fashioned" quality appealing (Kivy 1990, 85). Unless these conditions are met, there is no intentional object for the emotion to take, and consequently, no emotion.

I argued in chapters 2 and 3 that to grant that music is nonconceptual is not to grant the formalist point that it is nonrepresentational. As we shall see later on in this chapter, this has important implications for the arousal of emotion, including some garden variety emotions. But let us put issues of musical representation aside for the moment. I now shall argue that there is a garden variety emotion taking the *musical surface* as its object that arises during musical experience, that this emotion *initially* has nothing to do with the cognized structural-organizational properties of the music, and that its intentionality does not require apprehension under a potentially statable verbal description.

A flaw in the formalist argument just rehearsed is that it assumes the extreme "judgmentalist" theory of emotion adverted to in the previous section. According to the judgmentalist or, as it is sometimes called, the propositional attitude theory, an analysis of the concept of *emotion* (based on our relevant linguistic practice) shows that emotions require beliefs or evaluative judgments because they are individuated by the propositional contents of these beliefs (as well as by the valent attitudes adopted toward them). In the standard formulation, being in a state of fear, say, depends both on believing that one is threatened and taking a negative attitude toward those belief contents. One problem with this approach is that different theorists analyze the emotion concept differently. One (R. C. Solomon) tells us that an emotion *just is* an evaluative judgment (1980, 257). Another (Lyons) specifies two individually necessary and jointly sufficient conditions that establish a state as an emotional one: an evaluation based on a belief, say that a situation is dangerous and a physiological disturbance (1980, 57–58). A third (Kenny) stresses the centrality of belief (or "thought") for the individuation of emotion (1963, 64), but denies that physiological disturbance is a necessary condition. A fourth (Greenspan 1988), while weakening some of the more extreme claims of judgmentalism, still adheres to the conceptual analysis methodology, relying largely on an examination of how we talk about emotions and what it "makes sense" to say about them. Like Nussbaum (2001), however, Greenspan is willing to allow perception, as the facts seem to require, to fulfill the cognitive role, especially in the cases of animals and infants, thereby taking a position closer to the one I favor.

Moreover, although Greenspan does not characterize it this way, she develops an interesting variant of Sellarsian verbal behaviorism, so as to accord emotions appropriate justificatory force and subject them to rational evaluation. Just as, on Sellars's sccount, a spontaneous and unjustified verbal report (or a suppressed inclination to make such a report) may enter the space of reasons and justify a perceptual knowledge claim by being judged by the speaker or hearer to be a reliable differential response, so may an emotional reaction take on justificatory status by being judged a reliable perceptual response.[18] While agreeing with cognitivist philosophers that beliefs play the primary role in determining the intentionality or object-directedness of emotions, Greenspan also argues that emotions are more loosely constrained by standards of consistency than are beliefs: preserving a friendship or a marriage may require one to be simultaneously in contrary emotional states, say, states of happiness and annoyance (1988, 117). She suggests that the way in which emotions may flout certain canons of doxastic rationality is useful for the establishment of appropriate habits of ethical behavior, particularly in cases of akrasia (ibid., 168, 174).

In the previous section, we took note of Griffiths's argument that the conceptual analysis approach, even one as nuanced as Greenspan's, is misconceived because it misconstrues a problem that requires empirical-theoretical investigation as a problem likely to yield to conceptual analysis. If this is right, it would suggest that as students of musical aesthetics, we should not allow the judgmentalist account of emotions and their intentional objects to determine our view of what emotion in the musical-aesthetic context must be. "'Scientific' theories of the emotions come, and they go," Kivy (1990, 149) tells us. But the same can be said for any empirically responsible theory; and any *philosophical* theory of the emotions that claimed exemption from empirical pressure on the grounds that it is engaged in pure conceptual analysis would, in light of the naturalist explanatory principles assumed in the general introduction, be a nonstarter. On what, we may ask, *should* we rely if we want to know what an emotion is, if not a "scientific," that is, a psychobiological theory? Recent developments suggest, moreover, that the philosophical theory of the emotions on which Kivy relies may itself have come and gone (see, in addition to Griffiths 1997, Farrell 1988).

With these considerations in mind, let us look at the question of musical arousal of the garden variety emotions in the light of Ekman's affect programs (see the previous section). He claims to have identified six such species-specific programs: surprise, anger, fear, disgust, sadness, and joy,[19] all garden variety emotions. I shall argue later in the chapter for the "weak" arousal by pure music of *affective feelings*, and perhaps off-line emotions, of fear and sadness. Concerning anger I am somewhat less confident, and disgust may not be an emotion that can be enlisted for musical aesthetic effects at all. (This is not to deny that it may be aesthetically relevant in musical contexts; but if it is, it will likely be the result of the perception of some aesthetic defect or other). Putting anger, fear, disgust, and sadness aside, then, we are left with two emotions remaining from Ekman's list: surprise and joy.

Lazarus (1991, 54) holds that surprise is problematic as an emotion because it is not unambiguously valent, since it may be positive or negative: surprise, along with other "non-reflex reactions" like curiosity and attentiveness, is a "pre-emotion." The same, however, may be said for startle, perhaps the most primitive variety of surprise. For some, startle is a bona fide, if very primitive, emotional response (Robinson 1995, 2005); for others it is a mere reflex (Lazarus 1991, 53). Frijda, as we saw, notes the difficulty that attends making a clear-cut distinction between reflexes and emotions, and Griffiths claims (1997, 84) that the affect programs themselves "are rather like reflexes, but more complex and coordinated." It may be argued against Lazarus, moreover, that both surprise and startle really are negatively valent: even the shock of a totally unexpected surprise birthday party can be initially unpleasant (I speak from experience). Prinz (2004, 153) suggests that "in ancestral environments, fight and flight may have

Example 5.1

Mozart, Piano Quartet in G Minor, *Rondo: Allegro.*

been the safest responses to anything completely novel or unexpected. It is tempting to conclude," he continues, "that surprise and panic began as one emotion. Surprise may be a mild form of panic (low-arousal panic)." I see no reason, therefore, to quarrel with Ekman's inclusion of surprise on his list of basic emotions. I shall be arguing that unlike any arousal of emotions or affective feelings of fear or sadness, and unlike any arousal off-line of the corresponding emotions in fictional contexts, the emotions of surprise and joy are regularly aroused "on-line" by music. That is, during a successful musical performance the arousal of these two emotions is real and tends to result in appropriate behavioral responses.

Consider surprise first. The turns a piece of music takes often surprise us. Actual surprise behaviors (e.g., showing startle, raising the eyebrows and opening wide the eyes, and contractions of the neck and body) are not uncommon when a sensitive but unfamiliar listener is confronted with musical surprises like the climactic E-flat major deceptive cadence in the *Rondo* of Mozart's G-minor Piano Quartet (example 5.1), or the abrupt breaking off of the trio tune at the end of the *Scherzo* of Beethoven's Ninth Symphony (example 5.2), or the sudden outburst that begins the development section in the first movement of Tchaikovsky's *Pathetique* Symphony (example 5.3), or, perhaps most obviously, the surprise *fortissimo* G chord in the appropriately named Haydn symphony (example 5.4). Admittedly, such reactions depend on prior cognitive processing: to be surprised by such musical events, their structural significance must be understood. Nonetheless, the fact that these and similar musical episodes retain some of their effect even with increased familiarity also suggests the operation of a modular affect program.[20] Such claims about the role of surprise in musical experience are hardly unheard of. Nor are they particularly controversial. Indeed, they figure prominently in one well-known and well-regarded version of musical arousal theory, namely

Example 5.2

Beethoven, Symphony No. 9 in D Minor, *Scherzo*.

Example 5.3

Tchaikovsky, Symphony No. 6 in B Minor, *Allegro vivo*.

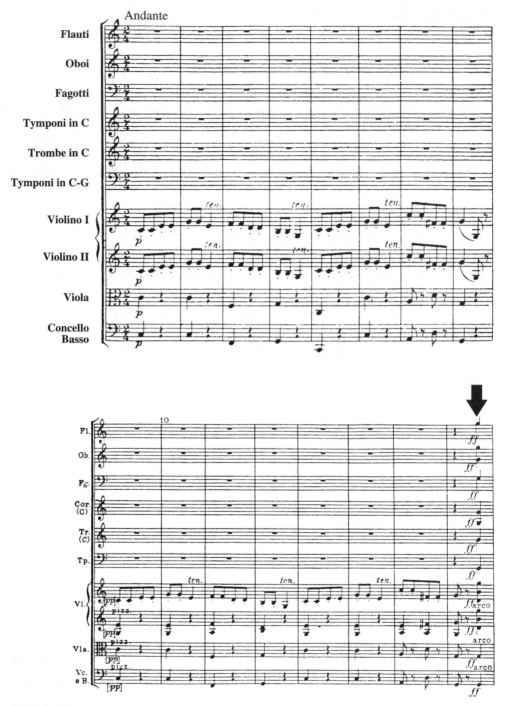

Example 5.4
Haydn, Symphony No. 94 in G, "Surprise," *Andante*.

Leonard B. Meyer's (1956) implication-realization theory, as well as in the more psychologically sophisticated contemporary version of this theory developed by Eugene Narmour (1990) discussed in chapter 2. Since we will be returning briefly to the implication-realization theory later in the chapter, let us also put surprise to one side for now.

There remains, then, for our consideration right now only one of the six basic emotions from Ekman's list, namely joy. There is nothing special in the choice of "joy" as the category-word for this "basic" emotion: it is a label for a group of related positive emotions, and any of its close cognates would have done as well. Indeed, in his 1984 essay Ekman uses "joy" interchangeably with "happiness." Still, the claim that joy is aroused on-line by music with attendant behavioral manifestations is, I think, a controversial one, at least in formalist circles. This thesis must be carefully distinguished from the fairly commonplace idea that music is productive of pleasure. What I shall argue is that any and every successful musical performance, before it does anything else it may do, and while it is doing everything else it does do, arouses in the listener the basic *emotion* of joy, and not just pleasurable *sensation*. I shall also argue, against the formalist position, that this emotion of joy is, as an emotion, a genuinely intentional state taking the musical surface as object, albeit a state not dependent, initially at least, on any propositional content or attitude.

We saw in chapter 2 that the specialized human sensory systems share a remarkably common plan, all coding for stimulus modality, intensity, duration, and location. We also saw that they use three different modes of stimulus transduction, and that only two of these systems function by means of mechanoreception: the touch component of the sensory-somatic system (as opposed to the heat-sensitive, the nociceptive, and the proprioceptive components), and the auditory system. Finally, we noted the homologous relationship between the lateral line organ in fishes, an organ of touch, and the organ of Corti in the human inner ear. Although musical sounds are (acoustically) periodic waveform phenomena, they in fact form a distinct subclass of such phenomena. Any sound with a definite pitch will be a periodic waveform phenomenon; but many a sound of this kind, say a blaring car or train horn, even one approximating a triadic major, augmented major, major-seventh, or diminished-seventh chord (as so many these days do), is hardly a musical sound. Here the unreconstructed formalist will treat us to an "I told you so." "Of course such a sound is not a musical one," he will say. "It lacks requisite intentionality in two ways. A musical sound is an interesting, complex artifact and is directed to the listener by the performer. And it must be an intentional object for the listener: the listener must hear it and recognize it as such under a description. But this requires belief and language."

I do not deny much of what is claimed here. My previous characterization of a musical performance as a pushmi-pullyu representation should signal agreement with the first claim: the performance must be understood by the listener as a syntactically organized symbolic utterance. I do, however, deny the second claim (or at least limit its scope), the claim that apprehension of the musicality of the *sound* requires belief and that the sound can be recognized as such only *under a description* after central cognitive processing has taken place. The results of Zajonc and others point us in a very different direction. They suggest that the qualities of a musical performer's tone can be processed and very likely are processed *initially* at a much shallower "input system" level[21] and recognized long before any judgments are made or descriptions applied, just as an animate touch to the body can be recognized almost instantaneously as such and just as quickly recognized as friendly or unfriendly. Very much the same holds true regarding animate touch for nonlinguistic infrahuman animals, as anyone who has attempted to stroke a cat can attest. To insist that an intentional object must be bound up with some propositional attitude or other is just an ill-founded prejudice of a certain brand of outmoded linguistic philosophy. And as a matter of fact, this judgmentalist view is not in accord with compelling experimental results that show that certain emotional responses in humans tend to precede the formation of any beliefs whatsoever (Zajonc 1980, 1984).

In his now rather well-known article, Zajonc (1980) cites a number of studies by various investigators supporting this claim. A study of his own is particularly representative. All things being equal, subjects prefer the familiar to the unfamiliar. Zajonc and a colleague presented 24 subjects with randomly constructed polygons, with each exposure lasting for the very brief interval of one millisecond. Subjects then rated another set of polygons on a preference scale and were tested for recognition memory. Some of these polygons were new, but others had already been presented in the first round. While *recognition* remained at a chance level (48 percent), in fact 60 percent of the *preferred* polygons were old and 40 percent were new. Of the 24 subjects, 16 liked old polygons better than new ones, but only 5 of the 24 recognized them *as* old at better than chance level. Perhaps most significantly, 17 of the 24 subjects showed better discrimination between old and new stimuli in their "affective judgments" (preferences) than in their recognition responses, but only 4 subjects showed superiority of recognition over affective judgments. The affective judgments, that is, tracked the objective familiarity/unfamiliarity ratios between the sets of polygons *better* than straight recognition judgments. The subjects, Zajonc (1980, 163) concludes,

were able to distinguish between the old and the new stimuli if they used liking as their response, but they were not able to distinguish between them if they had to identify them as "old" or "new." This result may be taken as evidence that a class of features (preferenda) exists that allows individuals to experience affect toward objects but does not allow them to accomplish cognitive tasks as simple as those in recognition memory tasks.

Why, then, the formalist may ask, are cats and other touch-sensitive animals not music lovers? Notice that I have not claimed that full-blown musical experience derives from the touch effect alone, or even that the entire range of affective musical experience derives from it alone. In fact, I indicated the opposite, and have been at pains in earlier chapters to agree with the formalist that cognitive factors, both conceptual and nonconceptual, make indispensable contributions to musical experience that must be acknowledged. The musical performance must be syntactically parsed and understood as a pushmi-pullyu representation. The listener must be able to deploy appropriate plan structures and mental models. Nonetheless, it is, I submit, nothing other than the real touch effect of music that endows it with its curiously immediate emotionally gripping quality, and that contributes to its distinctive affective impact, an impact that many have considered unequaled throughout the fine arts.

The touch of a fine musical sound is more than a friendly one, however. It has the characteristics of a loving touch, not always gentle, but loving nonetheless.[22] It "touches" us, as one says. It possesses a tactual texture fully congruent with the touch of a skilled performer on a stringed instrument as he presses down on the fingerboard and draws his bow across the string. It is as if he were playing on us. Even in very loud musical passages, "forcing" the sound of a stringed or wind instrument and pounding the keys of a piano are considered faulty execution. The sound, musicians say, must be "coaxed"; an indication of *fortissimo* is not a license for the commission of rapine on an instrument.[23] Similar considerations concern other aspects of physical musical touch: the felt quality of attacks and releases, of vibrato, of accents, of crescendos and diminuendos, and of the dynamic shaping of the musical phrases. After all, the longitudinal compression waves that impinge on our eardrums and set them into sympathetic motion emanate from the musician's motions and vibrating instrument. But in touching this body part in this way, and so in "touching" us, the musical sound engenders joy, because to experience a touch (under appropriate circumstances) that is nearly instantaneously perceived as overwhelmingly benignant and as promising more of the same engenders joy. That is how the lovely musical sound and execution strike us, and what initially draw us in, whatever particular emotionally expressive contours and structural properties the musical work turns out to possess. Moreover, the characteristic bodily comportments exhibited by engaged musical listeners regularly include joy behaviors, if "joy" is taken, as suggested above, as a placeholder label for a range of cognate positive emotions.

After a public presentation of mine on these ideas, a commentator[24] remarked that she detected a sexual hue in the descriptions. I did not, at the time, intend to suggest this, but thought the remark apt. I now believe that the idea of the musical touch effect captures much of what is correct in Edmund Gurney's appropriation of Darwin (see chapter 3 above). Gurney (1880/1966) claims that all "impressive" music, that is, all music that strikes us as beautiful and captivating, is found to be so because of an "association" with the ancient function of vocalization as a sexual lure. But without

pointing out discernible vestigial traces of this ancient function that play a significant role in modern musical experience, this is an instance of the genetic fallacy. It is
fallacious, that is, to endorse the part of "Darwin's thesis" (the part, recall, ignored by
Donald) that holds that sexual attraction was the original function of the vocalization
behaviors from which both music and speech derived, and then to conclude from this
that musical feeling arises in contemporary humans *by way of association* with ancient
sexual function without directing attention to specific and historically traceable effects
of such associations in contemporary musical response. Without this, music's having
originated in vocalization for the purpose of attracting a mate, if it did so originate,
says little about the *current* causes of musical excitement, which operate as strongly
within the sexes as they do between them. And as a matter of fact, ancient sexual function does seem a thin reed upon which to rest the rich panoply of musical affective experience. Such association casts little if any light, for example, on the "Ideal Motion"
that Gurney (1880/1966, 141) himself rightly finds so central to musical experience:

We have seen how, among changes of sense impression, [change of pitch] is unique in giving the
impression of passage from point to point. Rhythm clearly does nothing of the kind: however
much it may suggest movement, it does not suggest advance: whereas no change of pitch can
take place without involving this feature; and the most formless fragment of transition presents
this fundamental attribute of what will be afterwards described as the Ideal Motion.

And to conclude that Ideal Motion, like sexual experience, is pleasurable because
the former derives from the latter may not only be fallacious; it may actually mislead
us in our attempts to understand exactly what Ideal Motion might be. Budd (1985,
181n10), who finds the following passage from Gurney "unsurprisingly reminiscent
of sexual pleasure," may have been misled in this way:

[Music] must be judged by us directly in relation to pleasure, and that pleasure is the only criterion by which we can measure specimens of it. The pleasure, from its peculiarity, its power of
relieving the mind and steeping it as it were in a totally new atmosphere, its indescribable suggestions of infinity, and its freedom from any kind of deleterious after-effects, is of an extremely
valuable kind. (Gurney 1880/1966, 369)

To my mind, this language is far less reminiscent of sexual pleasure than of mystical
ecstasy,[25] though these two may not be entirely unrelated.[26] After all, sexual activity
is not exactly renowned for its "freedom from any kind of deleterious after-effects":
Post coitum omne animal triste est, goes the ancient wisdom.[27] Particularly salient, I
think, is the reference to "indescribable suggestions of infinity." But whichever it is,
whether the pleasure peculiar to musical experience is more akin to sexual pleasure or
mystical ecstasy, either claim needs to be explained in some detail and justified. Merely
pointing to hypothesized origins accompanied by a wave of the hand in the direction
of "sublimation" (ibid., 120) constitutes, it seems to me, not even a convincing evolutionary "just-so" story.

"There is one characteristic of melody," Gurney (1880/1966, 166) writes,

which attention to its aspect as motion brings out with special clearness; and that is our sense of entire oneness with it, of its being as it were a mode of our own life. We feel in it, indeed an objective character, inasmuch as we instinctively recognize that it has for others the same permanent possibilities of impression as for ourselves; but our sense of it nevertheless is not as of an external presentation, but of something evolved within ourselves by a special activity of our own.

Gurney's description of the phenomenology of musical experience is typically perceptive. And who would deny that the experience here described is pleasurable? But the connection between this pleasure and sexual pleasure is no more obvious than is the connection between sexual pleasure and yet another distinctive mode of musical delight to which Gurney (ibid., 72) draws attention:

when the unity [of a form] is apprehended with ease and certainty, this principle [the love of unity in diversity] in turn comes under the head of another still more general than itself, the delight, namely, in the exercise of *power*, in doing with facility a thing which seems to contain in itself the elements of difficulty.

While only tenuously, if at all, related to sexual pleasure, all of the phenomena singled out for comment by Gurney—Ideal Motion, simulation and animation, ease and power of active accomplishment—can, I submit, be explained using the theoretical apparatus of musical representation developed here in earlier chapters. Satisfying musical experience involves simulated acting on a well-devised plan in virtual musical space. Whatever in musical experience demonstrates any affinity with sexual response is comprised, as already suggested, in what I have called the musical touch effect. And as a matter of fact, Gurney himself notices the strong affinity between sound and touch without drawing what seems to me to be the obvious conclusion about the musical case (ibid., 37, emphasis mine):

We carry about an habitual instinct of having around us a certain amount of space in which we are alone, and any sudden violence to this instinct is very unnerving. That this is the true explanation seems to be shown by the fact that the gentlest possible touch, if it gives the same impression of unexpected nearness to a living creature, causes a similar start. . . . But in the starting caused by sound, there seems to be often a large element which lies quite outside these instincts: a loud sound will startle us violently without being conceived of as *due to* anything close to us.

Sound, that is, even if not traced to a *cause* in personal space affects us as if it were an animate presence *in* personal space.[28] This will prove to be quite important in later discussion. But where touch is concerned, relaxed intimacy is the contrary of startle: it is what startle gives way to when touch is expected and welcomed. I believe that this is why music, as unique among all the arts, has the special intimacy it has: if the musical sound, as an intimate presence in personal space, is well produced, it gives rise to a delight in intimacy. And because the delight is specifically the joy at the touch of a beautifully produced musical sound, its arousal is not guilty of the heresy of the separable experience, for this delight could be produced in no other way.

To say that one is "touched" in this way, however, is to say that one is *moved*, an aspect of the musical experience that formalists from Hanslick to Kivy have failed to explain adequately. Such failure is a direct result of the formalist horror of degrading musical art to mere sensuous stimulation, or worse, a mere aid to the digestion (cf. Kivy 1991, 250–264). One can sympathize with the formalist resistance to any sensualistic trivialization of musical experience. But the affect programs are far from trivial, for they do, as Gurney rightly suggests, recapitulate the cries and whispers of our ancient ancestors. Indeed, the formalists risk a trivialization of their own: for musical experience is no mere aural analogue to the apprehension of intricate recursive patterns, whether of the logical (Hofstadter 1979), mathematical (Rothstein 1995), kaleidoscopic (Hanslick 1891, 29), or Persian-carpet variety (Kivy 1993b, 349). Music literally presses our flesh. This much must be acknowledged if we are to begin to trace the source of its elemental emotional power.

5.5 The Musical Affordance, Nonconceptual Content, and Emotion

I argued in the preceding section that the basic emotion of joy is aroused on-line in a musical performance by a well-produced musical sound. Of course, this effect can be counteracted or swamped if the performance is defective. It is now time to begin to consider emotions aroused by cognitive engagement with the work itself, rather than those aroused by the lovely sounds and well-turned phrases produced by the players performing the work.

It should be fairly obvious how we will proceed, but there is quite a bit of theoretical groundwork to be laid. Emotions, recall, are to be construed as perceptions of situational meaning structures whose context components determine the nature of the emotion. The contents of the context components are Gibsonian affordances, the appearance of the environment to an organism as "actionable." To a fleet quadruped, a flat expanse appears runnable; to a hydrodynamic fish, a body of water appears swimmable. But actions are determined in accordance with action plans. In earlier chapters I proposed that we regard listening to a piece with understanding as an attempt to grasp a complex plan by trying it out, adopting it and acting on it by way of simulation or in imagination. Musical affective feelings would then arise out of an ongoing attempt to negotiate a musical virtual terrain, to act in accordance with its musical affordances, dealing with surprises, impediments, failures, and successes on the way, and requiring the constant reevaluation of strategy to which emotional response is keyed. This is a weak arousal theory that avoids the heresy of the separable experience precisely because it ties affective response to the negotiation of musical affordances provided by specific musical works.

5.5.1   Contrast with the Implication-Realization Arousal Theory

These claims may bring to mind Meyer's (1956) implication-realization theory of emotional arousal in musical experience, which bases the arousal of emotion (or affective feeling) on the elevation and reduction of informational uncertainty (cf. Meyer 1967). Unlike Meyer's theory, the present account is action oriented and simulational and therefore, I believe, can better establish the tie between musical experience and affect. Meyer's theory faces grave difficulties in explaining our continued, even heightened, responses to pieces we know intimately because we've heard them repeatedly. Surely we are not put into significant *informational* suspense with each subsequent hearing concerning what will happen next, even if we countenance musical "nuance properties" that are registered in peripheral modular input systems but not centrally represented or retained in long-term memory (cf. Raffman 1993). Although such loss of peripherally registered information does occur, any informational suspense it introduces seems scarcely robust enough to support our emotional responses to well-known works. Some nuance properties, moreover, *can* be held in memory. I retain a very nuanced aural image of a specific nuance property in my recording of Bruno Walter's rendition of the opening bars of Beethoven's *Pastoral* Symphony, which differs from the many other versions, live or recorded, I have heard. In this relatively late-career recording made with the Columbia Symphony Orchestra, Walter takes ever so slightly longer than usual to continue the opening phrase of the symphony after the fourth-bar fermata, thereby achieving what to my ear is an exceptionally beautiful and initially unexpected effect (example 5.5). I know it is there and now fully expect it whenever I listen to the recording, but I never fail to be affected by it, because the breathing room it affords has become my own as I negotiate the terrain of the piece.[29]

It is also not the case that informationally complex pieces are necessarily more affecting than informationally simple ones (cf. Budd 1985, 173–174). How many works of Western art music are informationally simpler than Schubert's *Der Lindenbaum*? Yet what is more moving than a fine recorded performance of it, even after repeated hearings of that very recording? The same could be said about a lesser, and even simpler, but still very fine musical item, the duet "I Have a Song to Sing, Oh!" from Gilbert and Sullivan's *Yeomen of the Guard*. Individuals given to snobbery may look down on this sort of thing, but considerable ability was required to craft a piece that achieves so lovely an effect by compositional means so modest: a gentle harmonic *ostinato* that rocks back and forth between tonic and dominant, relieved only momentarily by the late introduction of an unexpected lowered seventh (leading tone) in the melody. Informational surprise indeed! Yet it remains moving, to me at least, even after many hearings of the same (excellent) recording I own.

Lerdahl (2001, 172–173) has attempted to finesse this problem, the so-called Meyer paradox,[30] by arguing that the music processor is modular enough to offset the effects of learning and expectation. Roughly, just as one of two lines in the Müller-Lyer

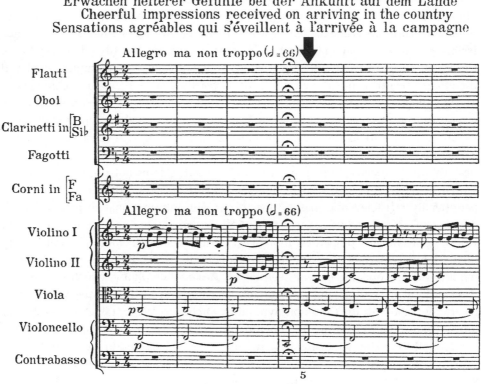

Example 5.5

Beethoven, Symphony No. 6 in F, *Pastoral, Allegro ma non troppo.*

diagram continues to look longer than the other, musical events are processed anew, even by the listener who is thoroughly prepared for them. I find this line of argument unpersuasive. At the end of chapter 2, I allowed for some local musical modularity effects. But the examples of musical affective response given in the preceding paragraphs do not seem similarly resistant to cognitive penetration. I anticipate Walter's deliberate pause in my mind's ear, and there it is, exactly as expected. Acquiring the same piece of information over and over again quickly palls. Indeed, any reaction, short of genuine reflex, to a novel event will be extinguished through repetition. But *doing* the same over and over again, even something as mundane as a challenging and varied daily exercise set, can maintain interest, because the interest lies in the doing. The powerful affective feelings that continue to attend the experience even of well-known recorded performances where nuances, even if some of them cannot be held in long-term memory in all their detail, remain exactly the same between hearings, far more plausibly derive from simulated action *undertaken* and experience *undergone*. They derive from off-line plan implementation, frustration, and, with understanding, successful realization, rather than from the increase and decrease of informational uncertainty. They derive from *doing*, not from *discovering*. With this issue now behind us, let us begin laying the theoretical groundwork necessary to develop a more adequate arousal theory.

5.5.2   Strawson, Evans, Peacocke, Cussins, and McGinn on Nonconceptual Content

Below our conceptual scheme—underneath the streets, so to speak—we find evidence of this more primitive system.
—Austen Clark (2000, 145)

If an informed reader of twentieth-century Anglo-American philosophy were to juxtapose the thought of music with the name of Sir Peter Strawson and then indulge in a bout of free association, the very next thing likely to come to mind would be the famous (or infamous) discussion of the ontology of pitched sounds in Strawson (1959/1963). Strawson asks whether particular tones (pitched sound events) could serve as "basic" (i.e., persisting, reidentifiable) particulars. After much tortuous thought experimentation, his tentative conclusion is that they could not, or at least that they could not without adding an apparatus of conceptual epicycles from which our "conceptual scheme" of basic material particulars occupying definite locations in three-dimensional space is mercifully free. From this he draws the further conclusion that it would be difficult or impossible for a nonsolipsistic consciousness to exist in a world limited to pitched sounds, because a necessary condition for nonsolipsistic consciousness is the possibility of there being unobserved but reidentifiable particulars *for that consciousness*.

Later on in the book there occurs a discussion apparently unrelated, but one in fact quite germane to our present concerns. That discussion treats the problem of what Strawson calls "term introduction." It is important to realize that Strawson's use of "term" is not the one currently standard. In the context of his discussion, a term is not a linguistic referring expression, but the *referent* of such an expression.[31] By employing linguistic expressions of certain types, we introduce corresponding terms. To the two fundamental components of sentential expressions (logical subjects and predicates) correspond two varieties of terms: particular-terms and universal-terms. Strawson emphasizes a crucial difference in presupposition between the respective introductions of the two varieties of terms. Introducing both particular-terms and universal-terms requires identification of the particular or the universal in question. But whereas the identification of a particular-term requires knowledge of an empirical fact serving to identify that particular uniquely, identification of the universal requires only knowledge that the predicate introducing the universal-term can be used in a meaningful empirical statement, whether such a statement is known to be true or not.

For example, to introduce the particular-term John Wilkes Booth, I must know some distinguishing fact about John Wilkes Booth, say, that he was the man who assassinated Abraham Lincoln. This fact is *presupposed* by the introduction of that term. To introduce the universal-term assassination, however, I need not know for a fact that any American president, or indeed that any particular person at all, was assassinated. I need only know that an existential statement like "Someone or other was assassinated in 1865" expresses a significant empirical proposition, whether or not someone actually was assassinated in 1865. It is true that this identifying fact for John Wilkes Booth introduces another particular-term, namely Abraham Lincoln, whose identification requires knowledge of some additional uniquely identifying fact (some fact other than the fact that he was assassinated by John Wilkes Booth), which is, in turn, presupposed. Although this creates what might be thought of as an ongoing presuppositional chain, we need not, Strawson assures us, fear vicious regress, for we will ultimately arrive at an existential statement, one which, moreover, most likely contains a demonstrative but contains no name or other singular referring expression, and therefore does not introduce a particular term. Such a statement, Strawson claims, *presents* a particular term, but it does not *introduce* it.[32]

This, however, is just one version of presupposition recognized by Strawson. We may also ask a different presuppositional question, one concerning the presuppositional chain that allows the introduction of a *class* of particular-terms—a question, that is, about the *general practice* of introducing such terms. Suppose we introduce the particular-term Lincoln's death. In order to do so, we must be able to state some true proposition about Lincoln's death in which "no particulars of the relevant kind are either introduced or quantified over, but which serves as a *basis* for the introduction of that particular" (ibid., 205). The presupposed proposition in question is expressed by the statement "Lincoln died," where "death" has been eliminated as a sortal universal, along with the class of particulars (deaths) that are its instances. The particular term Lincoln has taken its place; but Lincoln is a member of a class of a very different type: the class of basic particulars. It is clear that it is the basic particulars that serve as the "basis" for particulars of all other classes.

Is anything presupposed by this most basic level of term introduction? Strawson thinks that there is, and that we can get below this most basic level. But when we do, *we lose the subject-predicate structure of propositional language*. That is, in order to represent *in language* this subterranean level of presupposition, we must resort to a "feature-placing" language that lacks subject and predicate expressions and possesses no apparatus for the individuation of particulars. (Think back to chapter 3 and Kittay's "expressive" use of language, which serves to mark things off from one another.) Because a feature-placing language refers to no reidentifiable particulars, it also introduces no properties, for both particulars and properties belong to a higher level of term introduction. Hence Strawson's designation "feature-placing": features are properties not yet distinguished *as* properties.

The most obvious examples of the feature-placing use of language are expressions like "It's snowing" or "It's raining"; or, more simply, "snoweth" and "raineth." In these cases, "snoweth" and "raineth" indicate qualified *regions*, rather than determinate spatial locations, in the observer's vicinity. (This paragraph is indebted to Cussins [1992], who draws heavily on Strawson's discussion. See also Clark 2000, 2004 and Clarke 1987 [110] for useful discussion.) *"Fall of* snow" and *"Puddle of* rain" are sortals; but particular falls of snow or puddles of rain are not individuated by "snoweth" or "raineth"; nor are any particular places where it's snowing or raining fully individuated.[33] In ordinary language, "snow" and "rain" are quintessential mass expressions (or, as we would say in non-Strawsonian language, mass *terms*); and it would seem that sortals could play no role at all in a feature-placing language, since sortals are generally thought to presuppose principles of individuation for the members of the class they pick out: to apply the sortal "rabbit" properly is to possess criteria for the individuation of the particulars belonging to a certain class (rabbits, or undetached rabbit parts, or rabbit time-slices). "Snoweth" and "raineth," like "more snow" and "more rain," make sense; "rabbiteth" and "cateth," like "more rabbit" and "more cat," seem not to. Strawson, however, is willing to allow the use of sortals in feature-placing language, pointing by way of example to the "naming game" played by young children in the process of learning the language (ibid., 214). A child playing the naming game who says "cat!" might be taken to indicate the presence of certain characteristic patterns of feline motion through space, without any attempt to individuate or to reidentify particular cats. Since "features" are Strawson's substitute for what, in a more sophisticated linguistic practice, would be *properties*, the expressions of the feature-placing language are what would be *predicates* in the more sophisticated linguistic practice. Changing "snoweth" into "fall of snow," or "raineth" into "puddle of rain," does produce potentially individuating expressions: this fall of snow can be distinguished from that one, this puddle of water from that one. Notice, though, the introduction of *demonstratives* at this basic level of individuation.

In more recent times, Strawson's late Oxford colleague Gareth Evans (whom we encountered in chapter 2) argued that the demonstrative identification of any persisting object, be it a fall of snow or a puddle of water, requires more than a fleeting perceptual acquaintance or instantaneous causal information link with the object. It requires, as a necessary but not sufficient condition of identification, a *continuing* information link, an ability to *track an object in an egocentric behavioral space* (Evans 1982, 176), a three-dimensional space whose origin coincides with the observer's body and in which the observer can *act*. Such tracking abilities, while clearly involving an ability to discriminate, are still themselves nonconceptual, as Evans rightly observes. Not only do we share them with animals,[34] but human perceivers are able to locate objects demonstratively in egocentric space without possessing relevant concepts of geometry and trigoneometry (ibid., 146, 156ff), that is, without being able to say something like "it's close to 47 degrees off the sagittal plane," and even without being able, on some occasions, to locate this egocentric space in the objective public space required for full-fledged object identification: even if we happen to be disoriented, we can point and say "it's over there" without knowing where "there" is in public space. Successful location of the object, moreover, requires that it be tracked continuously.

Evans's pioneering investigation of the awareness of position in egocentric behavioral space as necessary for demonstrative identification provided much of the philosophical background both for Peacocke's (1992) later work on concepts and concept possession and for Cussins's (1990) attempt to provide a connectionist alternative to the language of thought hypothesis for the psychological explanation of conceptual thinking.[35] For Peacocke, nonconceptual "scenario content" is required for a noncircular account of the possession conditions for a perceptual concept like *red*, for the demonstrative concepts *here* and *there*, and for the "first-person concept" expressed by the token-reflexive "I."[36] A scenario is an array of surfaces in egocentric space not yet fully reified, or differentiated into persisting objects and properties. It is, in effect, an unconceptualized *feature domain*, an (as yet) unconceptualized content. Peacocke (1992, 242n16), we should note, suggests mental models as likely candidates for the *representational vehicles* that carry scenario content. According to Peacocke's "Principle of Dependence" (ibid., 5),

There can be nothing more to the nature of a concept than is determined by a correct account of the capacity of a thinker who has mastered the concept to have propositional attitudes to contents containing that concept (a correct account of "grasping the concept").

If possession of a concept consists in the capacity to assume propositional attitudes to contents containing that concept, then one must, he claims, be able to specify how the putative possessor of the concept is to demonstrate that capacity without, on pain of circularity, using that very concept in the description of the putative concept user's psychological state. In the case of perceptual concepts, indexicals, and the first-person concept, Peacocke argues, it is the ability to locate features in egocentric space that fits this bill.

Peacocke (1992, 74ff) also recognizes a further level of nonconceptual content, namely "protopropositional content," that is necessary for specifying the possession conditions for another group of perceptual concepts. Distinguishing a square from a regular diamond perceptually does not require having the concepts *square* or *diamond*. Indeed, it had better not if any account of such conditions is to avoid circularity. But distinguishing between these shapes does require imposing different axes of symmetry on the respective scenario contents: otherwise a diamond will simply be seen as a square from a different angle (or vice versa). The deciding factor is that the axis of symmetry of a square bisects opposite sides; that of a diamond bisects opposite corners. One need not possess the concept *axis of symmetry* to do this, but one must *perceive* the symmetry. Yet symmetry seems not to be merely an aspect of scenario content, located, as it were, among its surfaces presented in egocentric space. Hence, it is part of protopropositional content: one sees *that* the diamond is symmetrical about the angles (but without using the concept of *symmetry*). Peacocke (ibid., 85) observes that "symmetry and parallelism are not made salient in the protopropositional content of our tactile experience in nearly so wide a range of cases as they are in visual experience." But these particular protopropositional notions are made highly salient in the content of musical experience, as are the perceptions of gestalt groupings that Peacocke also counts as protopropositional (ibid., 79) and that play such an important role in Lerdahl and Jackendoff's generative theory.

It may seem that Peacocke's arguments for nonconceptual and protopropositional content are mere artifacts of his foundationalist and antiholist commitments regarding concept possession, and that their force could be blunted by forgoing these commitments. But the issue goes deeper than that. Following Evans, Cussins (1990) has argued that the sense of indexical expressions cannot be "canonically specified" by means of purely descriptive expressions. A canonical specification of any phenomenon is a characterization that captures the essential properties of the phenomenon (the essential properties, that is, as determined by a theory or as determined under a theoretical description). A canonical characterization of a baseball game, for example, would use descriptions employed in the rules of the game, and would describe events as the actions of pitching, batting, and catching the ball, not in terms of the physics of moving material bodies. "A [mental] content," says Cussins (1990, 282n25), "is canonically characterized by a specification which reveals the way in which it presents the world"; and the sense of indexicals cannot be canonically specified using concepts alone. The sense, or, speaking psychologically, the cognitive significance of the indexical or token-reflexive expression "I" is different from that of a uniquely referring descriptive phrase, "the person who is X," because, as Perry (1979) first explained, I may not realize that I am that person, as I may not know that I am the person who is spilling sugar all over the supermarket floor (I am unaware that the bag of sugar I just put into my cart is leaking). As we know, the Fregean test for difference of sense in the case of co-referential expressions is the possibility of rational assent to a sentence using one expression and denial of (or suspension of judgment regarding) a sentence using the other, as someone who is ignorant of historical fact may assent to the sentence "Benjamin Franklin was at one time the United States ambassador to France," but deny that the man who invented bifocals was. The cognitive significance of "I," as well as of other indexicals such as "here," "there," "near," "far," "up," or "down," Cussins argues, cannot be detached from the speaker's position in egocentric space and the *ability to act* in that space. Because the content of such expressions cannot in principle be canonically specified by purely descriptive means, Cussins concludes, it is in part nonconceptual.

In a recent postscript to his (1990) paper, Cussins (2003) makes explicit the link I have emphasized between nonconceptual content, motor organization, and environmental affordances. He contrasts two ways he might know the speed at which he is traveling on a motorcycle. He might have conceptual grasp of the speed as a definite quantity and be able to report it in miles per hour; or the speed may be given

not as a truth maker ... but made available ... as an element in a skilled interaction with the world, as a felt rotational pressure in my right hand as it [holds] the throttle grip, a tension in my fingers and foot in contact with brake pedals or levers, a felt vibration of the road and a rush of wind, a visual rush of surfaces, a sense of how the immediate environment would *afford* certain motions and *resist* others; *embodied and environmental knowledge* of what it would take to make adjustments in these felt pressures and sensitivities. (2003, 150, emphases in original)

In this case, the world is not given as realm of truth makers, as objects with properties standing in relations, but nonconceptually as a "realm of mediation." Passage through such an environment is, says Cussins, "intensely cognitive," but "thought free," just as musical experience, I would add, is intensely cognitive but, in this sense, thought free. The "trails" through such an environment "exist in ontologically distinct kinds of region; forest and savannah certainly, but also social, theoretical, linguistic, biological, psychological, and historical [and, I would add, musical] regions" (ibid., 157). Passage through any such region may be competent or incompetent, successful or unsuccessful. But for the comprehending listener,[37] passage through the virtual musical environment is *always* superbly competent or sure-footed, assuming the competence of the composer and the performers. That is one reason those who understand music love it as they do. We shall take up this important notion of "trails" in more detail in a moment.

Notice, however, how far Cussins's motorcycle scenario has moved from a mere feature-placing environment. The throttle, the brake pedals, the levers have been reified: they are objects that the rider identifies in some sense—in *some* sense, but not in the full-blown Strawsonian sense, for they are not separable from his experience, his knowing how to manipulate them, nor need we say that the rider must be able to report everything he has done once he has dismounted the motorcycle. The experience is "thought free" or, perhaps less controversially, not thought dependent. Perhaps we should say that it is protopropositional, not merely nonconceptual. The rider has cross-modal access to brake pedals, levers, and throttle via sight and touch, access that is lacking in acousmatic experience; and cross-modal access is an important stage on the way to perspective independence (Clark 2000, 204–205).

A pervasive theme in Cussins's (1990) paper, and one that will take on an important role later in this chapter, is that the capacity to think, that is, to apply concepts and to establish a mind–world distinction, is a phylogenetic and ontogenetic *achievement* that is built on and that gradually emerges from more primitive representational capacities.[38] This theme harmonizes with McGinn's defense of the theory of mental models, which, it will be recalled, are analog, topologically (but not sententially) structured representations that carry nonconceptual content. "What we seek," says McGinn (1989, 204),

is a general theory of representational content, applicable to any creature capable of bearing content [including humans]. Now some content-bearing creatures have a public language with which they talk to each other (and to themselves), but some do not—or so it seems. Anyone who believes that there can be content without public language will want a theory of content that allows for this possibility.... Thus, assuming we want to attribute contentful states to frogs and dogs and human infants, the sentential [i.e., the language of thought] theory has to credit these apparently infralinguistic creatures with a rich internal language; as it were, their brains can do what they cannot [overtly] do. Now while this does not seem a priori impossible (to me anyway), I think it is a consequence to be avoided if we can: for if they deploy a rich internal language, what is to stop them from going public?... is it really plausible to suppose that dumb creatures possess ceaselessly chattering brains?

Although it is controversial what level of computational abstraction connectionist modeling is supposed to be representing, it is fair to say that McGinn's discussion generally operates at a higher level of functional abstraction above the neuronal substrate than Cussins's and does not presuppose connectionism. Mental models, for example, are compatible with both von Neumann (see Johnson-Laird 1983) and connectionist architectures (see Rumelhart et al. 1986). Cussins does in fact allow that the construction of concepts from nonconceptual microfeature representations *could* itself be carried out on a von Neumann architecture, though it is obvious that he does not believe that this is how it is done in organic brains.

Strawson, Evans, Peacocke, Cussins, and McGinn are, then, in broad agreement concerning the indispensability of nonconceptual content in any account of human representational abilities;[39] and if nonconceptual (incuding protopropositional) content is present in the human representational system, *it is available for exploitation in musical experience.* But it is well to be clear about the fact that the five theorists arrive at that conclusion by different routes because they are engaged in distinct projects. This convergence by way of independent routes adds legitimacy to the notion of nonconceptual content. Whereas Strawson's project is the descriptive metaphysical project of constructing a transcendental argument in support of the conceptual scheme he takes to be presupposed by human linguistic practice, Peacocke's is the development of a metaphysics of concept identity based on the notion of possession conditions. Evans's project, by contrast, is located firmly within the philosophy of language; it is an attempt to account for certain modes of singular reference in a broadly Russellian manner.

Because of his Cartesian commitments, Russell was inclined to regard all reference to material objects as cases of knowledge by description and was inclined to limit the objects of perceptual knowledge by acquaintance to "sense-data."[40] Evans's strategy is to substitute for Russell's perceptual knowledge by acquaintance a causal information link that enables a subject to track a physical object in egocentric space. The aim is to reject Russell's epistemological Cartesianism, while vindicating his insight that in certain important cases of singular reference, chiefly those that make use of demonstratives, reference failure will preclude the expression (and indeed the possession) by the speaker of a thought at all, whereas in other cases of singular reference, chiefly those that make use of definite descriptions, reference failure will not preclude expression and possession of a thought. When reference failure rules out the possession of a demonstrative thought, the thought must include a nonconceptual content concerning object location in egocentric space; for if it did not, there would be available a description that could supply the requisite thought content, as in the case of definite descriptions that do not refer. Evans, that is, argues Russell's side against the Strawsonian view that utterances containing definite descriptions that do not refer say nothing (Evans 1982, 52–53). Russell, as we know, construed statements containing nonreferring definite descriptions as meaningful (but false) existential statements.

But are Russell and Evans right that reference failure precludes the expression and possession of singular demonstrative thoughts? Bilgrami (1992, 155ff) thinks not, for the Russell-Evans view would require us to deny that a real-life Macbeth would express or possess any thought at all when addressing his hallucinatory dagger token-reflexively, "Come, let me clutch thee:/ I have thee not, yet I see thee still."[41] And this, Bilgrami argues, is counterintuitive. It is hard not to agree. One might, however, reply in defense of Evans, if not Russell, that any such singular thought would be too short-lived to function in the cognitive economy as a belief, and that as a result, it is never endorsed. It is merely entertained: "Is this a dagger which I see before me,/ The handle toward my hand?" Demonstrative thoughts, the reply might continue, are "information-hungry": they dispose a speaker to establish and maintain ongoing, bi- or even multimodal information links with their putative objects if they are to be retained as beliefs and not suspended or eliminated, as even the fevered Macbeth eliminates his demonstrative thought of the dagger when he attempts (and fails) to establish a *tactual* information link with its putative object: "There's no such thing:/ It is the bloody business which informs/ Thus to mine eyes."

Cussins and McGinn, by contrast with Evans, may be said to be pursuing two different philosophy of mind projects. They both take aim at the language of thought hypothesis as an adequate empirical theory of the *psychology* of conceptual content. But their respective strategies are a little different. Cussins offers (as a viable *alternative* to the language of thought hypothesis) an account of the emergence ("construction") of conceptual structure out of the contextually embedded feature representations of a connectionist activation space; McGinn argues *against* the language of thought hypothesis in favor of a mental model theory of the psychology of representation. Placing sentences in the head, McGinn claims, gives no purchase on the problem of constructing a naturalistic account of intentionality, for it merely displaces the problem by "trad[ing] one intentional relation for another" (1989, 197). What needs explanation is how sentences are, in accordance with naturalistically acceptable principle, paired with content in the psychology of a believer. As we saw in chapter 3, McGinn proposes that sentence tokens instantiate propositions,[42] which *index* internal mental models. These mental models, in turn, "simulate" (represent in an analog manner) the states of affairs in the world that the propositions *describe* (ibid., 209). Since structural similarities abound in the natural world, all that is required for a naturalistic grounding of intentionality, he believes, is the exploitation of already available structural similarities for representational purposes, not a large leap.

This last argument of McGinn's reestablishes contact with the Lakoff and Johnson material explored in chapters 2 and 3. Like McGinn, Mark Johnson denies that the intentionality of sentences is self-explanatory. For Johnson (1987, 1–3), sentential intentionality depends on the deployment of nonconceptual "image schemata," which he characterizes as "nonpropositional," "preconceptual," "continuous, analog pattern[s] of experience," especially kinesthetic experience. Because images are contents of mental models, Johnson's image schemata and the mental models of Craik, Johnson-Laird, and McGinn are cognate notions.

5.5.3 Musical "Description," Resemblance, and the Expression of Emotion

Throughout his discussion of the ontology of sounds, Strawson remains confident that musical types or universals (he does not go to any great lengths to distinguish these), as opposed to particular sound events, are easily reidentifiable: we can identify something as *that theme again* or as *that work*. But these, of course, are not basic particulars; indeed, for Strawson, they are not particulars at all. Strawson also gives no attention at all to the issue of musical representation. He does not, that is, consider music as a symbolism; nor, given his concerns in that chapter, is there any reason why he should. For us, however, this is a major concern. Suppose, now, we approach musical performances as we have done as tokens in a symbolic system, but for the moment strain to assimilate musical representation (in a way I have counseled against) to linguistic representation. Would the musical symbol function as a logical subject or would it function as a predicate?

It is clear, I think, that the musical symbol would function as a predicate, and not a logical subject. This has no direct connection with our ability to reidentify musical types, or with our inability to reidentify musical particulars, the ontological issue that preoccupies Strawson in his chapter on sounds. Our issue right now concerns *representation*, not the ontology or the epistemology *of* the representation. The musical symbol would function as a predicate because, *qua* symbolic system, music cannot be credited with the grammatical apparatus required to make the metaphysical distinction between individuals and properties: it has nothing like singular terms, relative pronouns, or bound variables and quantifiers. Because it has not the representational resources to distinguish individuals from properties, then if it makes sense to speak of musical or "acousmatic" virtual space at all, such a space can be nothing other than an *egocentric feature space*, not a space (like physical space) containing fully reidentifiable particulars and places. Nonetheless, this feature space may contain objects and places that are reidentifiable in the more minimalist way we considered in the previous section.

To try to make this clearer, let us consider for the moment so-called representational painting. Considered as a token in a symbolic system, a representational painting also lacks the grammatical apparatus of language. But it does have something that music generally does not have: definite individuals can be "seen in" representational paintings, as the subject of a portrait can be seen in that portrait. The title of a representational painting, along with what can be seen in it, Jenefer Robinson (1994) has argued, allow us a certain license: we may treat the picture as something like a referring description, at least in cases like Gainesborough's portrait of Mrs. Siddons, where the painting depicts a real person. The painting, she claims, "ascribes" properties to an individual, namely Mrs. Siddons, as a statement "ascribes" a property to the referent of the logical subject. Notice that absent a pure causal theory of reference, both a title and "seeing in" are generally required to fix the "reference" of a painting. Without the title we generally will not know who the subject is, though in some cases we may; without "seeing in," the picture will refer (if it refers at all) in the manner of a Millian name, and not in the manner of a description. Pictures, Robinson concludes, may function as "predicates in schemes of predication" (ibid., 169). A similar case, she thinks, can be made for musical works. There is, however, an important difference. Music, she argues, is like *nonrepresentational* painting in that just as no individual can be "seen in" a nonrepresentational painting, with very few exceptions, no individuals can be "heard in" music. Musical works, insofar as they are treated as predicates in a scheme of predication, are, in her terminology, nonreferring *descriptions*; they are not referring *depictions, because they represent and purport to represent no particulars.*[43] Except for the occasional cuckoo (Beethoven, Respighi) or car horn (Gershwin), we do not hear particulars in music as we can see particulars in representational paintings. In music, says Robinson, we are able to hear only "qualities," that is, *universals*, or, as I prefer to say for reasons that will become evident, *features*: heroism, or the dynamic/kinetic features of events, or emotional mood qualities, to name three she specifically mentions.

Going along for the moment with Robinson's treatment of musical works (or epi-sodes) as predicates in a scheme of predication, I think that this is entirely correct. But when we press her and ask how a musical work functions as a description, her answer is that the music *possesses* the qualities we *hear in it*. But how is it possible for a piece of music like *Till Eulenspiegel's Merry Pranks* to be itself mischievous as she claims it is (ibid., 186)? How *can* a sequence of pitched sounds *be* mischievous? Yes, we hear it that way, we do hear the mischievousness in the music; but to say this is merely to point to the problem that has to be solved. Thinking back to earlier discussion in chap-ter 3, recall that Goodman, whose theory of aesthetic symbolism provides much of the background to Robinson's discussion of the "semantic" approach to pictorial symbol-ism, had already addressed this problem by invoking a distinction between literal and aesthetic metaphorical exemplification. In his terms, the *Till Eulenspiegel* music exem-plifies mischievousness metaphorically, not literally: the music *expresses* the quality. But once again, when we press Goodman for criteria whereby we can distinguish literal from aesthetic metaphorical exemplification, we come up empty-handed. In Good-man's case, the problem is exacerbated by his nominalism and antirealist (or irrealist) account of truth, for he countenances no properties or universals, only labels; and the correct application of a label is not grounded in an ontology of truth makers as much as it is validated by a pragmatic "rightness of fit" that realizes one or more of our mul-tifarious cognitive aims. So it is right to apply the label "is in the key of B-flat major" to extended episodes of *Till Eulenspiegel*, but it is also right to apply the label "is mischie-vous" to some of those same episodes. Why do these episodes literally exemplify one rightly applied label, but metaphorically exemplify the other rightly applied label? No satisfactory answer is forthcoming.

Goodman does direct our attention to "schemata," which do some of the work of the semantic fields discussed earlier in chapter 3, but in a purified, nominalistically ac-ceptable way. "We categorize by sets of alternatives," Goodman (1976, 71) tells us; and a schema is a set of alternative labels belonging to a single family of labels, say color labels. The "range" of the label "red" consists of red things, as the range of the label "green" consists of green things. But both red and green things belong to the same realm. The ranges of the labels "is in the key of B-flat major" and "is mischievous" be-long to different "realms"; and what makes the application of the latter to a musical work metaphorical is that musical works are not, according to established linguistic practice or habits of label application, normally included in the range of "is mischie-vous," while they are normally included in the range of "is in the key of B-flat major." But even if we were to grant that the distinction between the literal and the metaphor-ical is adequately explained on the basis of the habitual or the familiar versus the non-habitual and the unfamiliar application of labels, which is granting a great deal, we still cannot explain what makes the metaphorical application of "is mischievous" right in this case, and what would make the application of "is solemn" wrong.

Would a more relaxed attitude toward universals and shared properties help us here? Ridley's (1995) discussion suggests that it might, for he offers a resemblance theory, and resemblance depends on the sharing of properties. Following Kivy (1989), Ridley distinguishes between *expressing* an affective state and *being expressive of* an affective state. *Till*, being a piece of music and not an animate being, may not express mischievousness, but it may be expressive of it, just as the face of a St. Bernard (Kivy)[44] or the face of a (non-method) actor practicing in front of a mirror (Ridley) may be *expressive of* sadness without *expressing it* (see also Davies 1994, 240ff). Something is expressive of an affective state, or, as Ridley says, a "passion," if it "resembles" central cases of the actual expression of the "co-nomial" *emotion* by a human being. Ridley terms this sort of resemblance in the musical case "melisma." The least problematic, but also the least illuminating, case of melisma depends on a resemblance between music and the contours of the human voice; but there is another, more important variety, styled by Ridley "dynamic melisma," which is based in the resemblance between musical movement and other kinds of movement, chiefly, but not limited to, human bodily movement. Dynamic melisma, however, also comes in two flavors: co-nomial and non-co-nomial. Co-nomial dynamic melisma, which Ridley considers a phenomenon of relatively minor importance, occurs when music merely possesses, rather than being expressive of, the relevant property: "jaunty music," he says, "is not so much expressive of jauntiness as simply, itself, jaunty, so that it is related to its co-nomial state by resembling it (in its defining respect)" (1995, 100). In the case of non-co-nomial dynamic melisma, on the other hand, "the movements of music resemble human movements expressive of certain passions, which passions are not named after these kinds of movements" (ibid., 102).

No doubt Ridley would say that the *Till Eulenspiegel* music is genuinely expressive of mischievousness and is not merely mischievous in quality. Suppose it, then, to be a case of non-co-nomial dynamic melisma. How successful is Ridley in explaining our capacity to hear the mischievousness in Strauss's music? Not very, for when he feels himself pressed on this issue, all he has to say is that "this imaginative habit of ours...is maybe a brute fact about us" (ibid., 111). But he would be no better off if the music were held to be a case of co-nomial dynamic melisma. For contrary to what Ridley seems to think, co-nomial dynamic melisma is just as puzzling as non-co-nomial dynamic melisma. What makes a series of musical tones "jaunty" or "mischievous" in quality? Once again, we do hear it that way; but again, that is precisely what we want to understand. For as we have seen, nothing in the musical surface really moves at all.

To his credit, Ridley reaches the environs of what seems to me to be the critical issue regarding dynamic melisma as such, and that is the issue of simulation. "[I]n attending to the musical gestures [of the *Marcia funebre* of Beethoven's *Eroica*]," he says (ibid., 128–129),

I come to be aware of their heavyhearted, resolute quality through the very process of coming my-self to feel heavyhearted but resolute. It is rather like my coming to appreciate the melancholy of a weeping willow only as the willow saddens me: I could, of course, merely identify the expressive posture that the willow's posture resembles; but instead I apprehend its melancholy through a kind of mirroring response. I respond to it sympathetically...my response is grounded in the re-semblance that the willow bears to a particular human expressive posture.

Despite the reference to sympathy, I believe that by "mirroring response" Ridley means (or should mean) *empathy*, that is, simulation: he "apprehends" the "melan-choly" of the weeping willow by simulating its "posture" off-line. What Ridley seems not to realize is that there is a fundamental problem with the assertion of resemblance in the musical case that does not exist in the cases of the faces of St. Bernard dogs or even weeping willows: how is it possible for a temporally ordered sets of tones to con-stitute a *gesture* that *resembles* a human expressive physical *posture*? Another way to pose the problem is this: whereas Ridley could indeed "merely identify the expressive posture of the willow," that is, merely notice without any mirroring response the "resemblance it bears to a particular human expressive gesture," he could not "merely identify" in this way the resemblance between the musical gestures of Beethoven's *Marcia funebre* and the human expression of heavyhearted resolve, for, with the excep-tions of tempo and rhythm, there generally *is* no such dynamic resemblance between *temporally ordered sets of tones* and *human expressive behavior* merely to be noticed. Even the mere identification of musical dynamic melisma, whether co-nomial or not, that is, seems to *require* the mirroring response that is *optional* in the weeping willow case. But if we ask why this is, no answer is forthcoming: perhaps it is just a "brute fact" about us.

Kivy and Davies are no more helpful. Neither makes Ridley's distinction between co-nomial and non-co-nomial dynamic melisma, and Davies simply identifies all musical expression with the possession by music of expressive properties: "I argue, in particu-lar, that the emotions expressed in music are properties of the work" (Davies 1994, 201). Both writers emphasize, as I have done, the importance in musical experience of the human tendency to animate the inanimate, and both stress that "music presents not so much an appearance of the human face as one of human deportment, gait, or action" (Davies 1994, 292). Kivy (1989, 172–176), moreover, gestures toward an evolu-tionary cost–benefit explanation of the presence in humans of this animating ten-dency, and Davies allows that "music is experienced as spatial and as involving motion" (Davies 1994, 229). But when we ask how organized series of evanescent, motionless, nonspatial tones are even capable of "presenting" human deportment, gait, or action, no answer is forthcoming. For them, this may be where "the spade stops." Both Kivy and Davies seem to assume that the recognition of expressive proper-ties in music is no more (or scarcely more) problematic than is the recognition of them in the face of a St. Bernard dog or a weeping willow. But if I am right, this is just not the case.

While ever mindful of Kant's admonition that wisdom is required to know which questions may and may not be sensibly asked, I believe we can drive our spade a little deeper.[45] What none of these writers seems to realize is that (*interpreted*) *expression is a mode of representation.* Any expressive behavior or comportment, even a mere expressive symptom like an involuntary sigh of relief or grimace of pain, is an interpretable sign. An interpreted sign, in turn, is a representation. The face of the St. Bernard is not a symptom. But it functions *for its interpreter* as an iconic sign based on resemblance. In Davies's terminology (discussed in chapter 3), there is a "natural relation of resemblance" between the face of the St. Bernard and a sad human face. But as we saw in that discussion, natural relations of resemblance are inseparable from the interests of an interpreter. The face of the St. Bernard is taken as or seen as expressive of sadness by an interpreter. The comportment of the non-method actor is semiotically more sophisticated. Unlike the doggy face, it is an intentionally produced Meadian "significant symbol" (chapter 3): it is intended to affect the observer as it affects the actor himself.

The musical utterance is also a significant symbol. But it is semiotically even more sophisticated than the acting gesture, for melisma, whether co-nomial or non-co-nomial, does not depend on any direct relation of natural resemblance between musical representation and expression. As a pushmi-pullyu representation, a performance of *Till Eulenspiegel* is a representational token that enjoins the listener to implement a plan (off-line), which puts him into certain active bodily states whose muscular effects are inhibited, effects that, if not inhibited, would eventuate in the sort of behaviors, including deliberate inhibition of action,[46] that comport with a mischievous state of mind. We would immediately recognize these behaviors, which would most likely include facial expressions like smirks, winks, and twinkles of the eye, as mischievous were we to witness a mime attempting to communicate without props Till's doings to us, just as we would recognize a different set of behaviors as heavy-hearted but resolute. But in the musical case not only are there no props, there is no mime to witness: as already suggested in chapter 2, it is *we ourselves* who take on with our own bodies the miming or charade-like activity imaginatively or off-line (recall Gurney's telling remark that musical experience is like "a special activity of our own"). *That is why the mirroring response is required both for co-nomial and non-co-nomial dynamic melisma.* Reversing the order of dependence in Davies' claim that mirroring responses "are founded on a recognition of the expressive character of the musical work" (1994, 315), I submit, in the spirit of William James's theory of emotion, that *the expressive character of the work is founded on mirroring responses.* Here Goodman's pragmatist "rightness of fit" finds its proper home, because we are talking not of truth and denotation, but of the modeling relation. Under the influence of the musical pushmi-pullyu representation we construct a set of mental models representing a scenario as the locus of mischievous doings: the label "mischievous" fits the *Till Eulenspiegel* music whereas "solemn" does not because of the nature of these plans and mental models constructed in our heads.

As I proposed in chapter 3, a metaphor works or does not work, fits or does not fit, if and only if the mental models deriving from one semantic field can model (via our reformed version of exemplification) those belonging to another semantic field. What counts is the interaction of mental models within the psychology of the subject. The metaphor must feel right to the body, must use the body effectively, meaning that the motor plans evoked by it must generate mental models that allow themselves to be mapped onto and integrated with models in the topic domain, as T. S. Eliot's still arresting image of a surgical patient on an ether table, an image with very strong somatic and kinesthetic associations, endows the night sky with a disquieting emotional presence. The metaphor invites us to simulate the sky as if it were an animate, but anaesthetized, entity; it invites us to play a certain bodily charade, in which we "act out" the sky as an unconscious patient, flaccid and immobilized. If we can do this, the metaphor will have been successful. We may not be able to learn just from listening that the fourth movement of Schumann's *Rhenish* Symphony (marked "*Feierlich*," meaning "with solemn ceremony") was intended by the composer to represent the great cathedral at Cologne. But we do understand that whatever it represents is something vast, massive, and structurally intricate, with interlocking elements that demand repeated crisscrossing explorations.[47] How *do* we understand this? Certain bodily movements, eye movements, head movements, and slow walks round are required to take in such a structure. Models of observer and object located in musical virtual space complement the musical plan. But as already suggested in chapter 2, the musical listener takes on not only the body sets of the *observer* under these conditions, *but also simulates the "bodily sets" of the observed virtual object*, transformed under the influence of a kind of poetic animism. Just as the *Till Eulenspiegel* music gets us to mime Till-like behaviors, the Schumann movement gets us to mime not only the bodily comportment of the observer taking in (or perhaps also attempting to ascend) the awesome object, but the awesome object's "bodily comportment" as well. If we can "mirror" the weeping willow's "bodily comportment," so can we, under the influence of musical animism, "mirror" the "bodily comportment" of an awesome physical object. If this still seems puzzling, ask yourself how you would communicate by gestures alone the idea of a grand cathedral in a game of charades (recall the discussion from chapter 2).[48] Your movements, I suspect, would be slow, deliberate, and majestic, perhaps displaying a solemn, devotional character. Upward movements would predominate, most likely culminating full bodily extension with hands joined and arms raised above the head. Recall that for dynamic melisma, both co-nomial and non-co-nomial, simulation is not, as in the case of recognition of the "posture" of the weeping willow, optional; it is required.

There is nothing peculiar about this tendency to shift back and forth between viewpoints in the musical situation, for it is of a piece with what we do in other venues. Just as we go back and forth between sympathetic and empathetic emotions, say between empathetic grief and sympathetic pity in a bereavement situation, we tend to shift back and forth between observer and character viewpoints in grasping the structure of narratives. Compare Goldman (2006, 287): "either the reader or observer 'directly' simulates a character or she simulates a hypothetical-observer-of-fact simulating [or even just reacting to] a character." Interestingly enough, McNeill (1992, 94–104, 120–123) has found compelling evidence for this in the gestures employed by narrators. Not only did these gestures indicate this constant alternation of viewpoint, but they closely tracked which viewpoint was operative at a particular point in the narrative. Gestures, as I suggested in chapter 3, are a reliable indicator of what sort of mental modeling is occurring in the mind of a speaker. In the musical case, an appropriate set of imaginary motions, now in virtual acousmatic space, are mandated by the plan of the music, which also generates an appropriate set of complementary musical mental models. How good a fit is there, really, between the plan structure and the musical mental models of the *Marcia funebra* of the *Eroica* and the simulation of the strivings of a dung beetle in the Ridley thought experiment described in chapter 2?

With the notion of musical mental models now reintroduced, let us drop the strained assimilation of musical and pictorial representation to the predicates of linguistic representation. So-called nonrepresentational pictures and music refer to particulars, to the extent they do at all, by way of the modeling relation: the constructed models in the mind of the viewer or hearer share topological and perhaps also metrical properties with their target objects. They do not denote in the manner of linguistic representations. In the case of representational pictures, the construction of internal mental models based on the recovery of informational invariants from a two-dimensional surface, whether from the visual surface of a painting, or from the musical "surface" defined by axes of pitch and time, *is just what the obscure notions of "seeing in" or "hearing in" come to*. To say we can "see the subject in the portrait" is just to say that we are able easily to extract certain informational invariants by using mechanisms of visual perception in ways that comport with their evolved natural functions.

Goodman (1976, 1978), as we know, subjected this idea to unrelenting attack, arguing that any visual representation is a symbol that must be "read" properly, and that what usually is taken to be an issue of realism versus nonrealism is in fact an issue of habit, or the familiarity or unfamiliarity with a representational idiom and the conventions of a symbolic system. Although Goodman's admonitions are undeniably salutary to the extent that they force us to recognize that "realism" is a variable commodity, both historically and cross-culturally, admonitions, moreover, that are sensitive to the interests of the makers and users of visual representations, I do not believe his arguments are decisive (see Reed et al. 1980; Peacocke 1987; Robinson 1979, 2000; McIver

Lopes 2000). For he takes no account at all of what evolutionary psychologists have termed "the psychic unity of humankind" (Tooby and Cosmides 1992, 79) or of whatever modularity and domain specificity human perceptual systems may have. Some of the more sweeping claims of evolutionary psychologists, to be sure, have overreached themselves (see Griffiths 1997); and the modularity of perceptual systems easily can be exaggerated (see Churchland 1989, 255–279). But this much said, it is simply not credible to put a Norman Rockwell painting on all fours with a cubist portrait and to claim that the difficulties encountered in seeing the individual in the latter is simply a question of familiarity or lack thereof with a representational idiom.[49]

To say that we cannot usually hear objects in music is to say that we cannot easily extract informational invariants in the way we can with "realistic" pictures. In fact, as I shall be arguing presently, in a sense we *never* can do this. And it is obvious why we cannot. The human aural system is designed mainly to locate sounds in physical space, not to organize Hanslick's *tönend bewegte Formen* ("sounding forms in motion") in virtual musical space. The placement of the ears so as to enhance perception of the asynchronous onset of sounds and the structure of the tonotopic map in the primary auditory cortex show that this is so. This neocortical surface is organized vertically into a two-dimensional array of columns. Along one dimension, the columns vary in their sensitivity to sound frequencies; along the other, the columns alternate between summation and suppression function. The summation columns respond most strongly when a sound stimulus is presented *simultaneously* to both ears; the suppression columns respond most strongly in the case of monaural stimulus or temporal displacement of sounds (Matthews 1998, 455–456; Kandel et al. 1991, 494). We saw in chapter 2 that despite the effects of stereophonically recorded music, the binaural function, which is crucial for the location and individuation of sounds in physical space, is suppressed in the musical context, where pitch supersedes direction in physical space as an "indispensable attribute."

5.5.4   Aesthetic Mental Models and Simulation

Verse is a pedestrian taking you over the ground, prose—a train which delivers you at a destination.
—T. E. Hulme (1936, 135)

As we saw in chapter 3, Craik emphasized the predictive powers of working models in his original treatment of mental models. Working models facilitate prediction of the behaviors of their targets by simulating them, in one sense of "simulation": the working model functions like its target in relevant ways. But there is another important aspect of simulation via mental models to which he gave no attention at all, but which is hinted at by Johnson-Laird (1983, 243):

It is possible that from the meanings of sentences in a connected discourse, the listener implicitly sets up a much abbreviated and not especially linguistic model of the narrative, and that recall is very much an active reconstruction based on what remains of this model....A good writer or raconteur perhaps has the power to initiate a process very similar to the one that occurs when we are actually perceiving (or imagining) events instead of merely reading or hearing about them.

Generally, the mental models we construct in understanding ordinary discourse are very schematic and lack all nonessential detail, because the most economical cognitive strategy for grasping the sense of a statement is to construct the most minimal model of its truth conditions.[50] A "good writer or raconteur," however, invites us (or compels us) to expend considerable additional effort in order to construct mental models of un-accustomed richness and detail, which, in turn, makes it possible for us to initiate (in imagination) a process that is *like* an experience in its vividness and emotional effect, to *simulate empathetically*, to take a first-person and not merely a third-person attitude to the situations and events recounted, to "know what it is like" actually to undergo or to have undergone the experience. One attraction of this kind of writing is that, un-like ordinary description, it has the power to dissolve the standing epistemic barrier be-tween subjective points of view.

If this is what the "good writer or raconteur" does, what does the "good poet" do? He does what they do and more: like the good writer, he invites us (or compels us) by choice of language to construct unwontedly rich and detailed mental models that en-able empathetic simulation. But the mental models evoked by the poet are unwonted in an additional way, for not only do they render porous the standing *epistemic* barrier between subjective points of view, they also have a strong tendency to weaken (in our imagination) the standing *metaphysical* barrier between those entities that are subjects of experience and those that are not by invoking animism. The poet invites us to imag-ine that an inanimate entity like Eliot's evening sky is itself a subject of experience that could be simulated. "Animisim," as C. D. Lewis (1947, 106–107) observed, "lies surely at the very source of the poetic image." Although this view of the poetic image was pilloried by Ruskin and others as the "pathetic fallacy," this one-time fashionable charge has not stuck, as Guthrie (1993, 126ff) convincingly argues. Poetry does not, moreover, invariably rely on a radical animism. Sometimes it will rest satisfied with merely investing inanimate natural objects with unwonted intentional significance. Alfred Noyes's line, "The Moon was a ghostly galleon tossed upon cloudy seas," turns the moon into an artifact, an extension of human intentionality with strong kines-thetic and emotional associations, and therefore into something relevant to human planning, aspiration, and emotional response. The moon is just an impassive hunk of rock. The image of an old wooden sailing ship navigating by night through turbulent waters, on the other hand, is redolent with emotional significance, for its object is a frail nautilus in circumstances of danger and adventure. Notice how closely Noyes's image comports with the Lakoff and Johnson ontological metaphor,[51] *a natural object is an artifact*: the sailing ship, the metaphorical vehicle, is more intimately related to lived bodily experience than is the target, the moon. But Noyes does not go so far as to *animate* the moon. The musical environment, by contrast, as we saw in chapter 2, is radically animistic: everything in the musical environment is the product of a charade-like simulation.

If the mental models motivated by literature and poetry, unlike the minimalist models whereby discursive meanings are represented, are unusually rich and detailed, then the content of literary and poetical works cannot be captured by paraphrase: the work itself is required if the elaborate mental models that constitute its content are to be motivated. Although musical mental models carry only scenario and protopropositional content, representing feature environments that contain only virtual objects that cannot be individuated in the full-blown, metaphysical sense, the same point can be made of them, but even more strongly. For with music, the mental models in question are not, as with Johnson-Laird's mental models, constructed to represent propositional contents, but are constructed procedurally, on the basis of action plans; and a given set of models is a fortiori unavailable by verbal paraphrase, but requires the implementation of *those very action plans*. Such a plan, moreover, determines a very precise extended musical gesture, precise in that it differs from all others. These considerations, I believe, shed light on another issue whose importance Ridley recognizes but which he leaves mysterious, namely Mendelssohn's famous but puzzling claim that "a piece of music that I love expresses thoughts to me that are not too imprecise to be framed in words, but too precise. So I find that attempts to express such thoughts in words may have some point to them, but they are also unsatisfying" (quoted in Ridley, 116). Ridley (1995, 137–138) accounts for Mendelssohn's revealing avowal by pointing out that

although two sets of similar gestures, if regarded only robotically [i.e., without sympathetic or empathetic response] may equally convey a general type of psychological state, for example something funereal, in two infinitely particular ways, such gestures may also, if grasped through sympathetic response, convey by their infinite particularity two infinitely particular funereal states—*this* state, and *that*. And it is of these states that we feelingly judge this gesture and that gesture to be expressive. This explains, I believe, why we feel—and judge—the expressive characters of the [*Eroica*] marcia funebre and, for example, the funeral march from Chopin's B-minor [*sic.*, actually B-flat minor] Piano Sonata to be so different from one another, and respectively so precise, though both are funereal.

Passing over the fact that Ridley helps himself to the unexplained notion of music as gesture, we still don't quite understand how a gesture *could* be "infinitely particular," how something like the gestures (i.e., movements and facial expressions *without words*) of a practicing non-method actor could convey "two infinitely particular funereal states [of mind]." This, I fear, is beyond the powers even of a Gielgud or an Olivier. If we understood this we might have a line on how a musical "thought" could be so precise as to outstrip verbal characterization.

My principles, on the other hand, do give us a line on it. Mendelssohn's musical "thoughts," I suggest, are the elaborate (but nonconceptual) musical mental models constructed by the listener according to detailed musical action plans. These models may *motivate* thoughts, that is, mental states with propositional content, as when a listener thinks to himself (propositionally) that the fourth movement of Schumann's *Rhenish* Symphony suggests the presence of a massive, intricately structured object, or, more directly, just thinks propositionally of a massive, intricately structured object. But such *thoughts* will always fall short of the detail of the models, and anyway are secondary to the models to which they apply and which represent their truth conditions. That the action plan of Beethoven's *Marcia funebre* is very different from that of Chopin's funeral march is obvious. It is nearly as obvious that the difference between them could not be adequately captured in propositional language. But to discern the difference, the listener must *act* on them, if only off-line.

5.5.5   Feature Domains, Cognitive Trails, and the Egocentric Musical Environment

Does rejecting the comparison between musical works and predicates threaten the application of the feature-placing paradigm to music? I think not. Recall, feature-placing language is the way a feature domain might be represented *linguistically*. But children playing the naming game are not the only denizens of such domains, for feature domains constitute the environments inhabited by all nonlinguistic life, which includes all nonhuman terrestrial life. Nonhuman living things, that is to say, show in their discriminatory behaviors sensitivity to features of the world, including the higher-order features of persisting objects like continuity of motion, inertia, and resistance to penetration, without being able to reidentify persisting basic particulars in Strawson's strong sense. A living thing that can successfully engage the features of its environment, a living thing that (say) knows how to find the beneficial and avoid the deleterious, has established what Cussins (1992, 666) calls a "cognitive trail" through that environment:

We could also picture a non-linguistic mode of activity in which a theorist would use feature-placing sentences to describe the psychology of a simple marine animal. Suppose that the animal was capable of experience but had no use for the experiential detection of anything more than "warm/cold: in front/behind" and "bubbly/clear: in front/behind" as it floated through its liquid medium. The terms "in front" and "behind" which register the animal's experience, would gain their significance entirely by means of their connection with the two forms of locomotion available to the animal: move forwards and move backwards: they wouldn't function to identify places....It would be quite unwarranted to suppose in such a case that experiential responsiveness to "warm" and "bubbly" involved a sensitivity to conditions for reidentification.

Notice that such a creature, assuming its "experience" is conscious at all, will not have achieved a *nonsolipsistic* consciousness in Strawson's sense, precisely because it cannot fully identify and reidentify particulars. Strawson (1959/1963, 65–66) shrewdly observes that such "solipsism" would be "real," not "philosophical." Unlike the philo-sophical solipsist, our nonlinguistic creature cannot raise the philosophical question, cannot ask whether it alone exists, because it has no conception of its own identity. The philosophical solipsist can raise the question, but only, Strawson thinks, because he is covertly presupposing the "conceptual scheme" of persisting locatable material objects whose existence he now pretends to doubt. This, Strawson concludes, renders the position doubtfully coherent. Real solipsism, on the other hand, is just the non-achievement of subject–object differentiation. Cussins dubs this reciprocal differentia-tion of subject and object "S/Ojectivity," a notion that will loom large in our coming discussions.

When cognitive trails intersect in a feature domain, a "feature-domain landmark" is established (Cussins 1992, 675). Imagine that an animal knows how to reach a certain waterhole by way of only two trails. The intersection of these two trails at the water-hole constitutes it as a landmark in the feature-domain. But it is not yet, *for that ani-mal*, an object with a location, since the animal is unable to get to the waterhole by any route from any location in its territory. Much less is it able to get there, as are we humans, from any location on the planet. The animal has not achieved a very high de-gree of perspective independence.[52] Cussins terms cognitive trails "experiential lines of force" (ibid., 674) because they *afford* the animal paths through its environment that are relatively obstacle-free, thereby facilitating actions.

Let us now apply these considerations to the musical case. Rather than seeing a mu-sical episode as a symbol (or set of symbols) in a scheme of predication in the Robinson manner, I propose to construe it as a representation with nonconceptual content, a pushmi-pullyu representation mandating construction of a model of a *virtual feature domain*, through which the listener is able to move by following cognitive trails or ex-periential lines of force through that virtual feature domain. Suggestions of experiential lines-of-force intersections do commonly occur in music. At the conclusion of the introductory *adagio* in the first movement of Beethoven's Fourth Symphony, for exam-ple, the first theme of the exposition emerges in the key of B-flat major from a domi-nant seventh chord rooted on F. In the recapitulation, however, the theme appears rather differently. It emerges out of the home key of B-flat major, which (quite un-usually) had already been attained (albeit only in the form of a six-four chord or the second inversion of the tonic chord)—by way of a totally unexpected modulation from the distant key of B major—before the end of the development section (examples 5.6 and 5.7). This suggests a return to a landmark in a feature domain via a different route, and following very different lines of strong (harmonic) force: the prolongation reductions of Lerdahl and Jackendoff, it will be recalled, are intended to represent the "tension and release" of harmonic movement. The first route comes from the direction of the dominant; the second from the direction of the tonic, thereby reversing the usual direction. Is this location "the same" location in virtual musical space or just a

Allegro vivace ○ : 80

Example 5.6

Beethoven, Symphony No. 4 in B-Flat, *Allegro vivace.*

Example 5.6
(continued)

Example 5.7
Beethoven, Symphony No. 4 in B-Flat, *Allegro vivace.*

Example 5.7
(continued)

Example 5.7
(continued)

similar one? There is, metaphysically speaking, no answer, no determinate fact of the matter, because musical space does not have reidentifiable places, lacking as it does the metrical and topological properties of physical space (Scruton 1997, 75). Even simple repetition does not suffice for genuine reidentification of places, for such repetition occurs in virtual acousmatic space, *which remains egocentric*; it does not occur in a space that is objective and public.[53] There are also no Strawsonian reidentifiable particulars in acousmatic space, only musical virtual objects. A reidentifiable particular must maintain its identity while unobserved. This requires that it persist through time in space, and any such claim regarding musical virtual objects is doubtfully coherent.

But musical virtual objects may include Robinson's indefinite objects of "suggestion" like Debussy's sea, which is not any particular sea. Regarding virtual musical space as a feature space thus respects the metaphysics of musical space. The intersection of trails is subject to a variety of conditions in different musical contexts. Because the opening theme of the *Finale* of Beethoven's Fifth Symphony requires for its overwhelming impact emergence out of the eerie suspense of the concluding portions of the *Scherzo*, there is, in effect, only one satisfactory musical trail to that "location."[54] As a result, Beethoven opted to reintroduce a version of this *Scherzo* material before the theme's restatement in the recapitulation, a revolutionary move in 1807.[55] Occasionally a composer will render an intersection of trails with particular delicacy, subtlety, and ingenuity as Bizet does when he has the carillon bells return by emerging gradually out of the dreamy texture of the middle section of *Carillon* in the first *L'Arlesienne* Suite (example 5.8). (Is this the "same" church in the "same" place we encountered in the first section of the piece?)[56]

When a creature navigating a real (not a virtual) *physical* feature domain establishes a network of trails through a region such that *it is able to find its way to an arbitrary goal within that region starting out from any point within it*, that is, when it has constructed a genuine cognitive map of the domain, its degree of "perspective dependence" declines and its objective grasp of the region increases (Cussins 1992). If complete (or close to complete) perspective independence is achieved, we might say that the creature has evolved *concepts* of the objects in the region, of their properties, and of their locations. But this is to have transcended the *feature domain* in favor of an ontologically structured domain of objects and locations, and to have achieved S/Ojectivity. To achieve this is to satisfy what Evans (1982) first called "the generality constraint":[57] to possess a concept[58] of an object one must be able to conceive that object as satisfying a range of predicates, and one must also be able to conceive one of those predicates applying to each and every member of a class of objects. It is widely agreed that only a linguistic creature is capable of this, because doing so requires the syntactic and semantic scaffolding of language.

What is of particular interest for us is that complete perspective independence seems to be *in principle not achievable* in the musical feature domain, for the simple reason

Example 5.8

Bizet, "Carillon" from *L'Arlesienne* Suite No. 1.

Example 5.8
(continued)

that *there is only one way to move along the cognitive trails established by the composer*. In order to negotiate them, one *must* start the piece at the beginning and listen, seriatim, to the end, or at least begin an episode at the beginning and follow *it* seriatim to the end. There just is no entering the musical feature space at "any location" and proceeding to find one's way: this is not in accord with the metaphysics of musical space. The only paths to be followed are the ones the composer has carefully prepared, just as he has carefully prepared any apparent intersections of trails. But this is just another way of saying that musical space is nonconceptual, because conceptualization is the *achievement of perspective independence*.

Let there be no misunderstanding: there is no barrier to the conceptualization, either in music-theoretic or lay terms, of musical tonal structures themselves, say, certain chord progressions, or contrapuntal devices, or formal structures. There is also, as Strawson emphasizes, no difficulty in the identification and reidentification of musical types, motifs, and, of course, works themselves. It is even possible to conceptualize pitch classes, functional chord kinds, and keys ("regions") as a metrically organized space, with "distances" computed by degree of separation on the circle of fifths and by numbers of common tones between chords and keys as Lerdahl (2001) has done. For example, C and G are immediate neighbors on the circle of fifths; the C major and

G major triads lie close together because they share the pitch class G, which is the root of the G triad; and the keys or regions of C and G major are neighbors because they differ with regard to only one pitch class, with G major substituting F# for the F in C major.[59]

During musical listening, and not just during the listening of the music-theoretically informed, the conceptual apparatus is no doubt hard at work. In fact, it *must* be at work to some extent if the musical experience is to be properly "framed" so as to remain coherent. The listener must conceive the musical performance as an artifact, a production, a syntactically organized symbolic token. The listener must remain aware, or, shades of Kant, it must be possible for the listener to *become* aware that he is the subject of a unified, complex, extended experience *in real time*. It must, that is, be possible for the "I think" to accompany his musical representations, and this requires conceptualization. What *cannot* be conceptualized, according to the account I have proposed, is what is *represented* by or "heard in" the musical structures, namely virtual musical *space and its contents*. But from this it follows that musical or "acousmatic" space remains *really*, and not merely philosophically, solipsistic. And if this is right, then we have one explanation of *why the musical listener would naturally retain a powerful affective connection with the acousmatic virtual environment*. The "space" of emotional experience is intensely self-oriented: everything about it bears on the ego. Affective feelings, then, are aroused in the course of virtual action in this highly perspective-dependent, emotionally charged, egocentric musical space. The relatively "primitive" egocentric nature of the feature domain turns out to yield additional assets, however, for, as we are about to see, it enables us to rehabilitate the cliches of the rational "disenchantment" of the world and its aesthetic "reenchantment" by naturalizing them.

None of this, it should be noted, commits the heresy of the separable experience, for the arousal depends on acting off-line on a particular musical plan and interacting with a particular musical virtual environment, and could be produced in no other way. Affective feeling, or emotion off-line, functions, moreover, cognitively: one way we come to know what sort of a scenario and virtual object is represented in the fourth movement of Schumann's *Rhenish* Symphony is by way of the affective states we find ourselves in as we act out that musical plan and construct the musical mental models. The theory I have presented is, then, as already suggested, a weak arousal theory. Strong arousal theories, on the other hand, are unpopular among philosophers these days. But they are not entirely without adherents.

5.5.6 A Strong Arousal Theory and a Hybrid Theory

In recent times Derek Matravers (1998) has offered a vigorous defense of a strong arousal theory. In order to make his case, Matravers is prepared to grasp three very prickly nettles. First, he argues that the relation between musical work and listener is merely causal and entirely noncognitive and nonintentional: the belief that a piece is expressive of an emotion is *caused by* an emotional reaction, which is itself caused by hearing the piece (1998, 150, 154).[60] Second, he concludes from this that the heresy of the separable experience may not be a heresy at all. Third, he is prepared to assert the radical semantic claim that when we say that a piece of music is expressive, we are *not* attributing an expressive property to the work. What we *mean* by such a statement is that the piece causes certain affective feelings in us, not that the piece possesses this or that expressive property (ibid., 146).

When we look a little more closely at what Matravers has to say, however, the heresy of the separable experience ends up being heretical after all, and the relation between work and listener can be construed as noncognitive only on an unacceptably narrow view of cognition and intentionality. Matravers's rejection of the heresy seems to follow from his acceptance of the possibility of the proverbial "Beethoven's Fifth drug": a concoction that "could, in theory, provide all the feelings one could get on listening to the music with all the attention one could muster. Such a drug would provide about half an hour of tightly-packed feelings without an apparent cause" (ibid., 182). But then we see him insisting on the following page that

there are two ways in which music can arouse feelings: the first, in which we react to it simply as music, rather than reacting to it as expressive, and the second, in which our reaction is caused and sustained by attending to its properties. . . . The arousal theory is accused of elevating any emotional reverie provoked by hearing a piece of music to the aesthetically valuable. . . . But the accusation is unjust; the feelings which constitute the experience of musical expression are those which are aroused by close attention to the music, and which track the music in virtue of this.

The successful Beethoven's Fifth drug, then, would have to be a philter with some rather remarkable time-release mechanisms, because it would have to produce an *appropriate* sequence of feelings in the *right order*, and not just any emotional reverie. In fact, it would have to produce the sequence of feelings that would be produced by tracking the music closely and attentively. But this means that the drug would have to give rise to an appropriate set of brain states, even if not necessarily (given issues of multiple realizability) the very brain states realizing the affective feelings aroused by a given musical performance. As we saw in chapter 2, emotions implicate definite functional areas of the brain, and musical experience involves activity in the cingulate gyrus and prefrontal cortex, two important limbic areas. One would surmise that the drug would have to activate these areas in specified ways in order to produce anything that could reasonably be called Beethoven's Fifth feelings. Emotions, moreover, involve action tendencies, and musical affective feelings, I have argued, involve *inhibited* action tendencies. But, as we saw in chapter 2, there is empirical evidence that this involves activation of the supplementary motor cortex as well as Brodmann areas 5 and 7. Surely, then, the drug could not produce these musical affective feelings without activating these parts of the brain. Moreover, short of a brain-in-a-vat situation, sustaining these brain processes would be impossible without appropriate somatic feedback.

In order to be effective, then, the drug would have to produce a simulacrum of a significant portion of the musical experience itself. Indeed it might well have to produce just about everything but the hearing of the sounds (or the hearing of the sounds in one's imagination), assuming this is even intelligible. But to the extent the drug must do all this to be effective, it is weakened as a counterexample to the heresy of the separable experience, for Beethoven's Fifth *feelings* would seem to require a (large part of a) Beethoven's Fifth *experience*. Moving from the neurological up to the psychological level, could a "Schumann's *Rhenish* drug" produce six and a half minutes of the "tightly packed feelings" evoked by a performance of the fourth movement of the work without putting the subject into mental states involving an appropriate set of action plans and mental models? To assert that it could not would be to beg the question by assuming the correctness of my theory, but I am skeptical. For how could just *these* "feelings" in just *this* order arise without the specific action plans and mental models; and without them what would make this a Schumann's *Rhenish* as opposed to a Schumann's *Spring* Symphony drug at all?

As regards the issues of intentionality and cognition, it is well to point out that "attention" and "attending to" are intentional notions, and that "tracking" is a cognitive operation. True, these are not necessarily conceptual. But I have insisted all along that musical experience is (in important respects) not conceptual; and it is hard to see how Matravers can, on the one hand, deny that musical arousal requires cognition, but, on the other, attempt to defend the strong arousal theory against charges of philistinism by ruling out as irrelevant to musical expression aroused feelings that are the result of "reveries" that have only contingent causal associations with musical performance. "To experience the music in any depth," Matravers (1998, 177) tells us, "the listener must have some grasp of something analogous to narrative in fiction: he must have some idea of where the music has 'come from' and where it is 'going.'" I couldn't agree more: indeed, I have insisted on these points by emphasizing the plan structure of music. But can any of this talk of grasping a narrative structure fairly be called noncognitive? I conclude that without adherence to the principle of the heresy of the separable experience and without acknowledgment of a cognitive, if nonconceptual, element in the arousal by music of affective feeling, Matravers's strong arousal position collapses into incoherence.

Finally, if what we *mean* by calling a piece of music sad is that it arouses sadness, and not that music possesses this expressive property, how does Matravers deal with the celebrated Bouwsma observation, endorsed by just about everyone (including Matravers himself), that "the sadness is to the music rather like the redness to the apple, than it is like the burp to the cider" (quoted in Matravers 1998, 139)? His "solution," he tells us, is to be found in chapter 9, where he says (ibid., 177, emphasis mine):

The experience of expressive music is the experience of an organized structure of sound and the corresponding feelings it arouses. The feelings are aroused by paying close attention to the sound, and sustained by continued attention. The feelings being those usually aroused by the expression of a certain emotion in the central case is (for a qualified listener) sufficient to cause the belief that the music is expressive of that emotion. *This is simply a contingent fact about us and the world.*

We seem to be back to brute facts, with no idea how organized sequences of tones might arouse these feelings or why we would believe these sequences to be "expressive" simply on the basis of their power to cause certain feelings. We certainly would not believe that the Beethoven's Fifth drug was "expressive" on that basis.

I have proposed instead a weak arousal theory that is consistent with the Bouwsma observation and that does not distort the semantics of the attribution of expressiveness. Recall that emotional experience itself, human and infrahuman, is a primitive mode of perception. It is, as Frijda claimed, "objective" in its intentional structure: emotional experience is the perception of horrible objects, insupportable people, oppressive events, the valent perception of objects and their relational properties, objects evaluated or appraised with regard to the perceiver's weal and woe. Why, then, should *musical* affective experience be different? The musical scenarios and virtual objects we construct on the basis of musical plans are invested with the emotional qualities evoked in us as we comply with the pushmi-pullyus. When we say that a piece of music is sad, then, what we mean is that the music is sad because the virtual scenario which we hear in it is sad, just as we mean that certain of Picasso's blue paintings are sad when we call them sad because of what we see in them. When acting off-line in the virtual musical environment, however, we may, as we have already seen, alternatively adopt a character or an observer viewpoint, thereby giving rise to alternative affective feelings.

Robinson (2005) seems to be committed both to strong and weak versions of the arousal theory. On the one hand, she allows that music can function as a mere "stimulus object of emotion" (352), indeed can function, at least some of the time, like the epinephrine of Schachter and Singer fame (401). Although there is some controversy about what their experiment actually showed and the replicability of their results, Schachter and Singer (1962) were apparently able to induce anger and euphoria in different groups of subjects injected with identical doses of epinephrine by planting stooges who altered the cognitive contexts of the groups. Something similar, Robinson, believes, can happen in the case of musical arousal: musical audition produces arousal, while context provides the arousal with its specific emotional character. This suggests a strong arousal theory. But Robinson also insists that a musical performance functions as a communicative utterance (2005, 323), an utterance, moreover, that is no mere symptom with only "natural meaning." A musical utterance is not just a bit of evidence from which we infer a cause. Some responses to musical works are appropriate and some are not (369), and qualified listeners will respond appropriately at the right places (361). This suggests cognitive involvement with the music itself. How does she manage to reconcile these two approaches?

Following Lazarus (1991), Robinson holds an emotion to be an ongoing process of primary appraisals of circumstances and secondary appraisals of coping strategies and expectancies. An emotion, moreover, begins as an "affective" non-cognitive appraisal (2005, 41–42), which she conceives as an involuntary evaluative reaction rather like startle: Yes, good! Or No, bad! Cognitive appraisal, which in humans tends to enlist beliefs, then monitors the exigent situation. As the situation develops and elicits further appraisals (reappraisals), both affective and cognitive, the emotion will evolve. Fear may intensify and give way to terror or despair. It may also change into relief, or even into anger, say, if the relieved person is a parent concerned for the safety of a child. Diverging here from Lazarus, Robinson, in my view, exaggerates the "noncognitive" aspect of affective appraisal and assimilates it too closely to the case of startle, which straddles the border between genuine, cognitively impenetrable reflexes and semipenetrable emotional reactions.

This hybrid theory of musical emotional arousal seems to me to be problematic on two counts. First, with the possible exception of immediate emotional response to the sheer sensuous appeal of musical sounds, affective appraisals of musical events are more cognitive than Robinson allows. Few, if any, musical events are appraised only reflexively. To be appraised at all, the significance of a musical event must be understood, even if not conceptualized. Here, I believe, Robinson's assimilation of affective appraisal to startle comes back to haunt her: a musical appraisal is no mere subcortical response. Second, much cognitive appraisal on the part of competent, but music-theoretically unschooled, listeners remains nonconceptual, like the real-life cognitive appraisals carried out by emotional but nonverbal animals. Musical appraisal can be cognitive but nonconceptual; and some version of nonconceptual representational content seems required to support the arousal of finely differentiated, but unnamable, musical emotions.

Like Ridley, Robinson distinguishes mere resemblance from genuine expressiveness. But unlike Ridley, Robinson explains expressiveness in terms of an updated Romantic theory of expression. The older theory held that the composer communicated his own emotions by arousing similar emotions in listeners. Her new Romantic theory locates expression in the artwork itself by attributing the emotions expressed to an implied persona that may, but need not, be identified with the composer. A musical work is expressive to the extent it "articulates" an emotion (or an emotional process) by giving a reader, viewer, or listener the experience of what it is like to be in that sequence of states and facilitating reflection on the experience (2005, 271).

Unfortunately, Robinson is no more successful than Ridley in explaining dynamic musical resemblance, or "melisma." It may be true that "the rhythm of music is mirrored in our heart rhythms" (ibid., 376). But we are given no clue how the audition of rhythmically organized *sequences of pitches* "mirror" or "mimic" (model? simulate?) the dynamic structure of emotion (299), motor activity (311), and psychological events (345). Although Robinson's intuitions concerning the emotional content of Brahms's Intermezzo, Op. 117, No. 2, seem very much on target, we are not told how sequences of pitches could possibly mirror "the psychological development of the protagonist" of the piece (345) or how "pure instrumental music can be *about* [can denote? can exemplify?] the emotions it expresses" (328).

As I shall argue in the next section, music is *not* about emotions, but about an emotionally charged virtual musical environment, a very different matter.[61] In my view, Robinson systematically confuses the cognitive reappraisal of a developing emotional situation, a first-order mental process, with secondary appraisal, the cognitive monitoring of coping strategies and expectancies, a second-order mental process. Robinson's antiformalist commitments are laudable; but she provides no musical semiotic or theory of musical representation to secure their reflective equilibrium with principle.

5.6   The Affective Virtual Musical Environment

The inferential and referential apparatus of propositional thought, the compositionality, productivity, and the systematicity of its conceptual structure, its capacity to satisfy the generality constraint, have allowed human beings to achieve (or to approximate) an object-centered representational standpoint, a scientific, universalistic "view from nowhere" or, better said, "view from anywhere." Our social linguistic practices of "comparing, assessing, and correcting different repertoires of commitments one with respect to another—those we attribute to others and those we undertake ourselves—are," Brandom (1995, 431) reminds us, "what make them intelligible as *perspectives*, views *of* something, ways in which a perspective-independent reality can *appear*." But this massive cognitive development, this laborious self-extrication of the human cognitive subject from the limitations of the subject-centered perspective, has been bought at a price. Although emotions are psychological and physiological states of organisms subserved by genetically encoded internal mechanisms, the intentionality of emotion, as we saw, is such that objects appear to emotional creatures as imbued with emotional quality, just as objects appear to certain visually sentient creatures as imbued with color qualities.[62] Long before the appearance of sophisticated visual systems in animals, indeed long before the appearance of vertebrate central nervous systems, emotional (or protoemotional) response was in place as a primitive set of unconscious motivationally valent action tendencies. Even mammals cortically endowed, but less cognitively sophisticated than we, are far more dependent on affective experience for decision and action guidance than we are. Their environments come to them decked out in emotional qualities bearing immediately on their weal and woe. The same may be said for young children. That sound *is* threatening, that sight *is* appealing, that terrain *is* inviting.

For the adult human, the feeling-tones of the emotionally presented world are etiolated by the exigencies of propositional thought, which, because of its objectivist viewpoint, tends to insulate the subject from the affective importunings of the ambient surround. This is something the court of law, the academic study, and the scientific laboratory are specifically designed to do. Yet concepts and propositional thought also introduce ranges of intentional objects like past and future events, to which no creature incapable of concepts could have access, and bring with them cognitive abilities, like counterfactual thought and higher-order intentionality, again which no such creature incapable of concepts could possess. These cognitive abilities enrich the human emotional palette: to be able to conceptualize past and future events—to be able to think counterfactually and establish modal distinctions—makes the distinctively human emotions of hope and regret possible; achieving higher-order intentionality is a requirement for undergoing human emotions like pride and shame. These abilities also make possible the self-conscious simulation and role-playing we have recognized as essential to the aesthetic "distance" and the generation of off-line response. Propositional thought also vastly expands the repertoire of mental models and the complexity of task-level action plans available to a cognizer.[63] For the mental model theorist, to understand a proposition, any proposition, at least any proposition in context, is to construct a mental model of its truth conditions: what state of affairs would make it true.[64] The greater the number of propositions understood, the more extensive their systematic connections, the richer the corresponding array of mental models.[65]

These heightened cognitive abilities and the expanded emotional palette that goes with them have historically given rise to a human desire to retreat from the cool detachment of subject–object differentiation and to reenter imaginatively the wash of an undifferentiated, emotionally charged environment that allows an intense empathetic identification, but an environment now ontologically enriched with entities, properties, and relations introduced by those very powers of propositional thought, and correspondingly emotionally enriched as well.[66] Maintaining S/Ojectivity or subject–object independence exacts a prodigious psychic cost, and this, one may speculate, is a source of the desire in question.[67] All living things come into the world subject to powerful forces beyond their control, the most salient example of which is perhaps the inevitability of death; but the human achievement of S/Ojectivity renders us uniquely aware of the predicament we share with other living things. Our cognitive achievement makes evident our finitude, relative helplessness, and inevitable loss, for we are brought face to face with the fact that each of us is but a transient and insignificant configuration of a tiny portion of the eternal mass-energy that is the physical universe.

Psychologists give the name "depersonalization" to an awareness of loss of the sense of personal significance of events, even when their impact on the self may continue to be appreciated rationally. Such awareness of loss, it is claimed, enhances the sense of separation between subject and object, and is contrasted with "ego–object fusion," an awareness of oneness that occurs during mystical experiences, but also in experiences ecstatic, intimately interpersonal, and aesthetic (Frijda 1986, 214–215). How delightful, then, to ease the burden of S/Ojectivity by retreating to a genuinely egocentric musical realm, a totally benignant acousmatic environment (recall the musical touch effect) in which we are not buffeted about, an environment which, as Gurney so rightly says, encourages "our sense of entire oneness with it, of its being as it were a mode of our own life."[68] When we comprehend and accept a musical work, its plan becomes our plan. This retreat also makes it possible for the human subject to savor, to explore, and to exploit in idealized ways the expanded palette of emotions, including negative emotions, that has been won for it by its own cognitive virtuosity.[69] Such a retreat by a creature with these expanded cognitive and emotional capacities to a non-S/Ojective environment also gives rise to the animistic and numinous worlds of the poet and the religionist, emotionally saturated worlds where, as Sartre (1962) has it, consciousness "degrades itself" and the human being becomes a "sorcerer." In these "magical" realms mind and world are bound together by empathy and implicit intentional understanding. We have already given some attention to the animistic world of the poet; consideration of the numinous world of the religionist will have to wait for the next chapter.

Sartre's theory of the emotions repays some closer examination, both on account of its relevance to present concerns and to those that will be taken up in the next chapter. Immediately evident is Sartre's sure grasp of the intentionality of emotion, cited approvingly, as we saw earlier, by Frijda: "The emotional consciousness," says Sartre (1962, 56), "is primarily consciousness *of* the world." When we are in an emotional state we are not primarily aware of a feeling or a subjective state: we are aware of positively and negatively valent *objects*. Sartre borrows from gestalt psychology the expression *"Umwelt"* to characterize this emotionally charged environment, as well as the "hodological chart" that maps it. It is worth noting that this unusual expression derives etymologically from the Greek *odos*, meaning "way," "path," or, as we might also say, "trail": a hodological chart is a representation of "ways" through an Umwelt that "appears to be furrowed with strait and narrow paths leading to such and such determinate ends" (ibid., 62). "This world," Sartre observes, "is difficult." It constrains us. The difficulty "is out there, in the world, it is a quality of the world given to perception . . . it is the noetic correlate of the activity we have undertaken—or have only conceived" (ibid., 63). Translated from Sartre's phenomenological terminology into our preferred idiolect, the world of activity presents itself to the motivated human being as a demanding environment in which we search out affordances. It presents, as

Frijda said, "demand characteristics." To say that it is the noetic correlate of the activity we have undertaken *or have only conceived* is to say that it is the complement (in Shepard's sense) of motor schemata run on-line or off-line.

But how is it that emotion "degrades" consciousness? Sartre answers:

We can now conceive of what an emotion is. It is a transformation of the world. When the paths before us become too difficult, or when we cannot see our way, we can no longer put up with such an exacting and difficult world. All ways are barred and nevertheless we must act. So then we try to change the world; that is, to live it as though the relations between things and their potentialities were not governed by deterministic processes but by magic. (Ibid.)

When in the grip of abject fear, we cover our eyes, ostrich-like, in terror; or we fall down helplessly in a faint in a futile attempt to remove from our presence the horrific object before which we are powerless. We feign passivity, thereby shirking responsibility; but to respond emotionally is still to choose, for it is to adopt a strategy of sorts. Emotional life, Sartre would seem to be suggesting, is just a kind of bad faith, a combination of failure of nerve and self-deception, a retreat into a state of pretend that is childish, not childlike.

But there is no reason to accept this part of his doctrine. For these views exhibit the prejudices of Sartre the Cartesian, and as such constitute one more incarnation of what Damasio (1994) has styled "Descartes' error," the misguided ambition to set rationality against emotion, to tear it loose of its organic base, and to explain human cognition without taking account of its evolutionary prehistory. In Sartre's hands, to be sure, Cartesian rational autonomy has become an *irrational* ("absurd") radical existential freedom, absurd because it can be based on no preexisting rational ground: a radical choice is the ultimate *source* of all rational grounds available to the judging subject. But this is not so far from Descartes as might at first appear. Descartes had recourse to a similar act of radical choice that grounds rationality; but it was to God, and not to man, that he arrogated this ultimate founding decision, a decision, however, that is in this case redeemed from "absurdity" because rooted in God's perfect nature.[70]

We shall take up issues of religious experience in the next chapter. For now, let us recall that emotions (from the outside) are action tendencies or changes in action readiness. As such they are suited to *engage* the world; they are not a self-deceptive *flight from* the world. Because of their primitive origins, emotions can be "quick and dirty" in their operation, and thus can work at cross purposes to rationality; but, as a variety of recent studies have shown (Damasio 1994, 1999; de Sousa 1987; Plotkin 1993), they can also be enlisted as reason's ally, providing indispensable judgmental heuristics and helping to solve pervasive frame problems, in addition to assisting us in our moral deliberations and in the navigation of the social world by teaching us how we should feel in morally paradigmatic situations (de Sousa 1987; Sherman 1998). Making specific reference to Sartre's theory, van Fraassen (2002, 107–108) holds that emotions function cognitively by heating the cognitive "temperature" of the brain enough to allow assimilation of paradigm shifts in science. Dissonance between theory and evidence may produce higher than normal frustration levels. This, in turn, can bring about a reconfiguration of firing patterns in the brain that allows a new scientific paradigm, be it relativity or quantum mechanics, that initially seems senseless suddenly to make sense. As noted above (see note 7), certain connectionist architectures known as Boltzmann machines provide for a temperature parameter that affects the probability of firing of individual nodes in relative independence of the weights of their input connections. When the temperature is high, nodes fire almost at random. As the temperature is "cooled" over a training cycle during which the connection weights are modified, probability of nodal firing approaches either one or zero, that is, determinism. As heating and cooling cycles are repeated, this allows the machine to settle into weight settings that yield more optimal solutions to typical categorization problems than would be possible in a more conventional connectionist architecture trained by backpropagation alone. The temperature parameter in Boltzmann machines is thought to be similar in function to emotional arousal in organic brains.[71]

Nor need "the magical" be interpreted as the debased or the degraded, although the following passage suggests that Sartre (1962, 84–85) himself is not entirely of one mind about this:

There is an existential structure of the world which is magical. . . . the category of "magic" governs the interpsychic relations between men in society and, more precisely, our perception of others. . . . It follows that man is always a sorcerer to man and the social world is primarily magical.

Once again, when we get past the elliptical language, Sartre is calling attention to just the empathetic and simulational strategy directed toward achieving understanding of other minds that we have already recognized. The sorcerer animates the object, the nonliving, the nonconscious, the "in-itself," as the sorcerer's apprentice in Goethe's poem conferred life and consciousness on his broomstick, turned it into a subject, a fellow "for-itself," in order to command it. Mental simulation accomplishes a kind of animation. To simulate is to approach an object as a fellow subject. The emotions help the simulator to emulate the mental states of others, for as we simulate these states by running scenarios in our imagination we also undergo versions of the corresponding emotions. The simulated emotions are not "real" emotions: they are run off-line. But emotional states and the systems supporting them are modular enough for them to be sufficiently resistant to cognitive penetration so as to enable us to undergo an experience, to "know what it is like" actually to be in that simulated mental state, to enter into it in a way no merely descriptive expression of its cognitive content could possibly underwrite.[72] Think of how it can be helpful to remind ourselves, when viewing horrific but fictional dramatic cinematic images, that the depicted events are not actually occurring. To the extent the aroused emotional states remain resistant to this strategy (and they do), they display a degree of cognitive impenetrability. The acousmatic realm of organized tones is especially "magical" in this sense, for the physical world of nomic necessity is apparently transcended in imagination, and all that there is, and everything that happens, seems intentionally significant and transparent to the understanding.[73]

Notice Sartre's tendency to oppose the "magical" ("inter-psychological" communication) to the (causally) "deterministic" (ibid., 85):[74]

Not that it is impossible to take a deterministic view of the inter-psychological world or to build rational superstructures upon it. But then it is those structures that are ephemeral and unstable, it is they that crumble away as soon as the magical aspect of faces, gestures and human situations becomes too vivid.

But what is the musical utterance if not a gesture with a "magical" or even, as we shall see, incantational aspect? The magical aspect of the musical utterance is not, however, limited to its status as an interpsychological gesture in Sartre's sense. For the mental models it motivates provide (as their contents) a rich domain of affordances, but this domain is, as I have already suggested, entirely animistic, one from which material beings, all brutely existing psychically inert entities *de trop*, those disturbing sources of existential nausea, have been systematically excluded. Metaphorical transference in *Dichtung* (poetry) may or may not be invariably animistic (see the reference to C. D. Lewis above); but in *Tondichtung* (music), it is.

There is, however, nothing mysterious about this musical thaumaturgy, if by "mysterious" we mean something in principle inexplicable and not a result of our considerable ignorance concerning the brain and its remarkable powers, including its ability to construct mental models and to simulate. The acousmatic realm of tones is intentional through and through because we can understand the plan of the music, since a brain like ours ensconced in a body like ours arranged the tones that way. It is magical in the Sartrean sense because the plan of the music is also our plan, which we have adopted in coming to understand it. During a musical experience a performer sends a pushmi-pullyu representation the listener's way that both discloses this plan structure and enjoins him to implement it and to construct an appropriate set of mental models. Affective feeling in music arises in the course of making these plan structures our own and acting on them off-line.

5.7   Summary and Conclusion

The argument of this chapter has been a long and complex one. The main line of argumentation defends a weak arousal theory of musical experience against both formalist and strong arousal theories. Discussion of the biological and cognitive science of emotion showed emotions to be action tendencies (or changes in action readiness), as well as evaluative perceptions or appraisals of environmental affordances. From here, the line of argument led to the conclusion that the arousal of emotion by music results from the presentation of affordances in virtual musical space, activating motor schemata off-line and motivating the construction by the listener of appropriate mental models of musical scenarios or feature domains. The nonconceptual nature of these representations, I argued further, tends to dissolve epistemic and metaphysical barriers between subject and subject and between subject and object, a result that encourages simulation of virtual musical objects and further enhances emotional involvement with the musical scenario content. Finally, we considered Sartre's theory of the emotions, a theory that, despite its origins in phenomenology and existentialism, holds much in common with the views of Frijda I have endorsed and affords a transition to topics that will occupy us in the following chapter.

Let us end by taking special note of the fact that Sartre (1964, 22) explicitly excludes music from the nauseating press of brute existence:

The last chord has died away. In the brief silence which follows I feel strongly that there it is, that *something has happened.* . . . What has happened is that the Nausea has disappeared. When the voice was heard in the silence, I felt my body harden and the Nausea vanish. Suddenly: it was almost unbearable to become so hard, so brilliant. At the same time the music was drawn out, dilated, swelled like a waterspout. It filled the room with its metallic transparency, crushing our miserable time against the walls. I am *in* the music. . . . That is what has changed, my gestures. This movement of my arm has developed like a majestic theme, it has glided along the song of the Negress [*sic.*]; I seemed to be dancing.

His reason for the exclusion: music does not "exist" (ibid., 128):

If you existed, you had to *exist all the way*, as far as mouldiness, bloatedness, obscenity were concerned. In another world, circles, bars of music keep their pure and rigid lines. But existence is a deflection.

Is Sartre claiming that musical objects are "ideal" in the way mathematical objects are? Or is there another notion of ideal existence in play, perhaps a notion of incorporeality like that suggested by Scruton (1997, 333):

The organization of music is perceived not merely as movement, but as gesture. The activity which animates the musical surface is that which animates you and me—although transferred to another and inaccessible realm, the realm of pure sound, where only incorporeal creatures live and breathe.

If so, how should this rather wild and woolly suggestion be interpreted by the naturalist? It is to these and related issues that we now turn.

6 Nausea and Contingency: Musical Emotion and Religious Emotion

In the esthetic object tendencies are sensed as brought to fruition; in it is embodied a means-consequence relationship, as the past work of his hands was surveyed by the Lord and pronounced good.
—J. Dewey (1981, 314)

We do not actually want God to create the world we long for, but we want to be able to imagine it often.
—S. Neiman (2002, 79)

6.1   Introduction and Chapter Conspectus

6.1.1   The Horror of the Contingent

In nature there is nothing contingent.
—Spinoza (1985, 1, prop. 29)

*The sole aim of philosophical enquiry is **to eliminate the contingent.***
—Hegel (1975, 28, boldface emphasis in original)[1]

"The safest general characterization of the European philosophical tradition," goes Whitehead's (1978, 39) notorious claim, "is that it consists of a series of footnotes to Plato." Alternatively celebrated and reviled, Whitehead's provocative aperçu may be questionable as an exhaustive description of the history of European philosophy; but as an explicit recognition of the Platonic provenance of many of that history's perennial themes, it is unexceptionable.

The Sartrean existential nausea we encountered in the previous chapter surely reprises one such theme: the horror engendered in the Platonic imagination by the two lower segments of the "divided line," the realm of darkness, of chains and flickering shadows, of semblance and illusion, of generation and decay, of imperfection, and of contingency. I have chosen my emotion term carefully. One need not subscribe without reservation to a strictly componential account of the emotions to find the analysis of horror into more basic elements of fear and disgust compelling. This horror of the contingent, as it might be called, is at root a metaphysico-religious sentiment. Its fear component has been given eloquent expression in a famous *Pensée* (102) of Pascal (1670/1995, 26):

When I consider the short span of my life absorbed into the preceding and subsequent eternity, *memoria hospitis unius deis paetereuntis* [like the memory of a one-day guest], the small space which I fill and even can see, swallowed up in the infinite immensity of spaces of which I know nothing and which knows nothing of me, I am terrified, and surprised why it should be here rather than there, for there is no reason why it should be here rather than there, why now rather than then. Who put me here? On whose orders and on whose decision have this place and this time been allotted to me?

What terrifies Pascal, it is clear, is the suspicion that there might be no reason why his brief span of consciousness happens to have flickered where and when it has; he finds the possibility that this might be nothing more than a brute happenstance deeply disturbing. The fear expressed so poignantly by Pascal has served historically as a motivator of systems of religious belief, as well as of elaborate metaphysical cosmologies like those of Spinoza and Hegel that purport either to eliminate contingency as an illusion, or to sublate (*aufheben*) it into necessity.[2]

For the disgust component, we turn back to Sartre. Although nausea is not strictly speaking an emotion, it is the physiological counterpart of disgust, generally considered one of the basic emotions. Sartre's term, on the other hand, designates neither an emotion nor a physiological state. It is a term of art designating a fundamental ontological attitude: the claim of consciousness, the "for-itself," to radical freedom as against the passive and inert "in-itself," the intentional object of consciousness, as well as the claim of the for-itself on "negativity," its frantic resistance to objectification as a mere "thing." Nonetheless, Sartre's development of this idea unquestionably constitutes an important historical footnote to the Platonic horror of the contingent. Intensified by copious drafts of virulent misogyny and trading effectively on graphic images of sexual revulsion, Sartre's overheated language rises to a febrile pitch that goes far beyond even Plato's most immoderate expressions of his jaundiced attitudes toward the realm of becoming. Surely the Sartrean conceit "slime is the revenge of the In-itself" (1966, 777) is one of the most outrageous, if boldly imaginative, philosophical sentences ever crafted.

We took note in the previous chapter of Sartre's exemption of music from the nauseating slime of brute existence. He also, we may recall, exempts "circles," and, presumably, other objects of pure geometry and mathematics. Why are these two sorts of object "hard and pure," not slimy? Here is one Sartrean answer. Music and mathematical objects are not real, but "ideal"; they don't "exist": "In another world, circles, bars of music keep their pure and rigid lines. But existence is a deflection" (Sartre 1964, 128). Since it is existence that is nauseatingly *de trop*—pointlessly, superfluously *there*—music and geometrical objects remain uncontaminated. By "existence," Sartre clearly means spatiotemporal, causally implicated physical existence. There is no evidence he means to rule out the existence of Platonic abstract objects: the "another world" language suggests he may not be ruling them out. Whether or not Sartre accepted some version of mathematical Platonism (I don't know whether he did), a Platonic view of the ontology of musical works faces grave difficulties, for the musical Platonist must hold that musical works are discovered by their composers, not invented or created by them, and this is very problematic for reasons we have already considered. As I argued in chapter 4, musical works are ontological kin to biological species, reproductively established families of scores and performances; and these families surely exist (at some time or other). Sartre may also mean to tell us, however, that whatever a work of music is, it is not *experienced as* a mere physical existent, an inert in-itself, a thing set over against the for-itself. This is defensible and, in my view, correct. Indeed, it coheres with observations in earlier chapters concerning music's simulational function and the animism of its "magical" virtual world.

But there is also another, perhaps more profound, Sartrean answer on offer concerning the special status accorded music and geometry. In music contingency is eliminated by an "internal" necessity (1964, 133):

strains of music alone can proudly carry their own death within themselves like an internal necessity: only they don't exist. Every existing thing is born without reason, prolongs itself out of weakness and dies by chance.

But something similar holds in mathematics as well[3]: truths concerning mathematical objects, it is widely agreed, are true in all possible worlds,[4] and so necessary in the strictest sense. Whatever the sorrows of traditional essentialism in much recent philosophy of language and science, the mathematical properties of the objects of pure geometry are essential properties. The "internal necessity" of music rests, however, on a very different basis. Here necessity is achieved not by way of necessary truth, but by way of thoroughgoing intentional determination. Leaving aside the special case of aleatoric music, what distinguishes musical works, indeed, as I have argued elsewhere (Nussbaum 2003a), what distinguishes works of art in general from other purposive, but nonartistic artifacts, is a certain drive toward the elimination of the contingent. Otto Weininger, a late and grotesque but entirely characteristic product of the Viennese culture that generated much of the greatest music belonging to the style under consideration in this book, opined that "the greater the artwork, the less chance may it contain" (1980, 625).[5] To say that nothing in a successful work of art is contingent is to say that nothing about it is *de trop*: everything matters, every detail is potentially significant. Not only are all its aesthetically relevant properties essential properties,[6] but which of its properties are aesthetically relevant is a question not to be settled beforehand, but to be determined in the course of interaction with the work. This, however, is just to say that as symbol the artwork is, in Goodman's terms, "replete" as opposed to "attenuated."

Recall Goodman's (1976) celebrated example of two wiggly lines drawn on white backgrounds. One is an electocardiogram of the behavior of a patient's heart, the other a Hokusai drawing of Mt. Fujiyama. Both drawings function as symbols, but many details of the first are contingent: neither the color, nor its precise hue or degree of brightness or saturation, nor the precise thickness of the line matters. The case of the Hokusai drawing is quite different. Here every detail of the line is potentially significant and in this sense not contingent but necessary, because not dispensable. The art drawing requires a different kind of looking, a looking that is more flexible, more sensitive, more searching, more open-ended. Similar considerations apply to musical works, and a fortiori to their performances, which exemplify densely ordered sets of nuance properties not represented in the skeletal score.[7] The precise placement of a scored note by a performer in pitch or in time will be aesthetically significant.

Not only can we essay this more profound interpretation of Sartre's exemption of music from the nausea of existence. We can, on its basis, expand our account of musical aesthetic emotion on Sartrean grounds: an experience that assuages existential nausea by eliminating contingency can reasonably be held to give rise to powerful, positive emotions. But we look in vain in Sartre's philosophy for an explanation of how music might accomplish, or enable us to accomplish, this feat. Most important, Sartre gives us little help in understanding how music moves us as profoundly as it does. There are hints, of course, hints that suggest that any such explanation is likely to involve some connection between musical emotion and religious emotion (Sartre 1966, 268):

Beauty therefore represents an ideal state of the world, correlative with an ideal realization of the for-itself; in this realization the essence and the existence of things are revealed as identity to a being who, in this very revelation, would be merged with himself in the absolute unity of the in-itself. This is precisely because the beautiful is not only a transcendent synthesis to be effected but because it can be realized only in and through a totalization of ourselves. This is precisely why we desire the beautiful and why we apprehend the universe as lacking the beautiful to the extent that we ourselves apprehend ourselves as a lack. But the beautiful is no more a potentiality of things than the in-itself-for-itself is a peculiar possibility of the for-itself. It haunts the world as an unrealizable.

To the impossibility of this sort of "totalization," the impossibility of any ultimate unification of the "in-itself-for-itself" by the "for-itself," Sartre traces God's impossibility, or at least the impossibility of a conscious and omniscient God (ibid., 140):

Thus this perpetually absent being which haunts the for-itself is itself fixed in the in-itself. It is the impossible synthesis of the for-itself and the in-itself.... In short, this being would be exactly the self which we have shown can exist only as a perpetually evanescent relation, but it would be this self as a substantial being....

Let no one reproach us with capriciously inventing a being of this kind...it takes on the name of God.... The being of human reality is suffering because it rises in being as perpetually haunted by a totality which it is without being able to be it, precisely because it could not attain the in-itself without losing itself as the for-itself.

On Sartrean phenomenological principles, to be conscious is to be conscious *of something*, and to be conscious of something is to distinguish or "alienate" it, albeit non-reflectively, from the consciousness for which it is an object. Consciousness is negation because consciousness is, in this way, always other than its object. It cannot, therefore, "totalize" or complete itself, for its stance is inevitably proleptic. It may objectify itself psychologically by way of "impure reflection"; but in doing so it has already transcended itself, for its own objectification is only what it *was*, not what it is. Because consciousness cannot complete itself, a conscious, omniscient God is impossible. If God were conscious, his (or its) consciousness would not be an objectifying, cognizing consciousness at all. God could only "experience the world without knowing it" (Sartre 1966, 400). For Sartre, it is clear, all cognition is S/Ojective in Cussins's sense (see chapter 5). This will turn out to be important.

We shall not be concerned here with the ontological issue of God's existence, nor shall we grapple with the elusive idea of beauty. Nevertheless, these Sartrean remarks are suggestive with regard to the issue of the suspension of the horror of the contingent in the musical aesthetic context. But they are no more than suggestive. It is possible, however, to develop these suggestions further by invoking the theory of musical representation and meaning introduced in earlier chapters. But to bring this theory to bear, we must probe the horror of the contingent a little more deeply than we have done. Since the horror of the contingent is a psychological phenomenon[8] with a definite history of expression, any further probing will require that we consider this history more closely. Our approach in this chapter will, then, be historical; and our method will be primarily interpretive, "metarepresentational" in Sperber's sense, and not descriptive and explanatory,[9] for the horror of the contingent is, above all, an attitude, an emotionally charged evaluative stance taken with regard to human finitude. But how should we go about such an investigation? The obvious course of action would be to consider additional expressions of the horror of the contingent, that is, to consider additional footnotes to our original Platonic theme. But of these there are many, for this aspect of the Platonic legacy has cast a long shadow. Indeed, we have already taken passing note of three of them: Pascal's epigram and the metaphysical cosmologies of Spinoza and Hegel can all be seen as commentaries on it. We must make some tactical choices.

There is, however, a set of footnotes supplied by a towering historical philosophical figure who offers a far richer theology and aesthetics than does Sartre, in particular, a theory of aesthetic symbolism that sits particularly well with the theory of musical representation developed in previous chapters. This philosopher, moreover, shared with Sartre, as much as any other among Sartre's most directly influential predecessors, a similarly fervent commitment to radical human freedom, if not to Sartre's Cartesian (i.e., rule-*founding* not rule-*consulting*) version of it (see chapter 5, note 70). Just as important, the temperament of this philosopher, while considerably more sober, seems nevertheless to have been more than a little susceptible to something resembling Sartrean nausea, as we are about to see. The philosopher in question is Kant, and it is to his footnotes to Plato that we now turn.

6.1.2 Chapter Conspectus

Section 6.2 traces the horror of the contingent through Kantian theology, philosophy of mind, and epistemology. Section 6.3 then takes up Kantian musical aesthetics, criticizing one strand of Kant's theory, while arguing for convergence between another strand and the views put forward earlier in this book. Section 6.4 pursues the horror of the contingent into Nietzschean realms, but concludes, on a naturalistic note, with findings deriving from contemporary cognitive psychology and cognitive anthropology of religion. Section 6.5 then returns briefly to Kant, playing off the conclusions reached in this and earlier chapters against the seldom-noted fascination of this arch rationalist with a brand of Neoplatonic mysticism.

6.2 Contingency, Intuitive Understanding, and Religious Mysticism

And who does not feel himself compelled, notwithstanding all interdictions against losing himself in transcendent ideas, to seek rest and contentment, beyond the concepts which he can vindicate by experience, in the concept of a being, the possibility of which cannot be conceived but at the same time cannot be refuted, because it relates to a mere being of the understanding and without it reason must needs remain forever dissatisfied?
—Kant (1783/1977 4:352)

Like God, [music] sees only the heart.
—Schopenhauer (1844/1966, II, 449)

Kant is prone to make reference to illegitimacy and miscegenation, standard elicitors of sexual revulsion, when treating the empirical, both theoretical and practical. For example, in *Prolegomena* (1783/1977, 4: 257–258) he asserts that Hume "inferred that reason was altogether deluded with reference to [the concept of cause and effect], which she erroneously considered as one of her children, whereas in reality it was nothing but a bastard of imagination, impregnated by experience...." In *Grundlegung* (1784/1981, 4: 426) Kant denounces empiricist moral philosophies, where, he tells us, in "a dream of sweet illusions (in which not Juno but a cloud is embraced) there is substituted for morality some bastard patched up from limbs of quite varied ancestry and looking like anything one wants to see in it but not looking like virtue to him who has once beheld her in her true form." Kant's chief objection to empiricist moral philosophies, of course, is that they are one and all heteronomous: they subvert moral responsibility because they do not allow for autonomy, or self-determination. Locating the determination of action either in feeling or in social conditioning, factors that are imposed on or suffered passively by the moral subject, is to traduce moral responsibility by limiting freedom. Sartre's favored term of opprobrium for encroachments on the radical freedom of the in-itself, as in the bad-faith pretense involved in "magical" emotional strategies we considered in the previous chapter, is *degradation*. Yet he, too, has recourse to the image of bastardy when discussing the tendency to hypostatize the for-itself as an in-itself, an allegedly spontaneous ego *object*: "But this spontaneity, represented and hypostatized in an object, becomes a degraded and bastard spontaneity, which magically preserves its creative power while becoming passive" (Sartre 1960, 81).

Kant's expression *"reine Vernunft"* is a rendering of Christian Wolff's *"ratio pura,"* designating reason without any admixture of empirical content. There is no conclusive evidence of which I am aware showing that *"reine Vernunft"* was Kant's original coinage. G. E. Lessing, for one, had already used the expression *"reine Wahrheit"* ("pure truth") in *Eine Duplik* (*A Rejoinder*, 1778). Whether original with him or not, Kant's expression deviates from the apparently more entrenched *"lautere Vernunft,"* if H. A. Meissner's Wolffian *Philosophisches Lexicon* (1737, 650–651) be our guide to German philosophical usage standard at the time. There is no entry for *"reine Vernunft"* in Meissner's work. Now *"lauter"* and *"rein"* are quite close in meaning, both designating that which is pure because unalloyed. There is, however, a fine shade of connotative difference between the two. *"Rein"* is especially distinguished from that which is contaminated or polluted. It is, therefore, more strongly associated with disgust and bears a more potent emotional load. *"Rein"* and its verbal form *"reinigen,"* we may ruefully recall, were the terms employed by German speakers who subscribed to the theories of racial purity dominant within Germany's Third Reich. Kant's emotionally fraught distinction between pure and empirical origins ramifies throughout the Critical Philosophy, coloring such closely related distinctions as a priori–a posteriori, spontaneity–receptivity, intuitive understanding–discursive understanding, activity–passivity, and, last but not least, necessity–contingency.

The distinction between the intuitive and the discursive understanding is of particular interest in the present context. Kant invariably places the human understanding at a comparative disadvantage because it is *merely* discursive: it can only think, without being able actively to intuit. The intuitive content of human experience arises, that is, through passive affection of the senses. As a result, human knowledge that is not entirely a priori—knowledge that is not logical or mathematical—has a "material," "given" component that is *contingent*. The human understanding can conceptualize the given; but the given cannot be shown to be necessarily as it is. The specific empirical content of the manifold of intuition cannot be accounted for; it can only be organized. In the case of an intuitive understanding, things are otherwise. As creative, or original, it fully determines its objects because it actively produces them rather than being passively affected by them. For it, existence is not *de trop*. Although the intuitive understanding may perhaps be said to *know*, it does not, strictly speaking, *think*, since it does not conceptualize. "Through [intuitions] first an object is *given* to us, through [concepts] the object is *thought*" (Kant 1787/1963, A50/B74).[10] Concepts are, in Kant's view, "functions of unity": they function as rules for unification of given content, both for the unification of sensible manifolds or spatiotemporal arrays of empirical intuitions into measurable, persisting, causally interactive objects and for the unification of these objects into classes. Notice, in light of earlier observations concerning Sartre's critique of the idea of God, that an understanding that does not conceptualize *will not be S/Ojective in Cussins's sense*.

Palpable in the Kantian notion of an intuitive understanding is a considerable residue of theistic mysticism, undoubtedly derived by way of another extensive set of footnotes to Plato,[11] the Christian Neoplatonic theology[12] that was second nature to the rationalist philosophers of early modern Europe.[13] Indeed, faint echoes of Neoplatonism reverberate even in Sartre's own phenomenological descriptions of consciousness as completely "transparent," "diaphanous," and resistant to objectification. But this ceases to be particularly surprising when we appreciate the incalculable debt Sartre's ontology of being and nothingness owes to Hegelian determinate negation and the dialectical conception of mind as "pure negativity." Hegel's philosophy, in turn, has been aptly described[14] as "the crowning achievement of Neoplatonism."

In the Neoplatonic tradition, Christian theology was grafted, by Augustine and others, onto the Plotinian conceptions of the One and its emanations,[15] both conceptions deriving from Plato's metaphorical comparison in the *Republic* of the Good with the sun (Plotinus 1962, V. 5. 7–8; cf. Bussanich 1996, 41). Intuition, even the passive or receptive intuition that is required to supply any discursive understanding with its empirical content, is, according to standard Kantian doctrine, a mode of representation whereby cognition relates "immediately" to objects, meaning that there is direct connection between mind and object without any conceptual abstraction. In Kant's mature critical doctrine, concepts cannot relate directly to objects but are always "mediated" by intuitions. An intuitive understanding would also relate directly to its objects, but actively, not passively. The intuitive understanding affects, but is not affected: it is directly *present to* its objects, in direct causal contact with them, as the light of the sun directly affects the objects it illuminates. The Platonic comparison between intuitive understanding and the light of the sun is, of course, a metaphor; and there is an important difference between the two. Not only is active intuition unmediated by concepts; it is also unmediated by extended chains of material causes, whereas human sensible intuition is causally mediated.[16]

This Kantian notion of active intuition accords with a constant and pervasive theme in personal accounts of mystical religious experience, an awareness of the *immediate presence* of the deity.[17] This presence is, we should note, a *living* presence, the presence of a fellow subject, a "thou," with whom we can enter into personal relations. Karen Armstrong (1993, 104) maintains that the human susceptibility to religious mystical experience is a psychological universal: "It seems that when human beings contemplate the absolute, they have very similar ideas and experiences. The sense of presence, ecstasy and dread in the presence of a reality—called nirvana, the One, Brahman, or God—seems to be a state of mind and a perception that are natural and endlessly sought by human beings." According to Neoplatonism scholar W. T. Wallis (1995, 15), "the mystical experience [tends] to express itself in similar ways at all times and in all civilizations." William James (1902/1985, 503) tells us that "religion," that is to say religious sentiment, not theological dogma, "must necessarily play an eternal part in human history." Rudolf Otto (1950, 134ff) goes so far as to assert, in a Kantian vein, that "the holy" is an "a priori category." Although the tendency on the part of Otto and others to treat religious experience as psychologically *sui generis* has been pretty thoroughly discredited by recent cognitive science and anthropology of religion (Guthrie 1993; Boyer 2001),[18] religious mystical experience remains a widely reported phenomenon that does seem remarkably uniform across times and places. The following examples of personal testimony offered by James (1902/1985) are typical:

God surrounds me like a physical atmosphere. He is closer to me than my own breath. In him I literally live and move and have my being. (71–72)

I have the sense of a presence, strong, and at the same time soothing, which hovers over me. Sometimes it seems to enwrap me with sustaining arms. (72)

But in addition to an awareness of immediate presence, the mystical state of mind also has a quality of necessity and assurance, that everything is exactly as it should be and is unfolding according to plan (ibid., 392):

In that moment the whole of my life passed before me, including each little meaningless piece of distress, and I understood them. *This* was what it had all meant, *this* was the piece of work it had all been contributing to. I did not see God's purpose, I saw only his intentness and his entire relentlessness towards his means. He thought no more of me than a man thinks of hurting a cork when he is opening wine, or hurting a cartridge when he is firing. And yet, on waking, my first feeling was, and it came with tears, "Domine non sum digna [Lord, I am not worthy]," for I had been lifted into a position for which I was too small.

A special affinity between mystical religious experience and musical experience has been noticed by a number of writers. For Otto (1950), "Musical feeling is rather (like numinous feeling) something 'wholly other,' which, while it affords analogies and here and there will run parallel to the ordinary emotions of life, cannot be made to co-incide with them by a detailed point-by-point correspondence" (49). "Numinous" is Otto's term for the special feeling of mystery in the presence of the deity. The "wholly other" is the uncanny, the powerful, the awe-inspiring: "But the object of religious awe or reverence, the *tremendum* and *augustum*, cannot be fully determined conceptually: it is non-rational, as is the beauty of a musical composition, which no less eludes complete conceptual analysis." Otto (150–151) quotes Goethe to similar effect: "Such is the effect of music in the highest degree, for music stands too high for any understanding to reach, and an all-mastering efficacy goes forth from it, of which however no man is able to give an account. Religious worship cannot therefore do without music.[19] It is one of the foremost means to work upon men with an effect of *marvel*". Hinde (1999, 187) cites an empirical study carried out on a national sample in the United States showing that of all activities not explicitly religious, like prayer, reading the Bible, or attending services, listening to music was the most common trigger of religious experience among a group of subjects[20] who reported fourteen categories of such triggers and who claimed that "they had been close to a 'powerful spiritual force.'" Compare also Gabrielsson's (2001) data, consisting of 400 reports collected from 300 subjects of equally distributed gender, 60 percent between 20 and 40 years of age, 40 percent between 40 and 60, about 50 percent amateur musicians, about 33 percent professional musicians, and about 17 percent nonmusicians. About 80 percent of the reports derive from experiences as listeners. The following are representative of one variety of "strong experience with music" (2001, 442): "The music started to take command of my body. I was charged in some way...I was filled by an enormous warmth and heat." "I seem to be experiencing directly...feel the potential for anything to pass through me." "I felt like I was the receiver of a message...the feeling of being spoken to, strongly and directly, lived inside me."

For James (1902/1985, 420–421), the phrases of mystical literature

prove that not conceptual speech, but music rather, is the element through which we are best spoken to by mystical truth.... Music gives us ontological messages which non-musical criticism is unable to contradict.... There is a verge of the mind which these things haunt; and whispers therefrom mingle with the operations of our understanding, even as the waters of the infinite ocean send their waves to break among the pebbles that lie upon our shores.

In the light of observations of previous chapters, James's oceanic allusion is highly suggestive, as is the following (ibid., 279, emphasis mine):

Religious rapture, moral enthusiasm, ontological wonder, cosmic emotion, are all unifying states of mind, in which the sand and grit of the selfhood incline to disappear, and tenderness to rule. The best thing is to describe the condition integrally as a characteristic affection to which our nature is liable, a region in which we find ourselves at home, a region *in which we swim*. ...

The metaphor of immersion in water,[21] enriched by the idea of soft breath, also (rather remarkably) suggested itself to Helen Keller who, it will be recalled from chapter 2, claimed access to musical performance by way of the tactual sense of vibration: "And the ebb and flow of the great chorus beat sharply against my fingers. Then instruments and voices joined together—an ocean of wild vibrations—and died away like the breath of a mouth trembling in sweet softness" (quoted in Katz 1989, 193n9). Consider as well, in the light of our earlier observations (chapters 2 and 5) concerning the animistic quality of musical representation, James's description (1902/1985, 497–498) of the richly animistic aspects of nature in which "religion delights to dwell":

It is the terror and beauty of phenomena, the "promise" of the dawn and of the rainbow, the "voice" of the thunder, the "gentleness" of the summer rain, the "sublimity" of the stars, and not the physical laws which these things follow, by which the religious mind still continues to be most impressed; and just as of yore, the devout man tells you that in the solitude of his room or of the fields he still feels the divine presence. . . .

Finally, mystical religious experience involves, as Otto describes it, identification "of the personal self with the transcendent Reality," identification, moreover, with "Something that is at once absolutely supreme in power and reality and wholly non-rational" (1950, 22), and that brings with it a "self-depreciation which comes to demand its own fulfillment in practice as rejecting the delusion of selfhood, and so makes for the annihilation of the self" (ibid., 21).[22]

If we pause now to collate some of the preceding points, the contours of my proposal will begin to emerge. Consider: (1) the "inner necessity" of musical works; (2) the lack of S/Ojectivity on the part of the intuitive (divine) understanding; (3) the deity as a living presence with whom we enter into personal relations; (4) the necessity and rightness of the divine plan; (5) the tenderness of religious rapture; (6) the affinity between mystical experience, musical experience, and immersion in water; (7) the animism of the religious world; (8) the identification of the self with the supreme nonrational power and the submersion of the self. Combining these points with results from previous chapters, the proposal is this. As we saw in chapter 2, musical experience exploits anatomical structures (the cochlear structures in the inner ear) that are homologous with the lateral line of fishes, thereby yielding a quasi-spatial musical perception with a quality of immediate touch, a touch that, when properly executed by a skilled performer, affects us as tender and loving. This is what I termed (in chapter 5) the "musical touch effect." Music also encourages the construction of plans and mental models that guide movement through this spacelike environment, an environment, however, that is thoroughly animistic and that invites understanding via simulation as in a charade (chapters 2 and 5). Like the objects of an intuitive understanding, the virtual objects of musical experience are not *de trop*, superfluous, but created according to a coherent musical plan, a plan, however, with which the comprehending listener fully identifies, feeling, as it were, "Thy will be done" (chapters 2 and 3). Musical experience is nonconceptual and lacks S/Ojectivity: the listener is immersed in the musical environment as if in a watery surround.

It is these characteristics that allow the creation of a powerful illusion that assuages existential nausea and enables the listener to transcend the horror of the contingent by invoking a mood that is akin to the mystical religious mood of identification with a supernatural being, an experience that also has this palliating effect. Indeed, this powerful illusion *requires* that S/Ojectivity be suspended, since the mystical religious mood requires both the sense of immediate presence of the deity and the submersion of the self. These considerations, I suggest, elucidate the affinity between the mystical and musical moods and supply at least one reason, though not necessarily the *only* reason, why some music has the capacity to move us the way it does: the musical environment in which we find ourselves immersed is one which has become entirely plastic, cooperative, and directed toward "the good of the whole," an environment that has lost its contingent, brutely "given" aspect and has yielded completely to intentional design, as all of creation is considered to be plastic and yielding under the divine hand. "Why," asks psychologist Nico Frijda (1986, 357–358, emphasis mine),

should a work of art be moving, or staggering, or bring excitement, as even formal art can be or do? The nature of the emotion of "being moved" may give a clue. Being moved, to the point of tears, has been interpreted in an earlier section as surrender to something greater than oneself. It is, we argue, not mere tension release. The moving object of art is recognized as something that is greater than oneself and that one can surrender to.... That is to say: Aesthetic emotions result from the confrontation with objects that are recognized as challenging *and guiding* one's powers of assimilation, cognitive or emotional.

But this just constitutes the outlines of an account yet to be filled in. Let us now add some Kantian aesthetics to the Kantian theology already on the table.

6.3   Models and "Symbolic Hypotyposis": Reforming Kant's Musical Aesthetics

In a remarkable passage in the *Critique of the Power of Judgment* (1793/2000, 5: 328), Kant draws a parallel between music and what he calls the "affective tone" of speech. He first asserts that "every expression of language has, in context, a tone that is appropriate to its sense" and that "this tone more or less designates an affect of the speaker and conversely also produces one in the hearer." He then argues that since a musical expression is an expression of affective tone without sense or determinate thoughts (in contemporary terms, without conceptual content), it is able to communicate universally "by association" the "aesthetic ideas that are naturally combined with [those affects]." An aesthetic idea, Kant's readers will recall, is a counterpart or "pendant" to an idea of reason (ibid., 5: 314). An idea of reason, for example, the idea of the immortal soul or the idea of God, is a concept to which no sensible intuition is adequate, because its putative[23] object attains an unconditioned status that cannot be given within the scope of experience (since objects of experience are always conditioned by causes, by earlier and later times, by larger enclosing volumes of space, and by ever smaller spatially extended parts). Just as an idea of reason is a concept to which no sensible intuition is adequate, an aesthetic idea is a sensible intuition to which no concept is adequate, a product of the imagination that is too rich and elaborate in detail and too extensive in its subtle suggestions to be fully conceptualized. Aesthetic ideas, moreover, attempt by means of what Kant calls "indirect symbolic hypotyposis" or "indirect presentation," to make ideas of reason, which cannot be schematized or *directly* presented, sensible. Whereas a direct presentation or a "schema" for a concept is a product of imagination that includes a rule or procedure for the serial construction in time of the spatial configuration of a possible object of experience that will satisfy the concept in question, a symbol functions merely analogically or by reflection: properties of an object of experience are projected metaphorically onto another object that is not easily schematized because it is abstract or vague, or that cannot be schematized at all because it is not an object of possible experience. Thus a handmill, says Kant, may symbolize a despotic state (ibid., 5: 352), just as the streaming rays of the morning sun may, in a poetic context, symbolize the tranquillity that emanates from virtue (ibid., 5: 316). A despotic state is a political entity, albeit one that is quite abstract, and tranquillity is an emotional state, albeit one that is rather vague. Both are, nonetheless, experiential. Virtue, however, for Kant, is the object of a concept of reason and as such not an object of experience at all.

Kant's conception of the relation of indirect presentation between a handmill and a despotic state is, as a matter of fact, remarkably close to the paramorphic modeling relation we discussed in earlier chapters. "Presentation" is the standard English translation of Kant's "*Darstellung*," a rendering of the Latin "*exhibitio*." In Kant's usage, "*Darstellung*" contrasts with "*Vorstellung*" (Latin: *repraesentatio*), the term that entered the German philosophical vocabulary by way of Wolff as a translation of "idea" in seventeenth- and eighteenth-century anglophone philosophy. As a result, Kant's "*Vorstellung*" is narrower than the current term "representation" as it appears in the title of this book and as defined in the general introduction, since *Vorstellungen* are limited to *denotational* representations. Because of the conceptual link between exhibition and exemplification, "*Darstellung*" captures the *exemplificational* representational function that has been so central to our discussion.

Note also that Kant's term of art "*Symbol*" is orthogonal to my term "symbol," which I defined in chapter 3 as any conventional external representation, be it denotational or exemplificational, that is syntactically organized, or whose referent(s) may be separated in space and time from the occasion of its use, or both. Not only is a Kantian *Symbol* a *Darstellung* and not a *Vorstellung*, it is an *indirect Darstellung*, which is to say that it functions as a paramorphic, not isomorphic, model that involves a metaphorical transference of meaning between semantic fields or, in Goodman's more extensionalist terms, between objects belonging to different realms.[24] (Recall that isomorphism, or first-order similarity, requires metrical and topological mapping; paramorphism, or higher-order similarity, requires only topological mapping.) Finally, a Kantian *Symbol* may also involve the notion of a *working* model: "For between a despotic state and a handmill there is no similarity, but there is one between the rule for reflecting on both and their *causality*" (ibid., 5: 352, emphasis mine). How each of these objects *works* or *functions* is crucial for the rule of reflection involved. Also relevant to this "rule of reflection" on causality is the way in which *we operate* a handmill, what its mode of use is: as in the case of a despotic state, the user ("ruler") manipulates the mechanical device from the outside. With a constitutional monarchy ruled in accordance with laws "internal to the people," on the other hand, the appropriate symbol, says Kant, is not a handmill but a living body with a soul. The causal relation between body and soul is not one of external, manipulative causality.

Mark Johnson (1987) has drawn attention to Kant's further observations concerning the widespread presence in literal language of indirect presentation and to the connection between indirect symbolic hypotyposis and the Lakoff and Johnson metaphorical theory of meaning, the "body-in-the-mind" doctrine, which we discussed in earlier chapters. Symbolization is at work, says Kant, in our understanding of the concepts of *ground* (logical support), *dependence* (support from above), *flow* (entailment or causal production), *substance* (bearer of attributes), and, he claims, in "innumerable other" cases (ibid., 5: 352). According to the Lakoff and Johnson theory, we should recall, what Kant calls "indirect presentation" tends to invoke the lived bodily experience that is fundamental for metaphorical transference, which, in turn, is indispensable for the human understanding of abstract concepts like those cited by Kant. We should also recall the connection we established between metaphorical transference and the modeling relationship, and the function of musical mental models.

I propose that Kantian aesthetic ideas in general, intuitions to which no concept is adequate, and Kantian musical aesthetic ideas in particular are simply unusually elaborate and rich paramorphic mental models, that is, *nonconceptual analog representations*. Kantian intuitions, after all, are nonconceptual but spatiotemporally structured representations. Indeed, the Kantian distinction between intuitions and concepts and his insistence on their mutual irreducibility is perhaps the most significant source in early modern philosophy of the notions of nonconceptual representation and nonconceptual content. As we already have had occasion to observe (chapter 5), mental models are, in the interest of economy, normally schematic and minimal, containing only enough detail to facilitate efficient processing of the propositional content of linguistic expressions. In aesthetic contexts, and in richly metaphorical poetic contexts, the mental models evoked are exceptionally elaborate, as they are in musical contexts, which are nonconceptual but also elaborately structured because they are, as we observed in chapter 3, unusually rich in paradigmatic contrasts and affinities.[25] As a result, musical mental models are capable of "symbolizing," that is, representing by "indirect symbolic hypotyposis," the putative objects of metaphysical concepts or, in Kant's terminology, rational ideas.

Like rational ideas, aesthetic ideas "strive toward" a certain completeness, and the imagination that produces them "emulates the precedent of reason in attaining to a maximum" (ibid., 5: 314):

The poet ventures to make sensible rational ideas of invisible beings, the kingdom of the blessed, the kingdom of hell, eternity, creation, etc., as well as to make that of which there are examples in experience, e.g., death, envy, and all sorts of vices, as well as love, fame, etc., sensible beyond the limits of experience, with a completeness that goes beyond anything of which there is an example in nature.

An intuitive understanding (the divine mind) is the object of such a rational idea; and much (though not necessarily all) in the experience of modern Western art music that is especially engaging emotionally, I suggest, rests on the capacity of music to symbolize by indirect symbolic hypotyposis an intuitive understanding and its objects, along with the individual's identification with it, that is, the identification with Otto's "supreme in power" and its plan for the world it has created. Such musical symbolization, moreover, involves simulation, modeling by means of a working model, because musical experience includes the experience of virtual (off-line) bodily movement (chapter 2).

Eternity is one of the divine attributes, as well as the object of a rational idea that is, as we just saw, specifically mentioned by Kant. How *does* the poet go about making such an idea "sensible"? One naturally recalls Henry Vaughan's famous lines from "The World":

I saw Eternity the other night,
Like a great ring of pure and endless light,
All calm, as it was bright;
And round beneath it, Time in hours, days, years,
Driven by the spheres
Like a vast shadow moved; in which the world
And all her train were hurled.

Certain features of Vaughan's imagery, which, I think it is fair to say, displays a noticeable Neoplatonic hue, stand out: calm, pure, and endless light, contrasted with the complementary shadowing of the spatiotemporal world. In order to appreciate the significance of these lines, one must construct a set of vivid, elaborate, interrelated mental models.

Consider the poet's image of time moving like a vast shadow beneath a ring of light. To achieve a similar effect, the *tone poet* would have to enable the listener to simulate a scenario with the appropriate features; and this requires musical action plans that put the listener's body (off-line) into appropriate mimetic states. Because eternity is a temporal notion, the composer may have something of an advantage here, for one way such a effect can be achieved musically is by a radical slowing of rhythmic and harmonic motion, an effect that is enhanced by a change of key that moves in the "flat" direction along the circle of fifths, suggesting, for reasons I shall present in a moment, a move upward and away in space so as to produce a more comprehensive view, an exalted view, as one might say, *sub specie aeternitatis*.

Beethoven does all three in the sudden reduction of musical motion, both rhythmic and harmonic, coupled with an unexpected descent of a major third from brilliant *fortissimo* trumpet and horn calls on F, functioning as the B-flat major dominant (key signature of two flats), to a rich and darkly colored D-flat major chord (key signature of five flats),[26] all occurring in bar 133 of the *Adagio* of his Ninth Symphony (example 6.1). The rhetoric of these trumpet and horn calls is heraldic, as if to command attention for the imminent revelation of a mystery. Two bars later, the already dark harmonic texture darkens further when it moves briefly into E-flat minor (key signature of six flats). At this point, volume has decreased to a hushed *pianissimo*. Immediately thereafter, the home key of B-flat is restored and rhythmic and harmonic motion resume their previous pace. This short but striking passage can be heard as a musical attempt to arrest the passage of time, expand experiential scope, and render "sensible," by indirect symbolic hypotyposis, the rational idea of eternity.

Given the Gibsonian principles developed in chapter 2, however, we have available an entirely naturalistic explanation regarding how this remarkable musical effect might be achieved. With regard to ordinary spatial perception, apparent relative velocity between observer and object decreases with increased spatial separation: optical flow is such that an observer feels himself to be moving more slowly relative to objects further away (Gibson 1968). If this remains puzzling, think of the experience of take-off in a jet airplane. As the plane accelerates on the runway, we are aware of high velocity relative to nearby stationary objects. But as we become airborne, optical flow produces an illusion of abrupt reduction of motion (without significant inertial effects) coupled with a radical expansion of vista. At certain times of day and under certain meteorological conditions, the earth below will be cast into shadow. In the musical case we do not have optical flow, but we do have an analogue: a flow that is quasi-tactual. We also do not have in the musical case a diminution of light, but again, we have an intensively structured analogue, the rapid diminution of volume from *fortissimo* to *pianissimo*, an effect also exploited by Beethoven in this passage and enhanced by the abrupt change of key.

But why should this change of key, this movement from two to five flats along the circle of fifths, suggest shadowing? The flat keys, whether in major or minor mode, are generally heard as "darker" in coloration, whereas the sharp keys, albeit only in the major mode, are heard as "brighter." Although its key signature contains two sharps, B minor, the key of the first movement of Schubert's "Unfinished" Symphony, is generally considered a dark, indeed coldly dark, key, and contributes to the menacing quality of the symphony's cello and bass opening. It is also the key of Tchaikovsky's

Example 6.1

Beethoven, Symphony No. 9 in D Minor, *Adagio molto e cantabile, Lo stesso tempo.*

Pathetique Symphony, in particular of its truly morbid close.[27] D major, the relative major key of B minor, on the other hand, is considered a bright, "sunny" key. A major, the key of Beethoven's Seventh Symphony, Mozart's Symphony No. 29 and 23rd Piano Concerto, and Dvořák's *Carnival* Overture, is brilliant; but F-sharp minor, its relative minor, the key in which Tchaikovsky's *Romeo and Juliet* begins, is dark and foreboding. The slowly descending C-major scale that opens Beethoven's *Leonore* Overture No. 3 commences with Gs but ends on F sharps, presaging a brief modulation to B minor (example 6.2). Although extramusical meaning generally cannot, because it is nonconceptual, be this specific without title or verbal context, *given the operatic context of this music*, there can be little doubt that this scale is intended to represent, by indirect symbolic hypotyposis, descent into Florestan's cold, dark dungeon. (Leonore's first words in act 2, scene 1 of *Fidelio* are "Wie kalt ist es in diesem unterirdischen Gewölbe [How cold it is in this underground chamber]!") Beethoven used B minor very infrequently, and seems to have associated the key with feelings of abandonment and despair, emotions whose expression did not comport with his personal credo. Compare the B minor opening of the "Agnus Dei" (Lamb of God) in the *Missa Solemnis*. It must be acknowledged that not every great modern composer has so associated the key: the sprightly *Badinerie* from J. S. Bach's Second Orchestral Suite and Debussy's placid *Nuages* come to mind. These cases, however, are not prototypical.

Because of coloration, a radical change in key can, in the right context, produce an effect of depth and shadow. Taken together, these effects are capable of suggesting, by indirect symbolic hypotyposis, a sudden expansion of vista along with a radical slowing of time, thereby rendering the rational idea of eternity "sensible." Such musical indirect symbolic hypotyposis of the idea of eternity depends, if my argument has been convincing, on perception and the experience of bodily orientation and activity. But, as Lakoff and Johnson remind us, all metaphorical understanding, and not just musical indirect symbolic hypotyposis, depends ultimately on bodily experience. If this is right, poetic metaphor has, as suggested in chapters 3 and 5, more in common with musical metaphor than might at first appear. Recall, again with Vaughan's light imagery in mind, the radiantly bright coloration of the static, gently pulsating, thickly scored minor ninth chords over a pedal A in the bass that accompany the words "Über Sternen muss er wohnen [Beyond the stars must He abide]" in bars 647–654 of the *Finale* of the Ninth Symphony, a passage we noted in chapter 2.

There is a curious paragraph in Kant's third *Critique* that sheds considerable light on the symbolic relationship between musical organization and intuitive understanding. A discursive understanding (i.e., the human understanding), Kant holds (1793/2000, 5: 407), is one that that "must go from the **analytical universal** (of concepts) to the particular (of the given empirical intuition)." For such an understanding, as we saw, empirical content is contingent: concepts do not generate empirical intuitions, they only unify them once they are "given." But, Kant continues, "we can also conceive of

Example 6.2
Beethoven, *Leonore* Overture No. 3.

an understanding which, since it is not discursive like ours but is intuitive, goes from the **synthetically universal** (of the intuition of a whole as such) to the particular, i.e., from the whole to the parts, in which, therefore, and in whose representation of the whole, there is no **contingency** in the combination of the parts" (ibid.; all boldface in original). When attempting to clarify for his reader the nature of such a synthetically universal whole, Kant explains that although it has "some similarity" to the unity of space, it is also unlike space because space is "no real ground of generatings [or productions, *Erzeugungen*], but only their formal condition" (ibid., 5: 409). What are we to make of this? This much is clear. The synthetically universal is "holistic": it is like space to the extent that spaces, according to Kant's "Transcendental Aesthetic," are limitations of the whole in which they are contained and therefore are conditioned by the whole, as the parts of the synthetically universal are conditioned by the whole of which they are a part. But what about the puzzling reference to the "real ground of generatings"?

The distinction between mere spatial organization and "real grounds" no doubt harks back to theological debates in the mid-eighteenth century concerning the unity of the world, debates in which the pre-Critical Kant was a vigorous participant. However, Kant's characterization of the "synthetically universal" and his emphasis on the differences between the powers of a discursive and an intuitive (divine) understanding, along with the notion of holistic limitation, also recall Neoplatonic accounts of the generation of the diversity of the world from the unity of the One.[28] But in order to appreciate the full significance of Kant's paragraph, it must be placed in context. The immediate context is a discussion of the production of organisms, or "organized products of nature." Lacking as he does a theory of natural selection, Kant remains convinced that the human discursive understanding cannot explain how such intricately organized products could arise entirely on the basis of the efficient causality alone. Therefore we must, he thinks, invoke final causality, what he calls "teleology," as a heuristic principle of "reflecting," as opposed to "determining," judgment:[29] final causation is not an acceptable mode of scientific explanation. Kant is not merely recommending something like Dennett's reverse engineering, the adoption of a "design stance that is ultimately to be discharged by causal explanations at the physical level. Rather, he is claiming that we must regard organisms *as if* they were produced "intentionally," meaning produced according to a prior "idea of the whole," while we continue to pursue explanation by efficient physical causality, the only scientifically legitimate mode of explanation, as far as it will take us, even if it will never take us the entire way.

Kant explicitly denies, however, that the notion that such products could be produced by mechanism alone is *incoherent*: "it does not follow that the mechanical generation of such a body is impossible" (ibid., 5: 408). This remark may suggest that Kant wishes to allow for the possibility of something like undirected natural design after all. But he intends no such thing: by "mechanical generation," he means efficient causation, not the cloven hoof of ontological materialism;[30] and he goes on to assert that the impossibility of mechanical generation of organisms "would in fact follow if we were justified in regarding material beings as things in themselves. For then the unity that constitutes the ground of the possibly natural formations would merely be the unity of space," which is only the "formal condition" for causal production, the locus of all natural causal activity, but not itself causally efficacious. So the merely mechanical generation of *material organic beings that occupy space* indeed is, according to Kant, an impossibility.

What we have, then, is this. Kant seems to be suggesting a kind of production that achieves an overall unity that is *spacelike* but not spatial and that is intuitive and nonconceptual, that is, is *not* produced by final causation according to a prior concept. This is a mode of production *conceivable* but not *knowable* by the discursive understanding. There can be little doubt that Kant has here in mind a rational idea, the idea of an archetypal or original causality. But once again, although the object of such an idea is not an object of possible experience, the idea may be "made sensible" by indirect symbolic hypotyposis. And I suggest that musical aesthetic ideas are, given Kant's own principles, peculiarly effective vehicles for such symbolization, since music (or its mental representation in the listener) is, as we have seen, not spatial but suggests spatial organization; the "parts," the tones, the phrases, and the like of a musical piece, moreover, are holistically determined by their roles in overarching hierarchical structures; it is "productive" (*erzeugend*) because it is "generated" by the (off-line) implementation of action plans, as well as being generative in the Lerdahl and Jackendoff sense (derivative of Chomsky); and, finally, it is nonconceptually represented.

Glossed in this way, Kant's curious paragraph is certainly suggestive. But can we really find in Kant anything like a specifically *musical* indirect symbolic hypotyposis at all? To be sure, he does explicitly countenance musical aesthetic ideas (ibid., 5: 329–330). He claims, though, that they arise by "a mere mechanical association" with affective states evoked by the affective tone of the musical composition, presumably because *sentences* with the appropriate semantic contents express a similar affective tone. But if the connection is merely one of "mechanical" association between the affective tone of music and the affective tone of sentences, the sophisticated organization of the music itself would seem to have no cognitive significance for the listener at all and would play no role in determining which aesthetic ideas are evoked—a very implausible result. It is, moreover, most doubtful that the expression by music of aesthetic ideas can be achieved through mere association with the tone of sentences with the right semantic content.

This association story is not, however, Kant's only pronouncement on the topic. There is also the following (ibid., 5: 329, emphasis mine):

the form of the composition of these sensations (harmony and melody) serves only, instead of the form of a language, to express, by means of a proportionate disposition of them (which, since in the case of tones it rests on the relation of the number of vibrations of the air in the same time, insofar as the tones are combined at the same time or successively, can be mathematically subsumed under certain rules), *the aesthetic ideas of a coherent whole of an unutterable fullness of thought,* corresponding to a certain theme, which constitutes the dominant affect of the piece. On this mathematical form, although not represented by determinate concepts, alone depends the satisfaction that the mere reflection on such a multitude of sensations accompanying or following one another connects with this play of them as a condition of its beauty valid for everyone.

Here Kant seems to be thinking along the following lines (see Kivy 1991 and Butts 1993 for related discussions). Music is highly structured. This structure is mathematical because of the correlation between the mathematical proportions of vibrating bodies, the longitudinal compression waves produced by such bodies in the air, and the musical tones we hear sounding simultaneously (harmony) and successively (melody). The listener represents this musical structure nonconceptually, reflects on it, and thereby grasps an aesthetic idea, an intuitive product of the imagination. Such an idea is an intuition (i.e., an elaborate paramorphic mental model) of a mathematically complex and coherent whole that cannot be conceptualized. Thus the actual structure or organization of a piece of music, no less an object of sensible experience than a handmill, can indeed function symbolically, providing a bona fide Kantian alternative to the implausible "mere mechanical association" story.

Unfortunately, Kant's Pythagorean account of the represented structure of music is problematic, as he seems to recognize when he admits that mathematics "is only the indispensable condition [*condition sine qua non*] of that proportion of the impressions, in their combination as well as in their alternation, by means of which it is possible to grasp them together and to prevent them from destroying one another, so that they instead agree in a continuous movement and animation of the mind by means of consonant affects and hereby in a comfortable self-enjoyment" (ibid., 5: 329). The mathematics of music, that is, supplies only a necessary and not a sufficient condition for the sophisticated organization of the musical surface. There must, therefore, be another source of order to achieve sufficiency. The problem may be approached in this alternative way: in order for musical structure to supply for reflection a complex and coherent whole that "animates the mind," and thereby to suggest an "unutterable fullness of thought," that structure must be represented in the listener, even if nonconceptually. If the Lerdahl and Jackendoff theory, or some cognate theory of musical syntax, is correct, there is every reason to think that musical structure *is* nonconceptually represented in the listener who understands the music but is unacquainted with the principles of the theory itself. But this is a theory of rule-governed musical *syntactic* structure, of structure mandated by a set of well-formedness and preference rules, *not* a theory concerning the physical properties of sound.

To be sure, the mathematical relationships between tones are, as we saw in chapter 2, nonconceptually represented in the construction by the mind–brain of musical space and its "gravitational" dynamics. But that by itself is not by itself sufficient to support the production of musical aesthetic ideas, as Kant himself admits: "However, mathematics certainly has not the least share in the charm *and the movement of the mind that music produces*" (ibid., 5: 329, emphasis mine). He is therefore forced back to his affect arousal and mechanical association story to account for the evocation of aesthetic ideas in musical contexts. Kant certainly knew his physics, but seems to have had little knowledge of or appreciation for music. Since cognitive psychology and generative linguistics did not exist in his day, it may be that the mathematical physics of sound was the only candidate that occurred to him in his search for the formal relationships necessary, according to his general aesthetic position, to elevate music from a merely agreeable to a fine art. Such considerations may also account for his ambivalence concerning the status of music as an art. Most likely he would have been puzzled by any claim that music is syntactically organized. But we needn't be. For us, musical aesthetic ideas (elaborate musical mental models) do not result from mere "mechanical association" of the musical surface with the affective tone of sentences, but are constructed *from* the organized musical surface on the basis of hierarchically organized musical plans.

The failure of an exclusively Pythagorean approach to the representation of musical organization, incidentally, shows Schopenhauer's philosophy of music to have been much closer to the mark than Leibniz's Pythagorean theory, a result that is hardly surprising, given the fact that with the notable exception of Nietzsche (about whom more in the next section), Schopenhauer is the only major Western philosopher of the past whose principal writings demonstrate both serious engagement with and genuine understanding of music.[31] To Leibniz's claim that music is an unconscious exercise in arithmetic in which the mind is unaware it is counting, Schopenhauer replied (with deliberate parody) that music is an unconscious exercise in metaphysics in which the mind is unaware it is philosophizing (1844/1966, I, 256, 264). What Schopenhauer meant by this is that music "directly" represents what he took to be the metaphysical thing-in-itself, the Will, which is not spatial.[32] Music represents directly because its mode of representation is not, as in poetry and the plastic arts, mediated by spatially configured *visual* imagery, and therefore to this extent is not subject to the *principium individuationis*, the illusion of the "veil of Maya." Concerning the semiotic of this non-imagistic musical representation and how music might carry out its representational function, Schopenhauer has very little to say, and what he does say remains more Leibnizian than he might wish to admit, relying as it does on Pythagorean notions:

The connexion of the metaphysical significance of music with this its physical and arithmetic basis rests on the fact that what resists our *apprehension*, namely the irrational relation of dissonance, becomes the natural image of what resists our *will*; and, conversely, the consonance or the rational relation, by easily adapting itself to our *apprehension*, becomes the image of the satisfaction of the *will*. (Schopenhauer 1844/1966, II, 451)

We might, however, parody Schopenhauer's formulation, as he parodied Leibniz's, by saying that music is an unconscious exercise in metaphorical understanding in which the mind is unaware it is projecting lived bodily experience.

Still, Schopenhauer's position has much in common with the view I have advocated. First, like Schopenhauer, I hold that music is representational. But I also have a specific semiotic story to tell concerning how it represents: music represents nonmusical objects and situations by means of the modeling relation, that is, by way of the mental models constructed in the mind of the listener who reenacts the plan of the piece and moves through its virtual space in understanding it. Musical plans as action plans enable the listener to construct the virtual layouts, scenarios, and objects that constitute the contents of these models (chapter 2). Second, music's fundamental representational structure is nonconceptual, but also (as Schopenhauer claims) nonimagistic, because it is represented procedurally, in the form of plans or motor schemata, and because musical experience is more tactual than it is visual (chapters 2 and 3). Third, plans themselves may be interpreted as schemata for the exercise of what philosophers traditionally have termed "the will," as Miller, Galanter, and Pribram (1960, 11) explicitly suggest.[33] We need not, however, endorse Schopenhauer's extravagant and implausible metaphysics of the Will, nor need we agree that musical representation is invariably metaphysical in significance. Much less need we accept Steiner's rather grandiose claim that all of art must have metaphysical, indeed, theological significance.[34] Still, though the objects of musical modeling need not be metaphysical (or, in Kant's terminology, objects of rational ideas), they may be. And this, I think, is significant for an adequate understanding of the connection between musical and religious emotion. Music is particularly adept at generating models of the putative objects of such ideas by way of indirect symbolic hypotyposis.

6.4   Music, Mimesis, and Ritual: Naturalizing the Apollinian–Dionysian Distinction

However, it is noteworthy that for most cultures . . . the functions that music fulfills, the contexts in which it appears most efficacious, often lie in the realm of ritual and psychic healing. That is, music often functions in individual and group encounters with the numinous and in the modulation of affective state.
—I. Cross (2003, 53)

The contexts in which music is used and the function it appears to play in societies are also highly variable, with entertainment, the validation of social institutions, and the fostering of social bonds being particularly widespread. But the most prominent and perhaps the only *universal context* is that of religion: *music is used everywhere to communicate with, glorify and/or serve the divinities identified within any particular culture.*
—S. Mithen (2005, 13, emphasis mine)

Let us continue this necessarily selective survey of the historical expressions of the horror of the contingent by considering another set of footnotes to Plato deriving from that other major Western philosopher of the past whose writings demonstrate genuine understanding of and passionate concern for music. It is not clear, to me at least, that Nietzsche, any more than Schopenhauer before him, ever ceased to be affected by the horror of the contingent, despite his later, rather unvarnished criticisms of *The Birth of Tragedy*[35] and despite the emergence of a superficially more naturalistic style of thinking in his mature philosophy. Be this as it may, *The Birth of Tragedy*, which was written under the strong influence, if not the tutelage, of Schopenhauer, is permeated with it. Although Schopenhauer's metaphysical Will is in important respects fairly far removed from the Neoplatonic One, the contours of the monistic Neoplatonic metaphysics along with Plato's jaundiced view of the changeable world of sense experience are clearly discernible in Schopenhauer's philosophy.[36] Both these aspects of Schopenhauer's philosophy play paramount roles in Nietzsche's discussion. Indeed, the Apollinian–Dionysian distinction cannot be properly understood without taking account of Schopenhauer's distinction between representation and Will.

Just as Nietzsche's Apollinian is derivative of Schopenhauer's conception of the representational function of the imagistic, nonmusical arts, the Dionysian is derivative of the representational function of music, which forgoes visual imagery, thereby subverting spatial distinction and the "principle of individuation." All the arts, for Schopenhauer, represent the Will; but the imagistic arts do so "indirectly," by representing (Platonic) ideas[37] or unchanging essences of the four grades of "objectification" of the Will, that is, the Will as it manifests itself as spatiotemporal, causally linked individuals in the phenomenal world.[38] Schopenhauerian cadences resound in Nietzsche's very choice of words:

Apollo, however, again appears to us as the apotheosis of the *principium individuationis*, in which alone is consummated the perpetually attained goal of the primal unity, its redemption through mere appearance..., if we conceive of it at all as imperative and mandatory, this apotheosis of individuation knows but one law—the individual.... (Nietzsche 1886/1967, 45–46)

Under the charm of the Dionysian not only is the union between man and man reaffirmed, but nature which has become alienated, hostile, or subjugated, celebrates once more her reconciliation with her lost son, man.... Now, with the gospel of universal harmony, each one feels himself not only united, reconciled, and fused with his neighbor, but as one with him, as if the veil of *maya* had been torn aside and were now merely fluttering in tatters before the mysterious primordial unity. (Ibid., 37)

Equally evident is the extent to which the young disciple of Schopenhauer feels the horror of the contingent and imputes it to his adored ancient Greeks: "Oh, wretched and ephemeral race," he quotes Sophocles, "children of chance [*Zufall*; *Zufälligkeit*: contingency] and misery, why do you compel me to tell you what it would be most expedient for you not to hear? What is best of all is utterly beyond your reach: not to be born, not to *be*, to be *nothing*" (42). Somewhat less evident is the fact that he also seems to have anticipated something resembling Sartrean existential nausea:[39]

Here, when the danger to his will is greatest, art approaches as a saving sorceress, expert at healing. She alone knows how to turn these nauseous thoughts about the horror or absurdity of existence into notions with which one can live: these are the *sublime* as the artistic taming of the horrible, and the *comic* as the artistic discharge of the nausea of absurdity. (Ibid., 60)

Despite Nietzsche's rejection, already in *The Birth of Tragedy*, of Schopenhauer's life-denying philosophy in favor of a life-affirming one, this philosophy is not intended as an affirmation of the world of sense experience. Far from it, for tragedy provides a "metaphysical comfort": it leaves us with the conviction "that life is at the bottom of things, despite all the changes of appearances, indestructibly powerful and pleasurable" (ibid., 59). What "life" is this that is indestructibly powerful and pleasurable? Is it the undirected evolutionary phenomenon described a mere thirteen years earlier by one Darwin? Not on *your* life! It is "existence . . . justified as an aesthetic phenomenon" (ibid., 141), in which "the struggle, the pain, the destruction of phenomena, now appear *necessary* to us, in view of the excess of countless forms of existence which force and push one another into life, in view of the exuberant fertility of the universal will" (ibid., 104, emphasis mine).

Not only has the young Nietzsche, like so many before him, taken up the mantle of metaphysical necessity in the struggle against the horror of the contingent. He has also rung a change on one of the pervasive themes of the *philosophia perennis*, the Neoplatonic tradition stretching from Plotinus to Hegel and beyond, namely, the *principle of plenitude*, which holds that a more varied, more replete world, even a world that contains more apparent defect, is, provided it is coherent and unified, superior to a less replete one. The principle of plenitude, in turn, has been a long-standing staple of metaphysical theodicy, for it has provided a basis for arguing that evil in the world, both natural and moral, is a necessary ingredient in its plenitude: the world is just as it ought to be and is necessarily the way it is. Theodicy, that is to say, attempts a moral justification of the world by arguing that its defects contribute to, indeed are required by, the good of the whole. While Nietzsche's position is to this extent traditional, it is anything but orthodox. To say that the world is justified *only* as an aesthetic phenomenon (ibid., 52) is not just to suggest that the principle of plenitude is aesthetically motivated, nor is it merely to imply that the only successful "theodicies" are to be found in the imaginary worlds of works of art. It is to take the further, audacious metaphysical step of rendering the "universal will," the "primordial being," an eternal, aesthetically creative force: "it is precisely the tragic myth that has to convince us that even the ugly and disharmonic are part of an artistic game that the will in the eternal amplitude of its pleasure plays with itself" (ibid., pp. 104, 141). Moreover, "only music, placed beside the world, can give us an idea of what is meant by the justification of the world as an aesthetic phenomenon" (ibid., 141). And why is this? It is because "the joy aroused by the tragic myth has the same origin as the joyous sensation of dissonance in music. The Dionysian, with its primordial joy experienced even in pain, is the common source of music and tragic myth" (ibid.).

To say that the world is justified only as an *aesthetic* phenomenon is to reject any attempted *moral* justification of the world, or at least to reject any moral justification that does not subordinate moral values to aesthetic ones. It is also to doubt that the world in which we live is, morally speaking, the best of all possible worlds, a claim Schopenhauer had already countered with the characteristically acerbic retort that it is the *worst* of all possible worlds, since a world worse than ours would be so disorderly it would cease to qualify as a world at all (Schopenhauer 1844/1966, II, 583). But it is also to affirm something we have already recognized, namely that the successful work of art is so thoroughly intentionally determined that everything in its "world" is, in this special sense, "for the best," that is, serves the overall aesthetic aim, and that nothing in it is *de trop*. Nietzsche's metaphysics of the "universal will" in *The Birth of Tragedy*, like that of Schopenhauer before him, is the metaphysics of a nonbeliever. But it remains a metaphysics nonetheless, and one designed to assuage the horror of the contingent.

Let us, however, retreat from the rarefied heights of these descendants of Neoplatonic metaphysics and look to humbler origins. *The Birth of Tragedy* has a compelling historical story to tell, even if it is a historical "just-so" story. I shall now attempt a naturalistic reconstruction of an important aspect of Nietzsche's story, the Apollinian–Dionysian distinction, by considering the origins of that most ancient of palliatives of the horror of the contingent, namely religion. This exercise in reconstruction has intrinsic value, since the naturalization of any insightful piece of philosophical analysis is always to be welcomed in the interest of theoretical consilience with total science. But it has the further merit of providing additional support for the main thesis of this chapter concerning music and the horror of the contingent.

There can be little doubt that religious ritual, like music and prosody, originated in the mimetic culture we discussed earlier in chapter 3. Religious ritual's representational modes, even today, as Donald (1991) persuasively argues, are strongly rooted in the mimetic: the gestural and the nonverbal. In the present discussion, however, we shall be considering a considerably later phase of human development, the verbal but preliterate mythic culture that was the successor of mimetic culture, during which spoken language and music had come to be differentiated from rudimentary song.

No one knows with any certainty what the *ur*-arts,[40] the ancestors of what we in the modern Western tradition call the "fine arts," were. The archaeological record suggests that the first artifacts with demonstrably aesthetic attributes were the symmetrical hand-axes of *Homo heidelbergensis* dating from 1.4 million years ago, sometimes referred to as the "first aesthetic artefacts" (Mithen 2005, 188). Although such objects may have aesthetic properties, they are primarily functional. In my view, the most compelling hypothesis concerning the origin of the fine arts is that they derive from objects and performance-types that played ceremonial roles in the religious rituals of the Upper Paleolithic. The oldest known musical instrument, a bone flute, dates from about 36,000 years ago, a time roughly contemporaneous with the cave art of the Upper Paleolithic (Mithen 2005, 269). "Art and religion," as John Pfeiffer (1982, 100) says, "have been associated throughout history and they were probably associated from the very beginning."

This is an empirical hypothesis, and there are only two ways to evaluate it. The first is to examine the archaeological evidence; the second is to examine the ritual practices of extant human groups whose late-Paleolithic forms of life have remained relatively untouched by contemporary influence, and then to make some analogical inferences concerning prehistoric origins. In what follows, I take note of evidence of both sorts, although only at one remove, as filtered through reliable sources. My aim is not to establish the truth of the hypothesis. That would be a job for an anthropologist, not a philosopher. My strategy will be to accept it as plausible, based on theory and evidence derived from qualified authorities such as Pfeiffer (1982), Seeger (1987), Donald (1991), Guthrie (1993), Conkey (1999), Dissanayake (2000), Boyer (2001), Cross (2003), and Mithen (2005); then to use it to produce a naturalized version of the Apollinian–Dionysian distinction; and from there, to argue that the assuagement of the horror of the contingent came (by cultural exaptation) to be one direct proper function (though by no means the only one) of the musical representations belonging to the musical style under consideration in this book.

In chapter 4, I argued that representations, like the organisms comprised by species, form reproductively established families (REFs) whose members proliferate or fail to proliferate depending on their realization of proper functions, both direct and derived. Since, per hypothesis, the objects and performance-types of the *ur*-arts carried out symbolic functions in religious ceremonies, they count as representational. These symbolic objects and performances formed REFs whose members proliferated (i.e., were reproduced by their human makers) to the extent these objects and performance-types succeeded in carrying out their representational proper functions. But at some point such objects and performance-types took on different proper functions, that is, aesthetic as opposed to religious ones, and became subject to a different set of cultural selection pressures, just as at some point during biological evolution the direct proper function of the feathers of birds shifted from a thermal to an aerodynamic one. In chapter 3, I argued that musical performances are symbolic and that symbols are representations. I then argued in chapter 4 that musical works are reproductive families of performances subject to selection pressures. Assuming these arguments were in any degree convincing, we may conclude that musical performances have symbolic direct proper functions; and if, as seems plausible, the objects and performance-types of religious ritual did constitute the *ur*-arts, then inference to the best explanation (using the coevolutionary theory of the proliferation of cultural representations sketched in chapter 4) yields the conclusion that musical performances acquired these proper functions by way of a cultural exaptation. The task now is to fill in as many details of this exaptation as we can, relying on the best theory and evidence the anthropology and cognitive science of religion and ritual practice have to offer.

McCauley and Lawson's (2002) ritual form hypothesis is intended to explain (as dependent variables) both frequency of performance and comparative degree of sensory pageantry in religious rituals. The independent variable is the form of the ritual. According to the hypothesis, all religious rituals follow a standard tripartite format: an agent (1) carries out the ritual action on a patient (2) by means of some instrument or instruments (3). Their theory, which is empirically testable and supported,[41] divides all such religious rituals into two basic types. In rituals of the first type ("special agent rituals"), the god or the "culturally postulated superhuman agent" (CPS-agent)[42] is connected with the role of the agent in the ritual. Rituals of the second type ("special patient" and "special instrument rituals") are those in which the CPS-agent is connected with the roles of the patient or the instrument. Rituals also differ with regard to "depth," or number of links in the chain connecting the items filling the functional slots in the ritual schema and the CPS-agent itself. The greater the depth, the more distantly related the CPS-agent is to the ritual actions. Still, the basic typology remains constant: rituals in which the CPS-agent is associated with the agent role remain odd-numbered ones, whatever their depth or degree of separation; and those in which the CPS-agent is associated with the patient or instrumental role remain even-numbered ones, whatever their depth. The greater the depth, the higher the number, whether odd or even.

An example of the first type of ritual is a Catholic marriage ceremony: the priest performing the ceremony is invested with the authority of God, but he is several layers removed from God. The priest must have been ordained, and a chain of command, as it were, stands between the priest, the bishop, the pope, and God. Still, God is the ultimate actor in the marriage ceremony, the agent with whom "the buck stops"; and because the ritual represents a divine action ("Those whom God has joined, let no man put asunder"), the result is significant, and therefore difficult to reverse. The divine action, moreover, if actually consummated,[43] does not have to be repeated in the lives of two married individuals. As a result, such rituals occur infrequently in any given person's life. Because of this infrequency of occurrence, they tend, for mnemonic reasons, to be marked by rich use of multimodal sensory pageantry (rich relative to local mores, of course), and tend to be occasions of heightened emotion.

An example of the second type of ritual is the Catholic Eucharist. This occurs with great regularity, it involves little or no sensory pageantry, and it is not fraught with emotion.[44] In this case, the divine is implicated in the patient role in the ritual action: the wafer and the wine are, by means of transubstantiation, the body and blood of Christ, so the divine being is acted on by the congregant. Because these ritual types are "attractors" (in a possibility space) that show prototypicality effects, and not categories whose memberships are strictly determined by satisfaction of necessary and sufficient conditions, there are circumstances, say ones in which the CPS-agent is believed not to have acted, in which a special agent ritual may for a time be performed with relatively high frequency by a group of coreligionists, just as there are circumstances under which a special patient or a special instrument ritual may be infrequently performed. But these are, according to the theory, atypical.

The most important rituals in any system of religion are the special agent rituals with the smallest numbers, that is, those rituals which invoke superhuman agency, and so accord with "the principle of superhuman agency," or PSA, and which have the least amount of depth or the minimum number of layers of separation from the deity, and so accord with "the principle of superhuman immediacy," or PSI. Each type of ritual, the special agent ritual on the one hand and the special patient and instrument rituals on the other, tends to exploit one of two alternative strategies for enhancing memory in the preliterate mind: the strategy of producing so-called flashbulb memories, or the strategy of repetition. Flashbulb memories are those particularly vivid memories people have of significant events, for example, the ability of most American adults over fifty to remember exactly where they were and what they were doing when they received the news of John F. Kennedy's assassination. Citing Neisser's research on this topic, McCauley and Lawson argue that the centrally important mechanism at work in flashbulb memories involves an awareness of *participating* in an important event, as opposed to merely observing it, as if from the outside.

If the ritual origins of art hypothesis is true, which role, which slot in the McCauley and Lawson ritual action schema, would the various objects and performance-types of *ur*-art have been associated with? Not all varieties of art tend to arouse powerful emotions. Those arts whose objects or performances do arouse powerful emotions seem to fall among the fine, as opposed to the merely decorative or "agreeable," arts: music, painting, sculpture, poetry/literature/drama, and dance. I intend here a distinction of kind, not a criterion of quality. Chadwick and Beethoven, Kinkade and Rembrandt, Kilmer and Shakespeare all count, in the context of the present discussion, as producers of fine art. And the objects and performance-types of the fine arts, I propose, derive from *objects associated with special agent rituals*, or those rituals in which the CPS-agent was associated with the agent role, and not the instrument or patient roles, for the simple reason that *these are the rituals that tend to make heavy use of sensory pageantry and to be emotionally fraught*. They are the ones in which the god is present among participants *in act*, the ones in which participants as patients and spectators feel most strongly the presence of the numinous, the *tremendum*, the *augustum*.

The emotions of fear and awe evoked in the felt presence of CPS-agents may well be, as Boyer (2001, 145–148) proposes, products of a dedicated predator-detection system in the human brain. If so, they would be yet another example of cultural exaptation and the substitution of a cultural domain, namely religion, for the proper domain of a mental module. Perhaps God is, in part, powerful predator turned ally. But I would add that human predator detection has a long, prehuman phylogenetic history that has left in us vestigial remnants of very ancient bodily responses, for example, the piloerection and the "creeping of the flesh" that occur when we sense that we are observed by unseen agents. Understandably, bodily responses of this kind also occur in the felt presence of the *tremendum* and the *augustum*. Notice that these are responses of the mechanoreceptive somatosensory system and that they can also be triggered by musical experience. Weber claimed that certain eerie passages in the introduction of his *Der Freischütz* Overture made his flesh creep. The *pianissimo* opening of the *Scherzo* of Beethoven's Fifth Symphony produced in Berlioz the unsettling sensation of an unseen observer's gaze directed at his back.

Guthrie (1993, 52) hypothesizes that religious awe might have arisen from a tendency in humans and animals to animate violent natural events, pointing out that chimpanzees are known to exhibit threat behaviors in the presence of thunderstorms. Given the vivid effect of such events on all five sense modalities,[45] this suggestion is a particularly plausible one in the light of McCauley and Lawson's emphasis on sensory pageantry in special agent rituals. Because of the tactual immediacy and the sense of bodily immersion involved in the experience of violent meteorological events, moreover, it is relevant to my account of musical experience. "The moving atmosphere," says Katz (1989, 52n1), "strikes us subjectively as an immersed touch. This may well have prompted primitive people to make animistic interpretations of inanimate natural processes." Both powerful predators and animated violent meteorological events, we should note, engender feelings of absolute helplessness, which can easily become feelings of absolute dependence if propitiation of the fearsome agent is believed to have been achieved. Like Boyer, Guthrie postulates innate neural mechanisms, in this case mechanisms that support the inveterate tendency on the part of humans to anthropomorphize environmental features of all sorts, a tendency Guthrie documents by an extensive examination of perceptual phenomena and examples from literary and visual art, both fine and commercial. He explains the presence of these innate mechanisms by means of a standard evolutionary cost–benefit analysis: when it comes to detection of intentional agents, both human and nonhuman, the costs of false negatives tend to be great while the costs of false positives tend to be small. The logic of this evolutionary strategy, as Guthrie (1993, 4–6, 45) tellingly points out, is the same as that of Pascal's wager.

Let us, then, tentatively conclude that the modern Western fine arts are likely to have derived ultimately from special agent rituals. There is, however, a further distinction to be noted *within* special agent rituals. In such a ritual, some object or performance might stand in for the CPS-agent itself, the divine being; or it might stand in for the *patient* or the *instrument* of the CPS-agent. But how *does* something stand in for, or play the role of, the CPS-agent *in act*? Certainly, objects, both animate and inanimate, have traditionally been used to stand in for the god. But these stand-ins will be effective in a special agent ritual only if they are animated *by* the god and then incorporated within an orchestrated, coordinated group *event* so that the divine act itself can be mimetically represented and witnessed as it is occurring. The context for successful symbolization of divine agency in a ritual, that is, will be an event or set of events that involve mimetic enactment or role-playing, indeed an *organized, collective role-playing event*:

> When mimesis takes the form of a collective, or group, action, one common outcome is ritual. Ritual, and its derivatives in theatre, differs from most other forms of mimetic representation in that it is a collective act in which individuals play different roles.... The essence of the mimetic act in this case is not the action of a single individual but in the orchestration of several actors. Such representations are coordinated social efforts, dependent upon the actors', and the audience's, sharing a global cognitive model of the society. This is generally true of ritual. Even in modern society...the roots of public ritual are mimetic. (Donald 1991, 175–176)

Such collective "theatrical" role-playing also exploits another source of emotional arousal in the special agent rituals identified by McCauley and Lawson, namely strong feelings of group participation in the divine action invoked in the ritual, the factor that seems to play the central role in flashbulb memories. In these group mimetic events, however, the actors are still individuated by definite roles: it is difficult for everyone to enact or reenact the action of the CPS-agent at once. But when the mimetic representation is musical, or when it contains musical elements, this final barrier is breached and all the participants are unified in one orchestrated action plan, an action plan, moreover, whereby immediacy, that is, *simulational identification* with the CPS-agent (whose action plan this ultimately is), has been achieved, thus realizing, or coming as close as possible to realizing, the PSI simultaneously for all the participants.

Music is not just pageantry; it is socially coordinating pageantry:

> song bonds a congregation and moves emotion in a way that is hard for the verbal side of us to duplicate.... The bonding and emotive power of rudimentary song thus has an archaic, and profound, hold on human nature. The universality and robustness of the link between music and mass emotion speak to its deep roots in the past...the link between music and social ritual, and the evocative tie of song to emotion, are archaic vestiges and still in force. (Donald 1991, 40)

Paleolithic peoples are thought to have used song, rhythm, and declamation, along with dramatic illumination of the painted and sculpted images strategically located deep in caves like Lascaux,[46] to barrage the senses so as to produce a trancelike state of heightened awareness, a condition Pfeiffer (1982, 213) characterizes as the "twilight state," a mental state in which "you are ready to believe beyond belief, so totally and enthusiastically that the message comes through with a halo, with the force of religious revelation." The "twilight state" is just the mystical by another name. Pfeiffer offers the plausible, if speculative, evolutionary hypothesis that this process served a social bonding function that was adaptive for the hunter-gatherers of the Upper Paleolithic Magdalenian era, both for social cohesion and for the effective transmission of value commitments and a sense of cosmological orientation from the old to the young in the absence of literacy.[47] He is quick to point out that twilight-state thinking easily verges on the delusional. "But," he continues, "it is also the driving force behind efforts to see things whole, to achieve a variety of syntheses from unified field theories in physics to blueprints for utopias in which people will live together in peace" (ibid.). To these modes of synthesis we certainly may add those of metaphysical system building, most especially *monistic* metaphysical system building, and efforts to justify the world morally by way of theodicy, our topics earlier on.

We need not, however, content ourselves solely with rather spotty evidence concerning events in the distant past. There are contemporary groups of people living in remote areas who, with few exceptions (such as a handful of minor technological aids imported from surrounding modern civilization), still follow (or until very recent times followed) an Upper Paleolithic hunter-gatherer lifestyle, augmented by some minimal crop cultivation. The Suya of the Mato Grosso, a Native American tribe living in a remote Brazilian wilderness area, are one of these groups, a group whose musical practice has been the subject of close anthropological study in the ethnographical or interpretive style. Anthony Seeger, who lived with these people for extended periods of time and was accepted as a participant in their social life, describes in some detail (Seeger 1987) the "Mouse Ceremony," a rite-of-passage ritual of the special-agent type with the highest possible rating (or the lowest displacement number) on the PSI scale. During the course of the ceremony, men impersonate a CPS-agent, in this case a mythical mouse.

Suya legend has it that this CPS-agent taught one of their number the virtues of eating and cultivating corn, who passed the knowledge on to the rest of the village. Before they learned about the virtues of garden crops, the story goes, the Suya subsisted on rotten wood. The ceremony, which moves through an elaborate sequence of stages, lasts for a period of about two weeks, and includes feasting, dancing, and singing. The active participants, all men, paint their bodies and don capes crafted from burity palm buds. The capes are artfully painted with red, black, and white to indicate membership in various social subgroups or "moieties," and are the central ritual objects. Those who wear the capes actually become the mythical mouse, or at least share their essence with the mouse. But the musical component is just as important. With the approval of the mother of the initiate, a male relative begins the ceremony with a song. As others join in, they initiate a sequence of sets of choreographed movements which culminate in a simulated killing of the mouse (women drive arrows by hand through the participants' headgear) and a ritual bath in which the bodies of the men are cleansed of paint. At this point, the relative who began the ceremony declares it ended. Along the way, specially prepared foods are consumed by all, although who eats what when is carefully prescribed. The ceremony, it is clear, displays a high degree of sensory pageantry appealing to various modalities.

The music consists of two varieties of song, "shout songs" and "unison songs." Whereas the unison songs are, as the name suggests, highly coordinated, performances of shout songs are individual efforts that emerge polyphonically against the aural backdrop of the ongoing activity. Both types of song play a significant role in creating a singular atmosphere of euphoria that pervades the entire ceremony. The Suya are apparently a highly musical people with strong opinions regarding good and bad performance of their music. Music is not, however, mere entertainment for them, but serves to set ceremonial periods apart from nonceremonial ones; and Suya life is either in a ritual mode or in a nonritual mode. When music is heard among the Suya, Seeger (1987, 7) tells us,

something important is happening. Usually some connection is being created or recreated between different domains of life, the universe, or the human body and spirits. Music transcends time, space, and existential levels of reality. It affects humans, spirits, animals, and those hard-to-imagine beings in between . . . singing is associated with ceremonies taught men by spirit ancestors when they walked the earth, and music makes possible a return to and a renewal from the sacred past. . . . For the Ge-speaking societies that occupied a large expanse of the Brazilian interior, music communicates among human beings and creates a feeling of euphoria.

Most suggestive for our purposes, however, is this interpretative gloss (ibid., 46–47):

On the final night of the Mouse Ceremony the singers would undergo a metamorphosis in which they became a kind of being that was both human and mouse. . . . In song, the ambiguity is in the subject: is it a man or a mouse singing? Is it a man singing about an animal, or is it an animal singing through the mouth of a man? There is no simple answer.

Seeger asked several participants whether the singers were transformed into mice in the Mouse Ceremony, and was told that they were: "They are all mice (and also men) during the night" (ibid., 116). They are all, that is, identified with the CPS-agent.

It is in the context of such practices thought to have originated in the Upper Paleolithic that we are likely to find the actual historical basis for a Nietzschean Apollinian–Dionysian distinction, a basis that obviously long antedates the birth of ancient Greek tragedy in the sixth century B.C.E. The objects and performance-types of the fine arts, I have already argued, are likely to have derived from rituals of the special agent type because of their emotional load. The distinction (already noted) within the special agent rituals between superhuman animation of objects and participation by coreligionists in superhuman acts motivates the following naturalistic reconstruction of Nietzsche's distinction. The variety of art *objects* deriving from *ur*-artistic stand-ins for the CPS-agents, or for the patients or the instruments of divine actions in these special agent rituals, are objects of the Apollinian arts, the objects *animated by*, *acted on*, or *employed by* the god in the special agent ritual.[48] Consider once again Seeger's account of the Mouse Ceremony: "Before they are cut and painted by the formal friends,[49] the Mouse Ceremony capes are simply artifacts. Once they are painted they are in a sense activated, and the final phase of the ceremony has begun" (ibid., 107).[50] On the other hand, the art *performance-types* deriving from *ur*-artistic, coordinated group activities which allowed participants to *participate in* and (subsequently) to *reenact* (in order to commemorate and renew commitment to) the divine action by simulational identification, thereby achieving Pfeiffer's "twilight state," belong to the Dionysian arts, the *mimetic representation* of the CPS-agent *in act* among the participants.[51] Compare, once again, Seeger: "Every performance also reestablishes certain relationships between human beings and animals, between the village and its surroundings, and between the Suya and the cosmos they have created and within which they live" (ibid., 2). The paramount, though not necessarily the only, Dionysian art would, then, indeed be music, for it allows simultaneous group participation in and reenactment of divine agency and dispensation.

About Greek tragedy and its origins, I shall have nothing to say here. Greek tragedy may or may not have been born from the spirit of music;[52] but the "spirit" from which *Western musical performance art* seems to have been born is the more ancient spirit of human religion, including *the ritualistic, coordinated, collective, mimetic participation by human groups in superhuman interventions*.[53] At some point, these ritual practices were co-opted by musical performance practices that proliferated by producing cognate emotional effects. An important direct proper function of musical representations remains, even in today's Western societies, group unification and the evocation in performers and listeners of the emotionally charged twilight state. Both afford a temporary assuagement of the horror of the contingent, the original religious and didactic significance of such group experiences now having atrophied and fallen away.[54] Is this merely another just-so story, a plausible, but speculative, historical account? If compared with testable historical hypotheses in evolutionary biology, the answer must be yes. But not all just-so stories are equal. This one is consistent with a body of empirical anthropological and psychological evidence; it is not obviously false; and it helps explain the uncanny emotional power of paradigmatic examples of Western art music 1650 to the present.

A potential difficulty for the account is the fact that the EEG patterns generated by the brain states that realize the mystical "twilight state" differ markedly from the patterns associated with high sensory pageantry and emotional arousal. Mystical religious experience and most especially the intuition of immediate divine presence are associated with the abnormally synchronized alpha patterns characteristic of epileptic seizure, as presumably was the case with the ecstatic visions of Paul of Tarsus (see Sargant 1973, 63; Livingston 2005). But this problem is only apparent. Although trance states are commonly produced by meditative practices like yoga, they can also result from "parasympathetic dominance" brought on by intense arousal of the sympathetic branch of the autonomic system caused by sensory overload.

"In normal states of balance within the autonomic nervous system," cognitive anthropologist Michael Winkelman (1986, 177) informs us, "increased activity in one division is balanced by a response in the other." This claim of complementarity of function between the sympathetic and parasympathetic divisions of the autonomic system is consistent with the current neuroscientific thinking. According to Kandel et al. (1991, 760), "the sympathetic division of the autonomic system governs the fight and flight reaction, whereas the parasympathetic division is responsible for rest and digest." "However," Winkelman (1986, 177) continues,

Under intense stimulation of the sympathetic system, reciprocity breaks down and a collapse of the system into a state of parasympathetic dominance occurs. Sargant (1974 [1973]) noted this pattern of parasympathetic rebound or collapse can lead to erasure of previously conditioned responses, changes of beliefs, loss of memory, and increased suggestibility.

Sargant, a psychiatrist who treated war casualties and carried out extensive ethnological fieldwork, clearly differentiates the two methods of production of parasympathetic dominance:

So far, we have seen how the brain and nervous system of man can be furiously excited, by music, dancing, hell-fire preaching and the stirring up of great fear or anger. And it has been emphasized that this can induce various abnormal states of brain activity. There is another quite different method of achieving *the same results, by using an exactly opposite technique.* Here most of the nervous system is progressively relaxed, instead of being continuously excited. And as the mind becomes more and more quiescent, a state of generalized inhibition also finally results. Only a small part of the higher nervous system remains active and excited. (Sargant 1973, 73, emphasis mine)

Prolonged sensory stimulation, Sargant observes (ibid., 117), can cause overbreathing, leading to a high level of blood alkalosis associated with suggestible behavior and trance. He describes (ibid., 143) an exorcism he witnessed in Ethiopia, a high-pageantry special-agent ritual because the participants were partially naked and the healing in question was supposed to be God's doing:

Men and women alike were stripped to the waist and water was sprayed on to their faces and bodies. When they opened their mouths to breathe, they were forced to gulp down water, which gave them a feeling of suffocation and drowning, and their breathing was necessarily rapid and shallow.... Through rapid shallow breathing, the patient went into a state of trance and "possession" while being sprayed. The spirit possessing him would begin to speak and there was again a verbal battle between the priest and the spirit.... After a tremendous battle between priest and spirits, and the continued spraying of water on the patient's face and body, the patients finally dropped to the floor in a state of temporary inertia and collapse. It was expected that they would come round healed.

Parasympathetic dominance may also occur during the "strong musical experiences" discussed above. I have noticed in my own experience a marked tendency to engage in rapid, shallow breathing at times of extreme emotional involvement with musical works of a certain character, especially during live performances, and to slip into a trancelike state. An interesting experiment would be to ascertain to what extent this is common among subjects, and if it is, whether respiratory alkalosis is induced. To my knowledge, no one has carried out any such investigation.

6.5   Summary and Conclusion (On a Kantian Note)

Music is the sole incorporeal way of entry into a higher world of knowledge.
—Beethoven[55]

We began by glossing Sartrean nausea as an important "footnote to Plato," a commentary on the Platonic horror of the contingent. We then took notice of the fact that Sartre exempts both music and the objects of pure geometry from the nauseating press of contingent existence. We traced this exemption to two sources: (1) musical works and geometrical objects are "ideal" and "don't exist"; and (2) both music and mathematics eliminate contingency by means of an "internal" necessity. We also found in Sartre some hints concerning the possible connection between aesthetic and religious emotion. Intriguing as Sartre's observations are, they remain largely undeveloped in his writings. I suggested that the apparatus of earlier chapters might be useful in developing these themes, but that the notion of the horror of the contingent was a psychological phenomenon with a definite history requiring further elaboration if we were to bring that apparatus to bear.

To accomplish this, we turned to two other sets of footnotes. First we looked at some footnotes of Kant, who seems to have had some definite (proto)Sartrean sympathies. There we found the issues of disgust, contingency, necessity, theology, and musical art explicitly joined. By combining results derived from an examination of these Kantian footnotes with results reached in earlier chapters of this book, I offered an explanation of certain *central cases* of musical emotion as arising through assuagement of the horror of the contingent. This explanation drew parallels between musical experience and religious mystical experience. These parallels depended on certain distinctive aspects of musical experience, including its reliance on nonconceptual representations or mental models; its modification of S/Objectivity; its quality of immediacy or touch; and its thoroughgoing intentional determination and necessity.

We then took up a set of Nietzschean footnotes. We saw that like Sartre and Kant, the young Nietzsche remained, by way of Schopenhauer, firmly entrenched in the Neoplatonic tradition and, like them, strongly affected by the horror of the contingent. I then proposed a naturalistic reconstruction of the Apollinian–Dionysian distinction, deepening the account of the connection between musical and religious emotion by hypothesizing common origins of music and religious ritual in the preliterate culture of the Upper Paleolithic. Although affinities between musical and religious mystical experience have been noted by numerous other writers, few, I think, have succeeded in getting beyond the generalities and specifying the details of these remarkable affinities,[56] much less in accounting for them naturalistically, as I have attempted to do.

To many a sober-minded admirer of the Critical Philosophy, Kant's fascination with the mysticism of Emanuel Swedenborg, whom he genially lampooned in that curious early tract entitled *Dreams of a Spirit Seer Illustrated by Dreams of Metaphysics* (1766), might constitute something of an embarrassment. But this fascination really is fully in keeping with Kant's horror of the contingent and with his complex attitude toward metaphysics, "with which," he says in that early work, "it is my fate to be in love, although only rarely can I boast of any favours from her" (1766/1900, 112).[57] In a letter to Moses Mendelssohn dated that same year, Kant goes so far as to disclose something he never would have admitted in print,[58] namely that "I cannot help but be charmed by stories of this kind; but as regards the rational basis of such reports, I cannot rid myself of one or two suspicions of their correctness—leaving aside the absurdities, fancies, and unintelligible notions that undermine their value" (quoted in Zweig 1967, 55). The "stories" to which Kant refers concern the out-of-body mystical experiences reported by Swedenborg involving communication with an unseen spirit world, including souls of the dead. Particularly appealing to Kant, it seems, was Swedenborg's idealist vision of an immaterial world standing behind, as it were, the material world, a spirit world, as Kant says (1766/1900, 56–57),

regarded as a whole existing by itself, and its parts as being in mutual conjunction and intercourse without the instrumentality of anything corporeal. The relation by means of things corporeal is consequently to be regarded as accidental; it can belong only to a few; yea, where we meet with it, it does not hinder even those very immaterial beings, while acting on each other through matter, from standing also in their special universal relationship, so that at any time they may exercise upon one another mutual influences by virtue of the laws of their immaterial existence. Their relation by means of matter is thus accidental, and is due to a special divine institution, while their direct relation is natural and insoluble.[59]

This mystical vision, which, like Medieval alchemical theory, bears the stamp of magical animism, never entirely lost its hold over Kant, even after his critical turn, making its presence felt in later works, particularly in his discussions of moral philosophy.[60] Examples are the doctrine of the "Kingdom of Ends" of the *Grundlegung* and the related third *Critique* vision of "an intelligible world, in which everything would be actual merely because it is (as something good) possible" (1793/2000, 5: 404). In this intelligible world, everything that *ought to be* actualized, *is* actualized: every will is a "holy" will, and no right action is frustrated by akrasia or by brute circumstance. But, as a moment's reflection will show, a world in which every possible (or *compossible*) good is actualized is a world without moral contingency, since the contingent is precisely the possible that may (or may not) be actualized. Moreover, if no events in this world are morally irrelevant, such a world is also, like the world for an intuitive understanding (see my note 10 above), a world without contingency at all.

Toward the end of the *Dreams of a Spirit Seer*, Kant concludes, with characteristic resignation, that "human reason was not given strong enough wings to part clouds so high above us, clouds which withhold from our eyes the secrets of the other world" (121). What the imagination cannot *schematize*, however, it can *symbolize* by indirect symbolic hypotyposis. The autonomy (or heautonomy) of the reflecting aesthetic judgment whereby objects, both natural and artifactual, are judged beautiful is, along with the autonomy of the moral will, one of the consolation prizes offered human reason by the Critical Philosophy. This similarity between the two modes of autonomy, indeed, serves as the primary basis for the analogy whereby beauty, as Kant claims, may be a "symbol of morality" (1793/2000, 5: 353).[61] But beautiful art, if not beautiful nature, is not possible without the imaginative powers of genius, which is the capacity to produce effective aesthetic ideas. "The imagination (as a productive cognitive faculty)," Kant observes, "is, namely, very powerful in creating, as it were, another nature, out of the material which the real one gives it ... material can certainly be lent to us by nature, but the latter can be transformed by us into something entirely different, namely into that which steps beyond nature" (ibid., 5: 314). The imagination, that is to say, can, by means of aesthetic ideas (or, in our more cognitivist terms, exceptionally rich and detailed mental models), make "rational ideas," including the idea of "the other world," sensible by indirect presentation.

Because of the limitations of his musical aesthetics, Kant was not in a position to appreciate the fact that the *musical* imagination is especially powerful in this regard, first, as it were, among equals. For the fundamental "material" of Western tonal art music since 1650, well-tempered diatonic and chromatic scales and metrically segmented rhythms, is not "lent to us by nature." These things are not taken from nature, but are themselves products of human invention. Therefore, they, too, belong to "another nature." Because of the detachment of "acousmatic" experience (see chapter 2) from the locations in physical space of the sources of musical sound, this "material," when worked up into the astounding products of the musical imagination, induces the nearly irresistible illusion that it, this musical *material itself*, is somehow *immaterial*, as if it really somehow did derive from another world, a "spirit world"; and the musical work's virtual world, a world with which each and every performer and listener is at once in complete and intimate touch (see chapter 5), may seem "a whole existing by itself" and its parts "in mutual conjunction and intercourse without the instrumentality of anything corporeal." Moreover, in this musical virtual world, if we recall the discussions of animism and simulation in earlier chapters, everything can seem to be taking place in an "imaginary space [in which] there exists a universal community of spiritual natures" (Kant 1766/1900, 106). Scruton (1997, 76) maintains that

the causality that we hear in the musical foreground is therefore the "causality of reason" which, for Kant, was the ground of human freedom. It is the more easy to hear this "causality of reason" in music, in that the world of physical causes—the "causality of nature"—has been set aside, discounted, hidden behind the acousmatic veil. In music we are given an unparalleled glimpse of the reality of freedom; and because, as Kant reminds us, reason deals in necessities, we hear the free order of music as a necessary order: it is when each note *requires* its successor, that we hear freedom in music.

This is all unexceptionable, provided that (1) we remind ourselves that we are dealing with a skillfully produced illusion, and (2) we remain quite clear that because musical representation is nonconceptual, it cannot, like language, *express* logical relations. It can only *model* them, much as Narayanan's X-schemas were able to model (nonconceptually) the semantics of verbal aspect and fragments of logical inference (see chapter 3). As a result, the "necessity" Scruton descries in music is not logical, but *teleo-*logical:[62] the musical masterwork, it strikes us, *must* unfold exactly as it does, each note "requiring" its successor. Yet this necessity is nonconceptually grasped, because it is grasped by way of procedural, not declarative, representations: the planlike structure of the musical work, that is, its generative syntax considered as a hierarchically organized action plan (see chapters 2 and 3). What Sartre called the "inner necessity" of music derives, as we saw, from thoroughgoing intentional determination down to the finest details, the nuance properties of the successful performance.

The illusion of immateriality that music perpetrates, its seeming ability to "set aside the causality of nature," has, however, an additional source. I argued in chapter 4 that musical works are types and their performances tokens. But so are the themes and motifs contained in musical works; indeed, so are the materials of music themselves, the tonal scales, chords, and metrically segmented rhythms, although, as we saw, at this point structural considerations begin to trump historical ones in determining identity conditions. When we recognize a theme as "the same again," say, in the recapitulation of a sonata-form movement, what we are reidentifying is a type, not a token. The performance token itself is evanescent: *it* cannot be reidentified, for once it has ceased to sound it is gone forever. Yet the types that we hear in the musical surface present themselves *as if* they were reidentifiable *individuals*. We naturally use definite descriptions, as well as indexicals, when referring to them, as we say (or think to ourselves) "the principal theme has returned" or "there's that motif again" or "that's the *Tristan* chord." Types, as we observed in chapter 4, seem to straddle the ontological divide between particulars and universals; but to the extent a type is regarded as anything ontologically more weighty than a reproductively established family of tokens-of-a-type, it is some manner of abstract object. I do not want to claim that a musical type should, in terms of fundamental ontology, be regarded as anything more weighty than a REF of tokens-of-a-type. But however attractive so parsimonious an ontology may be in other respects, it does not capture the phenomenology of musical experience: during musical experience, we perceive musical types as if they were persisting individuals and their tokens as their successive appearances.

Abstract objects, however, do not themselves produce and suffer causal effects; only their tokens or their instances do. It is tokens, physical sound events, that affect us causally in musical experience; and we are aware of these as the particulars they are as they are occurring, even if, as events, they are not *basic* particulars in Strawson's sense. But the intentional objects especially significant for musical understanding, objects like recurring themes and motifs, the musical types that behave like reidentifiable individuals, not only are not *basic* particulars: they are not particulars at all. They have no spatial locations and we do not have the causal commerce with *them*, as opposed to their tokens, that would allow successful singular reference without presupposing the physical context of sound production (see chapters 2 and 5). But acousmatic experience, recall, abstracts from the locations of the sources of sound in physical space: they are hidden behind the "acousmatic veil." As a result, these musical types, these apparent "individuals," can *seem* to float free of physical causality, our commerce with them *seemingly* unmediated by physical causality. They, and the mental models (whose contents are layouts and scenarios in musical space) that we construct on their basis, come to us *as if* they were directly apprehended objects of a Kantian intuitive understanding, *thereby symbolizing such objects and such an understanding by indirect presentation.*

The deep irony is that the illusions[63] of immateriality and otherworldly significance, those aspects of the musical experience which, along with the inner necessity of music's thoroughgoing intentional determination, are most effective in assuaging the horror of the contingent, depend on the structure and the phylogenetic history of the human auditory apparatus and, crucially, on the phylogenetic origin of the brain as the organ of motor control (see chapters 2, 3, and 5). All of it is the result of an elaborate "body-in-the-mind" metaphorical transference, the structuring of the more abstract by the less abstract, of that which is more remote from lived bodily experience by that which is most intimately bound up with it, namely the sense of spatial orientation and intentional movement that is fundamental to the musical experience. "Being most metaphysical in its intonations, reaching deepest into the lit night of the psyche," says Steiner (1989, 80), "music is also the most carnal, the most somatically traceable of signifying acts." On the principles I have put forward here and in earlier chapters, we can well see why this should be so. If, *pace* Nietzsche, we must grant that musical dissonance really cannot rival the harrowing events of a *King Lear* in their ability to "tame the horrible" by (virtually) instantiating it, we may also rank the stark rhetoric of a *Tragic* Overture nonpareil in its ability to transfigure the horrible by (virtually) dematerializing it.

General Summary and Conclusion: Solving the Riddle

What is spatial and yet nonspatial, in motion and yet not in motion, meaningful and yet meaningless, sophisticated and yet primitive, universal and yet particular, voluptuous and yet austere, material and yet immaterial, religious and yet not religious?

Solving a riddle requires not just a correct answer, but an answer that "bestows a sense on the riddle question" (Putnam 1995, 274).[1] The solutions to some riddles, as a result, require not only an answer, but an elucidation. Without such elucidation, a correct answer may not by itself amount to a solution. "Man" was the correct answer to the riddle of the Theban Sphinx; but the elucidation that man crawls on all fours as an infant, walks two-legged as an adult, and uses a cane when aged was also required to untangle it. The preceding chapters have attempted to solve the riddle of musical experience, the answer to the riddle question having been obvious as soon as it was posed.

The answer is music, of course—specifically, the tonal, cadential-harmonic art music of the modern West. This music is spatial and yet nonspatial because its musical space is a virtual, not an actual space, constructed by the listener on the basis of frequency relationships and action plans (chapter 2). This music is in motion and yet not in motion—in motion because its action plans suggest modes of movement, both observer motion and object motion, an effect that is enhanced by the flow of stimulation along the tuned length of the organ of Corti in the inner ear; yet also not in motion, as the music itself consists of mere successions of evanescent tones (chapter 2). This music is meaningful and yet meaningless because it exemplifies by way of the elaborate mental models constructed by the listener while implementing (off-line) the musical action plans, but it lacks all propositional content: what it means cannot be said, and the nuances of its meanings exceed what can be said (chapters 3 and 6). This music is sophisticated in its various modes of hierarchical organization and its wealth of paradigmatic contrasts, yet primitive because it is a descendant of prelinguistic rudimentary song lacking grammatical categories, an expressive form whose contemporary linguistic residue is prosody (chapter 3). The musical work of this style is both universal and particular because it is a type, and types are able to straddle this ontological divide (chapter 4). This music is voluptuous because it comes to us by way of an intensely emotionally affecting touch; yet it is austere because it abjures the directly sensuous blandishments of graven or verbally mediated imagery (chapters 5 and 6). This music is material because its performances consist of physical sound events, yet immaterial to the extent that abstract types that seem to float free of the physical causal nexus supersede material, causally enmeshed events as the primary intentional objects in musical experience (chapter 6). This music is religious because it puts listeners into states of mind that have an affinity with states of religious mysticism, yet not religious because it arouses emotions off-line and expresses no religious doctrine, catechism, mythology, or theology (chapters 5 and 6).

The music that has been the subject of this book has spoken to me since my early childhood. Still, the results of these investigations have done much to enhance my musical experience. May they do the same for the person who has taken the trouble to read these pages! This, I believe, is the least that might be expected of any philosophy of music worthy of the description. It has been my ambition to do more, to solve the riddle of an important variety of musical experience and to turn this solution as a lens back on human cognition and emotion. Yet even if the riddle, as posed, has been solved, a mystery remains. There is a secret buried deep in the heart of modern Western tonal art music, some hidden nexus of touch, movement, cognition, emotion, and human ideals that resists the importunings of theory. It may be that the only initiates into this mystery are those whom Wittgenstein designated "true sons of God," the great composers of the modern West.

Notes

Chapter 1

1. Cf. Peirce's original definition: "A sign, or *representamen*, is something which stands to somebody for something in some respect or capacity" (1932, 2.228).

2. A grue object is green if examined before some stipulated future time; otherwise it is blue. All emeralds, therefore, may be said to be grue.

3. Derived from the proper functions of the mechanisms that produce them, or that produce the beliefs in which they occur.

4. Sperber: "In an oral tradition, all cultural representations are easily remembered ones; hard-to-remember representations are forgotten, or transformed into more easily remembered ones, before reaching a cultural level of distribution."

5. We shall revisit this distinction in chapter 3.

6. Even externalist semantic theories, if they are computational, must take account of syntactic norms.

7. Cf. Shaw, Wilson, and Wellman 1986 (64): "Chomsky has argued that a transformational grammar provides the operations defining the mapping of the generator set of clear-case utterances onto the corpus of all utterances; other theorists disagree. However, no one disputes that the acquisition of language requires cognitive schemata that are truly generative in nature."

8. Chomsky denies that public languages ("E-languages") are interesting or even identifiable objects of scientific study, whose proper objects are internal languages ("I-languages"). In recent times he has substituted talk of "principles and parameters" for the older "grammatical rules." Universal grammar (UG) is now taken to consist of an innate set of principles and parameters that govern the transition of the language acquisition device into a stable or "steady state" (an I-language) that is set when the normally endowed child is exposed to external linguistic utterances. The older rules (or some subset of them) now are seen as deducible from the underlying principles, with parameters set in one of a limited number of permissible ways. (See Chomsky 1986, 1995.)

9. It is not clear that these internal rules must be classically implemented as computational alogorithms. Horgan and Tienson (1996) argue for a connectionist version of the language of thought hypothesis that relies on syntactically structured representations, but without programmable representation-level rules that compute over these structured representations. In this case, I think we would have to grant the psychological reality of the language of thought within the connectionist system, but deny psychological reality to the universal grammatical *rules* postulated by generative linguistics, since these are not represented in the system. However, the Horgan and Tienson model would still be capable of providing an explanatorily adequate account of grammatical competence in Chomsky's sense, since it tells a biologically plausible, if alternative, causal story about the state transitions of the system, a story that is dynamic rather than algorithmic.

10. In a recent statement of the "minimalist" principles and parameters program, Chomsky seems to have abandoned the distinction between deep and surface structure deriving from the older extended standard theory (EST): "there are no levels of linguistic structure apart from the two interface levels PF [phonological form] and LF [logical form]; specifically, no levels of D-structure or S-structure" (1995, 219).

11. Abstracta are physically nonexistent but theoretically useful posits, as are centers of gravity (see Dennett 1987, 53; 1998, 96). (Centers of gravity, however, are posits of descriptive physical theory, and therefore not rule-constituted.)

12. Cf. Plotkin 2003 (266): "The 'confidence trick' that society plays is to present social reality to the child with much the same force as physical reality. Yet unlike natural objects such as mountains and chairs and people, which rest on a solid causal base within physical reality, social reality is poised on a seemingly unsubstantial and fragile base of what others agree is done or not done, is good or bad, and even exists or does not exist."

13. There is also a well-developed naturalist and pragmatist critique of reflective equilibrium (see Stich and Nisbett 1980; Stich 1988, 1993; Thagard 1988). Since this strain of critique concerns issues in epistemology and philosophy of science, its detailed consideration is beyond the scope of this book.

14. For an account with naturalist sympathies, see Gibbard 1990. For a brief sketch of an account with more limited naturalist sympathies, see Korsgaard 1996.

15. We shall take up proper functions in detail in chapter 4. See Millikan 1984 for extended discussion of this notion.

16. Cf. Brandom 1997 (196): "I accept Rosen's point that 'we sanction because we take a bit of behavior to be incorrect, so our taking the behavior to be incorrect cannot *consist* in our sanctioning it.' But I take this to be a sophisticated, late-coming possibility. The primitive practices I want to start with don't yet allow this sort of distinction. If that makes it inappropriate to call what they do 'sanctioning,' I am happy to mark the similarities and differences by retreating to 'proto-sanctioning.'"

17. Examples might be the ongoing reinterpretation of the principle forbidding cruel and unusual punishments and the modification of criteria for political enfranchisement in American constitu-

tional law. The debates concerning women's suffrage and the disenfranchisement of nonwhite citizens and citizens without property belong to the past; but recently a new debate concerning the disenfranchisement of convicted felons has arisen.

18. Cf. Elgin 1983 (192): "Philosophy then is viewed as an enterprise that seeks to achieve coherent, comprehensive systems in reflective equilibrium."

19. Pinker (2002, 404) endorses the stronger claim that acts of "criticism," i.e., "judging, appreciating, and interpreting" are "universal signatures" of artistic activity "recognizable everywhere."

20. Sperber dubs some representational types "semi-propositional" (1985, 51ff). A semi-propositional representation is a conceptual representation "that fails to identify one and only one proposition." Examples he gives include the relativist slogan ("people of different cultures live in different worlds"), the teachings of Zen masters, the philosophy of Kierkegaard, and poetical texts (53).

Chapter 2

1. The idea of a virtual musical space has been suggested before. Cf. Hatten 2004 (103): "music can create a virtual environment akin to the forces acting on our bodies in the world...." Clarke (2005, 154) offers a more developed account of virtual musical space that converges in some respects, but not all, with my own: "music can be understood as constituting a 'virtual world' into which a listener is drawn." I say "converges" because Clarke's book was published just as mine reached completion.

2. See Gibson 1947, 1954, 1960, 1966, 1971, 1977, 1986.

3. "Objects, for example, may be in part defined as those 'things' left invariant under certain transformations such as translation" (Jenkins, Wald, and Pittenger 1986, 118).

4. Inkblots and nonrepresentational paintings in general have been thought to be *in principle* incapable of representing individual virtual objects because no object can be clearly or unambiguously "seen in" such representations (see Robinson 1994). But this is a mistake; this distinction is not an absolute one, but merely a difference in degree, as Robinson herself seems to recognize: "It is not always clear when we can or cannot *see* an individual in a picture but that is precisely because it is not always clear whether a picture is or is not representational" (1994, 176). As a picture becomes more degraded or, alternatively, more severely stylized, more pattern-completion processes and more of the special skills that tend to result from training are required to see the virtual object in the painting, and the more "polysemous," or capable of supporting a range of different interpretations and of representing a multiplicity of alternative virtual objects, the picture becomes. The Rorschach test, recall, was designed to test a perceiver's contribution to the symbolic-perceptual situation. Any musical representation of virtual objects will tend to be highly polysemous.

5. In chapter 5 I shall qualify this loose talk of musical virtual objects.

6. Other attempts to apply a Gibsonian ecological approach to the problem of musical representation include those of Clarke (2005), Hatten (2004), and Windsor (1995). My treatment was,

however, developed independently of these writers and makes very different (indeed in some respects, diametrically opposed) use of Gibson's ideas.

7. The signal must depend nomically on (or reliably correlate with) events at the source, but signal and source need not be directly causally connected. Causal dependency of the signal on events at the source also need not be deterministic: the laws in question could be probabilistic (see Dretske 1981, 26ff). Dretske also recognizes "ghost" channels in which sender and receiver are not causally connected, but rather are correlated owing to causal dependence on a common source (1981, 38–39).

8. Cf. Aunger 2002 (150): "In the physicalist tradition of Pauling, information is determined by both a structure *and* a substrate. It is not disembodied, but always a function of some ordering of physical matter. By contrast, Shannon's mathematical theory of communication, information transmission is modeled as reduction in uncertainty about a message's content."

9. Cf. Gibson 1986 (136–137, emphasis in original): "A transparent sheet of glass in a window transmits both illumination and information, whereas a *translucent* sheet transmits illumination but not information." A light signal transmitted through a translucent sheet can surely be informational in the information-theoretic sense.

10. In one place Dretske (1981, 75–78) argues that since laws of nature are *intensional*, i.e., not purely extensional because they are modal (necessary and counterfactual-supporting), the informational content they support is therefore *intentional*. This transition from the intensional to the intentional turns on the referential opacity that attends both *intensional locutions* and *intentional states*. Dretske is, however, careful to point out that meaning (semantic content) has a "higher-order" intentionality than does informational content (ibid., 248n11). If all the "intentionality" of the *de re* information in a tree trunk amounts to is the intensionality of the relevant causal laws *in situ*, then the charge of absurdity does not stick. But this grade of "intentionality" falls far short of representation.

11. Cf. Dretske 1995 (4): "Not all events that carry information have the function of carrying it. . . . the angle a column of smoke makes with the horizon carries information about wind speed, but that, surely, is not the function of the smoke. The smoke cannot misrepresent wind speed. We may be misled by the column of smoke. We may take it to indicate something it doesn't (thus ourselves misrepresenting wind speed), but the smoke does not misrepresent wind speed the way an anemometer can." Cf. also Prinz 2004 (53): "But carrying information is not sufficient for representation. Smoke does not represent fires."

12. Strictly speaking, it is the use of putatively referring singular terms in fictional contexts that Evans designates as "conniving."

13. The distinction between an *a*-representation and a representation *of a* originally derives from Goodman (1976, 23, and earlier writings).

14. Cf. Clarke 1987 (111): "There is thus a fundamental contrast between an intentionally produced painting, map, or diagram as an iconic comsign [i.e., a conventional nonsentential representation] and a photograph or screen image as related causally to what it is a means of perceiv-

ing." Unlike Evans, Clarke seems to hold that photos and moving pictures never function as signs and hence never as representations at all, but exclusively as mere means of indirect perception like the mirror images in a telescope. I think this is overstated. For one thing, it renders the use of photographic and cinematic images for artistic ends unintelligible.

15. It could be argued that a photograph is never a mere informational vehicle but is both a representation of *a* and an *a*-representation, since it is a product of an artifactual device (a camera) whose function is to produce informational vehicles for our representational use. If this is right, then an accidentally exposed "swamp-camera" photo might be counted a mere informational vehicle.

16. Cf. Clarke 2005 (73): "Just as spatial arrangements of pigment in a painting can create a perceptual effect analogous to that produced by reflection, texture, and shadow in the real world, so music may create perceptual effects with temporal patterns of discrete pitches that reproduce, or approximate, those that we experience with the continuous acoustical transformations that are characteristic of real-world events." I do not mean to suggest that the musical surface lacks additional dimensions, including timbre and volume. These, however, are not "indispensable attributes" (see the next paragraph below).

17. Although pitched tones can be individuated, they cannot, except *qua* types, be *reidentified* once they have ceased to sound. We shall take up issues of musical ontology in more detail in chapter 4.

18. This is not completely accurate, since the viola, not the cello, sits on the extreme right in standard string-quartet seating.

19. Compare Schoenberg's observation that "a piece of music resembles in some respects a photograph album, displaying under changing circumstances the life of its basic idea—its basic motive" (quoted in Maus 1997, 125).

20. Cf. Julesz and Hirsch 1972 (333): "the visual image is integrated into a visual field from small samples collected by many quasi-random fixations, capitalizing on the fact that the visual environment is relatively stable in time. On the other hand, the auditory patterns are dynamic and ordered in time."

21. A similar idea has been suggested by Putman (1985) but remains undeveloped in his brief article.

22. Cf. Gibson 1963 (369): "In vision, we strive to get new perspectives on an object in order to perceive it properly. I believe that something analogous to this is what happens in the active exploratory touching of an object. The momentary visual perspectives, of course, are pictures or forms in the geometrical sense of the term, whereas the momentary tactual perspectives are not. Nevertheless they are similar since, for an object of a given solid shape, any change of cutaneous pattern like any change of retinal pattern is *reversible*."

23. Beethoven's cuckoo in the *Pastoral* Symphony and Respighi's in *The Birds* are examples (cf. Robinson 1994).

24. Cf. Bremner 1999 (517): "The Gibsonian version marks the extreme of ecological theorizing by dismissing the need for internal representation for most forms of interaction with the environment. The structure is in the environment, and the organism needs simply to pick it up. However, there are problems with this extreme, since the organism must be suitably adapted to pick this information up, and so there must be some form of internal structure, whether or not we want to call it representation." Cf. also Millikan 2004 (159): "Information 'picked up' by the organism would have to involve alterations to its inner states, which would be intentional signs of environmental affairs, these signs in turn guiding the organism's responses."

25. Cf. Johnson-Laird 1983 (466): "Some psychologists, notably J. J. Gibson (1979) [1986] have argued that there are no mental representations. Until they formulate their theories as effective procedures, though, they may be deemed to have been deceived by the adaptive nature of consciousness. Psychology is difficult precisely because of the evolutionary advantage of seemingly direct contact with the world—a phenomenon that makes the task of discovering the machinery of the mind that much harder." Marr, who developed what is to date perhaps the most detailed and sophisticated computational account of the extraction of visual information from retinal surfaces, makes a similar point. Gibson, Marr tells us, came nearest to the level of computational theory in vision, but "did not understand properly what information processing was, which led him to seriously underestimate the complexity of the information-processing problems involved in vision and the consequent subtlety that is necessary in approaching them" (1982, 29).

26. See the work of ecological psychologists Shaw and Hazelett (1986, 47): "Indeed, there exists a reciprocal interaction between the two types of schemas so we say that an organism behaves adaptively when one schema becomes calibrated in terms of the other. Put differently, the control processes for the execution of action schemas are perceptual schemas whereas the control processes for the pickup of perceptual information are action schemas. Every action, like every perception, is the achievement of a mission in the service of adaptation rather than a random behavior or a casual pickup of information."

27. Cf. Shepard 1981 (331):

Just as the basic six degrees of freedom of rigid motion are inherent in any solid object, the possibility of the set of such motions is implicit in its perception (or other internal representation). Indeed, the internal representation of the manifold of such possible motions may not only underlie our ability to manipulate the object either physically or mentally; it may also underlie our perception of the structure of the object itself.... Relevant to this conclusion are the further observations that subjects have to perform a mental rotation in order to determine that two differently oriented objects are nevertheless of the same intrinsic shape, and that there is a connection between the time required to perceive a rigid motion and the time required to perceive the full structure of a static object.

See also Shepard 1984 (439).

28. A "what else" argument, recall, may be bolstered by an "existence proof." I introduce one for the Lerdahl and Jackendoff theory in the next chapter.

29. Cf. Lerdahl 2001 (5–6): "it is known throughout cognitive psychology that learning and memory are enhanced if a subject is able to organize input in a hierarchical manner...."

30. This is one point (among others) concerning which Windsor's "ecological" approach diverges from mine: he takes examples of *musique concrète* (sound collages constructed from recorded snip-

pets that include everyday nonmusical sounds) as central cases. In a more recent publication, Lerdahl (2001) has offered a modified version of the generative theory that is applicable to atonal music.

31. The prolongation reductions, which represent harmonic tension and release by specifying the harmonic significance of tones in relation to cadences, also make use of the tree convention. In the interest of clarity when combining time-span and prolongation reduction analyses, Lerdahl (2001) has developed an alternative (but formally equivalent) notation for the time-span reductions, reserving the tree convention for the prolongation reductions alone. Because Lerdahl and Jackendoff's (1983) original notation for time-span reductions suits my purposes better, I shall continue to make use of it.

32. Cf. Donald 1991 (242): "Many of the features found in the articulation of speech segments are also found in other skilled motor behaviors. All conscious motor acts involve retrieving a plan, modifying for it the particular conditions of execution, and then unpacking it in a finely tuned temporal order under constant conscious supervision. Motor-learning theory has built these considerations into the concept of the 'motor schema.'"

33. But cf. Jeannerod 1997 (55): "Still, the level at which motor schemas are implemented neurally remains hypothetical."

34. Cf. Arbib 1985 (64): "Our actions are addressed not only to interacting with the environment in some instrumental way, but also to updating our 'internal model of the world.'" See also Pugh 1977 (27): "To predict the consequences of different action alternatives, both the artificial and the biological systems use a model of the environment....The model is used to calculate or simulate the consequences of different decision alternatives." Keijzer (2001) doubts that such internal models, or indeed any representations at all, are needed to explain behavior. See the appendix to this chapter for further discussion.

35. Cf. Johnson-Laird 1996 (102): "The simplest sort of model has an analogical structure that corresponds to the structure of the situation that it represents. And like diagrams, these simple models are isomorphic, or at least homomorphic, to what they represent."

36. The Roman alphabet, for example, is both disjoint and finitely differentiated. It is disjoint because there is no overlap between classes of characters: the class of As does not intersect the class of Bs, and neither intersects the class of Cs. The alphabet is also finitely differentiated. No mark may belong to two different letter characters; and any mark that is ambiguous, say between the As and the Ds, is excluded from one and included in the other. If there is no such procedure to differentiate ambiguous marks, the scheme counts as "dense." Consider a scheme with only two characters: lines that are 2 cm long and all other lines. The scheme is disjoint, because there is no overlap between these classes of marks, but it is not finitely differentiated and therefore is "dense": it may not be possible in principle to exclude a given line from the class of lines 2 cm long or those not 2 cm long. A dense scheme provides for an infinite number of characters which are ordered such that between any two there is a third less discriminable from each of them than they are from each other, and, as a result, is such that a given mark cannot be excluded from an infinite number of characters. (This and the following note are indebted to Elgin 1983.)

37. Consider once again a scheme with just two characters: lines less than 1 cm long and those 2 cm or greater. The scheme is disjoint, but there is a gap: there are no characters containing lines 1 cm or longer, but shorter than 2 cm. The scheme, however, is still dense. Since lines less than 1 cm long approach 1 cm but never reach it, the scheme satisfies conditions for syntactic density, for the following reason. Between any line shorter than 1 cm and any line 2 cm or longer there will be a third line, since there is an infinite number of lines approaching 1 cm. But because of the gap between 1 cm and 2 cm, the scheme is not "dense throughout." Insertion of a character that is exactly 1 cm will, however, "destroy" density, for then there will no longer be a third line allowable between 1 cm and 2 cm.

38. A piece of information is completely digitalized, in Dretske's sense, if it not only is not embedded in any larger information shells deriving from the same object, but also is not embedded in an informational shell deriving from another object.

39. Because these schemata or models are *representations*, they are also capable of *mis*representing BBs as flies.

40. Braddon-Mitchell and Jackson (1996) refer to "mental maps," but it is clear that they mean by this analog topological representations.

41. I do not claim that this *obscurum per obscurius* comparison does much to *explain* mental models; it just situates them intellectually and notes Johnson-Laird's (1983) Kantian allusion. We shall take up Kantian schematism and symbolism in Chapter 6.

42. On this point of comparison between pictorial and cinematographic representation, cf. Peacocke 1987 (394).

43. This is why Ridley's "dung beetle" scenario fits the finely contoured musical plan of the *Marcia funebre* of Beethoven's *Eroica* so *poorly*, rather than passably, as he so implausibly claims (1995, 110). To demonstrate the indeterminacy of musical scenario content, Ridley offers a thought experiment in which the strivings of a dung beetle, as opposed to the slow progression of a hero's funeral cortege, are imagined to occur in synchronization with strains of Beethoven. The aim is to show that the music fits the one scenario as well as the other. A dung beetle's micro-movements, however, are far too coarse to achieve any very satisfactory fit with the action plan of this music, providing the music is well performed.

44. Mental models are naturally associated with plans, since they are used in imagination and modified according to sequenced operations. (Cf. Arbib 1985, 64; Jeannerod 1990, 354; Miller, Galanter, and Pribram 1960, 17–18.) Cf. also Johnson-Laird 1983 (156): "[Models] may be dynamic and represent a sequence of events."

45. Cf. Gallese and Metzinger 2003 (374): "Interestingly, in systems capable of generating a PMIR [phenomenal model of the practical intentionality relation], the object component [of the relation] can now also be constituted by the output of ongoing phenomenal [motor] simulations, e.g., by the conscious representation of *possible actions*"; (383): "To have a PMIR means to have a phenomenal self-model. To be self-conscious does not imply having language, concepts, being able to mentally form a concept of *oneself*, etc. Body image and visceral feelings are enough."

46. Australian Aborigines are known to employ songs directly as maps of physical terrain:

In theory, at least, the whole of Australia could be read as a musical score. There was hardly a rock of creek in the country that could not or had not been sung. One could perhaps visualize the Songlines as a spaghetti of Illiads and Odysseys, writhing this way and that, in which every "episode" was readable in terms of geology....
Regardless of the words, it seems the melodic contour of the song describes the nature of the land over which the song passes. So, if the Lizard Man were dragging his heels across the salt-pans of Lake Eyre, you could expect a succession of long flats, like Chopin's "Funeral March." If he were skipping up and down the MacDonnell escarpments, you'd have a series of arpeggios and glissandos, like Liszt's "Hungarian Rhapsodies." (Chatwin 1987, 13, 108)

47. Clarke (2005, 75–76) also appeals to Gibson in an attempt to address this issue.

48. Cf. Jeannerod 1997 (168): "In this way, the visual centres could distinguish the retinal displacement related to a movement of the animal, from the displacement produced by moving objects. Visual changes produced by a movement of the animal were normally 'cancelled' by a corollary discharge of a corresponding size and direction, and had no effect on behavior." A variant, but closely related version of this function is sometimes characterized as matching an "efference copy" (of an executed motor command sent to short-term memory) to a reafference inflow signal" returning from peripheral effectors and sensory systems (Jeannerod 2006, 17–18).

49. Scruton (1997) uses the expression "acousmatic experience." The term "acousmatic" seems to derive from Pierre Schaeffer, the originator of *musique concrète*.

50. It also provides some explanation of music's emotional "touch effect," that is, its tactual and haptic quality (see chapter 5); and touch is, in point of phenomenology, spatial.

51. "In lower species of mammals...the thalamic auditory center also receives many fibers from the dorsal column via the medial lemniscus and secondary ascending projections from the trigeminal nucleus. This overlap is anatomic evidence that in support of the hypothesis that sound perception is a refinement of tactile vibratory sense, and is reminiscent of the phylogenetic origin of the auditory nerve from somatic sensory components of branchial nerves" (Sarnat and Netsky 1981, 183–184).

52. Based on a reading of Seeger (1987), Zbikowski (2002, 68) argues that the location of pitches as higher and lower in musical space is not, contrary to all expectation, a psychological universal. But I see no basis in Seeger's text for this conclusion. Although the Amazonian Suya people apparently classify musical *genres* by whether they are sung high or low in the throat (100), associating depth with the age of the singer, there is no evidence at all that they do not hear pitches as located in pitch space: "While the Suya apparently were unconcerned with absolute pitch, they were very concerned with relative pitch, which they used to establish differences among individuals and between age groups...the Suya did not talk about absolute or rising pitch [i.e., change of key]. A rise in absolute pitch, so important to *our* musical values, was itself neither commented on nor criticized....They were very interested in *relative pitch* (higher or lower than the midrange), which was associated with age, genre, and the authenticity of the singers" (Seeger 1987, 101–102, emphases original). We shall return to the music of the Suya in chapter 6.

53. Many of these ideas were presciently anticipated by David Katz, whose treatise *The World of Touch* (1989) first appeared in 1925 under the title *Der Aufbau der Tastwelt*. Katz emphasizes the

importance of tactual experience for these emergent concepts, and pays particular attention to the sort of linguistic evidence for metaphorical transfer based on bodily experience later collated by Lakoff and Johnson: "*Linguistic expressions derived from the tactile-motor sphere, particularly the activity of the touching hand.*... We posit transference of linguistic forms developed in the tactual domain to other sensory domains, on account of the primacy of touch within the whole province of perception" (Katz 1989, 238, 244, emphasis in original). Krueger (Katz's translator and editor) draws attention to the same asymmetry of transference (Katz 1989, 236): we talk of "sharp tastes," "dull sounds," and "soft colors," not of "loud or fragrant touches."

54. Although I arrived at the connection between musical experience and the Lakoff and Johnson "body-in-the-mind" theory independently, it must be acknowledged that Zbikowski (2002) got there first. As we shall see in the following chapter, however, my treatment differs from his in important respects. Lerdahl (2001, 191) notices a similar connection between music and the Lakoff and Johnson theory, but, surprisingly, recommends that we "drop gravity as a musical force," since "what is 'down' to us may be 'up' or 'away' in another culture." Whether and where this is (or has ever been) true are, of course, empirical questions, but I am skeptical. Fortunately, given the scope of my discussion, they are questions I need not attempt to answer. Levitin (2006, 19) holds that "high" and "low" are "culturally relative," since the ancient Greeks, he claims, called "low" those tones produced by short pipes whose tops were vertically close to the ground and "high" those tones produced by long pipes whose tops were vertically farther removed. I have not been able to document this claim about piped instruments, but neither does Levitin. The Greeks did call the low-pitched vertical string closest to a player on the harplike *kithara* "*hypate*," meaning "high". But this means "first" as in "first in line," not "high in pitch" (see Landels 1999, 54), and falls far short of showing that the ancient Greeks did not hear musical tones as located in pitch space. In classical Greek, the prefix *oxy-*, meaning "sharp" or "pointed," characterized musical tones high in pitch, while *bary-*, meaning "heavy," characterized tones low in pitch (whence our "baritone"), much as *aigu* and *grave* do today in modern French. See Lidell and Scott's standard Greek lexicon (1996, 308, 1236).

55. Quoted by Katz (1989, 192–193n5).

56. We are, of course, speaking phenomenologically, so the discrete molecular structure of water is irrelevant.

57. A diatonic scale consists of eight tones divided into two groups of four (two tetrachords), each of which contains two whole steps (major seconds) and one half step (a minor second). Among diatonic scales, only the harmonic minor scale is anomalous: its second tetrachord contains two minor seconds and an augmented major second.

58. According to Scholes (1955, 920), no interval, not even the octave, is common to all scales.

59. Certainly the Euclidean space of classical mechanics is entirely homogeneous. I am ignoring as irrelevant to the present point the local curvature of physical space in the vicinity of massive bodies posited by general relativity theory.

60. Levitin (2006, 72) identifies the tritone proportion as 43:32.

61. An exception seems to be the perfect fourth, which (to us) sounds more "deviant" or unstable than the major or even the minor third. This may be a result of harmonic considerations peculiar to Western cadential-harmonic music, where the fourth step of the diatonic scale tends to be heard as the seventh of the dominant seventh chord. Relative stability and instability of tones have their undoubted acoustic bases; but they are also sensitive to style.

62. I have always found the abrupt modulation from D major to F major that occurs between bars 213 and 219 in Movement 3 of Beethoven's *Pastoral* Symphony extremely disorienting and productive of a vertiginous sensation approaching nausea (see example 2.10). It may be that this passage was intended to suggest disorientation after whirling bouts of peasant dancing.

63. Cf. Sloboda 1985 (254): "Moreover, within most of these scales [across cultures] the octave appears to be a particularly privileged interval. The disposition of the pitches repeats within each octave, and the octave frequently appears as an interval in polyphonic music. It is particularly common to find the principal reference pitch being reinforced by voice or instruments at several different octaves. In addition, intervals close to our perfect fifth and fourth appear in the polyphony of most cultures." Cf. also Brown, Merker, and Wallin 2000 (14): "octaves are perceived as equivalent in almost all cultures [and] virtually all scales of the world consist of seven or fewer pitches (per octave)."

64. I am not counting the unison as a chord.

65. We shall take a closer look at these features from a logical and metaphysical standpoint in chapter 5.

66. Cf. Ferguson 1973 (141): "Such blitheness of motion as is here pictured [in Beethoven's Piano Sonata, Op. 101] is far beyond the limbs of man to execute; but it is not beyond his imagination to trip thus lightly upon whatever surface will give support to the limbs of fancy...."

67. Similar ideas have been suggested, but not really worked out in any psychological or neurological detail, by Ferguson (1973), Kivy (1989), Maus (1997), and Zbikowski (2002). I hope to provide a deeper account of animism in musical experience.

68. Cf. Lewis 1947 (106–107): "Animism lies surely at the very source of the poetic image."

69. Recall that for Gibson, animate objects and social situations also provide affordances.

70. Cf. Hatten 2004 (233): "Even the musical representation of natural objects (e.g., wind, or a storm) may be freighted with a human quality or amalgam of affective motivation...."

71. Cf. Callen 1985 (43): "But in order to hear fictive expressive movement in music (which is not movement of sound but of body), it helps for us to mediate what we hear through another mode of imagination, one more familiar: the movements of our own bodies and the feelings associated with those movements."

72. Robinson (2005, 446n35) takes note of some of these results but does not develop the idea.

73. One PET scan study (Parsons 2003) found no evidence of primary or supplementary motor area involvement during musical listening, but did find significant cerebellar activity, another important component of the motor system. But the author concludes that "the cerebellar activations

Example 2.10

Beethoven, Symphony No. 6 in F, *Pastoral, Scherzo.*

are not likely related to motor activity, since no overt motor activity occurred and there was little or no activity detected in neocortical motor areas" (256). This conclusion is open to question.

74. Norihiro Sadato, personal communication.

75. In contrast with these authors, Tomasello (1999) doubts that nonhuman animals are capable of such mind-reading.

76. Clarke (2005, 63) and Levitin (2006, 259–260) briefly note the possible relationship between mirror neurons and musical understanding.

77. Peel and Slawson (1984) take Lerdahl and Jackendoff to task because the generative theory allows fairly divergent analytical interpretations of the same passages, and they severely criticize some of Lerdahl and Jackendoff's interpretations. Peel and Slawson's alternative interpretations of two of Lerdahl and Jackendoff's stock examples, Bach's Chorale "O Haupt voll Blut und Wunden" and Mozart's Piano Sonata in A, K. 331, are certainly plausible, but I do not see allowing alternative interpretations as a problem for the theory, so long as it also supplies reasonable constraints. There certainly are interpretations that the theory decisively rules out. This is not, however, to dispute Peel and Slawson's claim that Lerdahl and Jackendoff's groundbreaking theory is in need of more work. More damagingly, Peel and Slawson question the theoretical integrity of preference rules at all, declaring themselves in favor of a theory that makes exclusive use of well-formedness rules. But they themselves provide only a very few examples of such rules and have no such theory on offer, thus failing to show the feasibility of such a theory. Finally, they question some of Lerdahl and Jackendoff's more sweeping pronouncements concerning so-called musical universals, a criticism with which I have some sympathy.

78. For a recent, more neuroscientifically oriented incarnation of the implication-realization approach, see Levitin 2006.

79. Other relevant parameters are those of duration, harmony, and meter. Expectations concerning all these parametric dimensions exert mutual influence during musical processing.

80. The late David Marr was a prominent example.

81. Connectionist explanations of gestalt phenomena are perhaps closer in spirit to the accounts of the original gestalt theorists (cf. Churchland's 1995 discussion of the holistic processing of informationally degraded pictures).

82. Handel's tuning fork (which still exists) set the tuning A at 422.5 Hz and Mozart used a piano tuned to 421.6 Hz, both closer to A-flat than to A by contemporary standards (Scholes 1955, 814). If A is set at 440 Hz, the current standard, the A-flat one half-step below will fall at about 415.3 Hz on the equally tempered scale (see Levitin 2006, 23).

83. A transposing instrument sounds the tonic of its own key when playing a written C. A trumpet in D sounds D when playing C, just as a clarinet in B-flat sounds B-flat when doing the same. Mahler specifies that each of the four strings of the violin be tuned up a whole step, to A, E, B, and F-sharp. The part must therefore be written a step lower (in B-flat minor) to sound in C minor.

84. Cf. Davies 1994 (354n35): "In almost all musics, some of the significant properties of the style depend on the possibilities of the instruments used in playing the music." Davies may, however,

go on to overstate the case. I can agree that a listener so unfamiliar with an instrument that "she cannot even identify its family affiliation" will miss these properties, but I doubt that "it will be difficult for her to make sense of the music heard under these circumstances." I am similarly skeptical of the claim that "it can be very difficult to locate the music in what one hears" if we are unfamiliar with the instruments involved and how their sounds are made (Davies 2001, 64). Recall the initial musical contact between humans and aliens in the motion picture *Close Encounters of the Third Kind*.

85. Cf. Benzon 2001 (150): "If tones played by two different people are close together in pitch and time, the ear will hear them as coming from the same source and place them in the same melodic stream. The mind thus infers the existence of virtual sound sources that are quite different from the real ones."

86. Lerdahl (2001, 171) takes note of the phenomenon of reversal expectation after leaps of large intervals but does not attempt to explain it. According to Lerdahl's theory, melodic "inertia" (the tendency for a melody to continue in the same direction) can *in general* be counteracted by the "attraction" of a less stable by a more stable tone of the scale.

87. I offer Warren's quotation of Piaget as an empirical observation, not as a blanket endorsement of Piagetian genetic epistemology.

88. Cf. Narmour 1990 (120): "F thus is an important note in an ascending-descending melodic pattern like C–D–E–F–E–D–C because it functions as an 'auditory corner,' terminating a rising process and then going on to initiate a falling one."

89. Cf. Hatten 2004 (129) on Alexandra Pierce's "spanning" exercises for musicians: "Spanning is embodied in two exercises, the first of which is stretching the hand from a loose fist outward to its full extent, timed to a felt climax in the music, and then gradually releasing the tension of the hand after the climax.... Pierce's second exercise ... is 'arcing,' which involves a stretch of the whole body directed by an arm that moves in a large, sweeping motion, as though outlining a giant clock face. The climax in this case is the point of maximum extension of the arm diagonally from the body, peaking at around 1:00 or 2:00 on the clock face if the right arm is arcing in a clockwise direction."

90. Countenancing only *relative* encapsulation allows for the possibility of cognitive penetration (cf. DeBellis 1995).

91. Because of the placement of the accompanying chords in the winds and contrabasses on the weak second and fourth beats of the common-time bar, the second and fourth beats of the cello melody that begins in bar 6 of the second movement of the Second Symphony (example 2.11) persistently sound like strong first and third beats, even though at a more global level we know they are not. Similarly, because of the placement of the accompanying pizzicato chords in the cellos and basses on the weak second beat of the three-quarter bar, it is difficult not to hear the motif introduced by the oboe and clarinet on the second beat of bar 16 of the Finale of the Fourth Symphony (example 2.12) as beginning on the first beat. When the same motif returns *fortissimo* in the violins and oboes in bar 200 (example 2.13) the *sforzando* repeated triplets in the

Example 2.11

Brahms, Symphony No. 2 in D, *Adagio non troppo*.

Example 2.12

Brahms, Symphony No. 4 in E Minor, *Allegro energico e passionato.*

Example 2.12
(continued)

Example 2.13
Brahms, Symhony No. 4 in E Minor, *Tempo I.*

Example 2.13
(continued)

winds and tympani and duplets in the cellos, contrabasses, and contrabassoon produce the same effect.

92. Jenefer Robinson (2005) has emphasized the importance of the activation of the motor system for the arousal of musical emotion, a topic we shall take up in chapter 5.

93. Exactly the same point applies to Clarke's (2005) connectionist antirepresentationalism.

94. We shall consider an existence proof that relies on two coupled or modularly connected neural nets in the next chapter.

95. See Clark 2003 for discussion of first- and higher-order connectionist systems and their representational capacities.

Chapter 3

1. Currie (2004, 121) takes an opposing view: "We should also distinguish between the symbolic and the representational, taking the latter category to be a special case of symbolism, where one object stands for another. Pictures and statues are representations in my sense, while rituals and their trappings would generally count as merely symbolic." Surely, though, natural representations, i.e., representational states of the mind–brain, cannot plausibly be counted a special case of the symbolic. Therefore, it seems unwise to regard representation as a special case of the symbolic. In my terminology, symbols are artifactual representations and, as such, a special case of the representational.

2. I exclude two other senses of meaningfulness as irrelevant to the issue of musical meaning. That which is important is sometimes termed "meaningful," as is human and animal behavior that can be rationalized or that "makes sense" using folk-psychological concepts.

3. Goodman (1978, 68) adds a fifth condition, "multiple and complex reference, where a symbol performs several integrated and interacting functions, some direct and some mediated through other symbols" (footnote omitted).

4. Recall that exemplification is for Goodman a referential relation.

5. That is, if we do not mean by "experiences," as Goodman surely does not, mental representations. More on this topic below.

6. No doubt the score possesses a variety of attributes, e.g., ink color, font type, having been printed on a Tuesday, etc. But it does not exemplify them, i.e., the score is not used to "refer" to these attributes.

7. "Mere reading" would presumably exclude the mental realization of a performance by a gifted musician (like Brahms's reputed mental performance of *Don Giovanni*), which would have aesthetic attributes.

8. Cf. Elgin 1983 (123): "Understanding a work of art involves discovering which of the labels in a dense field of reference its symbols exemplify. This is true in music as well as in the literary and visual arts, for a musical performance exemplifies not its score, but labels from a dense field of

sound." Cf. also Raffman 1993 (65): "Robison's C-sharps may be slightly lower than Dwyer's, or Steinhardt's D-sharps a shade higher than his E-flats; DuPre may narrow her vibrato on tense passages and widen it in relaxed ones, while Rampal's E-naturals tend to be slightly flat in the middle register. These fine-grained details of a performance—these *nuances*—are features the score does not (indeed *cannot*) dictate, hence precisely the sorts of features the performer can manipulate in forging his particular interpretation of the work."

9. We shall take up issues of musical ontology in the next chapter.

10. Goodman avails himself of both "attributes" and "properties" language. Levinson (1978) treats "attribute" as the genus-word for a category that includes both properties and qualities, but I shall not bother with this refinement here.

11. Davies (1994, 144) and Raffman (1993, 114) make similar criticisms.

12. In his (1976) book, Goodman limited representation to pictorial representation. Later (Goodman and Elgin 1988, 121n1) he termed this "depiction," preferring a "looser and more flexible use" for "representation."

13. See the end of section 3.7 below for qualifications.

14. Millikan points out (1996, 146) that the sentence, "No, Johnny, we don't eat peas with our fingers," directed by a parent to a child, is a propositional pushmi-pullyu representation because it combines descriptive and imperative functions. We might say that it possesses mixed illocutionary force.

15. Clarke (1987, 92) presents a similar notion under a different, less colorful name: "Nonconventional comsigns [non-linguistic communicative signals] such as the hissing sound of a snake [made by a communicator] are commonly objects of both cognitive and dynamic interpretation, and for them reference has a dual function. A pointing gesture accompanying the sound would indicate both the location at which the snake could be expected to be seen and from which there should be a retreat."

16. Mithen (2005, 172) endorses a version of the musilanguage hypothesis. He calls musilanguage, rather fetchingly, the "Hmmmmm communication system": Holistic (noncompositional), Multi-Modal (aural and gestural), Manipulative (imperative), Musical, and, Mimetic. He thinks that the more primitive animal pushmi-pullyus from which musilanguage arose are *only* manipulative and not referential at all, because he limits reference to conventional symbolic denotation.

17. Darwin (1871/1962, 875, notes omitted): "Insects and some few spiders are the lowest animals which voluntarily produce any sound; and this is generally effected by the aid of beautifully constructed stridulating organs, which are often confined to the males. The sounds thus produced consist, I believe in all cases, of the same note, repeated rhythmically; and this is sometimes pleasing even to the ears of man."

18. Tomasello (1999, 29ff) challenges such claims, holding that even chimpanzees do not imitate, they only "emulate." They are intentional agents; but because they have no second-order understanding of the intentional states of others, they are unable to (meta)represent the goal

representations of other intentional agents. They may notice a change brought about in the environment by the action of another agent and try to reproduce that change by any means available. But they do not imitate the action itself because the goal and strategy of the action are opaque to them.

19. Levitin (2006, 245–249) also endorses the sexual-selection origins hypothesis.

20. Benzon (2001, 176ff) has covered some of this ground.

21. Cf. Peters 1999 (864): "Mime and gesture, intelligently directed, offer a paratactic means for the communication of simple scenes without syntax, however, relying only on 'frame of dialogue' and the analogy of temporal order." Cf. also Molino 2000 (174): "a group of hominids would perform activities of collective imitation without language but accompanied by vocalizations and organized by rhythm; these would in fact be the first forms of the representation of scenes, that is, of narratives, leading to rite and myth."

22. Mimetic symbolism should not be confused with a non-mimetic, fully linguistic hand symbolism like American Sign Language (ASL).

23. Lerdahl and Jackendoff (1983) say that they intend their generative theory as a *"formal description of the musical intuitions of a listener who is experienced in a musical idiom"* (1, emphasis original). I think they should say that they intend their theory to be a formal description of the *rules and representations* that (adequately) *explain* those intuitions by psychological inference to the best explanation, and that metainterpret these rules and representations as norms, by standards of reflective equilibrium. By "the musical intuitions of a listener" they say they mean "not just his conscious grasp of musical structure; an acculturated listener need never have studied music" (3). If having studied music or not is what makes the difference, Lerdahl and Jackendoff should, it would seem, say "conceptual grasp" rather than "conscious grasp," assuming (as seems reasonable) that it is music-theoretic study and not performance study that is intended. To understand a piece of music the listener surely must have some *conscious* grasp of its structure, even if he cannot conceptualize it in music-theoretic terms and report it, and even if he does not have conscious grasp of the *formal rules* (the well-formedness and preference rules) he is implementing in grasping its structure, or even of the hierarchical representations he is implementing. On this issue see DeBellis 1995 (46ff). Cf. also DeBellis 1999 (491, emphasis original): Jackendoff "conflates not being aware of a structure *via certain music-theoretic concepts* with not being aware of it at all. But that is a mistake." Lerdahl and Jackendoff may also be conflating the structure of the musical surface with the structure of the internal representations, both conceptual and nonconceptual, that are deployed in parsing the musical surface. That is, they may conflate the representations with the *contents* of these representations. Discussion with Mark DeBellis helped me clarify this issue.

24. Cf. Wartofsky 1979 (144): "a model is an aid to the understanding or to the imagination. It is also a call to action in the sense of presenting some exemplary form of *how* things ought to be done or *what* ought to be done."

25. Cf. Scruton 1997 (333): "Musical activity is not just movement, but the peculiar form of movement we call action…an experience of movement, life and gesture, reaching through the imagined space of music." I have taken the liberty of connecting these two quotations and revers-

ing their original order. Cf. also Ferguson 1973 (176): "But to be expressive [i.e., to represent,] an image of motion must appear as more than an abstract pattern of movement. It must appear as the image of a motor impulse, sensed by the listener as suggestive of enactment by his own actual or imaginal [*sic*] motor equipment."

26. Cf. Johnson-Laird 1983 (447): "[A]nalogies may depend on procedures that apply a model of one phenomenon to another."

27. Cf. Molino 2000 (173): "[M]usic, language, dance, chant, poetry, and pretend play all have a partly common origin. Among the neural modules responsible for this activity, it would be necessary to give a central place to one or more rhythmic modules, which come into play in behaviors such as throwing and constructing and using tools.... In a general sense, this mastery of rhythm is the only imaginable route of access for the temporal organization of all activities: it is in this way that rhythmic modules are at the foundation of all types of syntactic constructions."

28. Peters 1999 (864): "The correlated theoretical assertion [correlated with modern structure of the vocal apparatus] is a hypothesis of the emergence of human vocalization in the form of sound symbolism in early *Homo sapiens*.... Theoretically these were vocal gestures that offered iconic representation, and which were organized into a system of contrasts."

29. Tomasello (1999, 122) endorses an ontogenetic version of it: "In combination with the principle of contrast as traditionally conceived, then, the child who knows some language can hear a new word and contrast it with others that the speaker might have chosen in its stead (paradigms), as well as with the other words in the utterance that are doing their part to express the entire utterance meaning (syntagms)." Clark (2000, chapter 6) argues that the sensory systems of vertebrates are designed to be far more sensitive to contrast between than to similarity between qualities.

30. This requirement of congruence is referred to by some theorists of metaphor (cf. Zbikowski 2002, 70) as the "invariance principle."

31. Cf. Chomsky 1986 (44): "I think that much of this work [misleadingly called 'the semantics of natural language'] is not semantics at all, if by 'semantics' we mean the study of the relation between language and the world—in particular, the study of truth and reference. Rather, this work deals with certain postulated levels of mental representation, including representations of syntactic and lexical form and others called 'models' or 'pictures' or 'discourse representations' or 'situations,' or the like."

32. Cf. Churchland 1979 (149): "the construction of an internal 'model' that can systematically mime sundry dimensions of the environment is presumably the essence of our own cognitive development."

33. Barsalou's (1992) "frames" are related structures that are not strictly binary.

34. Such structures are also known as "discrimination trees" (Clark 2003, 167).

35. Certain passages allow the *coordination* (by "fusion") of two notes of low structural importance into a single event (see Lerdahl and Jackendoff 1983, 153–154).

36. Hatten (2004, 3) claims that "tree hierarchies (as developed by Lerdahl and Jackendoff 1983) imply modes of cognitive processing that demand constant evaluations (yes/no, more/less) at every node—hardly an efficient model to explain the mind's constant leaps to coherent structures and meanings. It would be like trying to claim that the tongue needed to complete a detailed analysis of ingredients before concluding that something tasted good—whereas the senses synthesize on a routine basis." These comments confuse hedonic response with categorization and identification, and generally underestimate the complexity of the cognitive processing underlying the extraction of information from informationally structured objects. The objects of taste, recall from chapter 2, are not informationally structured in the Gibsonian sense.

37. Robert McCauley (pers. comm.) points out that mental modules are often quite *un*reliable.

38. Signification in Saussurian linguistics, it should be noted, differs fundamentally from signification in philosophical semiotic, where it usually (though not invariably) concerns the meaning of nonsymbolic signs and signals, both natural and conventional. See Clarke 1987 and Langer 1957.

39. Kittay (1992) argues that semantic field theory supports a local, as opposed to a global holism.

40. Think of the sentence "The apple is red" as a linear string in which "apple" and "red" contrast horizontally by virtue of their grammatical roles. "Pear" and "banana" may be placed vertically under "apple" as alternatives, while "yellow" and "green" may be placed vertically under "red."

41. Cf. also Ross 1992 (165n50): "Internal [semantic field] relationships of opposition, affinity, dominance, indifference, etc. are like the internal harmonic relationships *within* a composition among the 'notes' in diatonic music."

42. Cf. Levinson 1997 (159n1): "Aural cogency is manifestly not the same as visual coherence, nor is it the same as logical consistency, yet neither is it being such that no other continuation is thinkable."

43. Jenefer Robinson, to whose views we shall return in chapter 5, forcefully makes this point (Robinson 1994). See also Jones et al. 1980.

44. Agawu (1991) endorses a similar notion under the rubric of "introversive semiosis."

45. Cf. Saussure 1915/1959 (67): "I call the combination of a concept and a sound-image a sign, but in current usage the term designates only a sound-image, a word, for example (*arbor*, etc.)....Ambiguity would disappear if the three notions here were designated by three names, each suggesting and opposing the others. I propose to retain the word *sign* [*signe*] to designate the whole and to replace concept and sound-image respectively by *signified* [*signifé*] and *signifier* [*significant*]...." Kittay (1992, 237), I believe, misinterprets Saussure on this point: "Saussure distinguished value from signification. Signification is roughly what we speak of as the denotation of a term."

46. One further distinction: some semioticians, among whom I include myself, distinguish denotation from signification. For us, denotation requires a logical subject, which is lacking in nonpropositional representations (see Clarke 1987).

47. Cf. Davies 1994 (11): "In Coker's theory, sign and signified tend to collapse into each other...; a successful semiotic theory should be able to maintain their distinctness. Nowhere is this fault more obvious than in Coker's account of congeneric reference in music. A theme does not refer to itself simply because we recognize it when it recurs. That one musical gesture might lead us to think of another does not show that the first *says* anything about the second...."

48. Something similar seems to occur in the third section of the *Grosse Fuge*, where Beethoven quotes the principal motifs of the first two sections.

49. Elgin (1983, 135–136) likens musical quotation to onomatopoeia, the use of a word to denote a sound that is similar to the sound of the word. In the case of onomatopoeia, I would say, linguistic denotational function overlies an older musilinguistic modeling function.

50. Martha Nussbaum (personal communication) argues that Brahms both uses *and* mentions the student songs, given the occasion for which the Overture was composed: his receipt of an honorary doctorate from the University of Breslau. To my mind, this "quotation" is not *musical*, but *circumstantial*, like Beethoven's use of Russian themes in the Quartets Op. 59, Nos. 1 and 2 to compliment Count Rasoumovsky.

51. Gates (1988) and Zbikowski (2002) trace this idea to Mikhail Bakhtin.

52. "A piece of music is a constant metamorphosis of given material.... These *are* the meanings of music. And that is as close as I can come to a definition of musical semantics" (Bernstein 1976, 153).

53. Cf. Dretske 1981a (373): "we use contrastive focusing to indicate the range of relevant alternatives.... Someone claiming to know that Clyde *sold* his typewriter to Alex is not (necessarily) claiming the same thing as one who claims to know that Clyde sold his typewriter to *Alex*. The sentence we use to express what they know is the same, of course, but they reflect and are designed to reflect, different relevancy sets." Notice how language exploits prosodic effects to convey these contrasts.

54. Contrary to the opinions of those who have looked down on it, the *Pastoral* Symphony is not, for Beethoven, an anomalous or musically "weak" work because of its explicit program.

55. To Liszt (Cooke, n.d.) the movement suggested Orpheus taming the beasts.

56. Unfashionable, but not unprecedented. Cf. Ferguson 1973 (122): "The purist conceives [musical ideas] to arise and to be formed wholly within that region of the mind (fictitious to the psychologist) which is set apart from the rest of consciousness for musical conception and contemplation. We are contending that there is no such region, but that musical concepts are palpably relatable to large areas of non-musical experience"; (88): "[M]usic, like all the others, is thus a representative art." Cf. also Callen 1982 (387): "if one wants to think of hearing the expression in music as involving a conceptualization that might serve as a minimal program (not even as specific as Beethoven's [in the *Pastoral* Symphony]), so be it. But if the adequate apprehension of musical expression requires such conceptualization, as it often must, then to the extent that all music has such a character, and not just music standardly called program music, all music may be, even should be, heard programmatically." Also Walton 1997 (58): "Distinguishing 'absolute' music

from program music is not nearly as easy as one might expect. There is no sharp line between explicit and subtle program music, or between subtle program music and music that is unprogrammatic as it gets, and one can be puzzled about the location even of fuzzy lines."

57. Although I have enlisted Lakoff and Johnson as allies, I wish to sound a note of skepticism concerning their "experientialism" and the seemingly antirealist conclusions they draw from it, for they seem to me to commit a version of the genetic fallacy. From the unexceptionable claim that human *understanding* of abstract concepts, including the concepts of basic science, depends on human embodiment because human brains evolved from simple motor control systems, it does not follow that there is anything subjective or observer relative about the facts *described by* the statements of these sciences. Even if it is true (and this is controversial) that the physical theories we construct would be incomprehensible to us without the aid of nonpropositional models, there is no reason to think that we project the molecular structure of water onto water, as we project fronts and backs onto rocks and trees.

58. Cf. Goodman 1976 (260n9): "Music can inform perception not only of other sounds but also of the rhythms and patterns of what we see. Such cross-transference of structural properties seems to me a basic and important aspect of learning, not merely a matter for novel experimentation by composers, dancers, and painters."

59. Backpropagation is a directed learning regime because each change of connection weights during each training epoch is completely under the control of the human trainer. The connection weights between the layers of nodes of the network are gradually modified until the desired output results from a given input. There are, however, connectionist learning regimes that are to some degree self-directed. For an accessible account of backpropagation, see Churchland 1995 (42–45).

60. See figure 3.14 and related text for explanation of the fourfold grouping of input units.

61. A glance at the training set in example 3.4 shows that the smallest metrical value in different melodies could range from the sixteenth-note to the quarter-note.

62. I have simplified the account in the following way: Large et al. (1999) produced reconstructions using just the lower-level network (with encoding/decoding functions) as well as reconstructions using both lower- and upper-level modules together. Not surprisingly, accuracy of detail in the reconstructions was greater in the lower-level reconstructions.

63. The intriguing (but apparently apocryphal) story of Mozart's instantaneous mental grasp of a complete musical work nothwithstanding (see Kivy 1983c, 189–199).

64. Cf. Lerdahl and Jackendoff 1983 (310): "Many principles of pragmatics appear to have the nature of preference rules," and the reference to Grice that immediately follows. As we have seen, most of the rules of the generative theory of tonal music are preference rules, and not well-formedness rules.

65. Cf. Johnson-Laird 1983 (381): "Once models have been introduced as representations of discourse, they appear to be equally plausible candidates for representing the large-scale structure of discourse—the skeletal framework of events that corresponds to the 'plot' of a narrative, the 'argument' of a non-fiction work, etc."

66. This is a point of partial agreement with Levinson's "qualified concatenationism," which holds that the core of musical experience consists of sequences of episodes of "quasi-hearing," each such episode being the "vivid apprehension of a musical unit" (1997, 15). For Levinson, these units are more extended in time than perceptual instants, but remain quite small, paradigmatically no longer than a standard four-to-eight-measure phrase (87). Each instance of quasi-hearing includes three components: actual hearing, vivid remembering, and vivid anticipation. Apprehension of larger-scale musical structures, says Levinson, is an intellectual function that can enhance musical experience but is not necessary or even central to it.

I see Levinson's view as basically correct but overstated, for he underestimates the music-theoretically untrained listener's grasp of structures more extended than his units of quasi-hearing. There seem to be two reasons for this underestimation. First, although he emphasizes the contrast between the seriality of aural perception and the spatiality of visual perception, Levinson ignores haptic perception and any analogy between musical hearing and tactual exploration. Haptic perception, as I argued in chapter 2, is serial, but it is also spatial. Second, Levinson seems to want to limit the *conscious apprehension* of larger musical structures to cases of "contemplative," intellectual *recognition under a description*, that is, with the deployment of propositional representations. Still, the larger "structuring of the piece" is somehow "absorbed and retained unconsciously by the attentive listener" who lacks appropriate music-theoretical conceptual resources (105). The retention of larger structures may then have causal effects on such a listener (121), but these structures cannot, for that listener, be intentional objects of awareness. How this larger structuring of the piece is "absorbed" Levinson does not say. I maintain that some structures larger than units of quasi-hearing are represented nonconceptually.

67. Zbikowski (2002) considers two versions of metaphysical hierarchy, the Neoplatonic Great Chain of Being and the seventeenth-century compositional atomistic hierarchy, where indivisible atoms make up wholes, these wholes make up larger wholes, and so on. We shall take up related themes in chapter 6.

68. There are no entries for emotion, arousal, or affective response in Zbikowski's index.

Chapter 4

1. This chapter is a revised and expanded version of Nussbaum 2003b.

2. Wolterstorff (1974) remains uncommitted concerning the question of whether all *instances* of a musical work must be *performances*, that is, products of intentional action on the part of a performer. Ruth Lorand (2000, 139) claims that not all performances of musical works are *interpretations*. One may hum a tune to remind someone of it; a musician practicing a piece may play all the way through the score in the process of learning it. (But are these *performances*?) For the sake of present discussion I shall assume that instances are performances and that performances are (tokens of) interpretations.

3. *The grizzly* growls, and so do properly formed grizzlies, but not in the same sense: *The grizzly* produces no longitudinal atmospheric compression waves (128), but properly formed grizzlies do. Similarly, both the *Prelude* to Wagner's *Tristan und Isolde* and properly formed instances of it begin with the A below middle C in the cellos (example 4.3). But the A in the work, as opposed to

Example 4.3

Wagner, *Prelude* to *Tristan und Isolde*.

the A in a properly formed performance, is not a waveform acoustic phenomenon exhibiting a periodic frequency of approximately 220 Hz.

4. But cf. Gould 2002 (10).

5. Hull 1977; Ridley 1989; Rosenberg 1985; Sober 1984.

6. See Williams 1970. "Darwinian Clan," "Darwinian Subclan," "Darwinian Subcland" are technical terms introduced by Williams in her formal axiomatization of the theory of natural selection. A Clan is a set of biological entities and all the descendants of that set, and a Subclan is one or more branches of a Clan. Whereas the size of both Clans and Subclans remain relatively constant because of environmental limitations of space and resources, a Subcland is the Subclan of a Subclan that may expand, because of the differential fitness of its members, so as to take over the entire Subclan of which it is a part (see also Rosenberg 1985, 142).

7. See, e.g., Hull 1986; see also Rosenberg 1985 (213–216).

8. Cf. Rosenberg 1985 (205): "Because, according to the theory of natural selection, species evolve, they should not be treated as classes whose members satisfy some fixed set of conditions—not even a vague cluster of them—but should be treated as lineages, lines of descent, strings of imperfect copies of predecessors, among whom there may not even be the manifestation of central and distinctive, let alone necessary and sufficient common properties"; Sober (1984, 339): "it strikes me that there is no characteristic of an offspring that in itself is necessary or sufficient for its being in the same species as its parents. The reason is that species determination is retrospective."

9. If A and B have certain properties in common and B inherits these properties causally from A, then the properties in question are reproductively established characters (19–20).

10. Sharpe actually identifies interpretations of works, not the works themselves, as musical types, a view criticized by Kivy (1983a). As we shall see, construing musical performances as REFs can do justice to both positions.

11. Davies (2001, 38, 40) treats "abstract particular" and "abstract individual" as equivalent expressions. I counsel against this. A particular is normally an entity that cannot be either instanced or repeated. An individual, on the other hand, is any object of first-order quantification. It cannot be instanced; but it can be repeated. Nominalists, e.g., Goodman, have enlisted abstract individuals to do the duty of universals. A specific shade of color considered as an abstract individual is not multiply instanced, but multiply repeated.

12. Simons (1982) argues that types are exemplified patterns rather than classes of similar tokens. To the extent patterns are considered to be reproductively established characters, this view would be consistent with Millikan's conception of REFs. The REF interpretation of the type–token distinction I recommend is close to Hull's "evolutionary sense of 'term-type'" (1986, 233).

13. Scruton 1997 (104).

14. This includes the first performance of the score, even if it is the only performance the score ever receives. In this case, there is production of a single token, but no reproduction. Still, there is likely to be a REF of mental tokenings by the composer.

15. The printed copies constitute a higher-order REF because they are copies of the master template, not of earlier printed copies.

16. It is important to be clear about the different sorts of variation in play. There are three varieties of genetic mutation: (1) genome mutations, resulting from the missegregation of a chromosome pair during meiosis, which occur at a rate of 1 to every 25 to 50 meiotic cell divisions; (2) chromosome mutations, alterations of the structure of individual chromosomes, which occur at a rate of one rearrangement per 1,700 cell divisions; and (3) gene mutations, which include base-pair substitutions, insertions, and deletions. Although the first two varieties are associated with certain genetic diseases in humans (Downs syndrome and some cancers are due to genome mutations), they do not produce mutations that are significant for natural selection because they are rarely carried over from one generation to the next. It is the *gene* mutations in germline cells that have phenotypic effects that are the significant ones, for they are perpetuated across generations. In humans, the rate of replication error per base pair is, after replication error checking, a very low 1 error in 10,000,000,000 replications per base pair per cell division. Because genes vary in size (number of base pairs) and because every gamete (sex cell) is the ultimate product of numerous *mitotic* cell divisions, the rate of replication error at individual loci on the human chromosome is significantly higher: it ranges from 1 in 10,000 to 1 in 1,000,000 per locus per reproductive generation. See Nussbaum et al. 2001 (80–81).

17. So-called because these proper functions are derived from the neural mechanisms whose direct proper function it is to produce the representations. Considered as a first-order REF of tokens copied from other tokens, however, tokens of declarative sentences also have direct proper functions.

18. Precedent for the use of this expression can be found in Durham 1991 (360n66).

19. There are, however, cases of genetic adaptation to cultural environments. Durham (1991, 228ff) gives an example of a genetically based phenotypic trait that constitutes such an adaptation, the increased lactose absorption in the small intestine of members of populations engaging in dairying and milk use over extended periods of time.

20. Cf. Lock and Peters 1999b (386): "[T]he apparent course of modern cognitive economy need bear no straightforward relation to that of evolution, since in this case there is little reason to suppose cognitive development and the elaboration of socio-cultural systems are homologously motivated." Durham (1991, 452ff) holds that although the proximate selective force of cultural evolution is in some cases human preference, both conscious and unconscious, and not natural selection, this "secondary value system" remains responsive to the "primary value system," the human emotional/motivational system that is a product of natural selection, and that as a consequence, cultural practices that subvert biological purposes tend to be eliminated, either by choice or by group extinction. I submit that with regard to the biological adaptiveness of empirical science, a cultural artifact in existence for less than five hundred years, the jury is still out. Cf. McCauley 2000 on this issue.

21. Personal communication. In recent times Millikan has modified her view: "Beethoven's Fifth Symphony has many properties that are unlikely to vary from performance to performance" (2000, 27).

22. See Davies 2001 (ch. 7) for a subtle discussion of the differences between live and recorded performances of Western art music.

23. Dennett (1995, 356–360) gives this problem some attention.

24. Hull (1982, 277) points out that "most sexual species consist of only two sexes, but some have a half a dozen or so mating types." He goes on to suggest that "conceptual evolution has as many mating types as operative scientists." This analogy is rather bold, but perhaps not indefensible. A mating type is a subpopulation of individuals within a species that can mate, or exchange genetic material, with other members of the species. Certain fungi have tens of thousands of different mating types (Ridley 1993, 86–87). Unlike humans and most plants and animals, these organisms do not exchange genetic material by cellular fusion. Rather, they do so by "conjugation," via a pipe that forms between two cells. For evolutionary reasons that are quite complicated, almost all organisms that exchange genetic material by fusion are limited to two sexes. An exception is a variety of slime-mold with thirteen mating types (Ridley 1993, 102). The genotype of any newly formed slime-mold cell of this variety will have only two immediate ascendants, namely the genotypes of two of the thirteen mating types, though not just any two (see Ridley 1993 for details). But the genotype of the multicellular organism itself, however that may be defined, will have many.

25. Moreover, Sperber (1996) refers only to Williams's 1966 book *Adaptation and Natural Selection*.

26. Cf. Gould 2002 (641): "Williams' epochal book of 1966 set the intellectual basis for gene selectionism, and may justly be called the founding document for this ultimate version of Darwinian reductionism. But by 1992, Williams had realized that interactors, and not replicators, constituted units of selection, or causal agents in the usual sense of the term—and that hierarchy must hold because no level of interaction can be deemed exclusive, or even primary."

27. See also Durham 1991 (428): "In principle, of course, the potential exists for natural selection to operate at *any* level in the organizational hierarchy of life where there are variable, reproducing entities."

28. Notice that Durham's version of coevolution differs from Hull's in one important respect. For Durham, both systems of replicators, genetic and cultural, heterocatalyze the same interactors, the organisms, with each replicator system contributing to phenotypic expression: "genetic and cultural change...stand in symmetrical, 'instructive' relationship to human phenotypes" (1991, 457). Durham in fact recognizes five varieties of coevolution, two of which involve direct interaction between genes and culture and three that do not. Culture may affect the genes (as in the dairying example) or genes may affect culture (as in the evolution of color terms). Culture may also affect the phenotype nongenetically (through the secondary preference system) in an adaptively positive way (incest taboos), an adaptively neutral way (culturally relative food preferences), or in an adaptively negative way (disease-transmitting cannibalism). Although Durham, like Gould, recognizes units of selection at multiple biological levels, his double inheritance system approach seems to require that the analogy between memes and genes be paramount.

29. Comments from Stephen Hiltz and Robert McCauley helped clarify this issue for me.

30. Davies (2001, 180) holds that for simultaneous performance of two works, the "works in question must have an independent existence but be historically related." In this case, the second condition would not be fulfilled.

31. Davies (2001, 167) comes to a similar conclusion: "Despite its malformedness, a performance with errors instances the work at least because it possesses the same causal pedigree as correct performances."

32. See Ridley 1986. In his discussion of pheneticist metrics Ridley speaks generally of the distance between *species*, not *organisms*. But he is clear that these similarity measurements are to apply to biological taxa at any Linnaean level, as well as to the individual organisms themselves (36).

33. See Ridley 1986 (36–41) for further details.

34. Cf. Hull 1978 (353): "Right now all specimens of *Cygnus olor* are white. No doubt the type specimen of this species of swan is also white. However, if a black variety were to arise, *Cygnus olor* would not on that account become a new species. Even if this variety were to become predominant, this species would remain the same species and the white type specimen would remain the type specimen. The species description would change but that is all. Organisms are not included in the same species *because* they are similar to the type specimen or to each other but *because* they are part of the same chunk of the genealogical nexus."

35. Leif Inge's "9 Beet Stretch," a digitally temporally elongated version of Beethoven's Ninth Symphony lasting twenty-four hours, I hope you will agree, is not, despite its notational correctness, a recorded performance of Beethoven's work, but a new work based on that work. Counting Beethoven's metronome markings as notational will not help, since many genuine performances deviate from them.

36. Goehr (1992, chapter 7) argues that because of composition and performance practices common before 1800, our grip on the identity conditions even of much scored music is more tenuous than we might think.

37. Cf. Hull 1986. Gould (2002) characteristically injects a note of complexity into this "poster-child" example of evolutionary analogy: convergence at one level, constraint due to homologous developmental pathways at another. Although the close similarities in adult anatomy between single-lens cephalopod and vertebrate eyes are primarily due to convergence (1,128), there is evidence that all eye development even across phyla may be triggered by a set of "master control genes." Versions of these genes in nonvertebrates are homologous to mammalian *Pax* genes, "most notably the *Pax*-6" (1,123). *Pax*-6 genes from mice expressed in flies have been shown to be capable of inducing the formation of normal arthropod eyes (1,124).

38. Scott Cantrell, Dallas Morning News Classical Music Critic, August 27, 2006.

39. Incidentally, Davies (2001, 230) errs when he claims in the context of this discussion that Beethoven's student Ferdinand Ries received (actually *almost* received) a box on the ear for taking as a miscue the F major entrance of the first horn in bar 408 of the first movement of the *Eroica*. This entrance is the smoothly achieved result of a carefully prepared modulation. It was Ries's

comment concerning the unexpected E-flat major entrance of the second horn in bar 394, anticipating the recapitulation by four bars, which motivated that (threatened) fillip of annoyance.

40. Wagner's description.

41. The twenty-bar cello and bass *ostinato* in the *Finale* is alleged to have led Weber to declare Beethoven "ripe for the madhouse."

42. On this issue cf. Gould 2002 (8).

43. Ironically, Millikan seems in her latest major publication (2004) to have largely abandoned REF talk in favor of meme talk. I think this is unfortunate, for the REF idea is clearer, more flexible, and theoretically more powerful.

44. Robert McCauley (pers. comm.) made this objection, though the following example is not his.

45. Kivy (1983a, 41ff) doubts that it is all that entrenched, or at least that it has been in all times and places.

46. This should not be taken as an endorsement of mathematical Platonism.

47. An axiomatic system is finitary just in case it has a finite or a denumerable alphabet of symbols, well-formed formulas only finitely long, and rules of inference that use only finitely many premises.

48. Cf. Kripke 1971 (79): "Some things, perhaps mathematical entities such as the positive integers, if they exist at all, necessarily exist."

49. Kivy (1983a, 46) offers the following example: "I am told, in a recent issue of *Science News*, that the existence of 'the sporadic Group F1' requires a proof exceeding 5,000 pages in length. If logical space, or Platonic heaven, has room for that, surely it can find a niche for Beethoven's Ninth, or an itty bitty Wagner opera." But this is to miss the point entirely. It is not size, complexity, or the bounds of "logical space" that count against musical Platonism. It is the lack in musical organization of the necessary relations characteristic of deductive proof.

50. Numbers, for example, can be defined as sets of sets of unspecified elements. The natural number 0 may be defined in the Fregean manner as the set that contains the null set as its sole member. All the positive integers may then be defined using sets of unspecified elements, sets of these sets, and the successor function. The successor of any natural number is the set of sets that would become that natural number if a single member of each of the successor's constituent sets were removed. 1 is the successor of 0 because the set of singletons would revert to the set containing the null set if the lone member of each singleton were to be removed. The same strategy yields 2 (the set of all duples) as the successor of 1, 3 (the set of all triples) as the successor of 2, and so on. Zermelo and von Neumann later supplied alternative set-theoretical definitions of the natural numbers, but all three exploit the idea of sets of sets. Using Zermelo's version, which identifies 0 directly with the null set, 1 with the set containing the null set, 2 with the set containing the set containing the null set, etc., Quine (1969b, 83ff) proves various arithmetic theorems, including the Peano postulates. Cf. Quine 1982 (300): "One can go on to define the ratios, the irrational

numbers, the imaginary numbers, functions, indeed the whole apparatus of classical mathematics, without exceeding the frugal notation of set theory."

51. See Lewis 1986 (92ff).

52. Unlike mathematical objects, water is not a candidate for necessary existence. To say that water is necessarily hydrogen hydroxide is to say that this claim, *if true*, is necessarily true; and it is to say that in any possible world in which water does exist, it is necessarily hydrogen hydroxide.

53. Cf. Currie and Ravenscroft 2002 (9): "if we can place ourselves, in imagination, in situations other than our own, current situation, our capacity to engage with what is merely possible—and hence to make the possible actual—is greatly enhanced."

54. In order to keep set theory "pure" and noncommittal regarding the existence of individuals (and also for certain technical reasons), Quine (1969b, 31–32) treats individuals and their unit classes as equivalent:

none of the utility of class theory is impaired by counting an individual, its unit class, the unit class of that unit class, and so on, as one and the same thing. True, we are well advised now to adjust our terminology to the extent of ceasing to explain "individual" as "nonclass"; let us take to saying that what constitutes them individuals is not inclassitude, but identity with their unit classes (or, what comes to the same thing, identity with their sole members). . . . Everything comes to count as a class; still, individuals remain marked off from other classes in being their own sole members. . . . Still, if one wants to apply set theory outside pure mathematics, he may want any manner of odd things as members of his classes.

55. This objection is due to Denny Bradshaw.

56. Cf. Russell 1912/1959 (103): "*All* a priori *knowledge deals exclusively with the relations of universals*" (emphasis original).

57. Dennett (1995, 129) distinguishes between "deep" forced moves, those dictated by the laws of physics, mathematics, and logic, and "shallow" ones, those that are forced because, for historical reasons, there happens only to be one way of doing a certain thing at a particular historical juncture. In general, when a situation dictates a forced move, the language of discovery is appropriate.

58. If there had been only one way, then Edison's invention would not be a Good Trick, but a "shallow" forced move in design space.

59. Thanks to Kyle Stanford for bringing this point to my attention. Because of their relative accessibility in design space, however, it seems right to say that new species are invented, and not created by natural design, despite the fact that a species, once extinct, cannot be reconstituted.

60. Cf. Dennett 1995 (108): "Suppose that each book is 500 pages long, and each page consists of 40 lines of 50 spaces, so there are two thousand character-spaces per page. Each space is either blank, or has a character printed on it, chosen from a set of 100 (the upper- and lower-case letters of English and other European languages, plus the blank and punctuation marks). . . . Five hundred pages times 2,000 characters [i.e., character-spaces] per page gives 1,000,000 character-spaces per book." Dennett's formula seems counterintuitive until you try it with manageable numbers whose combinatorial possibilities can be exhaustively checked by hand using a brute procedure. How many possible "books" are there consisting of only one page, each page containing only four

character-spaces, and using only two characters, say the blank and one other? Two to the fourth power, or exactly sixteen. How many one-page books with five character spaces? Two to the fifth power, or thirty-two.

61. This is the figure given by Dennett (1995, 111). It is accurate to say that the human haploid genome consists of 3×10 to the 9th base pairs, with the diploid genome consisting of twice that number. Dennett, however, tells us that the human genome consists of 3×10 to the 9th *nucleotides*. Since each base pair contains two nucleotides, this number is either 6×10 to the 9th or 12×10 to the 9th, depending on whether we are referring to the haploid or the diploid genome.

62. Drawing attention to the issue of how the expression "*Tristan* chord" is written may, I fear, seem the height of pedantry. But it is an issue of some importance. Writing the expression without italics, as is Ridley's (1995) practice, suggests coextensionality with the music-theoretic expression "half-diminished seventh chord." Written with italics, as I have rendered it, it is not coextensional with the music-theoretic expression, and refers only to tokens of the chord in Wagner's *Prelude* and copies of it.

63. The distinction between "cranes" and "skyhooks" is a central metaphor of Dennett (1995). The idea is that although a range of highly organized phenomena in the natural world, including the products of organic design and of human creativity, seem to require "skyhooks," that is, nonnatural "mind-first" productive powers, Darwin has shown us how some such phenomena have been in fact and how others can be in principle built up incrementally and recursively by way of bottom-up undirected mechanistic processes ("cranes" and "cascading" series of cranes), which include natural-selectionist processes. Hence the "dangerousness" of Darwin's idea of natural selection: it works as a universal intellectual acid by systematically rendering skyhooks explanatorily otiose.

Chapter 5

1. Prinz (2004, 18–19) terms this the "problem of parts": how are these features to be theoretically unified? Theories that attempt to combine a variety of features by regarding them as inseparable functional aspects or separable components of a whole, or that single out some features as causal preconditions of others, are "encompassing theories." Such theories then face a complementary "problem of plenty." Some encompassing theories attempt to solve the problem of plenty by privileging one or more features as central.

2. Although Nussbaum's neo-Stoic account construes emotions as evaluative judgments, these "judgments" need not be propositional, but may include episodes of nonpropositional seeing-as, which allies her account with perceptual theories. Her main concern is to insist that emotions are cognitive and intentional, a point with which I agree. However, she also injects a metarepresentational, self-evaluative aspect into emotional perception, which I believe oversophisticates at least some emotions: "Chrysippus plausibly said that grief (along with other emotions) contains not only the judgment that an important event has gone, but that *it is right* to be upset about that: it makes a truth-claim about its own evaluations" (2001, 47). See Prinz 2004 (36).

3. According to Prinz's (2004) helpful taxonomy, Frijda's is an encompassing multifunction hybrid theory that privileges action tendencies. Hybrid theories combine cognitive and somatic elements. Encompassing multifunction theories include a variety of phenomena, including appraisal, arousal, motivation, and action tendency, within the emotion process as inseparable integrated functional aspects of a whole.

4. Prinz (2004, 173–174) construes valences as positive and negative "inner reinforcers," or "valence markers." They are inner "labels" that are associated with representations of stimuli. Once so associated, valence markers, depending on their sign, will tend to increase or decrease the probability of occurrence of future behaviors.

5. Cf. Nussbaum 2001 (45): "When I grieve, I do not first of all coolly embrace the proposition [or the perceptual content], 'My wonderful mother is dead,' and then set about grieving. No, the real full recognition of that terrible event (as many times as I recognize it) *is* the upheaval."

6. Cf. Dretske 1981 (172): "all information-processing systems occupy intentional states of a certain low order." Cf. also Dennett's well-known discussions of intentional systems and grades of intentionality (1987, 1995, 1996).

7. Standard feed-forward and recurrent connectionist networks are to be distinguished from Boltzmann architectures, which incorporate a cognitive temperature control parameter and therefore display some functional analogies to emotional arousal in organic brains. See my 2003c; see also Churchland and Sejnowski 1993; Hofstadter 1985; Levine 1991; Quinlan 1991.

8. "Events in the world are signaled as being good or bad, those we should attempt to attain or avoid, those associated with life and those associated with death ... that most fundamental of dichotomies is the most direct message that we can get from our genes as to what to do" (Plotkin 1993, 208). "Affect is the first link in the evolution of complex adaptive functions that eventually differentiated animals from plants. And unlike language or cognition, affective responsiveness is universal among the animal species" (Zajonc 1980, 156).

9. Prinz (2004, 175) highlights Solomon's results: "When a negative emotion kicks in, positively valent emotions automatically activate in response, and vice-versa."

10. Throughout his article, Solomon (1980) treats "motivational," "hedonic," "affective," and "emotional" as more or less equivalent in a rather rough and ready fashion.

11. I deny that the body is normally the intentional object of an emotion, agreeing with Prinz (2004) that if the body can be said to be the object of an emotion at all, it is the emotion's nominal, not real, object. Cf. also Nussbaum 2001 (118–119) in criticism of Damasio: "an awareness of self (and therefore, often, of one's body) is a part of the experience of any emotion. It does not follow from this that the emotion's [intentional] object is the body: the object is the goal or person or thing, whatever it is, to which the person is attending." I would, however, reverse Nussbaum's apparent order of dependence between self and body in emotion, saying instead that "an awareness of one's body (and therefore, often, of one's self), etc."

12. Cf. Lazarus 1991 (116): "Writing from an ecological perspective, Baron and Bordreau ... offer a pleasing metaphor that could help emotion and adaptation theorists grasp the idea of person-

environment relationships more clearly. Using Gibson's (1966, 1979 [1986]) concept of affordances to refer to the instantaneous perceptual recognition by an animal species that a female is receptive, a tree is for cooling off, a field is for grazing, a nipple is for nursing, these authors use a lock and key metaphor...to refer to how a particular person and a particular environment mesh or fit." Shepard, recall from chapter 2, also used the lock and key metaphor to explain his notion of "complementarity," the transformation functions by which internal representations decode the information concerning three-dimensional space encoded in two-dimensional sensory arrays. See Lazarus's reference to Shepard (Lazarus 1991, 154). See also Prinz 2004 (228): "Gibson (1979 [1986]) says that in ordinary perception we perceive the actions afforded by the objects in our surround....Emotions are perceptions of affordances in this sense." Affordances are relational properties *par excellance*. But they are surely experienced as out there in the world, not as subjective states.

13. Martha Nussbaum has suggested (in conversation) that the separation between emotions engaged off-line and on-line in aesthetic contexts is not as sharp or as exclusive as I have claimed. The grief we feel at Cordelia's death definitely occurs off-line. But the devastating emotional impact of this fictional event, she holds, requires that the emotion, or some closely related emotion, occur on-line as well: we must also experience a genuine emotion that concerns our actual status, perhaps sadness concerning the "fragility of goodness" or distress concerning our own vulnerability. For Nussbaum, this is one factor that separates great art, including great musical art, from lesser, but engaging and even gripping, simulational vehicles such as detective stories. I have no desire to deny that great art arouses real emotions as it forces us to reflect on our predicament. Any real distress occasioned by a clarified awareness of one's own vulnerability or even of human vulnerability in general, however, is no longer the simulated, off-line emotion of grief. I would also maintain that great art arouses positive real emotions bound up with the achievement of a certain mastery over suffering that is no longer senseless and meaningless. More on this in the next chapter.

14. Cf. Clark 2004 (463): "proto-objects include in their ranks some merely intentional objects, such as the ones that are perceived as moving objects in episodes of *apparent* motion."

15. Evelyn Glennie, celebrated deaf percussionist, in the film documentary *Touch the Sound*, quoted in the *New York Times*, September 7, 2005.

16. Some of the material in this section has appeared in Nussbaum 2005.

17. See Kivy's "anger at Uncle Charlie" discussion (1990, 148–153). More recently (1993a), Kivy has moderated his position.

18. Cf. Greenspan 1988 (87): "Here, perhaps, I should limit myself to a judgment that my reaction itself amounts to a sign that X is untrustworthy or gives me prima facie reason to think him untrustworthy, leaving unspecified its link to subliminal perceptual cues."

19. Some versions of this list also include contempt, which others regard as a variety of disgust. Others exclude surprise. See Griffiths 1997 (78).

20. It is important to distinguish the input and the output sides of the basic or "primary" emotions, and thereby to avoid the error of assuming that because the affect programs are innate

(pancultural) and because they give rise to stereotypical behaviors (output side), this means that they cannot be engaged by an "acquired" sensitivity to stimuli, i.e., by stimuli that reflect a learning history (input side). Nor does it mean that they cannot be triggered by higher cognitive activity of some kind (cf. Griffiths 1997, 102–106).

21. See Fodor 1983. See also Raffman 1993 for an informed cognitivist take on the role of these input systems in musical processing.

22. See Clynes 1989 for the classic treatment of the emotional qualities of touch.

23. These remarks are confined to performance standards of Western "classical" art music. Other idioms may apply different standards.

24. Lydia Goehr.

25. See Laski's (1968) interesting empirical study of ecstatic experience, including but not limited to mystical religious ecstasy, and the various "triggers" of ecstatic states. In two of the three groups of people she investigated (a group of individuals who answered a questionnaire and a selection of published literary authors) "music was the most frequently named art-trigger." Surprisingly, the third group, which comprised writers who had published accounts of personal religious experience, identified no art-triggers at all (190).

26. Both depend on complex interaction between the sympathetic and parasympathetic divisions of the autonomic nervous system resulting in so-called parasympathetic collapse (see Sargant 1973). We shall return to this topic in chapter 6.

27. Cf. also Schopenhauer's (1844/1966, II, 569) characteristic observation: "But the act by which the will affirms itself and man comes into existence is one of which all in their hearts are ashamed and which they carefully conceal.... A peculiar sadness and remorse follows close on it; yet these are felt most after the consummation of the act for the first time, and generally they are the more distinct, the nobler the character." Still less does musical experience seem comparable to dreaming, as Nussbaum (2001, 265ff) suggests. Musical experience is far too coherent and intensely focused for that and, as we shall see in chapter 6, is more plausibly compared to trance.

28. Cf. Putman 1985 (61): "The space each of us carries around us, the personal bubble as it is sometimes called, is pierced whenever we touch something or another entity touches us.... We feel profoundly annoyed when disturbing loud noise touches us without our permission. We feel invaded in a way analogous to something touching us physically against our will."

29. Cf. Davies 2001 (305): "I am not convinced by this last [Raffman's nuance-property] argument. I accept that people are not capable of 'replaying' a recording, with all its perceptible detail, in memory. The issue, though, is whether they can anticipate what is coming next as they listen to a recording. My experience suggests to me that this is possible. If I know the disc very well, sometime I have an eidetic aural 'picture' of what is about to happen a few milliseconds before it occurs."

30. Robinson (2005, 365) deals with the Meyer paradox by invoking an arousal theory of musical experience, construing initial emotional responses, including those caused by music, as "noncognitive." I shall defer discussion of this account until later in the chapter.

31. Strawson 1959/1963 (146): "It will be useful to have another way of speaking of this feature common to both 'Socrates' and 'is wise' in the remark 'Socrates is wise,' and common to both 'Raleigh' and 'smokes' in the remark 'Raleigh smokes.' Let us say that the expression 'Socrates' ('Raleigh') serves to *introduce* the particular person, Socrates (Raleigh), into the remark, and that the expression 'is wise' ('smokes') serves to *introduce* the quality, wisdom (the habit, smoking) into the remark. Let us say that anything which is introduced, or can be introduced, into a remark by an expression is a *term*."

32. Ibid. (197, emphases in original): "We can always count on arriving, in the end, at some existential proposition, which may indeed contain demonstrative elements, but no *part* of which introduces, or definitely identifies, a particular term, though the proposition *as a whole* may be said to *present* a particular term. (The simplest form of such a proposition is: 'There is just one so-and-so there.')"

33. Clark (2000, 138ff) takes issue with this claim, holding that places can be individuated on the basis of informational tracking alone. I suppose this depends on what level of individuation is in question. I agree with Evans and his followers that a grasp of the identity of places in allocentric space requires more than informational tracking. Clark admits that a bat locates the direction of its targets entirely in egocentric terms (140).

34. As best I can tell, Evans nowhere suggests that the human conceptual system is simply grafted onto an *unmodified* animal informational system; and there are no textual grounds to doubt that he was aware that the function of the human informational system displays considerable plasticity and allows for linguistic top-down effects, despite the modularity allegedly shown by the Müller-Lyer illusion, to which he adverts (1982, 123). McDowell (1996, 64), who sees no use at all for nonconceptual content, seems to have misinterpreted Evans this way: "If we share perception with mere animals, then of course we have something in common with them. Now there is a temptation to think it must be possible to isolate what we have in common with them by stripping off what is special about us, so as to arrive at a residue that we can recognize as what figures in the perceptual lives of mere animals. That is the role that is played in Evans's picture by informational states, with their non-conceptual content." Notice that Evans (1982, 124) claims that we share with animals only two (perception and memory), but not all, operations of the informational system: we, but not they, also acquire information from verbal reports.

35. "Thinking," for Cussins, characterizes the psychological aspect of concept application, "thought" the abstract, logical aspect.

36. Peacocke (1992, 71) dubs the following "Evans's Thesis": "It is partially constitutive of a subject's employing the first-person way of thinking that he is prepared to make noninferential, suitable first-person spatial judgments on the basis of his perceptions when these are taken at face value...."

37. The comprehending listener need not grasp every detail of the musical plan, but he must grasp it to some degree. I shall not attempt to specify to what degree (most likely a fruitless enterprise); but particularly important would be the grasp of metrical structure as well as of *local* grouping, time-span, and prolongation structures.

38. Bermudez (2003, ch. 6) distinguishes three distinct levels of nonlinguistic rationality. The first and lowest level involves merely tropistic behaviors based on evolutionarily designed mechanisms, the second involves the perception of affordances and genuine behavioral choice, and the third involves protoinferences concerning the causal consequences of behavioral choices. The lever-pressing behavior of the operantly conditioned rat will, for example, be extinguished if the reward of food is discontinued. These results, as well as findings concerning tool construction and use by wild chimpanzees, show according to Bermudez that some nonlinguisitc creatures are capable of instrumental protoinferences that go beyond the perception of affordances.

39. Cf. also Crane 1992, Currie and Ravenscroft 2002, and Gunther 2003 for further discussion of nonconceptual content.

40. Russell (1917/1957, 223): "We have acquaintance with sense-data, with many universals, and possibly with ourselves, but not with physical objects or other minds." In the version printed as chapter V in Russell 1912/1959, he includes the immanent objects of introspection and memory (51, 114).

41. This is not Bilgrami's example.

42. Propositions, for McGinn, are "abstract objects." If he means by this rule-constituted abstracta (see chapter 3), I have no objection to this construal. There is also no need to deny that sentence tokens are represented in the head, even if they are not represented as objects of classically computational, i.e., programmable representation level rules (cf. Horgan and Tienson 1996).

43. Robinson also recognizes an intermediate case, which she dubs "suggestion." Here an object may be vaguely "heard in" a piece of music, as we hear the sea in *La Mer*, without the music depicting any particular sea. More on this below, where I shall argue that musical suggestion may arouse emotions off-line as do fictional objects.

44. Robinson (2005) gently mocks this as the "doggy theory" of musical expression.

45. Kant's remark is directed at the question, "What is truth?," a question that is in his view illegitimate because to commit to an answer is implicitly to imply that we already know what truth is (1787/1963, A58/B82).

46. Think of Jack Benny's famous pauses.

47. Cf. Goethe's (and Schelling's) famous remark that architecture is "frozen music."

48. Here are a few equally or perhaps even more challenging material objects to mime, derived from the Milton Bradley charades game "Guesstures": sky, star, and water fountain.

49. Cf. Peacocke 1987 (408n35): "The evidence that those in other cultures are unable to appreciate Western pictures is shaky. . . . There is also evidence that the recognition of objects represented as outline drawings does not require prior instruction or substantial pictorial experience of any kind."

50. Johnson-Laird (1983, 244) seems to suggest that a simple sentence like "The elderly gentleman often walked the streets of the town," if entirely isolated from context of discourse, "gives

rise to a propositional representation" and can be understood without constructing any mental model, even a very minimal one, of its truth conditions. If so, this is a limiting case, for understanding a connected piece of discourse normally requires constructing and constantly updating a mental model: "A principal assumption of the theory I am developing is that the semantics of the mental language maps propositional representations into mental models of real or imaginary worlds: *propositional representations are interpreted with respect to mental models*" (156, emphasis original). Johnson-Laird does present empirical evidence for the psychological reality of propositional representations in addition to mental models: when discourse is indeterminate enough to motivate the construction of conflicting mental models, hearers show a marked tendency to hold the offending linguistic strings verbatim in memory as propositional representations until the conflict can be resolved (160–162). Generally, however:

there is a convention that speakers tend to abide by: they do not deliberately mislead their listeners. In other words, if you construct a mental model on the basis of my discourse, then I am likely to order the information in my description so as to prevent you from going astray. I owe you an account that you can represent in a single model without running into conflict with information that I only subsequently divulge. Of course, no speaker is likely to be able to live up to this principle all the time but nevertheless it is followed on most occasions. A mental model is in essence a representative sample from the set of possible models satisfying the description. (165)

51. An ontological metaphor identifies an object belonging to one ontological category, in this case the category of natural objects, with an object belonging to another, in this case the category of artifacts.

52. I have simplified Cussins's account. For him, the achievement of S/Ojectivity by humans involves a spiraling trajectory relative to two orthogonal axes: a horizontal axis of perspective independence (= high "perspective dependence [PD] ratio") and a vertical axis of conceptual stabilization (= "stabilization of cognitive trails") (see figures 5.1 and 5.2). The perspective dependence ratio is the ratio of an organism's "zone" of wayfinding competence to its entire territory. The

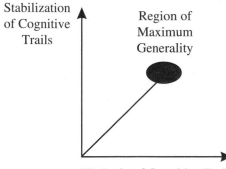

Figure 5.1
Concepts with maximum generality are both highly stabilized and highly perspective independent. (From Cussions 1992, reprinted by permission of Oxford University Press.)

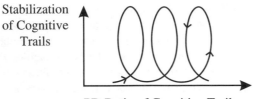

Stabilization
of Cognitive
Trails

PD Ratio of Cognitive Trails

Figure 5.2
Since stabilization and PD ratio are independent parameters, cognitive development spirals through this two-dimensional space, sometimes achieving high stabilization with low PD ratio, at other times achieving high PD ratio and low stabilization. (From Cussins 1992, reprinted by permission of Oxford University Press.)

higher this ratio, the larger the organism's zone of competence relative to its whole territory, the greater its perspective *independence*. A concept, which may abstract from a variety of experiential features as it unifies them, is stabilized to the extent that it is treated as a unified element of meaning that does not, for the moment, have to be renegotiated. Some concepts, like the concept of pain, Cussins claims, are highly stabilized but very perspective-dependent. Others, like the concepts of kinesthetic experience, he claims, are highly perspective-independent but poorly stabilized by names or predicates (we easily produce highly specific bodily postures in ourselves and recognize them in others) (1992, 683).

53. This objection is due to Robert McCauley.

54. Perhaps this is why taking the repeat of the exposition of the *Finale* is so unsatisfactory and, as a consequence, is rarely done, despite the fact that repeating the expositions of sonata movements is now far more common than it once was.

55. Stephen Hiltz suggests that this claim of uniqueness concerning the musical trail to the *Finale* opening might afford the musical Platonist some succor, for, as unique, the trail begins to look like an object of discovery. But, as I argued regarding this very example in chapter 4, the alleged object of discovery could not predate the *creation* by Beethoven of the *Finale* opening. However, because the musical constraints imposed by this particular compositional problem situation are so strong, the case may approach Kivy's species counterpoint example where, as I argued, the musical problem situation and its solution come into existence together.

56. Cf. Clark 2004 (465): "Now feature-placing can give us the wherewithal to locate, track, and count some putative entities, such as the waves in the ocean as they come crashing onto the beach. But waves are still quite a ways from being individuals or 'objective particulars.' Consider: Two waves can fuse; one wave can split into two; 'a' wave has entirely different parts at different times; and if all those parts are arranged in just the same way at a different time, it is a purely verbal question whether we have the same wave again, or one that is qualitatively identical." Notice that discrete stationary elements can produce apparently continuous moving wave effects, as a visible wave travels around a sports stadium when seated spectators sequentially raise their arms.

57. Evans (1982, 75): "we cannot avoid thinking of a thought about an individual object *x*, to the effect that it is *F*, as the exercise of two separate capacities; one being the capacity to think of *x*, which could be equally exercised in thoughts about *x* to the effect that it is *G* or *H*; and the other being a conception of what it is to be *F*, which could be equally exercised in thoughts about other individuals, to the effect they are *F*." See also Cussins 1990 and Peacocke 1992 on the significance of the generality constraint for conceptual content.

58. Evans (1982) calls this the "Idea" of an object, wishing, in Fregean fashion, to regard only predicates as expressive of concepts.

59. Notice that Lerdahl's tonal pitch space differs from physical space in at least three important ways. First, it is not continuous. Second, although it is *metrically* organized, it is not *topologically* organized: one may "move" from one "location" to another without passing through all the intervening "locations." Third, it contains no places that could be occupied *by* a variety of basic particulars. The places are identified *with* the occupants; and the occupants are not particulars at all, but sets (pitch classes) and universals (keys and functional chord kinds).

60. Although this makes Matravers's theory a strong arousal theory, he implies that some versions of the strong arousal theory are stronger than his (1998, 12). But what he means by this is that his version of the arousal theory allows for the possibility of "dry-eyed criticism," i.e., the description of a piece of music as expressive of an emotion by a critic who claims not to have the appropriate feelings. Matravers attempts to account for this in two ways. Either the feeling aroused in the critic is "incipient" but suppressed, while still causally efficacious (201–202); or the critic is able to predict the affective impact of a musical work (on the basis of familiarity with the causal of effects of certain "basic properties" of music, i.e., rhythmic, registral, dynamic ones, on normal listeners), just as a chemist might predict the color of a substance from the "primary properties" of that substance (221).

61. Following Langer (1957), Addis (1999, 72, 80, 109) commits the same error. His account, like mine, is representationalist; but unlike mine, it invokes a mental–physical property dualism. There is also a fallacy, or, depending on how you count, two fallacies lurking at the center of Addis's account. Distinguishing between properties requiring time for their exemplification (T-properties) and properties that do not (N-properties), Addis claims that being-a-sound is the only *physical* T-property that does not require change in order to be exemplified (68). Being-a-birth, for example, is a physical T-property (it could not be exemplified in a timeless world); but its exemplification obviously requires change. Being-triangular does not: it could be exemplified in a timeless world, so it is an N-property. Token states of consciousness also exemplify T-properties without requiring change, but they are not physical (*vide* Addis's property dualism). Because of this alleged "isomorphism" (i.e., the lack of a change requirement) between the physical T-property of being-a-sound and the nonphysical T-property of being-a-state-of-consciousness, music, Addis claims, is uniquely suited to represent emotions, which he construes as states of mind. Unfortunately, Addis's use of "sound" equivocates between sound as a physical phenomenon and sound as the intentional object of aural experience. Being-a-sound, considered as a physical phenomenon, does require change: the ongoing compression and rarefaction of molecules in the medium of sound transfer. Being-a-sound considered as an object of aural experience, on the other hand, arguably does not

require change. But this makes sound (at least in part) experiential, which begs the question concerning its alleged special status as a *physical* phenomenon. Being-an-experience is a mental property. It is important, Addis warns us, "not to identify the property in question with the experience of it" (68). Saltiness, he says, the property of the ham, is not the *experience* of saltiness: it is not *that* taste. Fair enough. But is Addis's sound not *that* sound?

62. Cf. Hardin 1993 (80): "'Is unique green' turns out to be less like 'is water soluble' and more like 'is disgusting' than we might at first have supposed." See my 2003c for a more extended discussion.

63. Cf. McGinn 1989 (184): "Even if having a language confers greater richness on the models available to a creature, the mechanism of content is still essentially model-based—models do all the representational work." See also Pugh 1977 (108): "The great evolutionary advantage of man over animals lies fundamentally in the superior world model that is used by the human decision system.... Although at present we can only guess what levels of sophistication different animals may have in their world model, the existence of a world model appears to be a necessary precondition for the emergence of symbolic speech."

64. Cf. McGinn 1989 (181): "This is not, of course, to say that we cannot explain the meaning of sentences—overt or covert—in terms of associated mental models, pairing sentence and model to confer a semantics on the sentence." Cf. also Sloboda 1985 (58): "The 'meaning' of a sentence for a listener is, roughly, what he adds to his model of the situation being described as a result of hearing the sentence."

65. Cf. McGinn 1989 (195): "Think of your total worldview—your entire system of beliefs—as your overall model of the world, itself made up of a huge number of submodels. This big world-model is a bit like a toy city, composed of a large number of variously connected submodels—of houses, bridges, roads, parks, people, etc."

66. Prinz (2004, 232) terms the emergence of new emotions under the influence of judgments or beliefs "recalibration." "By establishing new calibration files," he says (100), "an embodied appraisal can be said to represent something beyond what it is evolved to represent."

67. Cf. Katz 1989 (243):

Where the object is not set off as an invariant opposite the ego, but rather the ego acts in the environment without sharply differentiating its own efforts, the linguistic expression that depicts the world as the gushing forth of the creative activity of the ego actually appears quite apt. Thus . . . the schizophrenic's form of perception represents a reversion to an earlier stage of phylogenetic development, whose linguistic form for the activity of perception strikes us as inadequate. . . . Normal visual perception is not interweaved with what is experienced. It is different with the sense of touch. . . . Object and subject cannot be imagined at all as separate factors of the tactual impression.

Katz seems to be making two points. First, there is the claim that schizophrenia involves a regression to a phylogenetically more primitive mode of cognition in which mind and world are not sharply differentiated, thereby encouraging a (pleasantly?) delusional view of the world as creative product of the subject rather than as a brute constraint on the subject. But second, he also seems to suggest that unlike vision, touch, even in cognitively normal modern humans, retains a similarly primitive quality of nondifferentiation between subject and object (recall the musical touch effect). I make no endorsement of Katz's eighty-year-old views of schizophrenia, but the observations are still acute. The ideas they contain will prove important for our discussion in the next chapter.

68. Trainor and Schmidt 2003 (321): "Thus, we are free to laugh and cry to music, to feel our heart race, to feel chills, and to hold our breath, and perhaps once again to feel like the infant who is exquisitely tuned to the emotion in its mother's voice."

69. Cf. Davies 1994 (271): "The mirroring feelings awakened in the listener are uncluttered by the motives, desires, and the need to act that are their usual accompaniments. The listener is able to reflect on his feeling as he could not normally do and, thereby, he may come to a new understanding of it."

70. Cf. Sartre 1955 (196): "Thus, in his description of divine freedom, Descartes ends by rejoining and explicating his primary intuition of his own freedom, of which he says that it is 'known without proof and merely by our experience of it' . . . man is the being as a result of whose appearance a world exists." It is significant that Descartes was an extreme apostle of the power of divine fiat. For him, not only could the laws of physical causation have been different, had God willed it so; the principles of mathematics and of logic itself could have been different as well (see Descartes 1644/ 1984, 291). In this, few were willing to follow him. How God could make reasoned, as opposed to utterly capricious, decisions *about* logic *without* logic greatly exercised Descartes's critics. See my 2003a for a fuller account.

71. See my 2003c for further details and bibliographic information.

72. Cf. Trainor and Schmidt 2003 (320): "Despite the fact that, for adults in the modern world, music does not command the same approach/withdrawal reactions as other emotion-laden stimuli, much evidence suggests that music does activate the same cortical, subcortical, and autonomic circuits as other emotions."

73. Cf. Zuckerkandl (1956/1969, 374): "It is true that the musical concept of the external world . . . much more nearly resembles the magical and mythical ideas of primitive or prehistoric peoples than it does the scientific conceptions of modern man."

74. This opposition between the magical and the deterministic will prove to be important when we discuss affinities between musical and religious emotions in the next chapter.

Chapter 6

1. Quoted in Neiman 2002 (89).

2. I argue for the metaphysical point at length in my 2003a. Cf. also Neiman 2002 (84–103) on Hegel.

3. Cf. Steiner 1989 (155): "Thus it may be that only pure mathematics, whose kinship with music so exercised Pythagorean and Platonic meditation, is phenomenally free, 'at liberty,' in the manner of the arts."

4. Possible worlds talk does not require that possible worlds themselves be considered existents in the manner of the modal realist.

5. "Je grösser das Kunstwerk, desto weniger Zufall darf darin sein." Cf. also Meyer 1956 (75): "Though seeming accident is a delight, we believe that real accident is foreign to good art." No doubt there are contemporary Western musical styles to which the comments of Weininger and Meyer apply minimally or not at all; but they surely apply to central cases of the style of musical art under consideration in this book.

6. "Essential" here connotes "aesthetically not dispensable," not "metaphysically necessary." The latter would conflict with the REF account of the identity of musical works offered in chapter 4. Thanks to Stephen Hiltz for bringing this point to my attention.

7. As Davies (2001) repeatedly emphasizes, some scores, e.g., those belonging to the Baroque period, are "thinner" or more skeletal than others, e.g., late Romantic scores.

8. "The drive to seek reason in the world," to unify the *is* and the *ought*, to eliminate the contingent may be, as Neiman suggests (2002, 322), "as deep a drive as any we have."

9. Toward the end of section 6.4 I shall revert briefly to the descriptive-explanatory mode of coevolutionary theorizing.

10. Kant, *Critique of the Power of Judgment* (1793/2000, 5: 402, emphasis mine): "if our understanding were intuitive, it would have no objects except what is actual. Concepts (which pertain merely to the possibility of an object) and sensible intuitions (which merely give us something, without thereby allowing us to cognize it as an object), would *both* disappear."

11. Cf. Rist 1996 (407–408): "Within us [say Plato and Plotinus] is a pearl in the oyster, a pure, uncontaminated part of the self, which we can with effort free of its contaminations derived from empirical life, so that once again we become perfect."

12. Bussanich 1996 (39): "[Plotinus] is convinced that discursive thinking is a weakened form of thought, which is inferior to and relies on intellection (noesis), the immediate, intuitive, and comprehensive understanding that, when we have access to it, provides the most accurate view of the One available to us."

13. Compare Sartre (1955, 195) on Descartes: "As for the difficulty of maintaining freedom in the face of truth, he glimpsed a solution to it in conceiving a creation which is at the same time an act of intellection, as if the thing created by a free decree somehow encounters the freedom that sustains it in being and thereby yields to understanding. In God, willing and intuition are one and the same; the divine consciousness is both constitutive and contemplative."

14. By the late Professor Ivor Leclerc, in conversation. See also Wallis 1995 (173), where he contrasts Hegel's Procline version of Neoplatonism with Schelling's more Plotinian version.

15. Early Christian theologians, e.g., the fourth-century thinker Marius Victorinus, "telescoped" the first two hypostases (the One and Intellect), combining them in the divine mind (see Rist 1996, 402). According to Blumenthal (1996, 100), Plotinus himself occasionally telescoped the second and third hypostases (Intellect and World Soul). Later Neoplatonic thinkers, including

Cusanus and Bruno, telescoped all three hypostases. This tendency to telescope the original Plotinian hypostases seems to have carried through to Kant's conception of the intuitive understanding.

16. Cf. Costa 1996 (360): "When Plotinus tries to explain how an indivisible reality can be a cause, he argues that it does not pass through matter, but 'remains' in itself."

17. Ibid. (362): "Plotinus points out the fact that the transcendence of the One cannot be separated from omnipresence."

18. But compare Guthrie 1993 (37): "From Schleiermacher, James, Otto, and Eliade I take recognition that religious experience seems (but only that it *seems*) direct and unmediated."

19. As a universal claim about worship, this is false. But it may have been true of the varieties of worship with which Goethe was familiar.

20. "These data must, of course," Hinde (1999, 187) is quick to point out, "be seen as specific to the particular society in which they were obtained."

21. Cf. Zuckerkandl (1945/1969, 276): "The step from visual to auditory [i.e., musical] space would be like a step from a static to a fluid medium"; and 289: "Depth in auditory space is only another expression of this 'coming from . . .' that we sense in every tone. It is as if a swimmer in a river felt, in the pressure of the water against his skin, the whole depth of the extent through which its waters are in motion toward him from its source. One and the same sensation makes us experience auditory space as possessing depth and as flowing." Zuckerlandl gets the phenomenology right, but makes no attempt to explain it.

22. Hinde (1999, 190–191) thinks that there is a distinction to be made between the experience of the numinous, which induces feelings of "dependence and awe," and the experience of merging with God or the Absolute, which involves a "feeling of profound peace." But he admits that "such categories may blend or overlap with each other, and many aspects of experience are shared."

23. Kant seems to have been convinced that God and the immortal soul exist. A naturalist would be inclined to regard these objects as imaginary idealizations.

24. Kant 1793/2000 (5:352): "All intuitions that are ascribed to concepts a priori are thus either schemata or symbols, the first of which contain direct, the second indirect presentations of the concept. The first do this demonstratively, the second by means of an analogy (for which empirical intuitions are also employed), in which the power of judgment performs a double task, first applying the concept to the object of sensible intuition, and then, second, applying the mere rule of reflection on that intuition to an entirely different object, of which the first is only the symbol."

25. Cf. the discussion in the last chapter of Mendelssohn's famous pronouncement that the "precision" of musical thought outstrips verbal expression.

26. "Since that summer in Karlsbad I read Goethe every day, that is, when I read at all. He (Goethe) has killed Klopstock for me. You are surprised? And now you laugh? Ah ha! It is because

I have read Klopstock. I carried him about with me for years while walking and also at other times. Well, I did not always understand him, of course. He leaps about so much and he begins at too lofty an elevation. Always *Maestoso*, D-flat major! Isn't it so? But he is great and uplifts the soul nevertheless. When I did not understand him I could sort of guess. If only he did not always want to die! That will come quickly enough. Well, at any rate what he writes always sounds well." Beethoven, in conversation with Friedrich Johann Rochlitz (summer of 1822), quoted in Thayer 1970 (246, 802).

27. Hatten (2004, 258) characterizes B minor as "dysphoric."

28. Cf. Proclus' paraphrase of the Plotinian position: "There are other authorities, however, who have said that since the first principle is cause of all things, notwithstanding its superiority in respect to the Life, to the Intellect and to Being itself, it possesses within itself in some way the causes of all these things unutterably and unimaginably and in the most unified way, and in a way unknowable to us but knowable to itself; and the hidden causes of all things in it are models prior to models, *and the primal entity itself is a whole prior to wholes, not having need of parts*" (quoted by Costa 1996, 377, emphasis mine).

29. Judgment is the mental faculty or "power of the mind" that relates representations of particulars (intuitions) to representations of universals (concepts). Determining judgment places particulars under concepts already in the possession of the mind; reflecting judgment attempts to find the universal exemplified by particulars not yet conceptualized.

30. For Kant, an *efficient* cause need not be a *material* cause. For example, in the ethical works of the 1780s, he understands the rational will as an efficient cause of action: "The rational being counts himself, qua intelligence, as belonging to the intelligible world, and only insofar as he is an efficient cause belonging to the intelligible world does he call his causality a will" (1784/1981, 4: 453).

31. This is not to deny that occasional remarks of other important philosophers, for example, Wittgenstein and Popper, show considerable love and understanding of music.

32. Although Schopenhauer identifies the thing-in-itself with Will, this is still "appearance," albeit freed from the phenomenal forms of space and causality. The form of temporality, however, remains. What the metaphysical reality is apart from all phenomenal forms is unknowable: "the thing-in-itself, which we know most immediately in the will, may have, entirely outside all possible phenomenon [*sic*], determinations, qualities, and modes of existence which for us are absolutely unknowable and incomprehensible" (1844/1966, II, 198).

33. Miller, Galanter, and Pribram (1960, 11): "No doubt it is perfectly obvious to the reader that we have here a modern version of an ancient puzzle. At an earlier date we might have introduced the topic [of plans] directly by announcing that we intended to discuss the will."

34. Cf. Steiner 1989 (227): "The questions : 'What is poetry, music, art?,' 'How can they not be?,' 'How do they act upon us and how do we interpret their action?,' are, ultimately, theological questions."

35. *The Birth of Tragedy* reacts against so-called Socratic "optimism," which Plato presumably shared, but not, as I shall argue, against the Platonic horror of the contingent.

36. Schopenhauer designated Plato, along with Kant, as his two major philosophical influences.

37. These ideas are universals *ante rem*, and not mere conceptual abstractions, which are universals *post rem*. As such, the Schopenhauerian idea is akin to the so-called concrete universal of German idealist philosophy. The distinction itself echoes the Kantian distinction between the analytical and the synthetically universal discussed above. Both versions of the distinction derive from Neoplatonic thought.

38. The four grades are nonliving material objects, plant life, animal life, and human life. This is one example of close alliance with the Neoplatonic doctrine of emanation.

39. This is noted by the translator, Walter Kaufmann.

40. Jerrold Levinson's (1979) expression.

41. See especially the detailed comparison in chapter 4 of the empirical adequacy of the ritual form hypothesis with that of Whitehouse's (2000) ritual frequency hypothesis.

42. Since the publication of the (2002) book, McCauley has abandoned "CPS-agent" in favor of "CI-agent" ("agent possessing counter-intuitive properties") (personal communication).

43. McCauley and Lawson (2002, 166ff) discuss cases in which special agent rituals are frequently performed because of perceived failure to trigger the divine intervention.

44. I am told (Martha Nussbaum, personal communication) that this is not true of all versions of the Eucharist, specifically the Anglican version.

45. If the claim of gustatory effects seems dubious, think of the sulphurous taste produced by volcanic eruptions.

46. Conkey (1999, 292) cautions that these locations might be the result of differential preservation and therefore might lack the intentional significance Pfeiffer and other theorists attribute to them. That is, the surviving paintings might tend to be found at deep locations simply because these locations afforded better protection over time.

47. Pfeiffer's theory, it must be said, is only one among a number of theories of the significance of Upper Paleolithic art, but it is a respected and influential one. See Conkey 1999 for a judicious review of available theories.

48. Updike (2005, 13): "[F]rom almost the start, clumsy as he could be, [Van Gogh] was able to endow landscapes and still lifes with an extra intensity manifesting his belief, as he expressed it in a layman's sermon, that 'God is using the things of everyday life to instruct us in higher things, that our life is a pilgrimage and we are strangers on this earth.'"

49. Formal friends are individuals who stand in a special ritual relationship that allow the performance of certain duties (107).

50. Cf. Dissanayake 2000 (405n7): "In traditional societies, visual forms are rarely created without the intention to use them in structured ceremonies, hence one might even propose that visual arts were initially developed to accent and make more salient the temporal arts in a multimodal event."

51. "Rhythmic dancing and leaping," Sargant (1973, 58) tells us, "are among the principal methods of inducing states of ecstasy in which a man feels taken over by a force or being greater than himself....The most famous of the animal dancers of prehistoric art, the 'great sorcerer' of the Trois Freres cave, wears the hide and antlers of a stag, the mask of an owl, bear-like paws and the tail of a horse. It seems likely that he was both a god and the priest who represented the god, not merely in the sense of impersonating him but in the sense of feeling himself to be the living god walking on earth."

52. For a compelling scholarly argument that it was not, but an argument that remains highly respectful of Nietzsche's prodigious feat of imaginative reconstruction in *The Birth of Tragedy*, see Else 1965.

53. Note that the claim concerns public musical *performance art*, not music as such. Some modes of musical expression almost certainly predate the Upper Paleolithic, having come into existence with the earlier separation of language and music from musilanguage, as argued in chapter 3. I also do not claim that this is the only proper function of Western art music.

54. For a very different but also very speculative story concerning the origins of music, see Dennett 2001, who lays down the following challenge, a challenge I believe I have met: "If you believe that music is *sui generis*, a wonderful, idiosyncratic feature of our species that we prize in spite of the fact that it has *not* been created to enhance our chances of having more offspring, you may well be right—*and if so, there is an evolutionary explanation of how this can be true*. You cannot evade the obligation to explain how such an expensive, time-consuming activity came to flourish in this cruel world, and a Darwinian theory of culture is an ally, not an opponent, in this investigation" (321).

55. "Musik ist der einzig unverkörperte Eingang in eine höhere Welt des Wissens." Quoted in Holl 1966 (8).

56. Benzon (2001), from whom I have learned and whose approach has much in common with my own, emphasizes the unifying effect of music on groups, but does not specifically address the relation between musical and religious emotion. Mithen (2005), whose mastery of the relevant archaeological evidence is second to none, also emphasizes music's unifying effect and does draw attention to the connection between musical and religious emotion; but he does not attempt to explain it in any depth.

57. We find Kant expressing similar sentiments fifteen years later in the *Critique of Pure Reason* (1787/1963, A 850/B 878): "we shall always return to metaphysics as to a beloved one with whom we have had a quarrel."

58. From the same letter: "Although I am absolutely convinced of many things I shall never have the courage to say, I shall never say anything I do not believe" (Zweig 1967).

59. The Platonic provenance of Swedenborg's imagery is evident: "[A]ll things which appear in the spiritual world exist immediately from the sun of heaven, which is the divine love of the Lord; whereas all things which appear from the natural world exist from the same source, but by means of the sun of this world, which is pure fire" (*On the Athanasian Creed*, quoted in the appendix to Kant 1766/1900 [125]). Equally evident are Swedenborg's Neoplatonic commitments: "It is, however, an eternal truth that influx is spiritual, and not physical; that is, it is from the soul, which is spiritual, into the body which is natural, and from the spiritual world into the natural; and further that it is the Divine Being proceeding from Himself. So also He sustains all things by it; and lastly, that sustenation is perpetual creation, as subsistence is perpetual existence" (ibid., 129). His vision is also a theodicy:

The laws of order are called the laws of Divine Providence, and of these the natural mind can have no knowledge, unless it is enlightened. And because man has no knowledge of them, and thus forms his conclusions concerning the Divine Providence from contingencies in the world, and by means of these falls into fallacies and thence into errors, from which he afterwards with difficulty extricates himself, they must therefore be brought to light. But before they are brought to light, it is of importance that it should be known, that the Divine Providence operates in all the several things which belong to man, even in the most minute of them all, for his eternal salvation; his salvation having been the end of the creation both of heaven and earth. (144)

60. Already in the *Dreams of a Spirit Seer* (65) we find Kant claiming that "[t]he moral quality of our actions can, according to the order of nature, never be fully worked out in the bodily life of men, but it can be so worked out in the spirit-world, according to spiritual laws."

61. Cf. Neiman's (2002, 323) peroration: "We experience wonder in the moments when we see the world as it ought to be—an experience so deep that the *ought* melts away. The disappearance of the *ought* in such moments leads some thinkers to describe them as the experience of being freed from human demands and categories. But it is equally the experience that all our demands have been fulfilled."

62. That is, purposive or intentionally determined, not, as in Kant's more narrow conception of the teleological, determined by final causality in accordance with a prior concept.

63. Illusions, assuming they are such, subscribed to by Beethoven, arguably the greatest composer of modern Western instrumental art music ever to have lived: "Musik ist höhere Offenbarung als alle Weisheit und Philosophie [Music is revelation superior to all wisdom and philosophy]" (quoted in Holl 1966, 8).

General Summary and Conclusion

1. Putnam (1995) cites Cora Diamond who cites an unpublished remark of Wittgenstein's as the source of this thought.

References

Addis, L. 1999. *Of Mind and Music*. Ithaca: Cornell University Press.

Agawu, V. K. 1991. Playing with Signs: A Semiotic Interpretation of Classical Music. Princeton: Princeton University Press.

Alperson, P. (ed.). 1974. *What Is Music: An Introduction to the Philosophy of Music*. University Park: The Pennsylvania State University Press.

Alvin, J., and A. Warwick. 1991. *Music Therapy for the Autistic Child*, second edition. Oxford: Oxford University Press.

Arbib, M. A. 1985. "Schemas for the Temporal Organization of Behavior." *Human Neurobiology* 4: 63–72.

Armstrong, K. 1993. *A History of God: The 4,000-Year Quest of Judaism, Christianity, and Islam*. New York: Alfred A. Knopf.

Aunger, R. 2002. *The Electric Meme: A New Theory of How We Think*. New York: Free Press.

Bachrach, J. 1971. "Type and Token and the Identification of the Work of Art." *Philosophy and Phenomenological Research* 31: 415–420.

Barsalou, L. 1992. "Frames, Concepts, and Conceptual Fields." In Lehrer and Kittay 1992, 21–74.

Bechtel, W. 1994. "Natural Deduction in Connectionist Systems." *Synthese* 101: 433–463.

Benzon, W. 2001. *Beethoven's Anvil: Music in Mind and Culture*. New York: Basic Books.

Bermudez, J. L. 2003. *Thinking without Words*. Oxford: Oxford University Press.

Bernstein, L. 1976. *The Unanswered Question: Six Talks at Harvard*. Cambridge, Mass.: Harvard University Press.

Besson, M., and D. Schoen. 2003. "Comparison between Language and Music." In Peretz and Zatorre 2003, 269–293.

Bilgrami, A. 1992. *Belief and Meaning: The Unity and Locality of Content*. Oxford: Blackwell.

Black, M. 1962. *Models and Metaphors: Studies in Language and Philosophy*. Ithaca: Cornell University Press.

Blackmore, S. 1999. *The Meme Machine*. Oxford: Oxford University Press.

Blumenthal, H. 1996. "On Soul and Intellect." In Gerson 1996, 82–104.

Boyer, P. 1994. *The Naturalness of Religious Ideas*. Berkeley: University of California Press.

Boyer, P. 2001. *Religion Explained: The Evolutionary Origins of Religious Thought*. New York: Basic Books.

Braddon-Mitchell, D., and F. Jackson. 1996. *The Philosophy of Mind and Cognition*. Oxford: Blackwell.

Brandom, R. 1994. *Making It Explicit: Reasoning, Representing, and Discursive Commitment*. Cambridge, Mass.: Harvard University Press.

Brandom, R. 1995. "Knowledge and the Social Articulation of the Space of Reasons." In Sosa and Kim 2000, 424–432.

Brandom, R. 1997. "Replies." *Philosophy and Phenomenological Research* 57, 1: 189–204.

Brandom, R. 2000. "Vocabularies of Pragmatism: Synthesizing Naturalism and Historicism." In *Rorty and His Critics*, ed. R. Brandom, 157–183. Oxford: Blackwell.

Brandom, R. 2002. *Tales of the Mighty Dead: Historical Essays in the Metaphysics of Intentionality*. Cambridge, Mass.: Harvard University Press.

Bregman, A. 1981. "Asking the 'What For' Question in Auditory Perception." In Kubovy and Pomerantz 1981, 99–118.

Bremner, J. G. 1999. "Children's Drawings and the Evolution of Art." In Lock and Peters 1999a, 501–519.

Brown, S. 2000. "The 'Musilanguage' Model of Music Evolution." In Wallin, Merker, and Brown 2000, 271–300.

Brown, S., B. Merker, and N. Wallin. 2000. "An Introduction to Evolutionary Musicology." In Wallin, Merker, and Brown 2000, 3–24.

Budd, M. 1985. *Music and the Emotions*. London: Routledge and Kegan Paul.

Bussanich, J. 1996. "Plotinus's Metaphysics of the One." In Gerson 1996, 38–65.

Butts, R. E. 1993. "Kant's Theory of Musical Sound: An Early Exercise in Cognitive Science." *Dialogue: The Canadian Philosophical Review* 32: 3–24.

Callen, D. 1982. "The Sentiment in Musical Sensibility." *Journal of Aesthetics and Art Criticism* 40, 4: 381–393.

Callen, D. 1985. "Moving to Music—for Better Appreciation." *Journal of Aesthetic Education* 19, 3: 36–50.

Chalmers, D. 1996. *The Conscious Mind: In Search of a Fundamental Theory*. Oxford: Oxford University Press.

Chatwin, B. 1987. *The Songlines*. New York: Penguin.

Chomsky, N. 1980. *Rules and Representations*. New York: Columbia University Press.

Chomsky, N. 1986. *Knowledge of Language: Its Nature, Origin, and Use*. New York: Praeger.

Chomsky, N. 1995. *The Minimalist Program*. Cambridge, Mass.: MIT Press.

Churchland, P. M. 1979. *Scientific Realism and the Plasticity of Mind*. Cambridge: Cambridge University Press.

Churchland, P. M. 1989. *A Neurocomputational Perspective: The Nature of Mind and the Structure of Science*. Cambridge, Mass.: Bradford/MIT Press.

Churchland, P. M. 1995. *The Engine of Reason, the Seat of the Soul*. Cambridge, Mass.: Bradford/MIT Press.

Churchland, P. S., and T. Sejnowski. 1993. *The Computational Brain*. Cambridge, Mass.: Bradford/MIT Press.

Clark, Andy. 1989. *Microcognition*. Cambridge, Mass.: Bradford/MIT Press.

Clark, Andy. 1997. *Being There: Putting Mind, Brain, and World Together Again*. Cambridge, Mass.: Bradford/MIT Press.

Clark, Andy. 2003. "Connectionism and Cognitive Flexibility." In Gunther 2003, 165–181.

Clark, Austen. 2000. *A Theory of Sentience*. Oxford: Oxford University Press.

Clark, Austen. 2004. "Feature-placing and Proto-objects." *Philosophical Psychology* 17, 4: 443–469.

Clarke, D. S. 1987. *Principles of Semiotic*. London: Routledge and Kegan Paul.

Clarke, E. 2005. *Ways of Listening: An Ecological Approach to the Perception of Musical Meaning*. Oxford: Oxford University Press.

Clynes, M. 1989. *Sentics: The Touch of the Emotions*, revised edition. Dorset: Prism Press.

Coker, W. 1972. *Music and Meaning*. New York: The Free Press.

Conkey, M. 1999. "A History of the Interpretation of European 'Paleolithic Art': Magic, Mythogram, and Metaphors for Modernity." In Lock and Peters 1999a, 288–350.

Cooke, D. N.d. Record sleeve notes to Beethoven's Fourth Piano Concerto, performed by Claudio Arrau with Alceo Galliera conducting the Philharmonia Orchestra. Angel Records.

Costa, C. 1996. "Plotinus and Later Platonic Philosophers on the Causality of the First Principle." In Gerson 1996, 356–385.

Cox, R. 1985. "Are Musical Works Discovered?" *Journal of Aesthetics and Art Criticism* 43: 367–374.

Craik, K. 1943. *The Nature of Explanation*. Cambridge: Cambridge University Press.

Crane, T. 1992. "The Nonconceptual Content of Experience." In *The Contents of Experience: Essays on Perception*, 137–157. Cambridge: Cambridge University Press.

Cross, I. 2003. "Music, Cognition, Culture, and Evolution." In Peretz and Zatorre 2003, 42–56.

Cummins, R. 1996. *Representations, Targets, and Attitudes*. Cambridge, Mass.: Bradford/MIT Press.

Currie, G. 1995. "Imagination and Simulation: Aesthetics Meets Cognitive Science." In Davies and Stone 1995b, 151–169.

Currie, G. 2004. "The Representational Revolution." *Journal of Aesthetics and Art Criticism* 62, 2: 119–128.

Currie, G., and I. Ravenscroft. 2002. *Recreative Minds: Imagination in Philosophy and Psychology*. Oxford: Clarendon Press.

Cussins, A. 1990. "The Connectionist Construction of Concepts." In *The Philosophy of Artificial Intelligence*, ed. M. Boden, 368–440. Oxford: Oxford University Press.

Cussins, A. 1992. "Content, Embodiment, and Objectivity: The Theory of Cognitive Trails." *Mind* 101, 404: 651–688.

Cussins, A. 2003. "Postscript: Experience, Thought, and Activity." In Gunther 2003, 147–159.

Damasio, A. 1994. *Descartes' Error*. New York: Avon Books.

Damasio, A. 1999. *The Feeling of What Happens*. New York: Harcourt.

Darwin, C. 1871/1962. *The Descent of Man*. New York: Modern Library.

Darwin, C. 1872/1965. *The Expression of Emotion in Man and Animals*. Chicago: University of Chicago Press.

David, E. D., Jr., and P. B. Denes (eds.). 1972. *Human Communication: A Unified View*. New York: McGraw-Hill.

Davies, M., and T. Stone (eds.). 1995a. *Folk Psychology*. Oxford: Blackwell.

Davies, M., and T. Stone (eds.). 1995b. *Mental Simulation*. Oxford: Blackwell.

Davies, S. 1994. *Musical Meaning and Expression*. Ithaca, N.Y.: Cornell University Press.

Davies, S. 2001. *Musical Works and Performances: A Philosophical Exploration*. Oxford: Clarendon Press.

Dawkins, R. 1976. *The Selfish Gene*. Oxford: Oxford University Press.

Dawkins, R. 1982. *The Extended Phenotype: The Gene as the Unit of Selection*. Oxford: W. H. Freeman.

DeBellis, M. 1995. *Music and Conceptualization*. Cambridge: Cambridge University Press.

DeBellis, M. 1999. "What Is Musical Intuition? Tonal Theory as Cognitive Science." *Philosophical Psychology* 12, 4: 471–501.

Dennett, D. 1987. "Three Kinds of Intentional Psychology." In *The Intentional Stance*, 43–68. Cambridge, Mass.: Bradford/MIT Press.

Dennett, D. 1995. *Darwin's Dangerous Idea: Evolution and the Meanings of Life*. New York: Simon and Schuster.

Dennett, D. 1996. *Kinds of Minds: Toward an Understanding of Consciousness*. New York: Basic Books.

Dennett, D. 1998. "Real Patterns." In *Brainchildren: Essays on Designing Minds*, 95–120. Cambridge, Mass.: Bradford/MIT Press.

Dennett, D. 2001. "The Evolution of Culture." *Monist* 84, 3: 305–324.

Descartes, R. 1644/1984. *Principles of Philosophy*. In *The Philosophical Writings of Descartes*, vol. I, 177–291. Trans. J. Cottingham, R. Stoothoff, and D. Murdoch. Cambridge: Cambridge University Press.

de Sousa, R. 1987. *The Rationality of Emotion.* Cambridge, Mass.: Bradford/MIT Press.

Dewey, J. 1981. *Experience and Nature.* Excerpted in *The Philosophy of John Dewey*, ed. J. McDermott. Chicago: University of Chicago Press.

Dissanayake, E. 2000. "Antecedents of the Temporal Arts in Early Mother-Infant Interaction." In Wallin, Merker, and Brown 2000, 389–410.

Donald, M. 1991. *Origins of the Modern Mind: Three Stages in the Evolution of Culture and Cognition.* Cambridge, Mass.: Harvard University Press.

Dretske, F. 1981. *Knowledge and the Flow of Information.* Cambridge, Mass.: Bradford/MIT Press.

Dretske, F. 1981a. "The Pragmatic Dimension of Knowledge." *Philosophical Studies* 40: 363–378.

Dretske, F. 1995. *Naturalizing the Mind.* Cambridge, Mass.: Bradford/MIT Press.

Durham, W. 1991. *Coevolution: Genes, Culture, and Human Diversity.* Stanford: Stanford University Press.

Edelman, G., and G. Tononi. 2000. *A Universe of Consciousness: How Matter Becomes Imagination.* New York: Basic Books.

Ekman, P. 1984. "Expression and the Nature of Emotion." In Scherer and Ekman 1984, 319–343.

Ekman, P. 1992. "Are There Basic Emotions?" *Psychological Review* 99, 3: 550–553.

Elgin, C. 1983. *With Reference to Reference.* Indianapolis: Hackett.

Elman, J. 1992. "Grammatical Structure and Distributed Representations." In *Connectionism: Theory and Practice*, ed. D. Davis. Oxford: Oxford University Press.

Else, G. 1965. *The Origin and Early Forms of Greek Tragedy.* Cambridge, Mass.: Harvard University Press.

Evans, G. 1982. *The Varieties of Reference.* Oxford: Oxford University Press.

Farrell, D. M. 1988. "Recent Work on the Emotions." *Analyse & Kritik* 10: 71–102.

Feagin, S. 1997. "Imagining Emotions and Appreciating Fiction." In *Emotion and the Arts*, ed. M. Hjort and S. Laver, 50–62. Oxford: Oxford University Press.

Feldman, J., and S. Narayanan. 2004. "Embodied Meaning in a Neural Theory of Language." *Brain and Language* 89, 2: 385–392.

Ferguson, D. 1973. *Music as Metaphor: The Elements of Expression.* Westport, Conn.: Greenwood Press.

Fodor, J. 1983. *The Modularity of Mind: An Essay on Faculty Psychology.* Cambridge, Mass.: Bradford/ MIT Press.

Fodor, J. 1987. *Psychosemantics: The Problem of Meaning in the Philosophy of Mind.* Cambridge, Mass.: Bradford/MIT Press.

Fodor, J. 1998. *Concepts: Where Cognitive Science Went Wrong.* Cambridge, Mass.: Bradford/MIT Press.

Frijda, N. 1986. *The Emotions.* Cambridge: Cambridge University Press.

Gabrielsson, A. 2001. "Emotions in Strong Experiences with Music." In Juslin and Sloboda 2001, 431–449.

Gallese, V., and A. Goldman. 1998. "Mirror Neurons and the Simulation Theory of Mind-Reading." *Trends in Cognitive Science* 2, 14: 493–501.

Gallese, V., and T. Metzinger. 2003. "Motor Ontology: The Representational Reality of Goals, Actions, and Selves." *Philosophical Psychology* 16, 3: 365–388.

Gallistel, C. R. 1980. *The Organization of Action: A New Synthesis*. Hillsdale, N.J.: Lawrence Erlbaum.

Gallistel, C. R. 1981. "Precis of Gallistel's *The Organization of Action: A New Synthesis*." *Behavioral and Brain Sciences* 4: 609–650.

Gates, H. L. 1987. *Figures in Black: Words, Signs, and the "Racial" Self*. New York: Oxford University Press.

Gates, H. L. 1988. *The Signifying Monkey: A Theory of African-American Literary Criticism*. New York: Oxford University Press.

Gerson, L. (ed.). 1996. *The Cambridge Companion to Plotinus*. Cambridge: Cambridge University Press.

Gibbard, A. 1990. *Wise Choices, Apt Feelings: A Theory of Normative Judgment*. Cambridge, Mass.: Harvard University Press.

Gibson, J. J. 1947. "Pictures as Substitutes for Visual Realities." In Reed and Jones 1982, 231–240.

Gibson, J. J. 1954. "A Theory of Pictorial Perception." In Reed and Jones 1982, 241–257.

Gibson, J. J. 1960. "Pictures, Perspective, and Perception." In Reed and Jones 1982, 258–268.

Gibson, J. J. 1962. "Observations on Active Touch." *Psychological Review* 69, 6: 477–491.

Gibson, J. J. 1963. "The Useful Dimensions of Sensitivity." In Reed and Jones 1982, 350–373.

Gibson, J. J. 1966. *The Senses Considered as Perceptual Systems*. Westport, Conn.: Greenwood Press.

Gibson, J. J. 1968. "What Gives Rise to the Perception of Motion?" *Psychological Review* 75, 4: 335–346.

Gibson, J. J. 1971. "The Information Available in Pictures." In Reed and Jones 1982, 269–283.

Gibson, J. J. 1974. "Notes on Action." In Reed and Jones 1982, 385–392.

Gibson, J. J. 1977. "Notes on Direct Perception and Indirect Apprehension." In Reed and Jones 1982, 289–293.

Gibson, J. J. 1986. *The Ecological Approach to Visual Perception*. Hillsdale, N.J.: Lawrence Erlbaum.

Goehr, L. 1992. *The Imaginary Museum of Musical Works: An Essay in the Philosophy of Music*. Oxford: Clarendon Press.

Goldman, A. 1995. "Empathy, Mind, and Morals." In Davies and Stone 1995b, 185–208.

Goldman, A. 2006. *Simulating Minds: The Philosophy, Psychology, and Neuroscience of Mindreading*. Oxford: Oxford University Press.

Goodman, N. 1972. "Seven Strictures on Similarity." In *Problems and Projects*. Indianapolis: Hackett.

Goodman, N. 1976. *Languages of Art: An Approach to a Theory of Symbols*, second edition. Indianapolis: Hackett.

Goodman, N. 1978. *Ways of Worldmaking*. Indianapolis: Hackett.

Goodman, N. 1983. *Fact, Fiction, and Forecast*, fourth edition. Cambridge, Mass.: Harvard University Press.

Goodman, N., and C. Elgin. 1988. *Reconceptions in Philosophy and Other Arts and Sciences*. Indianapolis: Hackett.

Gordon, R. 1987. *The Structure of Emotions: Investigations in Cognitive Philosophy*. Cambridge: Cambridge University Press.

Gould, S. J. 2002. *The Structure of Evolutionary Theory*. Cambridge, Mass.: Belknap/Harvard University Press.

Grandy, R. 1987. "In Defense of Semantic Fields." In *New Directions in Semantics*, ed. E. Lepore, 259–280. London: Academic Press.

Grandy, R. 1992. "Semantic Fields, Prototypes, and the Lexicon." In Lehrer and Kittay 1992, 123–141.

Greenspan, P. 1988. *Emotions and Reasons: An Inquiry into Emotional Justification*. New York: Routledge.

Grice, H. P. 1957. "Meaning." *Philosophical Review* 66: 377–388.

Griffiths, P. 1997. *What Emotions Really Are: The Problem of Psychological Categories*. Chicago: University of Chicago Press.

Gunther, Y. (ed.). 2003. *Essays on Nonconceptual Content*. Cambridge, Mass.: Bradford/MIT Press.

Gurney, E. 1880/1966. *The Power of Sound*. New York: Basic Books.

Guthrie, S. 1993. *Faces in the Clouds: A New Theory of Religion*. Oxford: Oxford University Press.

Haack, S. 1993. *Evidence and Inquiry*. Oxford: Blackwell.

Hahn, L., and P. A. Schilpp (eds.). 1986. *The Philosophy of W. V. Quine*. La Salle, Ill.: Open Court.

Halpern, A. R. 2003. "Cerebral Substrates of Musical Imagery." In Peretz and Zatorre 2003, 217–230.

Hanslick, E. 1891/1986. *On the Musically Beautiful*, eighth edition. Trans. G. Payzant. Indianapolis: Hackett.

Hardin, C. L. 1993. *Color for Philosophers: Unweaving the Rainbow*, expanded edition. Indianapolis: Hackett.

Harrison, N. 1975. "Types, Tokens, and the Identity of the Musical Work." *British Journal of Aesthetics* 15, 4: 336–346.

Hatten, R. 2004. *Interpreting Musical Gestures, Topics, and Tropes: Mozart, Beethoven, and Schubert*. Bloomington: Indiana University Press.

Heft, H. 1996. "The Ecological Approach to Navigation: A Gibsonian Perspective." In Portugali 1996, 105–132.

Heft, H. 2001. *Ecological Psychology in Context: James Gibson, Roger Barker, and the Legacy of William James's Radical Empiricism*. Mahwah, N.J.: Lawrence Erlbaum.

Hegel, G. W. F. 1975. *Introduction to the Lectures on the Philosophy of World History*. Trans. H. B. Nisbet. Cambridge: Cambridge University Press.

Hinde, R. 1999. *Why Gods Persist: A Scientific Approach to Religion*. London: Routledge.

Hofstadter, D. 1979. *Gödel, Escher, Bach: An Eternal Golden Braid*. New York: Basic Books.

Hofstadter, D. 1985. "Waking Up from the Boolean Dream." In *Metamagical Themas: Questing for the Essence of Mind and Pattern*, 631–665. New York: Basic Books.

Holdcraft, D. 1991. *Saussure: Signs, System, and Arbitrariness*. Cambridge: Cambridge University Press.

Holl, K. 1966. *Horch auf die Musik*. Offenbach am Main: Kumm KG. Verlag.

Horgan, T., and J. Tienson. 1996. *Connectionism and the Philosophy of Psychology*. Cambridge, Mass.: Bradford/MIT Press.

Hull, D. 1977. "The Ontological Status of Species as Evolutionary Units." In Hull 1989, 79–88.

Hull, D. 1978. "A Matter of Individuality." *Philosophy of Science* 45: 335–360.

Hull, D. 1982. "The Naked Meme." In *Learning, Development, and Culture*, ed. H. C. Plotkin, 273–327. New York: John Wiley.

Hull, D. 1986. "Conceptual Evolution and the Eye of the Octopus." In Hull 1989, 221–240.

Hull, D. 1989. *The Metaphysics of Evolution*. Albany: SUNY Press.

Hulme, T. E. 1936. "Romanticism and Classicism." In *Speculations: Essays on Humanism and the Philosophy of Art*, second edition, 111–140. London: Routledge and Kegan Paul.

Jackendoff, R. 1987. *Consciousness and the Computational Mind*. Cambridge, Mass.: Bradford/MIT Press.

James, W. 1902/1985. *The Varieties of Religious Experience*. New York: Penguin.

Jeannerod, M. 1990. "The Representation of the Goal of an Action and Its Role in the Control of Goal-Directed Movements." In *Computational Neuroscience*, ed. E. L. Schwartz, 352–368. Cambridge, Mass.: Bradford/MIT Press.

Jeannerod, M. 1994. "The Representing Brain: Neural Correlates of Motor Intention and Imagery." *Behavioral and Brain Sciences* 17, 2: 187–245.

Jeannerod, M. 1997. *The Cognitive Neuroscience of Action*. Oxford: Blackwell.

Jeannerod, M. 2006. *Motor Cognition: What Actions Tell the Self*. Oxford: Oxford University Press.

Jenkins, J., J. Wald, and J. Pittenger. 1986. "Apprehending Pictorial Events." In McCabe and Balzano 1986, 117–133.

Johnson, M. 1987. *The Body in the Mind: The Bodily Basis of Meaning, Imagination, and Reason*. Chicago: University of Chicago Press.

Johnson-Laird, P. 1977. "Procedural Semantics." *Cognition* 5: 189–214.

Johnson-Laird, P. 1983. *Mental Models: Towards a Cognitive Science of Language, Inference, and Consciousness*. Cambridge, Mass.: Harvard University Press.

Johnson-Laird, P. 1996. "Images, Models, and Propositional Representations." In *Models of Visuospatial Cognition*, ed. M. de Vega and M. Marschark, 91–127. Oxford: Oxford University Press.

Jones, M. R., and M. Boltz. 1989. "Dynamic Attending and Responses to Time." *Psychological Review* 96, 3: 459–491.

Jones, R., E. Reed, and M. Hagen. 1980. "A Three Point Perspective on Pictorial Representation: Wartofsky, Goodman, and Gibson on Seeing Pictures." *Erkenntnis* 15: 55–64.

Julesz, B., and I. Hirsch. 1972. "Visual and Auditory Perception—An Essay of Comparison." In David and Denes 1972, 283–340.

Juslin, P., and J. Sloboda (eds.). 2001. *Music and Emotion: Theory and Research*. Oxford: Oxford University Press.

Kandel, E., J. Schwartz, and T. Jessell. 1991. *Principles of Neural Science*, third edition. Norwalk, Conn.: Appleton and Lange.

Kant, I. 1766/1900. *Dreams of a Spirit Seer Illustrated by Dreams of Metaphysics*. Trans. E. F. Goerwitz. New York: Macmillan.

Kant, I. 1783/1977. *Prolegomena to Any Future Metaphysics*. Trans. J. Ellington. Indianapolis: Hackett.

Kant, I. 1784/1981. *Grounding [Grundlegung] for the Metaphysics of Morals*. Trans. J. Ellington. Indianapolis: Hackett.

Kant, I. 1787/1963. *Critique of Pure Reason*. Trans. N. Kemp Smith. London: Macmillan.

Kant, I. 1793/2000. *Critique of the Power of Judgment*. Trans. P. Guyer and E. Matthews. Cambridge: Cambridge University Press.

Katz, D. 1989. *The World of Touch*. Trans. L. Krueger. Hillsdale, N.J.: Lawrence Erlbaum.

Keijzer, F. 2001. *Representation and Behavior*. Cambridge, Mass.: Bradford/MIT Press.

Keil, F. 1979. *Semantic and Conceptual Development: An Ontological Perspective*. Cambridge, Mass.: Harvard University Press.

Kenny, A. 1963. *Action, Emotion, and Will*. London: Routledge and Kegan Paul.

Kitcher, P. S. 1984. "Species." *Philosophy of Science* 51, 2: 308–333.

Kittay, E. F. 1987. *Metaphor: Its Cognitive Force and Linguistic Structure*. Oxford: Oxford University Press.

Kittay, E. F. 1992. "Semantic Fields and the Individuation of Content." In Lehrer and Kittay 1992, 229–252.

Kivy, P. 1983a. "Platonism in Music: A Kind of Defense." In Kivy 1993b, 35–58.

Kivy, P. 1983b. "Platonism in Music: Another Kind of Defense." In Kivy 1993b, 59–74.

Kivy, P. 1983c. "Mozart and Monotheism: An Essay in Spurious Aesthetics." In Kivy 1993b, 189–199.

Kivy, P. 1988. "Orchestrating Platonism." In Kivy 1993b, 75–94.

Kivy, P. 1989. *Sound Sentiment: An Essay on the Musical Emotions*. Philadelphia: Temple University Press.

Kivy, P. 1990. *Music Alone: Philosophical Reflections on the Purely Musical. Experience*. Ithaca, N.Y.: Cornell University Press.

Kivy, P. 1991. "Kant and the *Affectenlehre*: What He Said and What I Wish He Had Said." In Kivy 1993b, 250–264.

Kivy, P. 1993a. "Auditor's Emotions: Contention, Concession and Compromise." *Journal of Aesthetics and Art Criticism* 51, 1: 1–12.

Kivy, P. 1993b. *The Fine Art of Repetition: Essays in the Philosophy of Music*. Cambridge: Cambridge University Press.

Koffka, K. 1924. *The Growth of the Mind: An Introduction to Child Psychology*. Trans. R. M. Ogden. New York: Harcourt, Brace.

Korsgaard, C. 1996. *The Sources of Normativity*. Cambridge: Cambridge University Press.

Kripke, S. 1971. "Identity and Necessity." In S. Schwartz 1977, 66–101.

Krueger, L. 1982. "Tactual Perception in Historical Perspective: David Katz's World of Touch." In Schiff and Foulke 1982, 1–54.

Kubovy, M. 1981. "Concurrent-Pitch Segregation and the Theory of Indispensable Attributes." In Kubovy and Pomerantz 1981, 55–98.

Kubovy, M., and J. Pomerantz (eds.). 1981. *Perceptual Organization*. Hillsdale, N.J.: Lawrence Erlbaum.

Lakoff, G. 1987. *Women, Fire, and Dangerous Things: What Categories Reveal about the Mind*. Chicago: University of Chicago Press.

Lakoff, G., and M. Johnson. 1980. *Metaphors We Live By*. Chicago: University of Chicago Press.

Lakoff, G., and M. Johnson. 1999. *Philosophy in the Flesh: The Embodied Mind and Its Challenge to Western Thought*. New York: Basic Books.

Landels, J. G. 1999. *Music in Ancient Greece and Rome*. London: Routledge.

Langer, S. K. 1957. *Philosophy in a New Key: A Study in the Symbolism of Reason, Rite, and Art*, third edition. Cambridge, Mass.: Harvard University Press.

Large, E., C. Palmer, and J. Pollack. 1999. "Reduced Memory Representations for Music." In *Musical Networks: Parallel Distributed Perception and Performance*, ed. N. Griffith and P. M. Todd, 279–312. Cambridge, Mass.: Bradford/MIT Press.

Lashley, K. S. 1951. "The Problem of Serial Order in Behavior." In *Cerebral Mechanisms in Behavior: The Hixon Symposium*, ed. L. A. Jeffress, 112–146. New York: John Wiley.

Laski, M. 1968. *Ecstasy: A Study of Some Secular and Religious Experiences*. New York: Greenwood Press.

Lazarus, R. 1991. *Emotion and Adaptation*. Oxford: Oxford University Press.

Lehrer, A. 1974. "Semantic Fields and Lexical Structure." In *North Holland Linguistic Series*, ed. S. C. Dik and J. G. Kooij, 14–73. Amsterdam: North-Holland.

Lehrer, A., and E. Kittay. 1992. *Frames, Fields, and Contrasts: New Essays in Semantic and Lexical Organization*. Hillsdale, N.J.: Lawrence Erlbaum.

Lepore, E. (ed.). 1987. *New Directions in Semantics*. London: Academic Press.

Lerdahl, F. 2001. *Tonal Pitch Space*. Oxford: Oxford University Press.

Lerdahl, F. 2003. "The Sounds of Poetry Viewed as Music." In Peretz and Zatorre 2003, 413–429.

Lerdahl, F., and R. Jackendoff. 1983. *A Generative Theory of Tonal Music*. Cambridge, Mass.: Bradford/MIT Press.

Lessing, G. E. 1778. *Eine Duplik*. Braunschweig.

Levine, D. S. 1991. *Introduction to Neural and Cognitive Modeling*. Hillsdale, N.J.: Lawrence Erlbaum.

Levinson, J. 1978. "Properties and Related Entities." *Philosophy and Phenomenological Research* 39, 1: 1–22.

Levinson, J. 1979. "Defining Art Historically." In Levinson 1990b, 3–25.

Levinson, J. 1980a. "Autographic and Allographic Art Revisited." In Levinson 1990b, 89–106.

Levinson, J. 1980b. "What a Musical Work Is." In Levinson 1990b, 63–88.

Levinson, J. 1990a. "What a Musical Work Is, Again." In Levinson 1990b, 215–263.

Levinson, J. 1990b. *Music, Art, and Metaphysics*. Ithaca, N.Y.: Cornell University Press.

Levinson, J. 1990c. "Authentic Performance and Performance Means." In Levinson 1990b, 393–408.

Levinson, J. 1997. *Music in the Moment*. Ithaca, N.Y.: Cornell University Press.

Levitin, D. J. 2006. *This Is Your Brain on Music: The Science of a Human Obsession*. New York: Dutton.

Lewis, C. D. 1947. *The Poetic Image*. Oxford: Oxford University Press.

Lewis, D. 1986. *On the Plurality of Worlds*. Oxford: Blackwell.

Lidell, H. G., and R. Scott. 1996. *A Greek-English Lexicon*, supplemented ninth edition. Oxford: Clarendon Press.

Lidov, D. 1987. "Mind and Body in Music." *Semiotica* 66, 1/3: 66–97.

Livingston, K. 2005. "Religious Practice, Brain, and Belief." *Journal of Cognition and Culture*, 5, 1/2, 75–117.

Lock, A., and C. R. Peters. 1999a. *Handbook of Human Symbolic Evolution*. Oxford: Blackwell.

Lock, A., and C. R. Peters. 1999b. "Ontogeny: Symbolic Development and Symbolic Evolution." In Lock and Peters 1999a, 371–399.

Lorand, R. 2000. *Aesthetic Order: A Philosophy of Order, Beauty and Art*. London: Routledge.

Lyons, J. 1997. *Semantics*, vol. I. Cambridge: Cambridge University Press.

Lyons, W. 1980. *Emotion*. Cambridge: Cambridge University Press.

Margolis, J. 1977. "The Ontological Peculiarity of Works of Art." *Journal of Aesthetics and Art Criticism* 36: 45–50.

Margolis, J. 1980. *Art and Philosophy*. Atlantic Highlands, N.J.: Humanities Press.

Marr, D. 1982. *Vision*. San Francisco: W. H. Freeman.

Matravers, D. 1998. *Art and Emotion*. Oxford: Oxford University Press.

Matthews, G. 1998. *Neurobiology: Molecules, Cells, and Systems*. Oxford: Blackwell.

Maus, F. 1997. "Music as Drama." In Robinson 1997, 105–130.

May, L., M. Friedman, and A. Clark (eds.). 1996. *Mind and Morals: Essays on Cognitive Science and Ethics*. Cambridge, Mass.: Bradford/MIT Press.

McCabe, V., and G. Balzano. 1986. *Event Cognition: An Ecological Perspective*. Hillsdale, N.J.: Lawrence Erlbaum.

McCauley, R. 2000. "The Naturalness of Religion and the Unnaturalness of Science." In *Explanation and Cognition*, ed. F. Keil and R. Wilson, 61–85. Cambridge, Mass.: Bradford/MIT Press.

McCauley, R., and T. Lawson. 2002. *Bringing Ritual to Mind: Psychological Foundations of Cultural Forms*. Cambridge: Cambridge University Press.

McDowell, J. 1996. *Mind and World*. Cambridge, Mass.: Harvard University Press.

McGinn, C. 1989. *Mental Content*. Oxford: Basil Blackwell.

McIver Lopes, D. 2000. "From *Languages of Art* to Art in Mind." *Journal of Aesthetics and Art Criticism* 58, 3: 227–231.

McNeill, D. 1987. *Psycholinguistics: A New Approach*. New York: Harper and Row.

McNeill, D. 1992. *Hand and Mind: What Gestures Reveal about Thought*. Chicago: University of Chicago Press.

Meissner, H. A. 1737. *Philosophisches Lexicon*. Bayreuth: J. G. Vierling.

Meyer, L. B. 1956. *Emotion and Meaning in Music*. Chicago: University of Chicago Press.

Meyer, L. B. 1967. "Meaning in Music and Information Theory." In *Music, the Arts, and Ideas: Patterns and Predictions in Twentieth-Century Culture*, 5–21. Chicago: University of Chicago Press.

Miller, G., G. E. Galanter, and K. Pribram. 1960. *Plans and the Structure of Behavior*. New York: Henry Holt.

Miller, G., and P. Johnson-Laird. 1976. *Language and Perception*. Cambridge, Mass.: Belknap/Harvard University Press.

Millikan, R. 1984. *Language, Thought, and Other Biological Categories: New Foundations for Realism.* Cambridge, Mass.: Bradford/MIT Press.

Millikan, R. 1996. "Pushmi-Pullyu Representations." In May, Friedman, and Clark 1996, 145–161.

Millikan, R. 2000. *On Clear and Confused Ideas: An Essay about Substance Concepts.* Cambridge: Cambridge University Press.

Millikan, R. 2004. *Varieties of Meaning.* Cambridge, Mass.: Bradford/MIT Press.

Mithen, S. 1996. *The Prehistory of the Mind.* London: Thames and Hudson.

Mithen, S. 2005. *The Singing Neanderthals: The Origins of Music, Language, and Mind.* London: Weidenfeld and Nicolson.

Molino, J. 2000. "Toward an Evolutionary Theory of Music and Language." In Wallin, Merker, and Brown 2000, 165–176.

Nakamura, S., N. Sadato, T. Oohashi, E. Nishina, Y. Fuwamoto, and Y. Yonekura. 1999. "Analysis of Music–Brain Interaction with Simultaneous Measurement of Regional Cerebral Blood Flow and Electroencephalogram Beta Rhythm in Human Subjects." *Neuroscience Letters* 275: 222–226.

Narayanan, S. 1997. "Talking the Talk *Is* Like Walking the Walk: A Computational Model of Verbal Aspect." In *Proceedings of the Nineteenth Annual Conference of the Cognitive Science Society*, 548–553. Stanford University, August 7–10, 1997. Hillsdale, N.J.: Lawrence Erlbaum.

Narayanan, S. 1999. "Moving Right Along: A Computational Model of Metaphoric Reasoning about Events." *Proceedings of the Sixteenth Conference of Artificial Intelligence*, 121–127. Menlo Park, Calif.: AAAI Press.

Narmour, E. 1990. *The Analysis and Cognition of Basic Melodic Structures: The Implication Realization Model.* Chicago: University of Chicago Press.

Neiman, S. 2002. *Evil in Modern Thought: An Alternative History of Philosophy.* Princeton: Princeton University Press.

Nietzsche, F. 1886/1967. *The Birth of Tragedy Or: Hellenism and Pessimism.* Trans. W. Kaufmann. New York: Vintage Books. Original version published in 1872.

Nietzsche, F. 1883–92/1954. *Thus Spoke Zarathustra.* Trans. W. Kaufmann. In *The Portable Nietzsche*, ed. W. Kaufmann, 112–439. New York: Viking Press.

Nietzsche, F. 1889/1954. *The Twilight of the Idols.* In *The Portable Nietzsche*, ed. W. Kaufmann, 463–563. New York: Viking Press.

Nussbaum, C. 2003a. "Aesthetics and the Problem of Evil." *Metaphilosophy* 43, 3: 250–283.

Nussbaum, C. 2003b. "Kinds, Types, and Musical Ontology." *Journal of Aesthetics and Art Criticism* 61, 3: 271–291.

Nussbaum, C. 2003c. "Another Look at Functionalism and the Emotions." *Brain and Mind* 4: 353–383.

Nussbaum, C. 2005. "The Musical Touch Effect." *Transformation: A Journal of Literature, Ideas, and the Arts* 1, 2: 71–80.

Nussbaum, M. 2001. *Upheavals of Thought: The Intelligence of Emotions*. Cambridge: Cambridge University Press.

Nussbaum, R., R. McInnes, H. Willard, and C. Boerkoel. 2001. *Genetics in Medicine*, sixth edition. Philadelphia: W. B. Saunders.

Oatley, K. 1992. *Best Laid Schemes*. Cambridge: Cambridge University Press.

Oatley, K., and P. Johnson-Laird. 1987. "Towards a Cognitive Theory of Emotions." *Cognition and Emotion* 1: 29–50.

Ogden, C. K. 1932. *Opposition: A Linguistic and Psychological Analysis*. Bloomington: Indiana University Press.

Ortony, A., G. Clore, and A. Collins. 1988. *The Cognitive Structure of Emotions*. Cambridge: Cambridge University Press.

Otto, R. 1950. *The Idea of the Holy*, second edition. Trans. W. Harvey. Oxford: Oxford University Press.

Parsons, L. M. 2003. "Exploring the Functional Neuroanatomy of Music Performance, Perception, and Comprehension." In Peretz and Zatorre 2003, 247–268.

Pascal, B. 1670/1995. *Pensees and Other Writings*. Trans. H. Levi. Oxford: Oxford University Press.

Peacocke, C. 1987. "Depiction." *Philosophical Review* 96, 3: 383–410.

Peacocke, C. 1992. *A Study of Concepts*. Cambridge, Mass.: Bradford/MIT Press.

Peel, J., and W. Slawson. 1984. "Review of Lerdahl and Jackendoff's *A Generative Theory of Tonal Music*." *Journal of Music Theory* 28: 271–294.

Peirce, C. S. 1932. *Collected Papers*. Ed. C. Hartshorne and P. Weiss. Cambridge, Mass.: Harvard University Press.

Peretz, I., and R. Zatorre (eds.). 2003. *The Cognitive Neuroscience of Music*. Oxford: Oxford University Press.

Perry, J. 1979. "The Problem of the Essential Indexical." *Noûs* 13: 3–21.

Peters, C. R. 1999. "Tempo and Mode of Change in the Evolution of Symbolism (A Partial Overview)." In Lock and Peters 1999a, 863–876.

Pfeiffer, J. E. 1982. *The Creative Explosion: An Inquiry into the Origins of Art and Religion*. New York: Harper and Row.

Pinker, S. 1994. *The Language Instinct: How the Mind Creates Language*. New York: William Morrow.

Pinker, S. 2002. *The Blank Slate: The Modern Denial of Human Nature*. New York: Viking Press.

Plotinus. 1962. *The Enneads*. Trans. S. MacKenna. London: Faber.

Plotkin, H. 1993. *Darwin Machines and the Nature of Knowledge*. Cambridge, Mass.: Harvard University Press.

Plotkin, H. 2003. *The Imagined World Made Real: Toward a Natural Science of Culture*. New Brunswick, N.J.: Rutgers University Press.

Pollack, J., and J. Cruz. 1999. *Contemporary Theories of Knowledge*, second edition. Lanham, Maryland: Rowman and Littlefield.

Portugali, J. 1996. *The Construction of Cognitive Maps*. Dordrecht: Kluwer Academic.

Prinz, J. 2004. *Gut Reactions: A Perceptual Theory of Emotion*. Oxford: Oxford University Press.

Pugh, G. E. 1977. *The Biological Origin of Human Values*. New York: Basic Books.

Putman, D. 1985. "Music and the Metaphor of Touch." *Journal of Aesthetics and Art Criticism* 44, 1: 59–66.

Putnam, H. 1995. "Mathematical Necessity Reconsidered." In *On Quine: New Essays*, ed. P. Leonardi and M. Santambrogio, 267–282. Cambridge: Cambridge University Press.

Quine, W. V. 1969a. "Natural Kinds." In *Ontological Relativity and Other Essays*, 114–138. New York: Columbia University Press.

Quine, W. V. 1969b. *Set Theory and Its Logic*, revised edition. Cambridge, Mass.: Harvard/Belknap Press.

Quine, W. V. 1982. *Methods of Logic*, fourth edition. Cambridge, Mass.: Harvard University Press.

Quine, W. V. 1986. "Reply to White." In Hahn and Schilpp 1986, 663–665.

Quinlan, P. 1991. *Connectionism and Psychology*. Chicago: University of Chicago Press.

Radford, A. 1981. *Transformational Syntax: A Student's Guide to Chomsky's Extended Theory*. New York: Cambridge University Press.

Raffman, D. 1993. *Language, Music, and Mind*. Cambridge, Mass.: Bradford/MIT Press.

Rawls, J. 1971. *A Theory of Justice*. Cambridge, Mass.: Harvard University Press.

Reed, E., and R. Jones (eds.). 1982. *Reasons for Realism: Selected Essays of James J. Gibson*. Hillsdale, N.J.: Erlbaum.

Reisig, W. 1992. *A Primer in Petri Nets*. Berlin: Springer Verlag.

Rickheit, G., and C. Habel (eds.). 1999. *Mental Models in Discourse Processing and Reasoning*. Amsterdam: North-Holland.

Ridley, A. 1995. *Music, Value, and the Passions*. Ithaca, N.Y.: Cornell University Press.

Ridley, A. 2003. "Against Musical Ontology." *Journal of Philosophy* 100, 4: 203–220.

Ridley, Mark. 1986. *Evolution and Classification: The Reformation of Cladism*. London: Longman.

Ridley, Mark. 1989. "The Cladistic Solution to the Species Problem." *Biology and Philosophy* 4: 1–16.

Ridley, Matt. 1993. *The Red Queen: Sex and the Evolution of Human Nature*. New York: Macmillan.

Rist, J. 1996. "Plotinus and Christian Philosophy." In Gerson 1996, 386–413.

Rizzolati, G., and M. Arbib. 1998. "Language within Our Grasp." *Trends in Neurosciences* 21, 5: 188–194.

Robinson, J. 1979. "Some Remarks on Goodman's Language Theory of Pictures." *British Journal of Aesthetics* 19, 1: 63–75.

Robinson, J. 1994. "Music as a Representational Art." In Alperson 1994, 168–192.

Robinson, J. 1995. "Startle." *Journal of Philosophy* 92, 2: 53–74.

Robinson, J. (ed.). 1997. *Music and Meaning*. Ithaca, N.Y.: Cornell University Press.

Robinson, J. 2000. "*Languages of Art* at the Turn of the Century." *Journal of Aesthetics and Art Criticism* 58, 3: 213–217.

Robinson, J. 2005. *Deeper Than Reason: Emotion and Its Role in Literature, Music, and Art*. Oxford: Oxford University Press.

Rosen, G. 1997. "Who Makes the Rules Around Here?" *Philosophy and Phenomenological Research* 57, 1: 163–171.

Rosenbaum, D. A. 1980. "Human Movements Initiation: Specification of Arm, Direction, and Extent." *Journal of Experimental Psychology, General* 109: 444–474.

Rosenberg, A. 1985. *The Structure of Biological Science*. Cambridge: Cambridge University Press.

Ross, J. R. 1981. *Portraying Analogy*. Cambridge: Cambridge University Press.

Ross, J. R. 1992. "Semantic Contagion." In Lehrer and Kittay 1992, 143–169.

Rothstein, E. 1995. *Emblems of the Mind: The Inner Life of Music and Mathematics*. New York: Random House.

Rumelhart, D., P. Smolensky, L. McClelland, and G. E. Hinton. 1986. "Schemata and Sequential Thought Processes in PDP Models." In *Parallel Distributed Processing: Explorations in the Microstructure of Cognition*, vol. 2, ed. J. McClelland, D. Rumelhart et al., 7–57. Cambridge, Mass.: Bradford/MIT Press.

Russell, B. 1912/1959. *The Problems of Philosophy*. New York: Galaxy Press.

Russell, B. 1917/1957. "Knowledge by Acquaintance and Knowledge by Description." In *Mysticism and Logic*, 202–224. New York: Doubleday Anchor Books.

Sacks, O. 2004. "In the River of Consciousness." *New York Review of Books* 51, 1 (January 15, 2004): 41–44.

Sargant, W. 1973. *The Mind Possessed: A Physiology of Possession Mysticism and Faith Healing*. London: Heinemann Press.

Sarnat, H. B., and M. G. Netsky. 1981. *Evolution of the Nervous System*, second edition. Oxford: Oxford University Press.

Sartre, J.-P. 1955. "Cartesian Freedom." In *Literary and Philosophical Essays*, 180–197. Trans. A. Michelson. New York: Collier Books.

Sartre, J.-P. 1960. *The Transcendence of the Ego: An Existentialist Theory of Consciousness*. New York: Hill and Wang.

Sartre, J.-P. 1962. *Sketch for a Theory of the Emotions*. Trans. P. Mairet. London: Methuen.

Sartre, J.-P. 1964. *Nausea*. Trans. L. Alexander. New York: New Directions.

Sartre, J.-P. 1966. *Being and Nothingness*. Trans. H. Barnes. New York: Washington Square Press.

Saussure, F. de 1915/1959. *Course in General Linguistics*. Ed. C. Bally and A. Sechehaye. Trans. W. Baskin. New York: Philosophical Library.

Schachter, S., and J. Singer. 1962. "Cognitive, Social, and Physiological Determinants of Emotional State." *Psychological Review* 69, 5: 379–399.

Scherer, K., and P. Ekman (eds.). 1984. *Approaches to Emotion*. Hillsdale, N.J.: Lawrence Erlbaum.

Schiff, W., and E. Foulke (eds.). 1982. *Tactual Perception: A Sourcebook*. Cambridge: Cambridge University Press.

Scholes, P. 1955. *The Oxford Companion to Music*, ninth edition. Oxford: Oxford University Press.

Schopenhauer, A. 1844/1966. *The World as Will and Representation*, vols. I and II. Trans. E. F. J. Payne. New York: Dover.

Schwartz, D., C. Howe, and D. Purves. 2003. "The Statistical Structure of Human Speech Sounds Predicts Musical Universals." *Journal of Neuroscience* 23, 18: 7160–7168.

Schwartz, R. 1978. "Infinite Sets, Unbounded Consequences, and Models of the Mind." In *Perception and Cognition: Issues in the Foundations of Psychology*, Minnesota Studies in the Philosophy of Science, vol. 9, ed. C. W. Savage, 183–200. Minneapolis: University of Minnesota Press.

Schwartz, S. (ed.). 1977. *Naming, Necessity, and Natural Kinds*. Ithaca, N.Y.: Cornell University Press.

Scruton, R. 1997. *The Aesthetics of Music*. Oxford: Oxford University Press.

Seeger, A. 1987. *Why Suya Sing: A Musical Anthropology of an Amazonian People*. Cambridge: Cambridge University Press.

Sharpe, R. A. 1979. "Type, Token, Interpretation, and Performance." *Mind* 88, 351: 437–440.

Shaw, R., and W. Hazelett. 1986. "Schemas in Cognition." In McCabe and Balzano 1986, 45–58.

Shaw, R., B. Wilson, and H. Wellman. 1986. "Abstract Conceptual Knowledge: How We Know What We Know." In McCabe and Balzano 1986, 59–78.

Shepard, R. 1981. "Psychophysical Complementarity." In Kubovy and Pomerantz 1981, 279–341.

Shepard, R. 1984. "Ecological Constraints on Internal Representation: Resonant Kinematics of Perceiving, Imagining, Thinking, and Dreaming." *Psychological Review* 91, 4: 417–447.

Shepard, R., and S. Chipman. 1970. "Second-Order Isomorphism of Internal Representations: Shapes of States." *Cognitive Psychology* 1: 1–17.

Shepard, R., and J. Metzler. 1971. "Mental Rotation of Three-Dimensional Objects." *Science* 171: 701–703.

Sherman, N. 1998. "Empathy and Imagination." In *Midwest Studies in Philosophy*, vol. 22, ed. P. French and H. K. Wettstein, 82–119. Notre Dame, Ind.: Notre Dame Press.

Siegel, H. 1992. "Justification by Balance." *Philosophy and Phenomenological Research* 52, 1: 27–46.

Simons, P. 1982. "Token Resistance." *Analysis* 42, 1: 195–202.

Sloboda, J. A. 1985. *The Musical Mind: The Cognitive Psychology of Music*. Oxford: Oxford University Press.

Sober, E. 1984. "Sets, Species, and Evolution: Comments on Philip Kitcher's 'Species.'" *Philosophy of Science* 51: 334–341.

Solomon, R. C. 1980. "Emotions and Choice." In *Explaining Emotions*, ed. A. Rorty, 251–281. Berkeley: University of California Press.

Solomon, R. L. 1980. "The Opponent-Process Theory of Acquired Motivation: The Costs of Pleasure and the Benefits of Pain." *American Psychologist* 35: 691–712.

Sosa, E., and J. Kim (eds.). 2000. *Epistemology: An Anthology*. Oxford: Blackwell.

Sperber, D. 1985. *On Anthropological Knowledge*. Cambridge: Cambridge University Press.

Sperber, D. 1996. *Explaining Culture*. Oxford: Blackwell.

Sperber, D. 2000. "Metarepresentations in an Evolutionary Perspective." In *Metarepresentations: A Multidisciplinary Perspective*, ed. D. Sperber, 117–138. Oxford: Oxford University Press.

Spinoza, B. 1985. *Ethics*. In *The Collected Works of Spinoza*, I, 408–617. Trans. E. Curley. Princeton: Princeton University Press.

Stalnaker, R. 2003. "What Might Nonconceptual Content Be?" In Gunther 2003, 95–106.

Stanford, P. K. 1995. "For Pluralism and Against Realism About Species." *Philosophy of Science* 62: 70–91.

Steiner, G. 1989. *Real Presences*. Chicago: University of Chicago Press.

Stich, S. 1988. "Reflective Equilibrium, Analytic Epistemology, and the Problem of Cognitive Diversity." *Synthese* 74. Reprinted in Sosa and Kim 2000, 571–583.

Stich, S. 1993. *The Fragmentation of Reason: Preface to a Pragmatic Theory of Cognitive Evaluation*. Cambridge, Mass.: Bradford/MIT Press.

Stich, S., and R. Nisbett. 1980. "Justification and the Psychology of Human Reasoning." *Philosophy of Science* 47: 188–202.

Strawson, P. F. 1959/1963. *Individuals: An Essay in Descriptive Metaphysics*. New York: Anchor Books.

Thagard, P. 1988. *Computational Philosophy of Science*. Cambridge, Mass.: Bradford/MIT Press.

Thayer, A. W. 1970. *Life of Beethoven*. Ed. E. Forbes. Princeton: Princeton University Press.

Todd, N. P. 1999. "Motion in Music: A Neurobiological Perspective." *Music Perception* 17: 115–126.

Tomasello, M. 1999. *The Cultural Origins of Human Cognition*. Cambridge, Mass.: Harvard University Press.

Tooby, J., and L. Cosmides. 1992. "The Psychological Foundations of Culture." In *The Adapted Mind: Evolutionary Psychology and the Generation of Culture*, ed. J. Barkow, L. Cosmides, and J. Tooby, 19–136. Oxford: Oxford University Press.

Trainor, L. J., and L. A. Schmidt. 2003. "Processing Emotions Induced by Music." In Peretz and Zatorre 2003, 310–324.

Tramo, M. J., P. A. Cariani, B. Delgutte, and L. D. Braida. 2003. "Neurobiology of Harmony Perception." In Peretz and Zatorre 2003, 127–151.

Updike, J. 2005. "Determined Spirit." *New York Review of Books* 52, 19: 13–14.

van Fraassen, B. C. 2002. *The Empirical Stance*. New Haven: Yale University Press.

Vygotsky, L. 1986. *Thought and Language*. Trans. E. Haufmann and G. Vakar. Ed. A. Kozulin. Cambridge, Mass.: MIT Press.

Wallin, N., B. Merker, and S. Brown. 2000. *The Origins of Music*. Cambridge, Mass.: Bradford/MIT Press.

Wallis, R. T. 1995. *Neoplatonism*, second edition. Indianapolis: Hackett.

Walton, K. 1997. "Listening with Imagination: Is Music Representational?" In Robinson 1997, 57–82.

Warren, D. H. 1982. "The Development of Haptic Perception." In Schiff and Foulke 1982, 82–129.

Wartofsky, M. 1979. *Models: Representation and the Scientific Understanding*. Dordrecht: D. Reidel.

Weininger, O. 1980. *Otto Weiningers Taschenbuch*. In *Geschlecht und Charakter: Eine Prinzipielle Untersuchung*. Munich: Matthes & Seitz Verlag.

Whitehead, A. N. 1978. *Process and Reality*, corrected edition. Ed. D. R. Griffin and D. W. Sherburne. New York: Free Press.

Whitehouse, H. 2000. *Arguments and Icons: Divergent Modes of Religiosity*. Oxford: Oxford University Press.

Williams, G. C. 1966. *Adaptation and Natural Selection*. Oxford: Oxford University Press.

Williams, M. B. 1970. "Deducing the Consequences of Evolution: A Mathematical Model." *Journal of Theoretical Biology* 29, 3: 343–385.

Windsor, W. L. 1995. *A Perceptual Approach to the Description and Analysis of Acousmatic Music*. Unpublished doctoral dissertation, City University. Available at http//www.personal.leeds.ac.uk/~muswlw/wlw.html/.

Wing, L. (ed.). 1976. *Early Childhood Autism: Clinical, Educational, and Social Aspects*. New York: Pergamon Press.

Winkelman, M. 1986. "Trance States: A Theoretical Model and Cross-Cultural Analysis." *Ethos* 14, 2: 174–203.

Wollheim, R. 1970. *Art and Its Objects*. Cambridge: Cambridge University Press.

Wolterstorff, N. 1975. "Toward an Ontology of Art Works." *Noûs* 9: 115–142.

Zajonc, R. B. 1980. "Feeling and Thinking: Preferences Need No Inferences." *American Psychologist* 35: 151–175.

Zajonc, R. B. 1984. "On Primacy of Affect." In Scherer and Ekman 1984, 259–270.

Zbikowski, L. M. 2002. *Conceptualizing Music*. Oxford: Oxford University Press.

Zuckerkandl, V. 1956/1969. *Sound and Symbol: Music and the External World*. Trans W. R. Trask. Princeton: Bollingen/Princeton University Press.

Zweig, A. (ed.). 1967. *Kant: Philosophical Correspondence, 1759–99*. Chicago: University of Chicago Press.

Index